D1276820

PRINCETON **P** POCKET GUIDES

MAMMALS OF CHINA

Andrew T. Smith and Yan Xie
Editors

Robert S. Hoffmann
Darrin Lunde
John MacKinnon
Don E. Wilson
W. Chris Wozencraft
Contributing Authors

Federico Gemma
Illustrator

Professor Wang Sung
Honorary Editor

PRINCETON UNIVERSITY PRESS
PRINCETON AND OXFORD

PRINCETON ℗ POCKET GUIDES

Wildlife of Australia, by Iain Campbell and Sam Woods
Wildlife of East Africa, by Martin B. Withers and David Hosking
Wildlife of the Galápagos, by Julian Fitter, Daniel Fitter, and David Hosking
Wildlife of Southern Africa, by Martin B. Withers and David Hosking
Coral Reef Fishes: Indo-Pacific and Caribbean, Revised Edition, by Ewald Lieske
and Robert Myers
A Field Guide to the Birds of New Zealand, by Julian Fitter
The Kingdon Pocket Guide to African Mammals, by Jonathan Kingdon
Mammals of China, edited by Andrew T. Smith and Yan Xie
Reptiles and Amphibians of East Africa, by Stephen Spawls, Kim M. Howell,
and Robert C. Drewes

Copyright © 2013 by Princeton University Press
Published by Princeton University Press, 41 William Street, Princeton, New Jersey 08540
In the United Kingdom: Princeton University Press, 6 Oxford Street, Woodstock,
Oxfordshire OX20 1TW

press.princeton.edu

Cover illustrations © Federico Gemma

ISBN (pbk.) 978-0-691-15427-5
Library of Congress Control Number 2013930079

British Library Cataloging-in-Publication Data is available

This book has been composed in Minion Pro

Printed on acid-free paper

Printed in Singapore

1 3 5 7 9 10 8 6 4 2

Contents

List of Figures

List of Maps

List of Habitat Images

Preface

This Princeton Pocket Guide to the mammals of China is designed to give ready access to those encountering the diverse mammal fauna of China. This book is an outgrowth of the earlier comprehensive *A Guide to the Mammals of China* (Smith and Xie 2008). The full guide contains additional information on the identification of Chinese mammals, including comprehensive keys and descriptions of skulls and osteological features, as well as thorough reviews of systematic controversies concerning Chinese mammals and a history of Chinese mammalogy. It also contains a lengthy bibliography to lead readers to pursue additional background information concerning Chinese mammals. Those interested in these details of Chinese mammals are encouraged to consult this longer treatment. Here, however, we have presented material that can serve directly to identify mammals encountered in the field—concentrating on range maps and descriptions of the external appearance of species and their natural history. Increasingly, people are becoming interested in ecotourism and natural history. We hope that this book engenders enthusiasm for the study of Chinese mammals, especially in their natural and wild state.

Andrew Smith, Tempe, and Xie Yan, Beijing

Contributors

FEDERICO GEMMA
Species Plates
  Viale Marconi 19
  Rome 00146 Italy
  f.gemma@quipo.it
  www.federicogemma.it
ROBERT S. HOFFMANN*
Sciuridae, Cricetinae, Gerbillinae, Erinaceomorpha, Soricomorpha
  Division of Mammals
  Department of Vertebrate Zoology
  National Museum of Natural History
  Smithsonian Institution—MRC-108
  Washington, DC 20013 USA
DARRIN LUNDE
Arvicolinae, Murinae, Erinaceomorpha, Soricomorpha
  Division of Mammals
  Department of Vertebrate Zoology
  National Museum of Natural History
  Smithsonian Institution—MRC-108
  Washington, DC 20013 USA
  lunded@si.edu
JOHN R. MACKINNON
Proboscidea, Primates, Artiodactyla
  11 Leycroft Close
  Canterbury CT2 7LD United Kingdom
  arcbc_jrm@hotmail.com

ANDREW T. SMITH
Introduction, Proboscidea, Sirenia, Scandentia, Sciuridae, Gliridae, Castoridae, Dipodidae, Platacanthomyidae, Spalacidae, Cricetinae, Gerbillinae, Hystricidae, Lagomorpha, Pholidota, Cetacea, Maps, Appendixes

School of Life Sciences
Box 874501
Arizona State University
Tempe, AZ 85287-4501 USA
a.smith@asu.edu

WANG SUNG
Honorary Editor

Institute of Zoology
Chinese Academy of Sciences
1-5 Beichenxilu, Chaoyang District
Beijing 100101 People's Republic of China
wangs@panda.ioz.ac.cn

DON E. WILSON
Chiroptera

Division of Mammals
Department of Vertebrate Zoology
National Museum of Natural History
Smithsonian Institution—MRC-108
Washington, DC 20013 USA
wilsond@si.edu

W. CHRIS WOZENCRAFT*
Carnivora

Division of Natural Sciences
Bethel College
1001 West McKinley Avenue
Mishawaka, IN 46545 USA

XIE YAN
Introduction; Maps

Institute of Zoology
Chinese Academy of Sciences
1-5 Beichenxilu, Chaoyang District
Beijing 100101 People's Republic of China
xieyan@public3.bta.net.cn

deceased

Introduction

China is a magnificent country and one of the most diverse on Earth. Its size ranks fourth among the world's nations (9,596,960 km²), and it is home to over 1.3 billion people. The topography of China ranges from the highest elevation on Earth (Mount Everest, or Chomolungma; 8,850 m) to one of the lowest (Turpan Basin; 154 m below sea level). Chinese environments include some of Earth's most extensive and driest deserts (the Taklimakan and Gobi) and its highest plateau (the Tibetan Plateau or "Roof of the World"). Habitats range from tropical to boreal forest, and from extensive grasslands to desert (see the habitat images, map 1, and map 2). This wide variety of habitats has contributed greatly to the richness of China's mammal fauna. Additionally, the geographic location of China, at the suture zone between the Palaearctic and Indo-Malayan biogeographic regions, further contributes to the country's mammal diversity. Overall, more than 10 percent of the world's species of mammals live in China (556/5,416); an additional 29 species of cetaceans live in offshore waters (see Appendix I). Almost 20 percent (106/556) of China's mammals are endemic, and one of these is among the most recognizable of the world's mammals, the Giant Panda. China is considered a "megadiversity" country and has the third highest diversity of mammals among all countries (following Brazil and Indonesia).

China's Geography and Mammal Biogeography

There have been many attempts to describe China's diverse landscape. Conventionally, China has been divided into three major physical geographic regions: the Tibetan (Qinghai-Xizang) Plateau, northwest arid China, and eastern monsoon China (map 3).

The Tibetan Plateau is one of the highest and most remote landscapes on Earth. The plateau averages between 3,000 and 5,000 m in elevation and encompasses roughly a quarter of China. The word "plateau" is a misnomer, as this area is crisscrossed by numerous impressive mountain chains, such as the Anyemaqin Shan, Bayan Har Shan, and Tanggula Shan, and many smaller spur ranges. Nevertheless, approximately 70 percent of the plateau is composed of alpine meadow or semisteppe vegetation. The Qaidam Basin, an interesting area of tectonic collapse, is found at the northern extreme of the plateau at an elevation of only 2,600 m.

The arid northwest encompasses about 30 percent of China and represents an eastern extension of the great Eurasian deserts and grasslands. One of the world's most desolate deserts, the Taklimakan (translation: "those who go in do not come out alive") lies north of the Tibetan Plateau and the Kunlun Mountains. The cooler Dzungarian Basin, China's second-largest desert, lies in the far northwest. Various smaller deserts extend to the east, increasingly interspersed with semidesert and temperate steppe grasslands. Finally, the rocky Gobi Desert occupies the northern part of China and extends into Mongolia. Two of Asia's major mountain ranges break up this barren expanse in the northwest: the Tian Shan and the Altai. One can stand below sea level in Turpan Basin and clearly see the snow-capped top of Bogda Feng (in a spur of the Tian Shan) at 5,445 m.

Eastern monsoon China comprises about 45 percent of the country but is home to roughly 95 percent of China's human population. This land is crossed by major rivers that originate on the Tibetan Plateau, most notably the Huang He (Yellow River), Yangtze and Mekong. Almost all of the arable land has been converted to agriculture, and much of the original forest habitat has been destroyed. Most of this landscape is low in elevation and consists of broad alluvial valleys, coastal plains, and modest ancient mountain ranges. The south is seasonably humid, and the plains are punctuated by dramatic limestone pillars. The climate becomes increasingly temperate toward the north, with deciduous trees giving way to expansive coniferous forests in the far northeast.

These physical geographical regions, however, do not adequately define the major biogeographic divisions in China. Biogeographically, China's flora and fauna have been affected by both historical factors (their derivation from two formerly isolated biogeographic realms—the Palaearctic and the Indo-Malayan) and their relative ability to colonize new habitats.

The southern boundary of the Palaearctic realm varies in breadth from western to eastern China. The zone of overlap between the Palaearctic and Indo-Malayan realms along the southern boundary of western China is compressed, as this region is defined by high elevational relief. In contrast, in areas of low relief (such as in eastern central China), the zonation is determined more by latitude than elevation, and there is a broad latitudinal band of overlap between forms that originated from the Palaearctic and Indo-Malayan realms. In the south this zone extends from about 28° N on the coast to roughly 25° N in the area in northern Yunnan where the three great rivers (Yangtze, Mekong, Salween) lie in close proximity. The northern edge of this zone essentially follows the Yangtze River from the east coast to the area where the three great rivers come together. This description contrasts with previous opinions that the southern limit of the Palaearctic in China largely corresponds to the latitude of the Huang He in eastern China (about 30° N).

An objective and comprehensive approach to understanding the zoogeography of Chinese mammals has been developed recently (Xie et al. 2009). This approach defined 124 biogeographic units in China based on a comprehensive suite of factors (elevation, landform, climate, vegetation, hydrology, etc.); maps of 171 diagnostic mammal species were then overlaid on these units. A statistical analysis identified aggregations of biogeographic units based on mammal distributions, and this information was used to create cluster dendrograms. This analysis produced a classification of the boundaries dividing the mammal fauna at different spatial scales across China. A similar analysis was performed on 509 representative plant species.

The biogeographical divisions of mammals and plants in China determined by the methodology outlined above contrast significantly with the commonly used physical geographical regions for China. Additionally, there are distinctive differences between the biogeographical divisions using the plant and mammal data. Four major biogeographical divisions occur in China based on vegetation: northeast, southeast, southwest, and northwest. These in turn can be broken down into 8 subareas and 27 regions (see map 2 and table 1). Compared with the physical geographical regions, the major divisions based on plants separate the arid northwest into western and eastern sections, and eastern monsoonal China into northern and southern parts. The southwest China biogeographical region for plants is basically similar to the Tibetan Plateau physical geographic region, although both the northern and southern boundaries of the biogeographical region are found farther south than the physical geographical region (map 3).

There are three major biogeographical divisions for mammals (map 3 and map 4). As with the plants, the mammals have distinctive western and eastern distributions in the arid northwest geographical region; the divisional boundary

Table 1. China's Biogeographic Divisions

Areas	Subareas	Regions
I. Northeast China	Ia. Inner Mongolia steppe and northeastern China plain	1. Greater Xing'an Mountains
		2. Northeastern China plain
		3. Nei Mongol arid steppe and desert grassland
		4. Ordos Plateau arid and desert grassland
	Ib. Lesser Xing'an and Changbai mountains	5. East of Northeast China
	Ic. Northern China	6. Northern China
		7. Huangtu Plateau forest grassland and arid grassland
II. Southeast China	IIa. Central China	8. Huaibei Plain and plains of the middle and lower Yangtze River
		9. Qinling and Daba mountain mixed forest
		10. Sichuan Basin agriculture
	IIb. Highlands and plains in the south to Yangtze River	11. Southeast China hills and basins evergreen broadleaf forest
		12. Yangtze River southern bank evergreen broadleaf forest
		13. Yunnan-Guizhou Plateau evergreen broadleaf forest
	IIc. Coast and islands of southern China	14. South to Nan Ling evergreen broadleaf forest
		15. Southern Yunnan tropical monsoon forest
		16. Hainan and Leizhou Peninsula tropical rain forest and monsoon forest
		17. Taiwan island evergreen broadleaf forest and monsoon forest
		18. South China Sea islands tropical rain forest
III. Southwest China	IIIa. Southeast and south of Tibetan Plateau	19. Southern Sichuan and Yunnan Plateau evergreen broadleaf forest
		20. Eastern Tibet and Western Sichuan incisive hill coniferous forest and alpine meadow
		21. Himalayan Mountains
	IIIb. Central and northern Tibetan Plateau	22. Northeast Tibetan Plateau
		23. Western and central Qinghai-Tibetan Plateau
IV. Northwest China		24. Alashan Plateau temperate desert
		25. Eastern Tian Shan temperate desert
		26. Northern Xinjiang
		27. Tarim Basin and Kunlun Mountains

for mammals occurs farther west than that for plants (map 3). The mammals also separate eastern monsoonal China into northern and southern areas, and the boundary for mammals is further south than that for plants. In the large arc from northwest to southeast China, there is a single mammal biogeographical boundary compared with two for plants. Mammals in the interior drainage area on the Tibetan Plateau have northern affinities. The southeastern plateau region shows a continuous extension in faunal affinities to the southeast, maintaining a mammal fauna more similar to that of monsoonal southeastern China.

In northwest China the montane forests and grasslands of the Tian Shan and the Altai Mountains clearly are distinct from the surrounding arid landscape. The Altai (region F3, map 4) shows clear ties to the fauna of Russia's boreal forest. As a result, some biogeographers link the Altai with the Greater Xing'an Mountains of northeast China. However, more than twice as many Altai mammals occur simultaneously in the Tian Shan and the arid Dzungarian Basin as in the Greater Xing'an Mountains. In northeast China there are distinct differences in vegetation between the Greater and Lesser Xing'an mountains (regions 1 and 5, map 2), whereas mammal distributions are similar between these ranges, and the area can be classified as a single region (region A, map 4).

Overall, this analysis demonstrates that the ability to colonize varies between plants and animals, producing distinctive differences in the cluster analysis and the designation of major biogeographic areas in China. While plant distributions tend to be closely tied to prevailing environmental conditions, mammals generally exhibit broader geographic tolerance. Additionally, mammal distributions appear to be truncated by major rivers and mountain chains, whereas these do not appear to be as stringent barriers to plant distributions. Thus plant divisions appear to be more reliable than those of mammals as a general descriptor of China's biogeography.

Mammal Conservation

The mammals of China have been seriously threatened by a variety of anthropogenic causes. Few Chinese landscapes appear today as they occurred in the past; there has been an extreme loss of natural habitat, and natural habitats have increasingly become fragmented and isolated from one another. Chinese mammals have been harvested or poached heavily and unsustainably for food, products, and the pet trade. Native species have been subject to widespread poisoning campaigns. Additionally, the presence of alien invasive species, pollution, and litter has degraded many natural habitats. We fear that finding many Chinese mammals in the regions indicated on our distribution maps may not be possible today. One of our motivations for writing this guide is to attract attention to the Chinese mammal fauna so that effective conservation measures can be enacted.

The government of China understands the gravity of biodiversity loss. China is signatory to most major conservation conventions, such as the Convention on International Trade in Endangered Species (CITES; 1981), the Convention on Wetlands (Ramsar; 1992), the World Heritage Convention (1985), and the Convention on Biological Diversity (CBD; 1993). China has hosted a large number of major conservation workshops and congresses. The China Council for International Cooperation in Environment and Development (CCICED) has served as a model organization linking Chinese and international specialists in order to address issues of conservation and sustainable development. These efforts, however, often fall short in their implementation, resulting in ongoing threats to China's mammal diversity.

A first step in any conservation agenda is to recognize those species most in need of protection. In the species texts, we have listed the threatened species categorizations for Chinese mammals using four separate criteria, in this order: China (national) Species Red List, China State Key Protected Animal List, CITES appendix designation, and IUCN (global) Red List. We also present additional conservation information, when available, for each species. The instruments used for categorizing threatened species have distinctive characteristics and notations, as given below.

IUCN Red List

The IUCN (International Union for Conservation of Nature) Red List is one of the most respected indicators of the threatened status of species. The IUCN Red List presents the global status for a species using five independent quantitative criteria: (A) Population Reduction (measured as declines in population over time); (B) Geographic Range (extent of occurrence or area of occupancy); (C) Small Population and Decline; (D) Very Small or Restricted Population; and (E) Quantitative Analysis. Within each of these main criteria are additional refined criteria. Threatened species may qualify under any of these criteria for a listing as Critically Endangered (CR), Endangered (E), or Vulnerable (VU). Additionally, species can be listed as Near Threatened (NT), of Least Concern (LC), Extinct (EX), or Extinct in the Wild (EW). Some species cannot be listed because they are Data Deficient (DD), and others have not been evaluated (NE). In 2008 IUCN completed the Global Mammal Assessment, which classified the global Red List status of all mammals. These results are reported here for all Chinese mammals, unless updated subsequently (through January 2012; http://www .iucnredlist.org/initiatives/mammals).

China Species Red List

To complement the IUCN global Red Listing process, and to allow countries and regions to develop their own conservation priorities, IUCN developed a parallel mechanism for listing threatened species at national levels. These quantitative criteria take into consideration the extent of a species' range within a host country and other applications to tailor the IUCN Red Listing process to national levels. These criteria were followed in an ambitious effort to determine the Red List status all of China's mammals (Wang and Xie 2009). These evaluations include two additional categories: Regionally Extinct (RE), for those species that are now extinct in China although they exist elsewhere in the world; and Not Applicable (NA), for those species that are distributed at the margin of China and for which data are lacking (even though there may be sufficient data for a global assessment). All of China's mammals were assessed against these regional criteria; the only species for which we do not present a China Species Red List category are those whose taxonomy has changed since the workshops were held to produce the China Species Red List.

China State Key Protected Animal List

China's State Key Protected Animal List identifies select mammals as either Category I or Category II species. This national schedule of protected fauna is heavily skewed toward charismatic megafauna and is primarily composed of primates, carnivores, marine mammals, and ungulates. The representation on this list is not truly indicative of the overall threat across all taxa of mammals in China. The formulation of this list was initiated by the Chinese Endangered Species Scientific Commission and authorized by the Ministry of Forestry. Inclusion of species on the list was derived by consensus at an interactive workshop comprised of species specialists from throughout China. The State Key Protected Animal List was finalized soon after the People's Congress issued China's Wildlife Law in 1989.

Convention on International Trade in Endangered Species of Wild Fauna and Flora—CITES

Those species of mammal believed to be negatively affected by trade are listed in CITES appendixes. The Appendix I classification incorporates those mammals that would be threatened with extinction if traded. Trade in specimens of these species is permitted only in exceptional circumstances. Appendix II includes species not necessarily threatened with extinction, but for which trade must be controlled in order to avoid utilization incompatible with their survival. Listings on CITES Appendix I or II are current to late December 2011 (http://www.cites.org/eng/app/index.php).

China's Protected-Area System

Biodiversity conservation can take many forms, but one of the most recognizable is the establishment of nature reserves and protected areas, coupled with their effective management, to ensure that a decline in biodiversity does not occur. Thus, protected areas remain one of the best ways for governments to ensure biodiversity preservation, as well as serving as magnets for eco-tourists who desire to observe native species. Initially, few areas were protected, but the Chinese government has recently stepped up efforts to protect areas rich in biodiversity. By the end of 2010 over 8,000 protected areas had been established in China (not including Taiwan and Hong Kong), encompassing over 18 percent of China's land area (see map inside back cover).

Most of these were established after 1980, many after 1995. Of these areas, over 2,500 nature reserves (under the management of more than 10 governmental agencies) cover over 15 percent of the land area. Additionally (and sometimes overlapping) are 2,800 forest parks (State Forestry Administration), over 800 scenic landscape and historical sites (Ministry of Housing and Urban-Rural Development), over 300 geological parks (Ministry of Land and Resources), over 100 national wetland parks (State Forestry Administration), nearly 500 national water conservation scenic areas (Ministry of Water Resources), and 2,500 above A-grade scenic spots (National Tourism Administration).

The decision to protect species-rich areas in China stems from the belief that these lands will help define the national culture, assist in economic development among rural people, and provide destinations for tourists. Their function is to promote the retention of natural capital, provide flood control, and preserve biodiversity. However, in spite of the positive strides made in protected-area management in China, more work needs to be done to ensure that these lands will continue to support mammal biodiversity. China's protected areas are mainly found in the sparsely populated west. Many protected areas in China are small and isolated, minimizing their effectiveness in the preservation of biodiversity. Often they are poorly managed and insufficiently funded; in some instances key programs have been initiated that are actually counterproductive to the preservation of biodiversity (such as poisoning native wildlife). Incursions and poaching by people living outside of protected areas jeopardize their success. Nevertheless, the protected-area system in China has great potential to protect mammal biodiversity. With improved management, China's protected areas can become sites in which the study and viewing of mammals are enhanced.

How to Use This Book

We present available data on the systematics, distribution, and natural history of the 556 species of mammals found in China. The order of presentation follows the higher-level classification (from order to family to subfamily) as outlined in *Mammal Species of the World*, third edition (Wilson and Reeder 2005). Genera (within a family or subfamily) and species (within a genus) are alphabetized within a taxon. All taxa are identified by both their scientific and common names in English. Chinese names are given in both character and pinyin format. We have given a single English common name for each species, basically following the naming convention used in *Mammal Species of the World*. Many species are known by more than one common name, but we believe that the application of a single name will, over time, eliminate confusion and enhance the ability of mammalogists to communicate.

We present brief descriptions at each level of classification. Information given for each species includes distinctive characteristics, distribution, natural history, and conservation status. The depth of treatment reflects the information available for each species.

Distinctive Characteristics

Standard specimen measurements are given for each species, when available. These include head and body length (HB); tail length (T); length of hind foot (HF); and ear length (E) (fig. 1); as well as greatest length of skull (GLS). Bat measurements include forearm length (FA) (fig. 2). Shoulder height (SH) is presented for most larger mammals. These measurements are given in millimeters, unless otherwise stated for large mammals. Body mass (Wt) is given when available. The dental formula for a species (or other taxon) is presented as the upper incisors (I), canines (C), premolars (P), and molars (M)/lower incisors (i), canines (c), premolars (p), and molars (m), followed by the total number of teeth (e.g., 2.0.3.3/1.0.2.3 = 28).

A description of the appearance of each species and its distinctive characteristics follows. Drawings of 384 species (69 percent of Chinese mammals) accompany these descriptions. Our artist, Federico Gemma, examined specimens from the Institute of Biology, Chinese Academy of Sciences, Beijing, as well as the

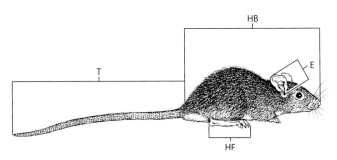

Figure 1. Standard external measurements used in the species accounts: HB = head and body length; T = tail length; HF = hind foot length; E = ear length.

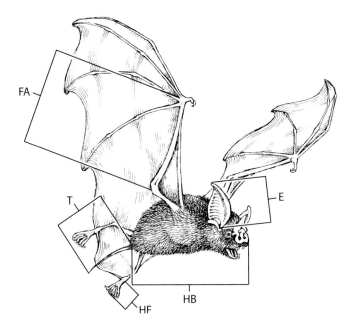

Figure 2. Standard external measurements used in the species accounts for bats: HB = head and body length; T = tail length; HF = hind foot length; E = ear length; FA = forearm length.

American Museum of Natural History, New York, and Smithsonian Institution, National Museum of Natural History, Washington, DC, to capture the color and nuances of each species; only a few drawings depict species that were not represented in these collections. He also visited the Beijing Zoo collection, which contains most of the large mammal species found in China. Additionally, authors made available to Gemma original photographs, other printed material, and Internet sources to assist with his depiction of species.

Distribution

A brief description of the distribution in China is given for each species, along with its range outside of China or the statement that the form is endemic to China. Every species description is accompanied by a map of its distribution in China. In a few cases we present separate maps of the historical and contemporary distribution of a species; otherwise the maps depict the original range of the species in China before any potential recent contraction of the range due to anthropogenic factors (see Mammal Conservation). Each map portrays the actual localities (dots) where a species has been found (or collected) in China. We present the maps in this manner, rather than as shaded range maps, for several reasons. First, the topography of China is so varied that any attempt to shade in a distributional range would inevitably present a misleading indication of the area(s) the species actually inhabits. Second, dot maps, such as we present, provide a gestalt for how well known or represented the species is in China; for example, common species are represented by hundreds of dots and tend to be very well understood, whereas those portrayed by only a few localities are generally poorly known.

The localities presented on maps were derived from data from the China Species Information Service. Data in CSIS were gathered using a variety of sources and recorded at the county level. The primary data included original locations from specimens housed at major mammal collections in China (Institute of Zoology, Chinese Academy of Science) and the United States (American Museum of Natural History; National Museum of Natural History), as well as published locality records from Chinese scientific surveys, journal articles, and Chinese provincial and regional mammal guides. All data added to CSIS were cross-referenced to their source, so that in verifying maps each author had available the data source for each locality. The original data entered for each map could have been corrupted for a number of reasons, including misidentification of specimens and out-of-date nomenclature. Thus, every map was reviewed carefully and updated. We believe that these maps portray the distribution of all mammal species in China in the most accurate form possible at the present time, although some of these distributions may need further definition.

Natural History

While information on the natural history of many Chinese mammals is fragmentary, some species are among the most widely recognized on Earth. We focus on the habitat requirements, mode of life, diet, and reproduction for each species, drawing from a variety of sources.

Conservation Status

We list the conservation status as determined by the China Species Red List analysis, the category from the China State Key Protected Animal List, the appropriate CITES appendix, and the IUCN global Red List analysis. Not all species have been categorized using all four of these criteria; we include only those that have been so evaluated. Details on each of these forms for assessing conservation status are found above.

Additional Material

Appendixes review those marine mammals that are found off the coast of China but are not included as a part of the Chinese fauna (Appendix I), those species whose distributional ranges appear very close to the Chinese border and may eventually be found in China (Appendix II), and those mammal species that have been introduced into China (Appendix III).

Acknowledgments

Financial assistance for this project was provided by the China Council for International Cooperation in Environment and Development, from funds made available by the governments of Norway (with special thanks to Peter Schei) and Sweden. We also received support from Arizona State University (ASU), Bethel College, Indiana, the National Museum of Natural History (Smithsonian Institution), and the American Museum of Natural History. The assistance of staff in the Beijing office of the Biodiversity Working Group, including Wu Lihui, Yin Songxia, Du Youmei, Du Youcai, Li Shengbiao, and Du Langhua, was invaluable. The administration and staff of the CAS Institute of Zoology mammal collection in Beijing were very helpful, and it is a pleasure to acknowledge their support. We benefited also from the mammal collections at the American Museum of Natural History, National Museum of Natural History (Smithsonian Institution), and the Chicago Field Museum (with thanks to Larry Heaney and Bruce Patterson). We appreciate the consultation and advice given by many of our colleagues, which greatly enriched our accounts: Alexei Abramov, William Bleisch, Thomas Geissmann, Colin Groves, Richard Harris, Mike Hoffmann, Charlotte Johnston, John Koprowski, John Lamoreux, Long Yongcheng, Richard Thorington, Wang Yingxiang, Peter Zahler, and Zhang Jingshuo, and Zhang Yingyi. William Bleisch and Richard Harris kindly reviewed selected color plates and range maps. We thank Crystal Palmer, Erin Gibbon, Hayley Ivins, Mary Boise, and Scott Holtz for their assistance with the manuscript. Brenda Flores and Crystal Palmer assisted with the final formatting of the range maps. We are grateful to the following for their assistance in translating scientific research papers: Eileen Westwig (Russian, French, and German); Margarita Uvaydov (Russian); and Julie Wozencraft, Chien Hsun Lai, Yu Xiang, Zhang Jingshuo, Chen Yanxi, Yan Rongsheng, Chen Yi, Badingqiuying, and Zhou Jiang (Chinese). We appreciate the talents of Patricia Wynne, who drew figures 1–2, and the unidentified Chinese artist(s) who drew figures 3–12 (these were composed during the Cultural Revolution when it was politically incorrect to bring attention to oneself by signing artwork). Staff at the ASU School of Life Sciences Visualization Center, in particular Jacob Sahertian, Allyson Moskovits, and Sabine Deviche, helped format the baseline map of China, prepared various black-and-white figures for publication, and assisted with the final preparation of the color maps. Larry Heaney and Harriet Smith kindly edited selected portions of the manuscript. Finally, we are indebted to the talented and supportive staff at Princeton University Press. Robert Kirk guided and encouraged our efforts, and the completed project is a direct result of his vision. We are also grateful for the meticulous attention that Terri O'Prey, Beth Clevenger, Kathleen Cioffi, Dimitri Karetnikov, Amy K. Hughes, and Anita O'Brien brought to this project.

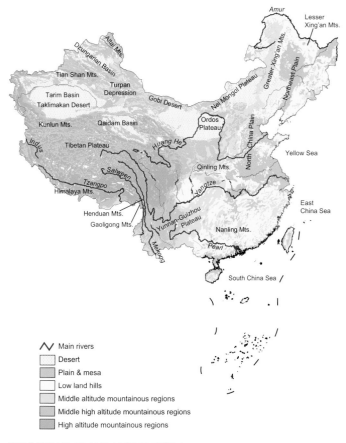

Map 1. Major Rivers and Landforms of China.

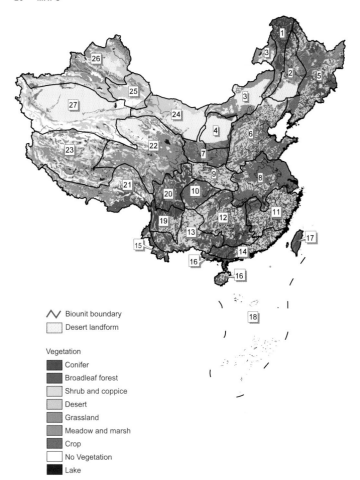

Map 2. Biogeographic Regions of China. The 27 biogeographic regions are based on vegetative characteristics. Regions 1–7 = Northeast China Vegetational Area; Regions 8–18 = Southeast China Vegetational Area; Regions 19–23 = Southwest China Vegetational Area; Regions 24–27 = Northwest China Vegetational Area (table 1). Background highlights vegetational zones across China.

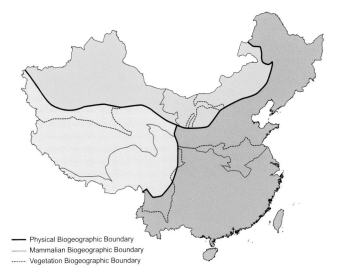

Map 3. China's Physical Geographic Regions and Major Biotic Divisions. The three physical geographic regions in China are shaded (salmon = Northwest Arid China; blue = Tibetan Plateau; purple = Eastern Monsoon China). The biotic divisions based on vegetation and mammal distributions are compared.

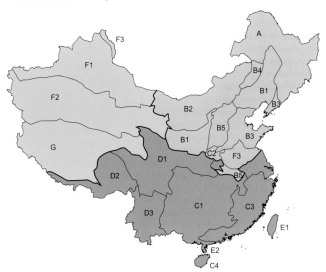

Map 4. Mammal Biogeographic Divisions and Regions of China. The major mammal biogeographic divisions (thick lines; blue = Northeast; green = Southeast; pink = West) and regions (thin lines) are portrayed.

Habitat 1. Tian Shan Grassland and Forest; Xinjiang (Andrew Smith)

Habitat 2. Tamarisk Riparian Habitat; Xinjiang (Andrew Smith)

Habitat 3. Bogda Feng from Turpan Basin; Xinjiang (Andrew Smith)

Habitat 4. Gobi Desert Habitat; Gansu (Andrew Smith)

Habitat 5. Nei Mongol Grasslands; Nei Mongol (Jingle Wu)

Habitat 6. Tibetan Plateau Grasslands; Qinghai (Andrew Smith)

Habitat 7. Tibetan Plateau Wetlands; Qinghai (Andrew Smith)

Habitat 8. Upper Yangtze River; Qinghai (Andrew Smith)

Habitat 9. Juniper Forest, Tibetan Plateau; Qinghai (Andrew Smith)

Habitat 10. Bamboo Forest, Dujiangyan Longqi-Hongkou Reserve; Sichuan
(Andrew Smith)

Habitat 11. Coniferous Forest, Juizhaigou; Sichuan (John MacKinnon)

Habitat 12. Forest Understory, Dahonggou Creek; Sichuan (W. Chris Wozencraft)

Habitat 13. Wolong Nature Reserve; Sichuan (Andrew Smith)

Habitat 14. Karst Forest; Maolan Protected Area; Guizhou (John MacKinnon)

Habitat 15. Xishuanbanna National Nature Reserve; Yunnan (Xie Yan)

Habitat 16. Mengla Forest; Yunnan (W. Chris Wozencraft)

Habitat 17. Damingshan Nature Reserve; Guangxi (John MacKinnon)

Habitat 18. Hainan Forest; Hainan (John MacKinnon)

Habitat 19. Mangrove Habitat; Hainan (John MacKinnon)

Habitat 20. Mixed Forest, Changbaishan; Jilin (Xie Yan)

Habitat 21. Mixed Conifer Forest, Changbaishan; Jilin (John MacKinnon)

Habitat 22. Northern Tundra, Changbaishan; Jilin (John MacKinnon)

Habitat 23. Northern Coniferous Forest, Changbaishan; Jilin (John MacKinnon)

Habitat 24. Grassland and Forest Edge, Changbaishan; Jilin (John MacKinnon)

Habitat 25. Forest Understory, Mudangjiang; Heilongjiang (John MacKinnon)

CLASS MAMMALIA—The Mammals

哺乳类 Burulei

Mammals belong to the class Mammalia, subphylum Vertebrata, phylum Chordata, kingdom Animalia. In spite of considerable variation in morphological structure among mammals, there is a suite of unique characteristics that defines the class. Pelage, or hair, is present in at least some stage of development in all mammals. It completely covers the bodies of most species, although it may be restricted to specific areas in some forms or occur only during embryonic development in others (such as whales). All young mammals are nourished with milk provided from mammary glands. A muscular diaphragm separates the lungs from the posterior body cavity. Mammals possess a four-chambered heart with only a left aortic arch (the right aortic arch is lost during development). Red blood cells lack nuclei at maturity in most species. And all mammals have three middle ear bones (malleus, incus, and stapes), and a single (dentary) bone comprises the lower jaw. The jaw articulates with the squamosal bone of the cranium. Additionally, nearly all mammals are viviparous (except monotremes), quadrupedal (except bats, some bipedal species, and those aquatic forms that have developed front flippers and lost their hind limbs), and have an external ear opening surrounded by a well-developed pinna (although the pinna may be reduced or absent in some aquatic species). Mammals are primarily endothermic, maintaining a relatively high and constant body temperature most of the time. Consequently, many of their adaptations revolve around the necessity to acquire significant amounts of food. Thus, most mammals have heterodont dentition, with teeth specialized to their diet in nature.

Mammals evolved from a lineage of primitive synapsid reptiles, and many of the most important fossil records of these early mammal-like creatures have been discovered in China. The last 65 million years of Earth history, the Cenozoic, is considered the age of mammals, and the major branches of the mammalian evolutionary tree (monotremes, marsupials, and placentals) diverged during this period, giving rise to the exciting diversity of mammals found on Earth today. The current (third) edition of *Mammal Species of the World* (Wilson and Reeder 2005) portrays living mammals as represented by 5,416 species in 1,229 genera in 29 orders. Past attempts to organize the higher categories of mammals have been varied, and an explosion of recent molecular and paleontological investigations has led to significant alterations in our efforts to characterize the phylogenetic relationships of mammals since the previous edition of this work. We follow the order of presentation of mammals in the third edition to describe the 556 mammal species in 14 orders that are found in China.

ORDER PROBOSCIDEA

FAMILY ELEPHANTIDAE

GENUS *ELEPHAS*—Elephants

长鼻目 Changbi Mu; 象科 Xiang Ke; 象属 Xiang Shu—象 Xiang

The elephants are unmistakable. There are two genera of elephants, one in Africa (*Loxodonta*) with two recognized species, and one in Asia (*Elephas*), the range of which includes China. The Asian Elephant is distinguished from the African forms by having smaller ears and a single lip on the end of its trunk, compared with two lips in African elephants. Dental formula: 1.0.3.3/0.0.3.3 = 26 (but tusk usually absent in female *Elephas*).

Asian Elephant *Elephas maximus*

亚洲象 Yazhou Xiang—**Distinctive Characteristics:** HB 550–650 cm; SH 320 cm (male), 250 cm (female); T 120–150 cm; Wt 4,160 kg (male), 2,720 kg (female). Uniquely large mammal with long proboscis, large triangular ears, thick gray skin with only a few bristly hairs (especially as tail tuft and on infants). Males have large ivory tusks; tusks of females at most protrude a few cm. Large rounded, flat feet. **Distribution:** Once ranged widely over much of S China, including Fujian, Guangdong, and Guangxi. The species disappeared from S Fujian and N Guangdong during the 12th century (Song dynasty) but held on in Guangxi into the 17th century (Ming dynasty). Now confined to Xishuangbanna prefecture of S Yunnan; extending to the Indian subcontinent, including Sri Lanka, through Indochina, Malay Peninsula, Sumatra, and NE Borneo. **Natural History:** Inhab-

its lowland and hill forests (generally at elevations <1,000 m) in evergreen and semievergreen tropical zone, often with bamboos. Eats a wide range of vegetation, with a strong preference for grasses and palms. Raids fields of rice, sugar cane, bananas, and papayas. May consume over 200 kg of vegetation per day. Diurnal and nocturnal, but usually rests at midday. Lives in small matriarchal family herds. Males solitary, or two or three males may travel together. Several female-led families may congregate at favored salt licks and mud wallows. Herds visit water every day. Various low rumbling sounds and loud trumpeting vocalizations are used to maintain social contact. Males have large tusks used in fighting and defense, to move obstacles in the forest, and to excavate mineral-rich earth at salt licks. Single young (rarely twins) weighing about 100 kg are born at intervals of several years. Gestation lasts 18–22 months. **Conservation Status:** Rare, restricted, and endangered by poaching and loss of habitat; also persecuted by farmers for raiding crops. While poaching continues, a ban on this activity is strictly enforced. There is evidence that the Chinese population had grown from approximately 100 in the 1970s, to 180 in the 1980s, to perhaps 150–250 by the mid-1990s. However, the sex ratio increasingly favors females, and an increasing percentage of males are tuskless because poaching is changing the gene pool. China RL—EN A1acd. China Key List—I. CITES—I. IUCN RL—EN A2c.

ORDER SIRENIA

FAMILY DUGONGIDAE

GENUS *DUGONG*—Dugongs

海牛目 Hainiu Mu; 儒艮科 Rugen Ke; 儒艮属 Rugen Shu—儒艮 Rugen
This order of large herbivorous marine mammals contains three families (one extinct) totaling five species and is characterized by paddle-like forelimbs, heavy bones, no hind limbs, and no dorsal fin. The dugongs (Dugongidae) can be distinguished from the other living family, the manatees (Trichechidae), by possessing an incisor (versus no functional incisors in manatees) and a notched tail (versus a spoon-shaped tail), and lacking nails on the flippers (versus flippers with nails in two of the three manatee species). The Chinese representative is in the monotypic Dugongidae.

Dugong *Dugong dugon*

儒艮 Rugen—**Distinctive Characteristics:** HB 240–400 cm; Wt 230–1,000 kg. Body fusiform, and hind limbs absent; head round; tail a deeply notched fluke with a crescent shape; forelimbs paddle-like and without nails. The short hair is distributed sparsely over the body, with the exception of dense bristles on the muzzle. Dental formula: 2.0.3.3/3.1.3.3 = 36. **Distribution:** East China and South China seas, at Guangdong, Behai City (Guangxi), Hainan, and Dashufang in S Taiwan; extending to the coasts of the Indian Ocean and SW Pacific Ocean. **Natural History:** Live in small groups in shallow coastal waters, although they can sometimes be found in deeper offshore waters. Most animals remain submerged for several minutes at a time, surfacing for a short time to breathe. Dugongs are not built for speed. They are herbivorous, subsisting largely on sea grass. Reproductive season primarily from June to September but may extend throughout the year. Males fight for access to females in a polygynous mating system. Gestation lasts 12–14 months. The single offspring is weaned at about 18 months but may remain with its mother for several years. **Conservation Status:** The Taiwanese population is believed to have been extirpated; there have been no recent sightings on the island. The mainland population is very poorly known. In the mid-1980s, dugongs mostly occurred along the coast of Guanxi and W Guangdong, and rarely on the coasts of Dianbai and Yangjang counties, Guangdong, in addition to the west coast of Hainan Island. However, most recent sightings have come only from Hainan, although even there coastal development and harbor construction have eliminated key sea-grass beds, causing dugongs to disappear. While dugongs have historically occurred in the Pearl River estuary, none have been seen in recent years in spite of intensive research on dolphins in this area. China RL—CR A1c; B1ab(i,iii) + 2ab(i,iii)c; C; D; F. China Key List—I. CITES—I. IUCN RL—VU A2bcd.

ORDER SCANDENTIA

FAMILY TUPAIIDAE

GENUS *TUPAIA*—Tree Shrews

树鼩目 Shuqu Mu; 树鼩科 Shuqu Ke; 树鼩属 Shuqu Shu—树鼩 Shuqu
These squirrel-like animals are distributed across SE Asia. They possess large eyes and lack long vibrissae in the facial region. Dental formula: 2.1.3.3/3.1.3.3 = 38. There are five genera and 20 species in the Scandentia; only a single species, one of 15 in the genus *Tupaia*, occurs in China.

Northern Tree Shrew *Tupaia belangeri*

北树鼩 Beishuqu—**Distinctive Characteristics:** HB 160–195; T 150–190; HF 36–45; E 12–20; GLS 41–49; Wt 110–185 g. Pelage olive green to dense brown; shoulder with faint vertical stripes. Tail bicolored, olive brown above and whitish underneath; tail hairs long, and overall the tail has the appearance of being flat. All five toes developed on feet; claws strong and sharp. The rostrum is elongated, and the ears are short and rounded. **Distribution:** S China; extending south through Thailand, Myanmar, India, Cambodia, Laos, Vietnam, and associated coastal islands. **Natural History:** Occupies tropical to subtropical forests from low elevations up to 3,000 m. Lives in tree holes (not of its own making). Arboreal and primarily crepuscular, but may be active at any time. Omnivorous, feeding on fruits and seeds in addition to insects, small vertebrates, and bird eggs. Territorial. Mates from March through August. Estrus lasts approximately 10 days, and gestation about one and a half months.

Females produce one or two litters of two to four young per year. **Conservation Status:** China RL—LC.

ORDER PRIMATES—Primates

灵长目 Lingzhang Mu—灵长类 Lingzhanglei
The order Primates includes humankind and its nearest relatives, including apes, monkeys, lemurs, and lorises. Most species have five digits on each limb, usually with an opposable first digit and mostly with flattened nails rather than claws. The brain is well developed. Only two pectoral mammae are present. Primates have two sets of teeth, the deciduous juvenile set being later replaced by permanent adult teeth. Upper canines, especially in males, are generally tusk-shaped. Molars have blunt cusps. There are two suborders of Primates, the Strepsirrhini, with seven families, one of which (Lorisidae) is found in China; and the Haplorrhini, with eight families, two of which (Cercopithecidae, Hylobatidae) are found in China.

FAMILY LORISIDAE—Lorises

懒猴科 Lanhou Ke—懒猴 Lanhou
Lorises are compact, small nocturnal primates with flat faces and large reflective eyes. Arms and legs slender and about equal in length. They have short tails, and their short ears are covered in fur. Second digit of forearm is reduced; second digit of hind leg possesses a claw. Rostrum long. Dental formula: 2.1.3.3/2.1.3.3 = 36. Upper incisors are small and separated from each other to form a comb. The Lorisidae contains five genera and a total of nine species; most forms are African, but two genera occur in Asia, of which only *Nycticebus* reaches China.

GENUS *NYCTICEBUS*—Slow Lorises

蜂猴属 Fenghou Shu—蜂猴 Fenghou
Nycticebus differs significantly from other genera of Lorisidae, bearing a compact form and short limbs. Short, thick fur; vestigial tail; grasping hands. Of three species, two occur in China.

Bengal Slow Loris *Nycticebus bengalensis*

蜂猴 Feng Hou—**Distinctive Characteristics:** HB 260–380; T 22–25; E 20–25; GLS 61–68; Wt 1–2 kg. Small nocturnal primate with very fluffy pelage. Dark brown stripe down back, short fluffy tail, and broad flat face with large eyes and moist rhinarium. General color varies from whitish to pale yellowish brown. The big toe on the hind foot is set apart from the other toes, allowing for greater gripping power. Second digit on front foot is reduced in size, and second toe has a long, curved claw used for scratching (fig. 3). The Bengal Slow Loris is much larger, paler, and has a more pronounced dark dorsal stripe than the Pygmy Slow Loris, also found in S China. **Distribution:** S China; extending to NE India and Indochina. **Natural History:** Inhabits tropical forest, scrub, bamboo thickets, and orchards. Occurs in both evergreen and deciduous formations. Feeds mostly on large insects such as katydids and crickets but also eats fruits and some young leaves and buds. Occasionally catches small birds, lizards, or larger prey. Strictly nocturnal. Mostly seen alone, moving slowly and cautiously within the canopy or in small trees. Can walk quite fast when crossing the ground from one tree to another. Sleeps by day curled up in a ball in dense vegetation or tree hole. Both sexes are territorial and mark territories with

Figure 3. Feet of the Bengal Slow Loris showing the reduced second digit and enlarged and separated big toe (a = front foot; b = hind foot).

urine. Ranges of the two sexes overlap, and animals may engage in social grooming. The large eyes possess pronounced *tapeta lucida*, giving the animal excellent night vision. The animal stalks prey by slow, stealthy movements, then grabs it with front feet in a fast and accelerating move followed by a bite. Second digit on each hind foot has an elongated toilet claw used for grooming; other digits have flat nails. Estrous females emit a loud whistle that attracts males. Gestation lasts about six months. Single young, or rarely twins, cling on their mother for about three months but may be "parked" on a branch while their mother forages alone. **Conservation Status:** China RL—EN A2cd; B1ab(iii). China Key List—I. CITES—I. IUCN RL—VU A2acd + 3cd + 4acd.

Pygmy Slow Loris *Nycticebus pygmaeus*

倭蜂猴 Wo Fenghou—**Distinctive Characteristics:** HB 210–260; T 10; GLS <55; Wt 250–800 g. Small, rufous-orange-colored loris. In winter, grayer, with a faint dorsal stripe and curly hair; in summer, without dark dorsal stripe and with little curly hair. **Distribution:** Recorded only in SE Yunnan, however, it is unclear whether these are wild-caught local animals or animals brought into the country from Vietnam in the wildlife trade; extending into NE Laos, Vietnam, and E Cambodia. **Natural History:** Inhabits low-lying evergreen forest, secondary forest, and scrub. Diet consists of insects, fruits, young leaves, and presumably small vertebrates. Also known to gouge trees and eat the resulting gum exudate. Behavior similar to that of the Bengal Slow Loris. **Conservation Status:** China RL—EN A2cd; B1ab(iii); D. China Key List—I. CITES—I. IUCN RL—VU A2cd.

FAMILY CERCOPITHECIDAE—Old World Monkeys and Baboons

猴科 Hou Ke—猴类 Houlei

The suborder Haplorrhini is commonly divided into three infraorders containing the tarsiers, New World monkeys (Platyrrhini), and Old World monkeys (Catarrhini), respectively. The catarrhine lineage is further divided into two superfamilies: the Cercopithecoidea and the Hominoidea. Within the Cercopithecoidea is the single family Cercopithecidae, containing two subfamilies, the Cercopithecinae and Colobinae, and representatives of both are found in China. The Cercopithecidae are medium-large apes and monkeys, with tails and limbs equal in length or with hind limbs slightly longer than forelimbs. Dental formula: 2.1.2.3/2.1.2.3 = 32.

SUBFAMILY CERCOPITHECINAE—Old World Monkeys

猴亚科 Hou Yake—猴类 Houlei

The Cercopithecinae represents the main branch of Old World monkeys, including many African genera such as mangabeys, baboons, and guenons. Of 10 total genera, only one, *Macaca* (the macaques), reaches Asia. Quadrupedal, omnivorous monkeys with both arboreal and terrestrial abilities. Tails long to short. Most live in large multimale groups; weakly territorial.

GENUS *MACACA*—Macaques

猕猴属 Mihou Shu—猕猴 Mihou

Macaques are highly intelligent, versatile monkeys. They are to varying degrees adapted to terrestrial life, with their quadrupedal stance and reduced tail length. They usually jump to the ground to flee predators rather than stay in the canopy. Some species can swim. They live in large multimale groups. Females show a bright red face and ischial swellings to indicate estrus. Diet is omnivorous, and most are wily crop raiders. Typical pelage color is agouti brown, with alternating light and dark bands of color in the hairs producing a grizzled appearance. Possess cheek pouches. Upper canines of males strong, with a groove on the labial surface. Of 21 species of *Macaca*, six occur in China. A seventh species, the Long-tailed Macaque (*M. fascicularis*), has been introduced into Hong Kong and now ranges feral there, where it hybridizes with *M. mulatta*.

Stump-Tailed Macaque *Macaca arctoides*

短尾猴 Duanwei Hou—**Distinctive Characteristics:** HB 485–650; T 45–50; HF 145–177; GLS 120–157; Wt 7 kg (male), 5 kg (female). Pelage is dark brown, varying from blackish to reddish. The face is bare and reddish brown in color, becoming bright red when excited or in estrus. Tail is very short (ca. 10% of HB length), so short the species sits on its tail. Skull has pronounced brow ridges. **Distribution:** S China; extending to Bhutan, Assam (India), Myanmar, Indochina to N Malay Peninsula. **Natural History:** Occurs in upland forests in mountainous regions. Feeds on fruits, seeds, insects, small vertebrates, and young leaves. Regularly raids crops for maize, rice, and potatoes. As in other macaques, has cheek pouches to carry food while foraging.

Lives in multimale groups of up to 50 individuals, occupying very large ranges and sometimes moving from one hill range to another. Female face and bare skin around ischial callosities become red during estrus. Mating is baboon-style, with male grasping the female's legs with his feet. Single births occur at about one- to two-year intervals. Males form affiliations with infants and sometimes care for them. **Conservation Status:** China RL—VU A2cd + 3cd. China Key List—II. CITES—II. IUCN RL—VU A3cd + 4cd.

Assam Macaque *Macaca assamensis*

熊猴 Xiong Hou—**Distinctive Characteristics:** HB 515–665; T 170–250; HF 155–175; E 35–37; GLS 131–159; Wt 6–12 kg (male), 5 kg (female). A brown, short-tailed macaque with bare brown face. Distinguished from the Rhesus Macaque by gray rather than rufous hindquarters and hair extending up to ischial callosities. Distinguished from the Northern Pig-tailed Macaque (but not from the Rhesus) by its hairy, pendulous tail. Slightly smaller, longer-tailed, and paler than the Tibetan Macaque. Tail much longer than the Stump-tailed Macaque's. Sagittal crest of skull conspicuous; face long, nose flat. **Distribution:** SW and S China; extending to E Himalayas, Bangladesh, Bhutan, and Assam (India) through Myanmar and through N Indochina as far south as the Tenasserim Hills and W Thailand. **Natural History:** Occurs in both evergreen and deciduous forests in hill and mountain terrain. Feeds on fruits, young leaves, insects, and small vertebrates. Typical diurnal, quadrupedal macaque. Lives in small groups of 10–15 animals, usually with only one adult male per group; sexually dimorphic. Travels mostly on ground and spends long periods resting and grooming on ground or rocky terrain, but feeds mostly in trees and bushes. Has large cheek pouches for carrying food while foraging. Female posterior becomes red during estrus. Single births occur at about one-year intervals. **Conservation Status:** China RL—VU A2cd + 3cd. China Key List—I. CITES—II. IUCN RL—NT.

Formosan Rock Macaque *Macaca cyclopis*

台湾猴 Taiwan Hou—**Distinctive Characteristics:** HB 360–450; T 260–456; GLS 96–117; Wt 4–5 kg. Typical pink-faced macaque with a medium-length tail and grayish-brown pelage. Similar to Rhesus Macaque but grayer, with dark tail. Some rufous on crown. Head round, face flat. **Distribution:** Taiwan

(most common in northeastern and southwestern parts). Endemic. **Natural History:** Mostly confined to main mountain chain and wild coastlines. Eats fruits, leaves, seeds, insects, crustaceans, and small vertebrates. Diurnal and quadrupedal; lives in small to medium-sized, multimale groups containing up to 60 individuals. Due to population reduction in recent years, most groups are small and may contain only a single male. Habits similar to those of other macaques. Red perineum swells in estrous females. Reaches maturity at five to six years. Single young are born and stay with their mother for about two years. **Conservation Status:** China RL—EN B1ab(i,iii). China Key List—I. CITES—II. IUCN RL—LC.

Northern Pig-Tailed Macaque *Macaca leonina*

北豚尾猴 Beitunwei Hou—
Distinctive Characteristics:
HB 440–620; T 120–180; GLS
111–142; Wt 11–14 kg. Powerful, stocky macaque with short, sparsely haired tail. Tail is normally pendulous, but is held erect at times of high excitement. General color agouti brown. Sexual dimorphism is high, and males have a broad ruff of grayish hair around face with a concave dark patch on their crown caused by shorter vertical hairs. The bare face is generally pink, but bluish above the eyes; males give threat signals by raising their eyebrows to give a blue flash. **Distribution:** W Yunnan; extending to N Indochina, Bangladesh, and Assam (India). **Natural History:** Inhabits tropical and subtropical evergreen and semi-evergreen forests in hilly terrain. Eats fruits, leaves, shoots, and some insects, small animals, and eggs. Lives in large multimale troops, often of 30 or more animals, which range over very large home ranges of many square kilometers. Troops feed in trees but travel mostly on the ground. Dispersed groups maintain contact with low hoots and grunts. When alarmed, animals drop from trees and flee on ground. The species is a serious and wily crop raider, especially of maize fields. Males can be aggressive and have been known to kill dogs. A single young is produced following a gestation of 171 days. **Conservation Status:** China RL—EN A1cd; B1ab(i,iii); D. China Key List—I (as *M. nemestrina*). CITES—II. IUCN RL—VU A2cd + 3cd + 4cd.

Rhesus Macaque *Macaca mulatta*

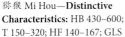

猕猴 Mi Hou—**Distinctive Characteristics:** HB 430–600; T 150–320; HF 140–167; GLS 95–122; Wt 7–10 kg (male), 5–6 kg (female). Medium-sized brown macaque with moderate sexual dimorphism. Pelage light agouti brown with contrasting orange tinge on cap, lower back, and base of tail. Tail medium length and not very fluffy. **Distribution:** From the eastern valleys of the Tibetan Plateau to the east coast, Hainan Island, and as far north as Beijing; introduced into Hong Kong; extending to N Indochina, N Thailand, N India, and Afghanistan. **Natural History:** Inhabits forests, woodlands, coastal scrub, and rocky areas with scrub and trees. Feeds on fruits, leaves, shoots, insects, small vertebrates, and eggs. Lives in large multimale troops of up to 50 animals. Troops occupy large to small home ranges, depending upon the suitability of habitat. In areas where monkeys are provisioned, such as S Hainan and Guangdong, high densities and considerable overlap of group ranges can occur. Noisy squabbles over food, females, dominance, or territory are accompanied by barking and fear squeals. Animals are quite terrestrial but also feed in trees. On Hong Kong where *M. fascicularis* has also been introduced, mixed-species groups and hybridization have occurred. **Conservation Status:** China RL—VU A2cd. China Key List—II. CITES—II. IUCN RL—LC.

Tibetan Macaque *Macaca thibetana*

藏酋猴 Zangqiu Hou—**Distinctive Characteristics:** HB 490–710; T 60–100; GLS 121–168; Wt 10–25 kg. Large, stocky, short-tailed macaque. Hair is long and thick; dark brown on back and paler buffy white ventrally. The bare face is generally pink, but red in adult females. **Distribution:** Wide ranging across C and SE China. Endemic. **Natural History:** Inhabits tropical and sub-tropical forests of mountainous regions up to 3,000 m. Eats fruits, young leaves, insects, small birds, and eggs. Lives in large multimale troops. A single dominant male leads in defense and arbitrates disputes. Low levels of aggression are expressed among group members, and females display consistently high levels of affiliative behavior based on kinship. Troops travel both through trees and on ground. Food is collected mostly in trees, but increasingly monkeys exposed to tourists have learned to pester visitors for food and eat off the ground. Breeding occurs throughout the year, primarily between January and August, most concentrated in March–April. Females, on average, become sexually active in their fourth year. Generally a single young is born every two years; gestation is approximately 70 days. Males deliver a significant proportion of the parental care of young. The thick coat enables the species to survive the extremes of winter weather in the mountains. **Conservation Status:** Widespread, but shy where persecuted. There are large groups of Tibetan Macaques in Mount Emei of Sichuan and Huang Shan of Anhui. China RL—VU A1cd. China Key List—II. CITES—II. IUCN RL—NT.

SUBFAMILY COLOBINAE—Leaf-eating Monkeys

疣猴亚科 Youhou Yake—疣猴 Youhou
The Colobinae are the leaf-eating specialists among the Old World monkeys. These animals are typically rather arboreal, with arms nearly as long as their legs and the ability to travel through trees in a semibrachiating manner. They have long intestines and sacculated stomachs for digesting cellulose. All species have long tails that are used for balance. Colobines live in single-male groups or aggregations of such groups. Some species are strongly territorial. Of 10 genera, three occur in China.

GENUS *RHINOPITHECUS*—Snub-nosed Monkeys

仰鼻猴属 Yangbihou Shu—仰鼻猴 Yangbihou
Rhinopithecus is a specialized group of colobines. Four of five species occur in China. All species have a sacculated stomach that allows them to digest very coarse and woody materials. This allows them to live at higher altitudes and in harsher environments than other primates, where they occur in huge aggregate troops sometimes numbered in hundreds of animals together. They are large monkeys and have a special upturned nose and small lappets at the sides of the mouth. All three Chinese endemic species were formerly considered a single species. A new, all black species, the Burmese Snub-nosed Monkey, was recently discovered in adjacent Myanmar and reportedly extends into the Gaoligong Mountains of W Yunnan.

Black Snub-Nosed Monkey *Rhinopithecus bieti*

滇金丝猴 Dian Jinsihou—**Distinctive Characteristics:** HB 740–830; T 510–720; GLS 104–135; Wt 17 kg (male), 12 kg (female). Large monkey with very long tail. Back, sides, sides of limbs, hands, feet, and tail all grayish black. Cheeks, ears, sides of neck, venter, and inner sides of limbs white. Bare facial skin is pink with

black patch on bluish nose. Lips are deep reddish pink. Infants are white and become yellowish before turning gray. Adult male has long hair on back and crown. **Distribution:** Confined to montane forests of Yun Ling Mountains in NW Yunnan and extreme SE Xizang to west of Yangtze River and east of Mekong River. Endemic. **Natural History:** Lives in high-elevation evergreen conifer forests and mixed conifer and oak forests from 3,400 to 4,100 m elevation. Eats mostly lichens, supplemented by bark, leaves, bamboo, acorns, and some berries. Has a sacculated stomach to assist in the breakdown of cellulose, allowing this species to eat tough and woody materials available in these forests through the winter. Live in large bands, up to 200 animals, composed of many smaller single-male groups. The bands break into smaller units, groups, and some all-male groups during the breeding season. Survives severe winters and deep snow. Long, dense hair is an adaptation to cold, damp local conditions. Animals are mostly arboreal and agile for their size, making great leaps and some semibrachiation. They feed and travel on the ground above the treeline. Groups proceed in single file and spend roughly a third of their time feeding actively and a third resting. Groups have large home ranges and may take several years to exploit their entirety. They move to lower elevations in severe winter weather. Vocalizations consist mainly

of soft murmurs; loud calls are heard only infrequently. Menstrual cycle is 26 days, and frequency of breeding peaks in spring and autumn. A single young is born. Females reach maturity in four to five years; males in five to six years. **Conservation Status:** China RL—EN A1cd; B1ab(i,iii); E. China Key List—I. CITES—I. IUCN RL—EN C1.

Gray Snub-Nosed Monkey *Rhinopithecus brelichi*

黔金丝猴 Qian Jinsihou—**Distinctive Characteristics:** HB 640–690; T 700–850; GLS 100–130; Wt 15 kg (male), 8 kg (female). Large, long-tailed monkey with dark pelage and blue face. Males are much larger than females and more brightly colored. Crown blackish with pale rufous central spot and pelage centrally parted, ears with whitish tuft of hair. Facial skin blue with pinkish above eyes and around mouth. Sometimes has pink lappet at corner of mouth. Fringe of hair around face grayish. Rest of pelage dark blackish gray with a chestnut band across chest, on back, and on upper forearms. Nipples and scrotum are white, contrasting with the darker body, and the penis is black. Tail black with whitish tip. **Distribution:** Guizhou; confined to mountain forests on and around Fanjing

Mountain in the Wuling Mountain Range. Endemic. **Natural History:** Lives in mixed deciduous and evergreen broadleaf forests at moderate elevations between 1,500 and 2,200 m. Like the other *Rhinopithecus* species, this is a folivorous monkey living in huge troops that consist of aggregations of several subgroups that periodically break up and recombine. Subgroups are generally single male or all male in composition. A wide range of flowers, shoots, twigs, bark, lichens, and fruits are consumed. **Conservation Status:** China RL—EN A1ac; B1ab(i,ii,iii); E. China Key List—I. CITES—I. IUCN RL—EN B1ab(iii,v); C2a(ii).

Golden Snub-Nosed Monkey *Rhinopithecus roxellana*

川金丝猴 Chuan Jinsihou— **Distinctive Characteristics:** HB 520–780; T 570–800; GLS 104–135; Wt 15–17 kg (male), 6.5–10 kg (female). A large, long-tailed monkey with golden-yellow pelage, long hair, and bluish face. Adult male much larger than female and has upturned nose and pink lappets at corners of mouth. Races vary in coloration: Sichuan forms are darker, those in Hubei are paler, and those in Shaanxi are bright golden. **Distribution:** C China. Endemic. **Natural History:** Inhabits subalpine conifer forests from 2,000 to 3,500 m, descending into broadleaf and mixed forests in winter months. Strongly prefers to live in primary (undisturbed) forests. Feeds on a wide variety of tree leaves, hemlock shoots, tree bark, some fruits, a few insects, and especially the cabbage lichens that festoon the tree branches in these damp, cold forests. Primarily arboreal, although it occasionally descends to the ground. Lives in very large troops reaching 100 or more animals. These seem to be composed of several subgroups that may disperse and reform in irregular patterns. The smaller family subgroups are composed of 5–10 individuals with a single adult male and form the primary social unit within this species. Groups range over many square kilometers. Most females first breed at age five, and males do not become reproductively competent until the age of six and a half. Mating occurs in the fall, and births occur six months later in the spring. **Conservation Status:** China RL—VU A1c. China Key List—I. CITES—I. IUCN RL—EN A2ac.

Burmese Snub-Nosed Monkey *Rhinopithecus strykeri*

缅甸金丝猴 Miandian Jinsihou—**Distinctive Characteristics:** HB 555; T 780. Predominantly black pelage, with the exception of white ear tufts, chin beard, and perineal area, and a "moustache" of whitish hairs above the upper lip. Tail long (140% of HB). **Distribution:** E Yunnan in the Gaoligong Mountains; extending into NE Kachin State, Myanmar. This newly discovered species is geographically isolated from other snub-nosed monkeys and separated from them by two major barriers: the Mekong and the Salween rivers. **Natural History:** Lives in high-elevation forest; its habits are presumably similar to those of *R. bieti*. **Conservation Status:** China RL—NA. IUCN RL—CR A4cd.

GENUS *SEMNOPITHECUS*—Sacred Langurs

长尾叶猴属 Changweiyehou Shu—长尾叶猴 Changweiyehou
The sacred langurs are larger, longer-legged, and more terrestrial than the closely related *Trachypithecus* (lutungs), and live in larger multimale groups. Once classified with *Trachypithecus* within the genus *Presbytis*. The young are born white and gradually assume darker adult coloration. Calls tend to be discrete barks. Of seven species in the genus, only one occurs in China.

Nepal Gray Langur *Semnopithecus schistaceus*

长尾叶猴 Changwei Yehou—**Distinctive Characteristics:** HB 620–790; T 690–1,030; GLS 120–145; Wt 9–24 kg (male), 7.5–18 kg (female). Large, rangy langur with long hind legs and tail held high when running across ground. Color pale gray to cream; back, tail, and outside of thighs darkest. Ears and almost bare face black. Hair of forehead forms a fringe over the brow. Himalayan race is a darker gray than forms from the Chumbi River region. **Distribution:** S Xizang; ranging to N Pakistan, Nepal, Sikkim (India), Bhutan, N Myanmar. **Natural History:** Occurs in high forests and mountain scrub of the Himalayas to elevations above 5,000 m. Omnivorous diet consists of leaves, fruits, and some insects and vertebrates. More terrestrial than most other leaf-eating monkeys, but also feeds in trees where it shows considerable agility and occasional semibrachiation and spectacular leaping. Lives in small to large troops containing up to 25 animals, formed as single-male or multimale units with adult males acquiring a harem of females. Groups show much allo-grooming behavior. Single births are the norm. Gestation is 168–200 days, and weaning takes up to 20 months. Mothers may allow other females to hold or care for their young. **Conservation Status:** Scarce and limited in distribution within China but able to escape persecution in rugged mountain terrain. China RL—EN A2c; B1ab(i,iii). China Key List—I. CITES—I. IUCN RL—LC.

GENUS *TRACHYPITHECUS*—Lutungs

乌叶猴属 Wuyehou Shu—乌叶猴 Wuyehou

Trachypithecus and *Semnopithecus* are similar genera, and formerly both were classified within the genus *Presbytis*. *Trachypithecus* young are born golden, then fade to pale yellow before assuming adult coloration. Groups usually contain a single male or represent associations of two single-male groups. Male territorial calls are harsh and repetitive. More arboreal than *Semnopithecus*. Of 17 species of *Trachypithecus*, five occur in China.

Tenasserim Lutung *Trachypithecus barbei*

缅甸乌叶猴 Miandian Wuyehou—**Distinctive Characteristics:** HB 520–620; T 600–880; Wt 6–9 kg. Back brown, nearly black; legs and tail paler dark gray with no black on distal part; underparts pale (gray). There is an asymmetrical white patch on the skin of the inside of the thigh in females. The upright crown hair forms a distinct crest. There are sparse white hairs on the upper lip and blackish hairs on the lower lip, and the lips are bluish black in coloration; the face has a soft violet coloration. **Distribution:** A few records exist from Yunnan (Hekou and Xishuangbanna); extending to Myanmar and N Indochina. **Natural History:** Gives birth to one offspring at a time. Its natural history is likely similar to that of other lutungs. **Conservation Status:** Very rare and poorly known. China RL—NE. CITES—II. IUCN RL—DD.

François' Langur *Trachypithecus francoisi*

黑叶猴 Hei Yehou—**Distinctive Characteristics:** HB 520–710; T 700–900; GLS 84–97; Wt 9–9.5 kg. Elegant black leaf-eating monkey with long tail and hair on crown forming pointed crest. Adults all black or may have white cheek fringes. Infant is orange, fading to yellow. **Distribution:** Guangxi and Guizhou; extending to N Vietnam, C Laos. **Natural History:** Confined to limestone outcrops with forest or scrub in monsoon evergreen rain-forest habitats. Seems to prefer steep slopes and deep valleys with complex topography. Occurs at low elevations. Lives in single-male troops. Eats leaves and some fruits. Uses caves for shelter and

giving birth. Moves slowly and rests for most of the day in sparsely vegetated areas. Behavior similar to that of other leaf-eating monkeys. **Conservation Status:** Rare; restricted range, fragmentation, and narrow habitat combined with persecution by farmers and hunters have made this species vulnerable. Its primary threat is the tradition of using the species to make a medicated wine. In Fusui Nature Reserve in SW Guangxi, the local population declined by over 50% between 1995 and 2000 due to severe loss of habitat. There are encouraging signs that hunting of this species is being controlled. China RL—EN A2cd + 3cd. China Key List—I. CITES—II. IUCN RL—EN A2cd.

Phayre's Leaf-Monkey *Trachypithecus phayrei*

菲氏叶猴 Feishi Yehou—**Distinctive Characteristics:** HB 550–710; T 600–800; HF 168–180; E 33; GLS 91–107; Wt 6–9 kg. Medium-sized, gray or pale brown leaf-eating monkey, with darker hands, feet, and head, and with conspicuous bluish-white eye-rings and whitish muzzle patch. Tail same color as back. Infant is orange. **Distribution:** SW China; extending to NE India, Bangladesh, Myanmar, N Thailand, N Laos, and N Vietnam. **Natural History:** Inhabits lowland and hill forests including deciduous forest. Feeds mostly on leaves and shoots, plus some seeds, and is fond of visiting salt licks. Females routinely disperse from family groups, and males are primarily philopatric. Females display a linear dominance hierarchy and appear more likely to squabble over food than expected. **Conservation Status:** Limited distribution and persecuted in China, but widespread elsewhere. China RL—EN A1c; B1ab(i,iii). China Key List—I. CITES—II. IUCN RL—EN A2cd.

White-Headed Langur *Trachypithecus poliocephalus*

白头叶猴 Baitou Yehou—**Distinctive Characteristics:** HB 520–710; T 700–900; Wt 6–9.5 kg. Graceful black langur with white head and neck and yellowish central crest. Tail basally black, but almost white at tip. Infant is golden. **Distribution:** S Guangxi; also on Cat Ba Island, Vietnam. **Natural History:** Lives on

limestone outcrops with scrub or forest cover, sometimes sympatric with *T. francoisi*. Stone caves on cliffs are used as sleeping sites. Lives in single-male troops, and group size ranges from 4 to 16 individuals. Rests more than half of daylight hours, and percentage of time engaged in play behavior increases with habitat quality. Leafy vegetation accounts for more than 90% of annual diet. Requires high-quality habitat for successful reproduction. **Conservation Status:** Habitat of the White-headed Langur is deteriorating and becoming increasingly fragmented; only 200 km^2 in 16 patches remain of its preferred habitat. Additionally, the species has been subject to a high level of poaching. Overall, its population has declined dramatically in recent years. China RL—EN A2cd + 3cd; C2a(i). China Key List—I. CITES—II. IUCN RL—CR A2cd.

Shortridge's Langur *Trachypithecus shortridgei*

戴帽叶猴 Daimao Yehou—**Distinctive Characteristics:** HB 498–716; T 767–1,041; HF 163–234; GLS 97–121; Wt 9–12 kg. Silvery-gray langur, with hands and feet darker gray, tail darkening toward tip. Legs slightly paler gray, underside more so. Facial skin shiny black, eyes startlingly yellow-orange. Narrow black brow band ending laterally in upward-pointed "spikes." Similarly, cheek whiskers at each corner of the mouth ending in downward-pointed spikes. Infant is orange. **Distribution:** SE Xizang and along Yunnan border on western side of Salween River; extending to N Myanmar. **Natural History:** Occupies dense, humid, monsoon evergreen broadleaf forests at low elevations (1,200–1,600 m). **Conservation Status:** Rare and restricted in China, where it is estimated that no more than 500–600 occur. China RL—EN A2cd; C2a(i). China Key List—I. CITES—I. IUCN RL—EN A2cd.

FAMILY HYLOBATIDAE—Gibbons and Siamangs

长臂猿科 Changbiyuan Ke—长臂猿 Changbiyuan
Hylobatids are small to medium-sized lesser apes. All species have no tail, but some have a pubic tuft. Forelimbs are very long, hanging below the knees. Upper

canines of both males and females well developed and tusk-shaped. Animals travel in a suspensory brachiation mode of arm swinging, although they can walk bipedally if they need to cross open ground. Gibbons are regarded as frugivorous, with a strong association with fig fruits, but up to half the diet may be composed of leaves. The social system is generally one of small territorial monogamous families. Families patrol and defend their territories from neighbors with loud chorus calls given in early morning. Some species are sexually dichromatic, males being dark and females light colored. Four genera of gibbons are recognized, three of which occur in China. These forms are anatomically very similar and were all formerly included in *Hylobates*.

GENUS *BUNOPITHECUS*—Hoolock Gibbons

白眉长臂猿属 Baimei Changbiyuan Shu—白眉长臂猿 Baimei Changbiyuan Formerly considered a single species, the Hoolock Gibbon has been split into western (*Bunopithecus hoolock*) and eastern (*B. leuconedys*) species, the latter of which occurs in China.

Eastern Hoolock Gibbon *Bunopithecus leuconedys*

西白眉长臂猿 Xi Baimei Changbiyuan—**Distinctive Characteristics:** HB 600–900; HF 140–153; GLS 93–99; Wt 6–8.5 kg. Males and females about the same size. Typical gibbon with very long arms used to hang and brachiate beneath branches. No tail, but male has long genital tassel. Both sexes have opposable but short thumb; curved fingers act as hooks in suspensory hanging. Female has small throat sac that helps to amplify territorial calls. Fur is dense and woolly. Male is blackish brown with white brows and buff-colored beard and genital tuft. Female is beige or buffy gray with dark brown cheeks and ventral area. Eyebrows are white, as is narrow edge to blackish face and a stripe beneath the eyes and across ridge of nose, giving face a skull-like appearance. Young are whitish at birth, but resemble male in pelage after a few months. **Distribution:** W Yunnan in Gaoligong Mountains, west of Salween River only; extending to Assam (India), Bangladesh, and Myanmar. **Natural History:** Inhabits a wide range of evergreen and semievergreen forest types from tropical to subtropical hill forest. Eats fruits supplemented by young leaves and occasionally flowers and insects. Lives in small monogamous family groups. Strongly territorial, with home ranges from 14 to 55 ha per family. Larger ranges may occur in poor habitat. Almost totally arboreal. Territorial duet calls are given frequently in early morning in summer, and later and less frequently in winter. Calls consist of loud wailing cries rising and falling in pitch and last about 15 minutes per session, and no sex-specific phrases are evident. Families sleep curled on large branches of emergent trees. Usually only one young born at a time at two- to three-year intervals. **Conservation Status:** China RL—CR A2cd; D. China Key List—I. CITES—I. IUCN RL—VU A3cd.

female

male

GENUS *HYLOBATES*—Gibbons

长臂猿属 Changbiyuan Shu—长臂猿 Changbiyuan
Of seven species of *Hylobates*, only one occurs in China.

White-Handed Gibbon *Hylobates lar*

白掌长臂猿 Baizhang Changbi-
yuan—**Distinctive Characteristics:**
HB 450–600; HF 130–155; E 33–37;
GLS 93–110; Wt 3.9–7 kg. Small gibbon with no genital tuft or throat
sac, white hands and feet, and clean
white margin around black face. Various color forms occur, from dark chocolate to pale buff, but these are not related
to gender. Long arms and curved fingers,
typical of all gibbons. **Distribution:** Only a
tiny distribution in the tropical zone of SW
Yunnan between the Salween and Mekong

rivers; extending to E Myanmar through W Indochina to Malay Peninsula and N Sumatra. **Natural History:** Inhabits tropical evergreen and semievergreen rain forests. Eats mostly fruits (especially those of the strangler fig), supplemented by leaves, buds, and some insects. Typical gibbon, living in small monogamous family units. Highly arboreal and territorial, defending territories with vocal "great calls" and aggressive chases and occasional fights. Travels in swift bursts of suspensory brachiation, feeding in many sites each day and sleeping on large branches or forks in the high canopy. Shy of water, and drinks from tree holes or rain on branches rather than visiting streams. Loud territorial chorus given at dawn and early morning consists of duet, with males giving many barks and whoops, and females giving the "great call" of prolonged wailing notes rising and falling in pitch. Normally only one infant is born at intervals of two to three years. **Conservation Status:** Very rare and restricted in China; some recent evaluations have indicated it may be extinct in China. China RL—CR A2cd; D. China Key List—I. CITES—I. IUCN RL—EN A2cd.

GENUS *NOMASCUS*—Gibbons

黑长臂猿属 Hei Changbiyuan Shu—黑长臂猿 Hei Changbiyuan
Of six species of *Nomascus*, four occur in China.

Black Crested Gibbon *Nomascus concolor*

黑长臂猿 Hei Changbiyuan—**Distinctive Characteristics:** HB 430–540; HF 150–165; GLS 90–115; Wt 7–8 kg. Largish gibbon. Male is all black; female is yellow, orange, or beige-brown with black crown and often a dark patch on ventral region. Both sexes have a blackish face and pronounced hair crest on crown. Races differ in the shape of the dark crown patch of females: forms east of the Black River have a small diamond-shaped patch, those between the Mekong and Black rivers have a round patch with trailing nape line, and those between the Salween and Mekong rivers have a large patch over entire crown with nape band. **Distribution:** S China; extending to N Vietnam. **Natural History:** Found in evergreen and semievergreen forests between 500 and 3,000 m. Eats mostly fruit, but supplemented with leaves, buds, and insects. As in other gibbons, the social structure consists of small territorial family groups with three to six individuals, but some with two adult females; home ranges 44–200 ha.

male

female

Highly arboreal; suspensory brachiation locomotion and early morning territorial duets. Call sessions last 10–13 minutes, with female giving the "great call" commencing with long notes, becoming faster and higher pitched as a series of barks to a climax followed by twitters. Male adds booms, staccato notes, and modulated phrases to the chorus. Subadults may join in. One young is born at a time at intervals of several years. **Conservation Status:** Becoming increasingly rare. Vulnerable to hunting, pet trade, and habitat destruction and fire. Main strongholds are in Ailao and Wuliang mountains. China RL—EN A1abcd; B1ab(i,ii,iii,iv,v); C2a(i); E. China Key List—I. CITES—I. IUCN RL—CR A2cd.

Hainan Gibbon *Nomascus hainanus*

海南长臂猿 Hainan Changbiyuan—**Distinctive Characteristics:** HB 480–540; HF 100–150; E 33–40; GLS 102–105; Wt 6.5–10 kg. Largish gibbon; males and females same size. Male is entirely black. Female is yellowish, orange, or beige-brown with a blackish cap and pale venter. Infants are born with a light coat, like that of females. At one year of age young turn dark, like males, but later only females will change again to a light coat color. **Distribution:** Hainan Island. Endemic. **Natural History:** As in the Black Crested Gibbon, with which it was formerly classified. Differs by uttering unique vibrato-type notes in the female territorial "great call." Lives in tropical evergreen rain forest where it obtains all its food, sleeps, and gives birth in treetops. Formerly occupied lowlands, but now confined to 800–1,200 m. Favorite foods include fleshy fruits, but will also eat animals and young leaves. Small family breeding groups defend territories against other such families. Females give birth to a single infant in alternate years, and young are carried by their mother for about two years. **Conservation Status:** Extremely precarious. It is believed that as many as 2,000 Hainan Gibbons inhabited the island in the 1950s, however, in 2003 only 13 animals were documented in Bawangling Nature Reserve. China RL—CR A1abcd; B1ab(i,ii,iii,iv,v); C2a(i); E. China Key List—I. CITES—I. IUCN RL—CR A2acd; B1ab(iii,v) + 2ab(iii,v); C2a(ii); D.

Northern White-Cheeked Gibbon *Nomascus leucogenys*

白颊长臂猿 Baijia Changbiyuan—**Distinctive Characteristics:** HB 451–525; HF 97–160; E 26–41; GLS 111–115; Wt 4.6–9 kg. Largish gibbon. Male is black except for white cheek patches that connect under black chin and extend over the ears; crown hair raised to form crest. Females are dark to light buff or creamy orange, often suffused with tan, gray, or black, with a black crown patch; crown hair not raised as in male. Females are sometimes larger than males. **Distribution:** S Yunnan; extending to N and S Laos, C and N Vietnam. In Yunnan the species is restricted to the southern parts of Xishuangbanna to the east of the Mekong River. A few families remain in Mengla County, Xishuangbanna. **Natural History:** As in the Black Crested Gibbon, with which this species was formerly classified. Songs in this species are given as duets between males and females, and the calls are highly dimorphic between the genders. **Conservation Status:** Rare and endangered. Extinct in much of its original and recent range. Found only in remote parts of Mengla and Shangyong nature reserves. Vulnerable to hunting, pet trade, and forest clearance. China RL—CR A2cd; D. China Key List—I. CITES—I. IUCN RL—CR A2cd + 3cd.

female

male

Cao-vit Crested Gibbon *Nomascus nasutus*

东黑冠长臂猿 Dong Heiguan Changbiyuan— **Distinctive Characteristics:** Wt 7–8 kg. Males and females same size. Largish gibbon, standing about 60 cm tall. Male is almost entirely black with a brownish tinge on chest and venter. Female is yellowish, orange, or beige-brown with a blackish cap and pale venter. Females have a distinctive white disk of fur around the face and a dark streak from the head down their back. This is the only gibbon in this genus in which babies are born black, as opposed to buff yellow or orange. Females later change to their light color. **Distribution:** SW Guangxi; extending into Vietnam. **Natural History:** Similar to that of the closely related Hainan Gibbon. **Conservation Status:** Considered extinct as recently as 2002, but small populations have been located on both sides of the China-Vietnam border; the Chinese population is highly vulnerable and consists of only 10 animals in two groups. China RL—NE. China Key List—I. CITES—I. IUCN RL—CR A2acd; C2a(i); D.

ORDER RODENTIA—Rodents

啮齿目 Niechi Mu—鼠类 Shulei

Rodents occur in nearly every habitat type present in China—from the high elevations of the Himalayas and the Tibetan Plateau to tropical rain forests, grasslands, dry deserts, agricultural fields, villages, cities, and even ships in port. They exploit terrestrial, arboreal, subterranean, and aquatic habitats. Some rodents are strictly herbivorous, but most are omnivorous, feeding on a wide variety of plants, fungi, insects, and small vertebrates. Often highly fecund, most rodents have an incredible capacity to populate their environment. Altogether there are more species of rodents in China than any other group (192 of 2,277 species recognized worldwide), and their impact on both the environment and society is enormous. They may be important agricultural pests, disease vectors, seed dispersers and seed predators, laboratory animals, keystone species, ecosystem engineers, and sources of food for wildlife and sometimes even for humans. Rodents are distinguished by a single set of large, ever-growing, chisel-like upper and lower incisor teeth. The rootless incisors are used for gnawing and enable them to gain access to a wide range of foods (lagomorphs are similar in this regard, but they have a second set of peg-like upper incisors just behind the first set). Canines are absent, leaving a long gap or diastema between the incisors and the cheek teeth. Dental formula: 1.0.0–2.3/1.0.0–1.3 = 16–22. Five suborders of Rodentia are recognized, four of which are represented in China (encompassing nine of 33 rodent families): (1) Sciuromorpha (Sciuridae, Gliridae); (2) Castorimorpha (Castoridae); (3) Myomorpha (Dipodidae, Platacanthomyidae, Spalacidae, Cricetidae, Muridae); and (4) Hystricomorpha (Hystricidae).

FAMILY SCIURIDAE—Squirrels

松鼠科 Songshu Ke—松鼠 Songshu

This family of rodents is extremely diverse in many aspects of its biology. It includes both arboreal and terrestrial forms and very small (mouse-sized) to large (dog-sized) species. Dental formula: 1.0.1–2.3/1.0.1.3 = 20–22. Sciurids possess five digits on their hind feet and four on their forefeet (a thumb is diminutive but present). The tail is well haired, but tail hairs are of variable length, longer on arboreal and shorter on terrestrial species. There are three broadly defined types of sciurids: flying squirrels, tree squirrels, and ground squirrels. The mostly nocturnal flying squirrels possess a furred gliding membrane (patagium) that extends between the limbs, as well as horizontally arranged hairs on the tails of small species (although not on *Petaurista*). Styliform cartilage extends from the wrist to add support to the patagium. Tree squirrels have rounded heads with prominent eyes and sharp, curved claws on their feet—traits they share with the gliding forms. Most tree squirrels, however, are diurnally active. The primarily diurnal ground squirrels have relatively flatter heads and straight claws. While living in burrows, they lack the extreme adaptations for life underground as found in some fossorial mammals. Sciurids are found worldwide except for Australia, Madagascar, S South America, and the extensive African and Arabian deserts. The family is comprised of 51 genera and 278 species; of these, 17 genera and 43 species are represented in China. The Sciuridae is divided into five subfamilies (Ratufinae, Sciurillinae, Sciurinae, Callosciurinae, Xerinae), four of which are found in China.

SUBFAMILY RATUFINAE

GENUS *RATUFA*—Giant Squirrels

巨松鼠亚科 Jusongshu Yake; 巨松鼠属 Jusongshu Shu— 巨松鼠 Jusongshu
Size large, habits arboreal; tail longer than HB length. Dental formula:
1.0.1.3/1.0.1.3 = 20. Three pairs of mammae. This subfamily is represented by a single genus, *Ratufa*, all forms of which occur in SE Asia from S India to Hainan Island, and four species, one of which is found in China.

Black Giant Squirrel *Ratufa bicolor*

巨松鼠 Ju Songshu—**Distinctive Characteristics:** HB 360–430;
T 400–510; HF 84–91; E 30–38; GLS 71–77; Wt 1,300–2,300 g. The Black Giant Squirrel is appropriately named, as the entire dorsal surface is covered by black fur, as is the entire tail; the ears have tufts. The nose and muzzle are white, and the ventral surface is buffy to rusty yellow, as is the small eye-ring. This species is highly variable throughout its range. **Distribution:** S China, including Hainan Island; extending to E Nepal, Assam (India), Myanmar, Thailand, Laos, Cambodia, and Vietnam, south through the Malay Peninsula to Java and Bali. **Natural History:** Arboreal; occupy tropical forests. On Hainan they are said to live in the forest canopy. They generally perch with their tail hanging down. They venture onto the ground only to chase another squirrel, or, during the breeding season, males descend to follow a female. At other times they are solitary or paired. Vocalization is a harsh short chatter. They are excellent climbers, able to leap 6 m or more. Their diet includes fruits, nuts, bark of some trees and shrubs, insects, and birds' eggs. Tree holes are used as shelters; during the breeding period they construct large nests of leaves and branches. Here the young are born and raised. May breed twice each year (in spring and fall), and gestation lasts 28–35 days. Litter size may consist of one to three young. **Conservation Status:** China RL— VU A1cd. China Key List—II. CITES—II. IUCN RL—NT.

SUBFAMILY SCIURINAE—True Squirrels

松鼠亚科 Songshu Yake—松鼠 Songshu

The Sciurinae comprises 20 genera and 81 species, of which eight genera and 15 species are represented in China. The Sciurinae can be divided into two tribes: Sciurini (tree squirrels) and Pteromyini (flying squirrels). The Chinese fauna contains only a single species in the Sciurini, *Sciurus vulgaris*; all others represent the Pteromyini.

GENUS *AERETES* (monotypic)

沟牙鼯鼠属 Gouyawushu Shu

Northern Chinese Flying Squirrel *Aeretes melanopterus*

沟牙鼯鼠 Gouya Wushu—
Distinctive Characteristics:
HB 275–355; T 275–362; HF 47–63; E 21–40; GLS 61–66. Not distinctively different from other large flying squirrels in form. No slender tufted hairs at base of ears. Sandy-brown or dusky dorsal pelage soft, long, and loose; tail brown, no black tip; feet black; venter pale buff to whitish, hairs shorter than on dorsum; edges of gliding membranes black dorsally; face and throat gray; upper incisors broad, grooved on anterior surface. **Distribution:** Two isolated populations in C China. Endemic. **Natural History:** Occupies mountainous forests. Information on the biology of this species is very scarce. **Conservation Status:** China RL—EN A1ac. IUCN RL—NT.

GENUS *BELOMYS* (monotypic)

毛耳飞鼠属 Maoerfeishu Shu

Hairy-Footed Flying Squirrel *Belomys pearsonii*

毛耳飞鼠 Mao'er Feishu—**Distinctive Characteristics:** HB 160–260; T 102–158; HF 31–47; E 31–40; GLS 40–44. Small flying squirrels with relatively large ears sporting threadlike black tufted hairs at their base. Tail relatively short and bushy; dorsal surface of patagium blackish, contrasting strongly with dark reddish brown of the dorsal pelage. Ventral side of patagium dark yellow-orange merging with the hoary, dark-gray-based ventral pelage. Three pairs of mammae. **Distribution:** C and SE China, to Taiwan and Hainan Island; extending to Vietnam, Thailand, and N Myanmar, and west in the Himalayas to E Nepal. **Natural History:** Occurs in dense subtropical and mixed forests at elevations of 500–2,400 m in the southern part of its range; to the north, lives in mixed broadleaf forest. Reported to feed on leaves and fruits, and in the north or at higher latitudes on oak leaves, but prefers needles of cedar and pine. Almost nothing else is known of its habits. **Conservation Status:** China RL—NT. IUCN RL—DD.

GENUS *EUPETAURUS* (monotypic)

棉毛鼯鼠属 Mianmao Wushu Shu

Woolly Flying Squirrel *Eupetaurus cinereus*

棉毛鼯鼠 Mianmao Wushu—**Distinctive Characteristics:** HB 515–610; T 370–480; HF 85–87; E 27–37; GLS 80–85; Wt 2.5 kg. A large and highly unusual flying squirrel. The hypsodont (high-crowned) dentition is unlike that of any other squirrel. Has a long, trumpet-shaped muzzle and possesses extremely dense, thick, woolly fur. Pelage is a grizzled gray dorsally and a paler gray ventrally. There is a black patch of hair on the muzzle and chin. The tail, unlike that of other flying squirrels, is thickly haired and cylindrical. The soles of the feet are heavily furred. **Distribution:** NW Yunnan and SE Xizang; the primary range of the species is in N Pakistan. **Natural History:** Very poorly known and unstudied in China. Lives in caves in high cliff faces between 2,400–3,800 m. Nocturnal, and very slow moving for a squirrel. Diet consists almost entirely of pine needles (which may explain its unique dentition). **Conservation Status:** China RL—NE. IUCN RL—EN A2c + 3c; C1.

GENUS *HYLOPETES*—Flying Squirrels

箭尾飞鼠属 Jianweifeishu Shu—箭尾飞鼠 Jianweifeishu
Size small, HB plus tail length less than 500 mm; tail wide and sometimes flattened, feather-shaped; three pairs of mammae. Distributed in tropical and subtropical zones of SE Asia. Of the nine species of *Hylopetes*, two occur in China.

Particolored Flying Squirrel *Hylopetes alboniger*

黑白飞鼠 Heibai Feishu— **Distinctive Characteris-tics:** HB 175–247; T 172–227; HF 36–45; E 27–36; GLS 41–52. Throat white, extending forward, as a gray band, onto the cheek below the eye and behind the ears, forming a half "collar." Both sides of the ears are covered with minute black hairs. Dorsal color dark rufous brown shading into blackish on the limbs, dorsal surface of gliding membranes, and underside of tail; ventral color white to creamy (except tail). Tail not strongly flattened, as in *H. phayrei*. **Distribution:** SE China including Hainan Island; extending broadly across SE Asia from the Himalayas to S Vietnam. **Natural History:** Much smaller than most other Chinese flying squirrels. They are arboreal and nocturnal, and nest in hollow trees, primarily in oak and rhododendron forests at middle to high elevations (1,500–3,400 m). *Hylopetes* and *Petaurista* are equally abundant in these forests. Nests consist of a ball of oak leaves and ferns lined with fine grasses. At night the squirrel's presence can be detected by a high-pitched trill or a repeated *scree* vocalization. The diet consists of fruits, nuts, leaves, and buds. The breeding season runs from April through mid-June, and there are two or three young born each litter. **Conservation Status:** China RL—NT. IUCN RL—LC.

Indochinese Flying Squirrel *Hylopetes phayrei*

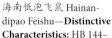

海南低泡飞鼠 Hainan-dipao Feishu—**Distinctive Characteristics:** HB 144–173; T 128–159; HF 32–35; E 23–25; GLS 36–42. Smallest flying squirrel in China. No slender tufted hairs at the base of the ear; tail flattened; dorsal pelage russet. Cheeks white, extending behind the ears. Ventral pelage generally white tinged with yellow. **Distribution:** S China, including Hainan Island; extending throughout SE Asia. **Natural History:** Occupies lower montane forests and mixed deciduous forests. These flying squirrels remain in hollow trees during the day and forage at night. *H. alboniger* and *H. phayrei* occur sympatrically on Hainan Island. **Conservation Status:** China RL—VU A1c. IUCN RL—LC.

GENUS *PETAURISTA*—Giant Flying Squirrels

䶄鼠属 Wushu Shu—䶄鼠 Wushu

This genus contains the largest forms in the tribe Pteromyini, with HB plus tail length clearly more than 500 mm, and more than 1,000 mm in the largest; no slender tufted hairs at base of ears; tail length close to or surpasses HB length; tail narrow, rounded, slightly broader in one or two northern species. Three pairs of mammae. Occurs primarily in the Indo-Malayan realm, extending to the Palaearctic. Seven of the eight recognized species occur in China.

Red and White Giant Flying Squirrel *Petaurista alborufus*

红白䶄鼠 Hongbai
Wushu—**Distinctive Char-**
acteristics: HB 350–580; T 430–615; HF 78–90; E 47–59; GLS 78–83. Largest species in the genus, with a thick, glossy pelage. Characterized by a large area of light speckling on the dorsum formed by mixture of wholly white or light russet hairs with maroon hairs; throat white; ventral pelage pinkish brown; base of tail possesses pinkish-brown or off-white rings. **Distribution:** Found throughout C and S China, including Taiwan; extending into Myanmar. **Natural History:** Has rarely been collected, and little is known of its natural history. It inhabits dense hillside forests in mountainous terrain, where nests are normally located high in tree hollows, although they may also occupy niches in limestone cliffs. In Taiwan it occurs in both hardwood and coniferous forests, preferring hardwood forest. Ranges from 800 to 3,500 m in elevation, but is most commonly found between 2,000 and 3,000 m. Nocturnal; it covers its home range by climbing high in trees and gliding distances of up to 400 m. Diet consists of acorns, other nuts, fruits, and leafy vegetation, as well as insects, larvae, and perhaps birds' eggs. The reproductive rate is low, most likely with litters of one or two young. It has been observed to be sympatric with *Hylopetes alboniger*, *P. philippensis*, and *Trogopterus xanthipes*. **Conservation Status:** China RL—LC. IUCN RL—LC.

Gray-Headed Flying Squirrel *Petaurista caniceps*

灰头小䶄鼠 Huitou Xiaowushu—**Distinctive Characteristics:** HB 300–370; T 360–400; HF 61–67; E 45–50; GLS 62–65. Size small. Dorsal pelage gray or dusky, pale brown at base of ears; ventral pelage whitish brown, throat pure white; upper side of feet orange; tail tip black. Lack of dorsal spots distinguishes

this form from the similar *P. elegans*. **Distribution:** C and S China; extending to Nepal and Myanmar. **Natural History:** Occupies oak-rhododendron forests from 2,100 to 3,600 m and temperate and alpine coniferous biotopes from 3,000 to 3,600 m. These squirrels are strictly arboreal and nocturnal and feed on rhododendron leaves, buds, and fir cones. Although pairs have been sighted in oak and fir forests 30–40 m above the ground, they usually occur singly. Nest in hollow oak trees or build a nest of ferns in tall rhododendron and fir trees. These squirrels can be located at night by their continuous cries. Little information is available regarding their breeding habits. Females usually give birth to one, but sometimes two, young. A lactating female was collected in October. **Conservation Status:** China RL—LC. IUCN RL—LC.

Spotted Giant Flying Squirrel *Petaurista elegans*

白斑小鼯鼠 Baiban Xiaowushu—**Distinctive Characteristics:** HB 296–375; T 347–405; HF 59–68; E 44–45; GLS 62–65. Size small; dorsal pelage dark gray, dark yellow, or russet-tinged, with many white-tipped hairs giving it a frosted or spotted appearance; gliding membranes darker reddish orange; tail color same as dorsum; rump and base of tail dark rufous and unspotted; lateral margin of gliding membrane to back of feet dark rufous brown; inside of ear bases and orbits russet; ventral pelage bright orange-brown. **Distribution:** Yunnan; extending to Myanmar, Vietnam, and Laos. **Natural History:** A species of mountain forests, where it is found in tall trees, but also often in rhododendron scrub and on rock cliffs. In the Himalayas it has been found to be quite common between 3,000 and 4,000 m. Nests in hollows in fir trees, breeding just before the rainy season. **Conservation Status:** China RL—LC. IUCN RL—LC.

Hodgson's Giant Flying Squirrel *Petaurista magnificus*

栗褐鼯鼠 Lihe Wushu—**Distinctive Characteristics:** HB 359–420; T 415–480; HF 72–78; E 41–43; GLS 65–74; Wt 1,350 g. Size large; dorsal pelage dark brown or russet with a dark brown to blackish stripe running from head to base of tail, contrasting strongly with yellow patches on shoulders, bordered laterally by deep russet sides and gliding

membranes; underparts and feet are light rufous and tail is deep brown at base, shading into rufous for most of its length, with a small black tip; feet black. **Distribution:** S Xizang; extending into Nepal, Sikkim (India), and Bhutan. **Natural History:** Lives in evergreen and broadleaf forests from the lowlands up to 3,000 m; it seems to prefer deciduous forests. It is about 25% larger than *P. elegans*, with which it shares the same habitat. Chiefly nocturnal and arboreal, it feed on leaves, buds, and flowers of rhododendrons and trees, fruits, and even grass. Highly vocal, these squirrels utter a deep monotonous booming call when emerging at dusk; they can be seen then gliding 60–100 m from oaks to the rhododendron below, landing in a short upward arc at the end of the glide. They occupy nests with a round entrance, 5–15 m above the ground, constructed with moss and other soft materials. Reproductive habits not known, except that only mothers occupy nests with their young. **Conservation Status:** China RL—NA. IUCN RL—LC.

Red Giant Flying Squirrel *Petaurista petaurista*

红背鼯鼠 Hongbei Wushu—**Distinctive Characteristics:** HB 398–520; T 375–630; HF 63–100; E 35–507; GLS 63–78; Wt 1,596–2,50 g. Large, bright-red squirrel. Dorsal pelage russet, the hairs white tipped and dark gray at the base, giving it a grizzled appearance; ventral pelage light brown, not gray at base; tail color the same as the back, with dark brown to black tip; ear pinnae, area around eyes, and lower jaw very noticeable dark brown; ear thin and nearly hairless. **Distribution:** Across S China; extending widely along the Himalayas from Afghanistan, Pakistan, India, and Nepal through Myanmar and Thailand and south into Sumatra, Java, Borneo, and Malaysia. **Natural History:** Occupies evergreen broadleaf and coniferous forests between 1,500 and 2,400 m elevation. These squirrels build nests in hollows of tall trees or on cliff crannies. They are primarily nocturnal and vocalize mainly at dusk. They are generally associated in pairs, both with and without young. Diet consists of young fir and pine cones, fruit, leaves, and shoots. Limited evidence indicates that two young are produced. **Conservation Status:** China RL—VU A1cd. IUCN RL—LC.

Indian Giant Flying Squirrel *Petaurista philippensis*

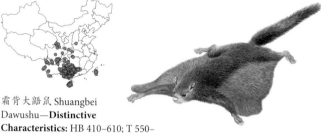

霜背大鼯鼠 Shuangbei Dawushu—**Distinctive Characteristics:** HB 410–610; T 550–691; HF 65–90; E 45–47; GLS 65–82. Second-largest species in the genus; entire dorsal pelage dark maroon to black, hairs with white tips, so whole dorsum shows a gray hue; ventral pelage russet to buff, somewhat sparse; tail very long, all black; ears black, but with conspicuous red front surface. **Distribution:** C and S China, including Hainan Island and Taiwan; extending to Thailand, Myanmar, India, Sri Lanka, and the Indo-Chinese peninsula. **Natural History:** On Hainan this squirrel is found only in large patches of forest, where it was considered abundant. On Taiwan it is most abundant in hardwood, compared with coniferous, forest and is most commonly found between 500 and 2,000 m elevation. Diet is broad in Taiwan and includes 30 plant species. Primarily eats young and mature leaves (74% of the diet). It is a seasonal breeder in Taiwan, with peaks in spring and fall. About half of all females become pregnant in each breeding season. Litter size is normally one, although occasionally a second young will be produced. **Conservation Status:** China RL—LC. IUCN RL—LC.

Chinese Giant Flying Squirrel *Petaurista xanthotis*

灰鼯鼠 Hui Wushu—**Distinctive Characteristics:** HB 325–430; T 294–350; HF 65–80; E 43–50; GLS 65–70; Wt 700–1,200 g.
Pelage grayish yellow, soft, and loose; dorsum dark, with black underfur, guard hairs black at base, with white to buff tips; large orange spot behind black-tipped, round ears, otherwise lateral base of ears bright russet; throat white, remainder of venter grayish, due to black underfur and white tips of guard hairs; feet black but legs and outer margins of gliding membranes orange; upper side of feet dusky. Tail long, covered with long, sparse black-and-orange-tipped hairs; sharp

contrast between light venter and dark underbase of tail. **Distribution:** C China. Endemic. **Natural History:** Poorly known. Records indicate that its range and numbers are extensive in spruce forest habitat at elevations of about 3,000 m in the highlands of C China. Nocturnally active; nests in cavities in trees. Diet consists of young shoots and leaves, as well as pine nuts. This species has been commonly collected for the fur trade, many specimens being secured in winter—evidence that the species does not hibernate. Reproduction occurs in summer; litter size is small, averaging two young. **Conservation Status:** China RL—LC. IUCN RL—LC.

GENUS *PTEROMYS*—Northern Flying Squirrels

飞鼠属 Feishu Shu—飞鼠 Feishu
Size small; four pairs of mammae. Distributed in broadleaf forests of the Palaearctic realm. There are two species in the genus, one of which is found in China.

Siberian Flying Squirrel *Pteromys volans*

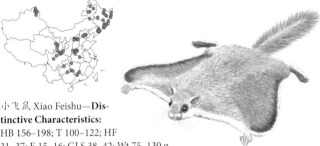

小飞鼠 Xiao Feishu—**Distinctive Characteristics:** HB 156–198; T 100–122; HF 31–37; E 15–16; GLS 38–42; Wt 75–130 g.
Size small; short, dense (soft and silky), closely fitting body hairs. Dorsal pelage dusky and usually darker than ventral surface; ventral pelage whitish to buffy; feet white ventrally, brown dorsally. Hair on tail grows in an arrowhead pattern; tail flattened, lateral tail hairs longer, grayish black at the tip. Eyes black and large. **Distribution:** NW China and NE China extending down into C China; extending from Hokkaido (Japan) and Sakhalin (Russia) islands across Siberia to Scandinavia. **Natural History:** Inhabits the boreal evergreen forests of the Old World from Scandinavia to E Siberia, including the fir forests of N China up to 2,500 m. Also frequents mature birch forests. Nests are constructed in hollows in trees, and these squirrels also construct dreys (leaf nests high in trees). Most occupy several nests, which they change frequently. They do not hibernate and are strictly nocturnal. Individuals are highly mobile, often moving up to 300 m per night. Diet consists of nuts, pine seeds, buds, shoots, leaves, berries, alder and birch catkins, and occasional birds' eggs and nestlings, mushrooms, and insects. They collect large food stores. Small litters of one to four young are produced in early spring. **Conservation Status:** China RL—VU A1cd. IUCN RL—LC.

GENUS *SCIURUS*—Tree Squirrels

松鼠属 Songshu Shu—松鼠 Songshu
Habits typically arboreal, form slender; tail long, its length more than half HB length. Some species grow long tufted hairs on their ears in winter. Dental formula: 1.0.2.3/1.0.1.3 = 22. Broadly distributed in both Palaearctic and Nearctic realms; of 28 species in the genus, a single species occurs in China.

Eurasian Red Squirrel *Sciurus vulgaris*

松鼠 Songshu—**Distinctive Characteristics:** HB 178–260; T 159–215; HF 25–70; E 33–36; GLS 44–48; Wt 200–480 g. In winter pelage, long tufts of upright hair grow on the ears; in summer, the ears are not tufted, but the tail hairs are very long and bushy. Two color phases occur: winter pelage gray or brown on dorsum, whitish on venter; summer pelage black or brownish black on dorsum, whitish at venter. Four pairs of mammae. **Distribution:** NW and NE China; extending across the forested regions of the Palaearctic, from Iberia and Great Britain east to the Kamchatka Peninsula and Sakhalin Island. **Natural History:** Occupies northern evergreen forests, where it is diurnally active. Does not hibernate. Diet consists largely of conifer seeds, acorns, fungi, bark, and sap tissue. Individuals store food in larder hoards (hollow trees) or scatter hoard (food buried in shallow holes or under surface litter). They maintain home ranges 2–10 ha in size that usually overlap. Both sexes also build one or more dreys within their home ranges. The peak of mating activities is early spring (January–March) followed by birth of first litters (March–May), or later (July–September). Litter size ranges from one to eight. Young are weaned after 7–10 weeks and are independent at 10–16 weeks. **Conservation Status:** China RL—NT. IUCN RL—LC.

GENUS *TROGOPTERUS* (monotypic)

复齿鼯鼠属 Fuchiwushu Shu

Complex-Toothed Flying Squirrel *Trogopterus xanthipes*

复齿鼯鼠 Fuchi Wushu—**Distinctive Characteristics:** HB 200–300; T 260–270; HF 56–60; E 30; GLS 55–61. Size medium, dorsal pelage light reddish buff, dark gray at base; ventral pelage light gray at base, russet at tips; lateral margin of gliding membrane and central ventral side bright brown. Tail slightly shorter than HB length and slightly flattened. Long black hairs predominate on the tip of the tail. A prominent characteristic is the tuft of slender black hairs around the base of the ears. **Distribution:** Widely distributed across C China. Endemic. **Natural History:** Closely associated with forest habitats, in particular temperate forests. Feeds from the canopy of oaks and pines, primarily eating oak leaves. Apparently nests in caves, which provide a stable microclimate for this species, and glides between cliff faces and nearby trees. Nocturnal. Litter size ranges from one to four, gestation is 78–89 days, and sexual maturity is attained at 22 months of age. **Conservation Status:** China RL—VU A1cd. IUCN RL—NT.

SUBFAMILY CALLOSCIURINAE—Oriental Tree Squirrels

丽松鼠亚科 Lisongshu Yake—丽松鼠 Li Songshu
Generalized diurnal squirrels, most forms arboreal. Tails moderately bushy; no distinctive ear tufts. Dental formula: 1.0.2.3/1.0.1.3 = 22. The Callosciurinae is comprised of 14 genera and 64 species; of these, four genera and 14 species occur in China.

GENUS *CALLOSCIURUS*—Beautiful Tree Squirrels

丽松鼠属 Lisongshu Shu—丽松鼠 Lisongshu
Habits typically arboreal, similar to *Sciurus* in size and form, no tufts of hair on ears; tail long, no stripes on dorsum. *Callosciurus* effectively fills the tree squirrel niche in southern Asian tropical forests that is occupied by *Sciurus* in Holarctic forests. Two or three pairs of mammae. *Callosciurus* is comprised of 15 species, five of which live in China.

Pallas's Squirrel *Callosciurus erythraeus*

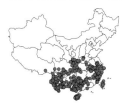

赤腹松鼠 Chifu Songshu—**Distinctive Characteristics:** HB 175–240; T 146–267; HF 41–55; E 18–23; GLS 48–56; Wt 280–420 g. The pelage characteristics of this widespread species are highly variable. Dorsal pelage olive gray; ventral pelage a rich red, maroon, brown, or buffy; an olive or olive-gray line is present at midline in some forms; ear same color as dorsum. The tail shows diffuse banding, flecked with black and tan, and is sometimes black tipped. **Distribu-**

tion: Widely distributed in SE China, including Hainan Island and Taiwan; extending to India, Myanmar, Thailand, Malay Peninsula, Indochina. **Natural History:** Mainly inhabit tropical and subtropical forests at low elevations, although they may be found in subalpine coniferous forests or in a mix of conifers and broadleaf trees at elevations above 3,000 m. Primarily active at dawn and dusk, they are very active jumping among trees. They make leaf nests high in trees that are used throughout the year; underground nests may be made during winter. Individuals maintain traditional home ranges, although these are more fixed in the case of females; males and young animals are more likely to shift home ranges seasonally in response to population density or varying food availability. Highly vocal, including a variety of warning calls that elicit predator-specific antipredator behavior. Males produce two types of mating vocalizations: precopulatory calls and postcopulatory calls. Postcopulatory calls may last up to 17 minutes and allow males to efficiently guard their mate without interruption. Feed on different kinds of nuts, berries, insects, even birds' eggs and fledglings. Reproductive rate low; only litter sizes of two have been reported. **Conservation Status:** China RL—LC. IUCN RL—LC.

Inornate Squirrel *Callosciurus inornatus*

印支松鼠 Yinzhi Songshu—**Distinctive Characteristics:** HB 218–291; T 176–210; HF 46–49; E 20–22; GLS 51–52. Ventral pelage light violet gray from chin to wrists and ankles; chin almost invariably bluish gray; dorsal pelage agouti, with two or three light bands on individual hairs, and deep olive in color; ears and feet same as dorsal pelage. The tail is colored dorsally the same as the dorsal pelage, and often black tipped. *C. inornatus* is smaller than *C. erythraeus*, with which it is almost completely sympatric (see above); comparatively, *C. inornatus* lacks the lighter color markings on the hip of *C. erythraeus*; also the feet and forelegs are colored like the dorsum instead of being noticeably more gray. **Distribution:** S Yunnan; extending into Laos and Vietnam. **Natural History:** Occupies a variety of habitats: scrub, degraded evergreen forest, and pristine evergreen forest. **Conservation Status:** China RL—VU A1cd; B1ab(iii). IUCN RL—LC.

Phayre's Squirrel *Callosciurus phayrei*

非氏松鼠 Feishi Songshu—**Distinctive Characteristics:** HB 190–220; T 160–210; HF 50–54; GLS 46–54. This species has a distinctive color pattern: a diffuse lateral dark stripe as wide as 1 cm runs from the base of the forelimbs to the base of the hind limbs, separating the dorsal and ventral pelage. The rostrum, ears, crown, and side of the neck are agouti gray like the dorsum. The ventral pelage varies from rich orange to very pale orange but is never red or gray. All four feet are yellowish buff to pale orange. The tail is black tipped, and a bright yellow stripe, 12–15 mm wide, runs ventrally down the tail. **Distribution:** W Yunnan; extending into Myanmar. **Natural History:** This species appears to inhabit the rain-forest vegetation area from the mouth of the Salween River northward. Normally represents the medium-sized tree squirrel in these tropical deciduous forests. **Conservation Status:** China RL—NA. IUCN RL—LC.

Irrawaddy Squirrel *Callosciurus pygerythrus*

蓝腹松鼠 Lanfu Songshu—**Distinctive Characteristics:** HB 190–230; T 110–220; HF 43–48; E 17–20; GLS 49–52; Wt 230–300. Dorsum dark olive brown. The light bluish-gray ventral pelage is not uniform, as these colors grade into cream and orange-buff. Pale red patch on hip. Tail gray and with an evident black tip. Front legs and all feet are grayer than the back. **Distribution:** E Xizang; extending into Myanmar, Nepal, India. **Natural History:** Primarily occupies rain-forest habitat at 600–1,300 m elevation. Often found in cane shrubs at forest edges or in banana plantations. Lives in the holes of trees. Throughout its range *C. pygerythrus* is sympatric with a larger species of tree squirrel; in China, *C. erythraeus*. Normally solitary, although sometimes seen moving in pairs, and diurnally active. Diet consists of flower buds of bananas or other fruit, but also insects. Reproduces once each year, and litter size averages three or four young. **Conservation Status:** China RL—NA. IUCN RL—LC.

Anderson's Squirrel *Callosciurus quinquestriatus*

五纹松鼠 Wuwen Songshu—**Distinctive Characteristics:** HB 200–222; T 180–210; HF 44–55; E 18–23; GLS 50–55; Wt 258–315 g. Dorsum a grizzled olive brown or olive yellow, but with a rufous tint. Ventral pelage white, but marked with one to three black midline or lateral stripes; one of these runs along the midline of the chest from the belly to the vent. These stripes are separated by white, and one is apparent when viewed from the side, distinctly dividing the ventral and dorsal pelage. The chin and throat are gray. The tail is the same color as the dorsum, but with black and rufous annulations (rings), and is tipped in black. **Distribution:** W Yunnan; extending into Myanmar. **Natural History:** Occurs primarily in mountain forests above about 1,000 m but can also be found in the lowlands. It lives alone or in small family groups. Nests are built of twigs and placed on the outer branches of small trees. Diet consists of vegetation and a fair proportion of insects. One female pregnant with a single embryo was recorded in March. **Conservation Status:** China RL—VU D2. IUCN RL—NT.

GENUS *DREMOMYS*—Red-cheeked Squirrels

长吻松鼠属 Changwensongshu Shu—长吻松鼠 Changwen Songshu
Habits semiarboreal; tail hairs not fluffed out; ears lack tufted hairs; some species possess reddish marks on venter and cheeks. Dental formula: 1.0.2.3/1.0.1.3 = 22. Of six species of *Dremomys*, five occur in China.

Red-Throated Squirrel *Dremomys gularis*

橙喉长吻松鼠 Chenhouchangwen Songshu—**Distinctive Characteristics:** HB 187–230; T 145–180; HF 42–50; E 23–26; GLS 58. Similar to *D. pyrrhomerus* and *D. rufigenis*, but chin, throat, and neck a rich ochraceous tawny in abrupt contrast to other underparts; ventral pelage dark blue-gray; flank patch obsolescent and reduced to a narrow line; entire ventral side of tail red. **Distribution:** Yunnan; extending into Vietnam. **Natural History:** The type specimen was collected at high elevation (2,500–3,000 m) from Mount Fan Si Pan, near Chapa Tonkin, Vietnam. It was the only *Dremomys* found at this high elevation, but it was found in company with *Tamiops swinhoei*, microtines, and other typically Palaearctic species. Little else is known of its ecology. **Conservation Status:** China RL—NT. IUCN RL—LC.

Orange-Bellied Himalayan Squirrel *Dremomys lokriah*

橙腹长吻松鼠 Chenfuchangwen Songshu—**Distinctive Characteristics:** HB 165–205; T 135–220; HF 38–48; E 15–24; GLS 46–53; Wt 150–240 g. A dark rufous-brown animal; back of ear with white spots; ventral pelage orange to buffy; ventral side of tail black with a mixture of orange hairs, although not red. **Distribution:** Xizang and W Yunnan; extending into Myanmar, Bhutan, Nepal, India. **Natural History:** Occupies a variety of habitats from 1,500 to 3,400 m elevation, including oak-rhododendron forests to subtropical forests at lower elevations and conifer forests at high elevations. Strictly diurnal. Nests in tree hollows close to the ground. The nest consists of fern and oak leaves with a lining of fine grasses. Frequently comes to the ground to search for fruits, nuts, and other plant materials. A favorite food is mistletoe, but fruit and insects are also an important part of the diet. Utters loud, sharp, squeaky vocalizations, which are often repeated. Young are born from May to August in litters of two to five young. Lactating females have been seen in May, June, and August. **Conservation Status:** China RL—NT. IUCN RL—LC.

Perny's Long-Nosed Squirrel *Dremomys pernyi*

珀氏长吻松鼠 Poshichangwen Songshu—**Distinctive Characteristics:** HB 170–230; T 156–180; HF 43–54; E 19–28; GLS 46–55; Wt 160–225 g. Dorsum olive brown; ventral pelage buffy white; ventral and dorsal side of tail reddish at base,

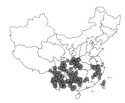

other parts russet or isabelline. This is a fairly distinct, large northern species distinguished by its lighter gray dorsal pelage and tail. Venter is white from chin to anus, while anal area and inner sides of hind limbs are bright rusty brown; lacks red markings on chin and throat. Yellow tufts behind ears. **Distribution:** Throughout C and SE China, including Taiwan; extending into Vietnam, Myanmar, and India. **Natural History:** Typically found in forest uplands from 2,000 to 3,500 m in elevation, where they live in evergreen broadleaf and coniferous trees. They are diurnal and primarily terrestrial (commonly seen running along fallen tree trunks). Highly vocal; they utter cries that have great power and resonance. **Conservation Status:** China RL—LC. IUCN RL—LC.

Red-Hipped Squirrel *Dremomys pyrrhomerus*

红腿长吻松鼠 Hongtuichangwen Songshu—**Distinctive Characteristics:** HB 195–210; T 140–162; HF 50–55; E 22–24; GLS 55–58. Evident reddish spots present on thigh; cheek and sides of neck conspicuously reddish. Dorsum olive gray; venter gray and white; yellowish spots behind eyes; tail is white-grizzled above and brilliant red below. **Distribution:** Central S China, including Hainan Island. Endemic. **Natural History:** These squirrels are apparently almost entirely terrestrial, living in holes in their rocky habitats. During the winter months they are infrequently active. The species seems to have a very spotty distribution. **Conservation Status:** China RL—NT. IUCN RL—LC.

Asian Red-Cheeked Squirrel *Dremomys rufigenis*

红颊长吻松鼠 Hongjiachangwen Songshu—**Distinctive Characteristics:** HB 170–228; T 130–180; HF 44–54; E 23–25; GLS 46–51; Wt 210–335 g. Dorsal pelage buffy brown. No reddish spots on thigh; pelage of cheeks is red. Ventral pelage is grayish white; the ventral surface of the tail is a rich red; the throat is not red. **Distribution:** S China; extending into Vietnam, Thailand, Laos, peninsular Malaysia, Myanmar, and India. **Natural History:** This is a semiterrestrial foothills species, generally found at less than 1,500 m elevation. **Conservation Status:** China RL—NT. IUCN RL—LC.

GENUS *MENETES* (monotypic)

线松鼠属 Xiansongshu Shu—线松鼠 Xiansongshu

Indochinese Ground Squirrel *Menetes berdmorei*

线松鼠 Xian Songshu—**Distinctive Characteristics:** HB 162–210; T 130–175; HF 40–47; E 18–22; GLS 45–51; Wt 213 g. Body dusky, dorsum with blackish-brown and buffy short stripes; ventral pelage buffy white. Dental formula: 1.0.2.3/1.0.1.3 = 22. **Distribution:** S Yunnan; extending into Vietnam, Cambodia, Laos, and Thailand and to C Myanmar. **Natural History:** Forages on the ground in forests and along the forest edge; lives at elevations up to 1,200 m. Known to enter rice and corn fields to dig up and eat planted grain. Often caught in traps baited with bananas. Although this species spends most of its time on the ground, occasionally it may be seen running along railings or up and down slanting or broken bamboos, but never far from the ground. **Conservation Status:** China RL—NA.

GENUS *TAMIOPS*—Asiatic Striped Squirrels

花松鼠属 Huasongshu Shu—花松鼠 Huasongshu
Size smallest of Asian Sciuridae; chipmunk-like. Tufted white hairs present on ears; dorsum with dark and light longitudinal stripes; pelage highly variable in color; tail narrow. Dental formula: 1.0.2.3/1.0.1.3 = 22. Three pairs of mammae. Of four species in *Tamiops*, three occur in China.

Maritime Striped Squirrel *Tamiops maritimus*

倭松鼠 Wo Songshu—**Distinctive Characteristics:** HB 105–134; T 80–115; HF 25–30; E 9–17; GLS 36–38. Dorsal pelage short and olive gray; ventral pelage buffy; lateral light stripes short and narrow, dusky white. Medial pair of light stripes faint, lateral pair more distinct, but not as pronounced as in *T. mcclellandii*. Pale stripe under eye not continuous with other light stripe on back. Pelage short; ventral pelage buffy. **Distribution:** SE China, including Hainan Island and Taiwan; extending to Vietnam and Laos. **Natural History:** A relatively low-elevation species occupying the southeastern coastal region of China. In Taiwan, however, it is most common at elevations between 2,000 and 3,000 m. On mainland China it occurs in two general forest types: evergreen broadleaf forest with evergreen oaks, laurels, and conifers in secondary stands; and mixed mesophytic forest. Dietary habits include the very specialized habit of robbing nectar from ginger plants. Highly arboreal, it is

known to make long leaps between trees. Its characteristic vocalization sounds are a *cluck* or short *chirrup*. **Conservation Status:** China RL—LC. IUCN RL—LC.

Himalayan Striped Squirrel *Tamiops mcclellandii*

明纹花松鼠 Mingwenhua Songshu—**Distinctive Characteristics:** HB 100–125; T 86–120; HF 27–32; E 15–22; GLS 30–34; Wt 27–51g. Dorsum olive yellow, with three brownish-black or grayish-black longitudinal stripes separated by buffy longitudinal stripes; the medial pair of light stripes is faint, the lateral pair bright. There is a pale stripe under the eye that is continuous with the lateral light stripe

on the back. Pelage short; ventral pelage ochraceous; tail tip black. **Distribution:** S China; extending to Nepal, India, Myanmar, Thailand, Cambodia, Laos, and Vietnam, to the S Malay Peninsula. **Natural History:** Commonly found high in tropical and subtropical forest trees above 1,700 m elevation. They are also found in association with humans in fruit trees and coconut palm plantations. While they usually occur in mountains above 700 m, they occur also in low plains in the southern part of their range. Generally seen alone or in pairs. They are rarely seen on the ground, preferring to run up and down tree trunks. The dorsal stripes serve as camouflage when the squirrels are on the bark of a tree; when frightened they often spread themselves out against the bark to heighten the effect. They use holes in trees for shelter, and they often move through trees by making long leaps. The diet consists of insects and some fruit and vegetable matter, including mistletoe. Vocalization is a harsh *chick*. They are sometimes sympatric with *Dremomys lokriah*. **Conservation Status:** China RL—LC. IUCN RL—LC.

Swinhoe's Striped Squirrel *Tamiops swinhoei*

隐纹松鼠 Yinwen Songshu—**Distinctive Characteristics:** HB 140–164; T 67–116; HF 28–35; E 9–16; GLS 31–41; Wt 67–90 g. Dorsal pelage long and soft, olive brown or olive gray in color; five dark dorsal stripes, the central one black; four light dorsal stripes that may be olive yellow, olive gray, or even buffy; ventral pelage is whitish. Pale stripe under the eye not continuous with the barely discernible lateral light stripe on the dorsum. Although there is considerable overlap, *T. swinhoei* is usually larger than other species of *Tamiops*. **Distribution:** C China; extending to N Myanmar and N Vietnam. **Natural History:** Where the range of this species overlaps with that of *T. mcclellandii*, there are significant differences in elevation between the two, *T. mcclellandii* occupying tropical habitat between 300 and 600 m, while *T. swinhoei* is most common in evergreen broadleaf trees or conifers at elevations between 2,500 and 3,000 m. It is almost exclusively arboreal, living in holes in trees, although it can be found on the ground. Takes long jumps between trees. The call is high pitched, like that of a bird. It is primarily active at dawn and dusk. Diet consists of young shoots, fruits, and insects. **Conservation Status:** China RL—LC. IUCN RL—LC.

SUBFAMILY XERINAE—Afro-Asian Ground Squirrels

非洲地松鼠亚科 Feizhoudisongshu Yake—非洲地松鼠 Feizhoudisongshu
The subfamily Xerinae consists of 15 genera and 128 species, divided into three tribes: Xerini, Protoxerini, and Marmotini. The Xerini are confined to Africa, with the exception of *Spermophilopsis*, which extends into Central Asia (but not as far as China), while all representatives of the Protoxerini are found in Africa. All Chinese Xerinae are placed in the tribe Marmotini; four genera and 13 species are represented in China.

GENUS *MARMOTA*—Marmots

旱獭属 Hanta shu—旱獭 Hanta
Size large; habits terrestrial. Body stout; tail short, with tip flat; ears short and round; limbs stout; forefeet with four digits, the first reduced, middle digit longest, and with robust claws modified for burrowing; hind feet with five toes. Female has five pairs of mammae. Dental formula: 1.0.2.3/1.0.1.3 = 22. Diurnally active; all forms hibernate. Occurs in Asia, Europe, and North America; of 14 species, four occur in China.

Gray Marmot *Marmota baibacina*

灰旱獭 Hui Hanta—**Distinctive Characteristics:** HB 460–650; T 130–154; HF 74–99; E 22–30; GLS 83–100; Wt 4,250–6,500 g. Size similar to *M. caudata*; tail short, less than one-third of HB length; dorsum buffy or sandy yellow, sprinkled with black or dark blackish brown; ventral pelage dusty or dark russet; ears sandy yellow; rostrum dark brown. **Distribution:** Xinjiang; extending into Mongolia, Russia, Kyrgystan, and Kazakhstan. **Natural History:** Preferred habitats include montane steppe spreading over low mountains with gentle slopes. Fewer live in stony mountain steppes strewn with boulders or in the alpine zone. It is highly social and lives in colonies with many burrows. Summer and winter burrows are usually separate; winter burrows are deeper, while summer burrows are just as long, but not as deep; both types may hold two or three marmots, but winter burrows hold up to 10. Marmots eat a wide variety of food plants, which vary with season. Early spring foods include the sagebrush *Artemisia frigida*; by late spring and early summer the diet consists mainly of grasses; and by late summer, other herbaceous vegetation. Mating begins in early May and ends by the beginning of June. Gestation lasts 40 days. Hibernation is initiated at different times in different places, from August to October, and appears influenced by local weather and food resources. Enemies include large raptors, wolves, and other smaller predators such as foxes, Steppe Polecat, and Pallas's Cat. **Conservation Status:** China RL—LC. IUCN RL—LC.

Long-Tailed Marmot *Marmota caudata*

长尾旱獭 Changwei Hanta—**Distinctive Characteristics:** HB 426–570; T 185–275; HF 63–92; E 18–30; GLS 87–105; Wt 4,100–4,600 g. Form stout. Tail is longest within *Marmota*, up to half of HB length, and black at the tip. Whole body orange or pale brown; ventral pelage essentially the same color as the dorsum, with no evident boundary. **Distribution:** Xinjiang (Tian Shan); extending throughout Central Asia, Afghanistan, Pakistan, and N India. **Natural History:** A montane animal, it inhabits the coniferous forest zone but also penetrates the alpine zone, chiefly on open stony stretches, although it does not avoid forests. This species is less common in feather-grass and fescue areas, and it is uncommon in semidesert tracts with shrub cover (winter-fat, sagebrush); it shuns saline soils. Prefers dry, cliff-like mountain slopes covered mainly by short grasses, or at lower elevations, stands of junipers up to 3–4 m high. Like other marmots, it is strictly diurnal. Emerges from burrow shortly after sunrise, when the ground surface has begun to warm. If disturbed by an intruder, it utters a call resembling a bird call that is unique to this species. Diet consists of the leaves and stems of various grasses, and legumes, which it prefers. Frequently found in monogamous situations consisting of one adult male and one adult female, although social groups of up to seven adults may be formed. When multiple females share a common home range, only a single adult female lactates and weans young. Litters of two to five are seen outside burrows by late April or early May. Shortly after the young emerge, adults begin to molt, ending by mid- or late August. Two weeks after the end of molt, they enter their burrow to begin hibernation, about mid-September. **Conservation Status:** China RL—LC. IUCN RL—LC.

Himalayan Marmot *Marmota himalayana*

喜马拉雅旱獭 Ximalaya Hanta—**Distinctive Characteristics:** HB 475–670; T 125–150; HF 76–100; E 23–30; GLS 96–114; Wt 4,000–9,215 g. Form stout. Tail very short—less than twice HB length. Dorsum grass yellow or buffy, sprinkled with many irregular black spots; ventral pelage buffy or light brown; ears dark yellow or russet; rostrum often with black or blackish-brown spots. **Distribution:** C to W China; extending to Nepal, India. **Natural History:** Inhabits upland grassland mostly from 3,750 to 5,200 m (but up to 5,670 m). This species is adapted to alpine meadows and desert conditions with very low rainfall, typically inhabiting steep bush-dotted slopes. Lives in small or large colonies, depending on local resources, and feeds on grasses by preference, although it also consumes roots, leaves of herbaceous plants, and seeds. It excavates unusually deep burrows, which are shared by colony members during hibernation. Females give birth toward the end of hibernation, from April to July; litter size reported to be 2–11 (average 7 at low density; 4.8 at high density). Gestation is one month, and young are generally weaned at 15 days of age. Young normally remain with their family, and females become reproductively active only in their second spring. **Conservation Status:** China RL—LC. IUCN RL—LC.

Tarbagan Marmot *Marmota sibirica*

草原旱獭 Caoyuan Hanta—**Distinctive Characteristics:** HB 360–495; T 112–121; HF 72–82; GLS 80–104; Wt 5,000 g. Size slightly smaller than other species. Dorsum light brown or light rusty, sprinkled with light whitish yellow; ventral pelage brown; rostrum and top of forehead dark brown; ears light orange; tail dark brown without black hue. **Distribution:** NE China; extending across Mongolia and Russia (Siberia, Tuva, Transbaikalia). **Natural History:** Primary habitat is steppe grasslands; highly colonial. Forages on grasses, but also on herbs and woody plants such as sagebrush. Autumn hibernation is initiated in September but is influenced by summer food conditions and fall weather. Hibernates in groups of 5–20 in a single burrow. Enemies include wolves, red foxes, and several species of large eagles and hawks. May carry and transmit bubonic plague and is therefore subject to stringent control measures in many parts of its range. Mating begins in April, after it has aroused from hibernation. Gestation lasts 40–42 days. Young appear above ground in June; typical litter size is four to six, occasionally eight. Molting of winter hair in adults occurs about two and a half to three weeks after the birth of young. **Conservation Status:** China RL—LC. IUCN RL—EN A2ad.

GENUS *SCIUROTAMIAS*—Rock Squirrels

岩松鼠属 Yansongshu Shu—岩松鼠 Yansongshu
Medium-sized, bushy-tailed squirrels. Habits terrestrial. Both species of *Sciurotamias* are restricted to China.

Père David's Rock Squirrel *Sciurotamias davidianus*

岩松鼠 Yansongshu—**Distinctive Characteristics:** HB 190–250; T 125–200; HF 45–59; E 20–28; GLS 52–58. Dorsum olive gray; ventral pelage yellowish white or ochraceous. No pale stripe on side. A dark line crosses the cheek. Soles of feet densely haired. Dental formula: 1.0.2.3/1.0.1.3 = 22. **Distribution:** Throughout C China. Endemic. **Natural History:** Favors rocky terrain and make dens in deep crevices between rocks. Shows great agility, and while capable of climbing trees, apparently rarely does so. Does not hibernate. Known to collect and eat seeds that it carries in large cheek pouches. Particularly adept at scatter-hoarding the large acorns of the oak *Quercus liatungensis*. It may reach high densities in places and may constitute an agricultural pest on occasion. **Conservation Status:** China RL—LC. IUCN RL—LC.

Forrest's Rock Squirrel *Sciurotamias forresti*

侧纹岩松鼠 Cewen Yansongshu—**Distinctive Characteristics:** HB 194–250; T 130–180; HF 47–54; E 25–27; GLS 54–60. Dorsum of head and body dark grayish brown, the hairs ringed with black and buff. On the side, a narrow white line runs from shoulder to hip; the dark line running below the white matches the back in color, turning ochraceous lower on the side; ears buffy brown; sides of head and throat also ochraceous; and with white patch from chin to chest. Ventral surface pale, creamy white. Dental formula: 1.0.1.3/1.0.1.3 = 20. Soles of hind feet almost naked. **Distribution:** Yunnan, S Sichuan. Endemic. **Natural**

History: Occupies scrub-clad cliffs at about 3,000 m elevation. Its biology is likely similar to that of its sister species, *S. davidianus*. **Conservation Status:** China RL—LC. IUCN RL—LC.

GENUS *SPERMOPHILUS*—Ground Squirrels

黄鼠属 Huangshu Shu—黄鼠 Huangshu

Size small; habits burrowing. Eyes large; ears small; limbs and tail short; claws robust; first digit on forefoot reduced; cheek pouch present. Females have five pairs of mammae (two on chest, three on abdomen). Dental formula: 1.0.2.3/1.0.1.3 = 22. Of 41 species of *Spermophilus* occurring across Asia, Europe, and North America, six are found in China.

Alashan Ground Squirrel *Spermophilus alashanicus*

阿拉善黄鼠 Alashan

Huangshu—**Distinctive Characteristics:** HB 190–210; T 55–76; HF 33–37; E 8–10; GLS 45–48; Wt 192–224 g. A pale form; summer pelage light russet to distinctly pinkish buff. Winter pelage lighter and yellower. Has a distinctive eye-ring, and a light brown spot is positioned below the eye and separated from the ring by a whitish stripe running from the base of the ear to the muzzle. Tail colored as the back, but rusty red beneath. **Distribution:** Central N China. Endemic. **Natural History:** Occupies deserts of C China, but also is found in grasslands at the edge of the Gobi. Its preferred habitat appears to be dry sandy areas; locally its common name translates to "sand rat." Occupies single, sloping burrow; no dirt mounds surround burrow entrances. Lives in small scattered groups. Diurnal. Hibernates, as do other *Spermophilus*. The species feeds on a variety of herbs and other plants, including cultivated grains. Vocalizations consist of frequently uttered high-pitched squeaks. Litter size ranges from one to nine, normally three to six; parturition most likely in June. **Conservation Status:** China RL—LC. IUCN RL—LC.

Brandt's Ground Squirrel *Spermophilus brevicauda*

阿尔泰黄鼠 Aertai Huangshu—**Distinctive Characteristics:** HB 165–210; T 31–50; HF 29–38; E 5–9; GLS 42–47; Wt 143–436 g. Smaller in size than some other *Spermophilus*; tail short, about one-fifth of HB length. Hind metatarsal region russet; dorsum ochraceous, with distinctive small light spots; tail rusty in some forms to light yellow in others. Noticeable rust-colored patches above and below the light eye-rings. **Distribution:** N Xinjiang; extending into Kazakhstan. **Natural History:** Inhabits dry steppes and semidesert brushlands. Its range, as presently understood, is restricted to NW Xinjiang, while *S. alashanicus* is found in the Alashan Desert, from Nei Mongol on the north to Gansu on the south, and *S. pallidicauda* is restricted to NE Gansu and Nei Mongol. These three closely related *Spermophilus* are allopatric in distribution. Chiefly vegetarian, they climb and dig in order to obtain whatever food is in season, enjoying the young shoots of certain shrubs as well as tulip

bulbs and wild onions. They may be either solitary or communal, and they spend much time in their burrows, in which they hibernate if the temperature is low enough, or aestivate if the summer heat becomes too high. Burrows are normally constructed at bases of shrubs. They rarely stand upright on their hind legs (as do other *Spermophilus*), and their alarm call is a very quiet squeak. **Conservation Status:** China RL—LC. IUCN RL—LC.

Daurian Ground Squirrel *Spermophilus dauricus*

达乌尔黄鼠 Dawu'er Huangshu—**Distinctive Characteristics:** HB 165–268; T 40–75; HF 30–39; E 5–10; GLS 42–50; Wt 154–264 g. Size small; tail short, about a fifth to a third of HB length; soles of forefeet naked; soles of hind feet covered with hairs; whole body buffy or gray russet, no light spots on dorsum. Tip of tail light yellow, with a distinctive black-brown preterminal band. A light eye-ring extends to the ear. Summer pelage relatively short and coarse; winter pelage significantly longer and softer. **Distribution:** NE China; extending into Mongolia and Russia (Transbaikalia). **Natural History:** Occupies open plains or deserts. It is considered a characteristic species of the northern edge of the Gobi in extreme N Mongolia and the adjacent borders of Siberia. It apparently does not extend far into the Gobi but follows around the northeastern edge to reappear in Chinese territory along the borders of Hebei and adjacent Nei Mongol. It is strictly diurnal and lives in dense colonies where it constructs relatively simple burrows, generally with only two entrances. Tunnels normally extend a maximum of 2 m, although some may reach as far as 6–8 m in length. A single nest, lined with grass, is normally found at a depth of 50 cm. Hibernates over winter. Feeds on various herbs and other plants, including those in grain fields. Single litters of two to nine young are produced in spring. **Conservation Status:** China RL—LC. IUCN RL—LC.

Pallid Ground Squirrel *Spermophilus pallidicauda*

内蒙黄鼠 Neimeng Huangshu—**Distinctive Characteristics:** HB 198–233; T 35–53; HF 36–41; E 5–9; GLS 42–46. This is a pale species characterized by a short tail that is whitish yellow with a rust-colored stripe extending along most of the upper side. The dorsum is pinkish buff to straw-sand in color. A weakly defined white line runs from the vibrissae on the cheek to the ear. Eyelids are white, but there is a rusty spot beneath each eye. Underside is white, faintly tinged with buffy. In the summer pelage, the coloring becomes more sandy and less buffy. **Distribution:** N China; extending into Mongolia. **Natural History:** Has a wide distribution in the grasslands of the Gobi and adjacent areas. Colonial and diurnally active. **Conservation Status:** China RL—LC. IUCN RL—LC.

Tian Shan Ground Squirrel *Spermophilus ralli*

天山黄鼠 Tianshan Huangshu—**Distinctive Characteristics:** HB 200–240; T 60–75; HF 33–42; GLS 47–50; Wt 290–405 g. Summer pelage is gray-brown to light yellow on the back, with lighter sides; ventrally yellow-gray. Light spots on the back are indistinct. Winter pelage is lighter and grayer. Dorsal surface of tail is rusty to light yellow; end of tail characterized by a band of dark coloration and a yellowish-white tip. There are no facial markings around the eye. **Distribution:** W Xinjiang; extending into Kazakhstan. **Natural History:** A meadow-dwelling ground squirrel. Burrow diameter averages 6 cm, and there are many openings close together and clumped. Diurnal, yet not active during the hottest part of the day. Often stands erect next to its burrow; highly vocal. Diet consists of grass, green vegetation, and insects. Hibernates between August–September and the end of February–beginning of March. Reproduces in spring following emergence. Litter size averages three to seven young born after a 25–27 day gestation. **Conservation Status:** China RL—NA. IUCN RL—LC.

Long-Tailed Ground Squirrel *Spermophilus undulatus*

长尾黄鼠 Changwei Huangshu—**Distinctive Characteristics:** HB 210–315; T 100–140; HF 45–50; E 10–11; GLS 46–56; Wt 250–580 g. Size large; tail long, more than a third of HB length. Upper parts with russet or dusky black-brown patterning; sides a gray-straw or yellow; underparts orange, reddish brown, or brown; sides and tip of tail tinged with white or yellowish white. Winter pelage

much lighter. **Distribution:** Extreme NW and NE China; extending into Kazakhstan, Russia, and Mongolia. **Natural History:** This large ground squirrel typically occurs in thinly wooded savannahs and grassy steppes bordering the Gobi Desert. In addition to grasslands, it occupies bushy terrain among oaks and in white or black beech groves, alpine meadows, and wet areas along river valleys. Lives in colonies with a labyrinth of burrows. Burrows are characteristically 8–13 cm in diameter and surrounded by a large mound of soil (up to 2 m in diameter and 40 cm high). Diurnally active; although most active at dawn and dusk. The alarm call is soft and unlike that of most other ground squirrels, more closely resembling the call of a chipmunk. Diet consists of green vegetation and seeds, but also insects. Before hibernating, makes a store of vegetation to utilize following arousal. Hibernates from

October until late March–mid-April. Reproduces once per year in spring; litters of three to nine young are produced following a 30-day gestation. **Conservation Status:** China RL—LC. IUCN RL—LC.

GENUS *TAMIAS*—Chipmunks

花鼠属 Huashu Shu—花鼠 Huashu
Size small. Pelage thick; dorsum with five brown to brownish-black longitudinal stripes. Dental formula: 1.0.2.3/1.0.1.3 = 22. Well-developed internal cheek pouches. Four pairs of mammae. Of 25 species, all but one occupies the Nearctic realm, the single species that occurs in China.

Siberian Chipmunk *Tamias sibiricus*

花鼠 Hua Shu—**Distinctive Characteristics:** HB 120–165; T 90–130; HF 28–40; E 13–20; GLS 34–48; Wt 78–102 g. Dorsum russet, with five conspicuous brown or brownish-black stripes; ventral surface buffy white. **Distribution:** NW, C, and NE China; extending to N European and Siberian Russia to Sakhalin Island, including Kazakhstan, Mongolia, Korea, and Japan (Hokkaido Island). **Natural History:** Nests and burrows near tree roots. Diet consists of pine nuts and young shoots and leaves of vegetation. In summer and fall also eats flowers, mush-rooms, and occasionally insects. Hibernates from September to March–April. In late summer constructs large winter stores, carrying seeds back to nest in its cheek pouches. Diurnally active, with activity concentrated in the early morning. Tends to run along the ground, but also ascends trees. Utters a "chirping" vocalization when alarmed. Females enter hibernation first, followed by males; this order may allow males to learn where females are for mating upon emergence in early spring. Normally produces a single litter of four to six young each year, although there are reports of two litters in some populations. **Conservation Status:** China RL—LC. IUCN RL—LC.

FAMILY GLIRIDAE—Dormice

日本睡鼠科 Ribenshuishu Ke—日本睡鼠 Ribenshuishu

Most dormice resemble small squirrels with soft thick fur, a heavily furred tail, and large eyes, although some are mouselike. One of their unique traits is their ability to regenerate the tail. Forefeet with four digits; hind feet with five. Undersides of feet and digits naked; toes have short, curved claws. Generally arboreal, they store food in nests made in tree holes and add body fat prior to entering hibernation in winter. Dental formula: 1.0.1.3/1.0.1.3 = 20 (compared to 16 in spiny dormice); incisors sharply pointed. Of nine genera and 28 species within the Gliridae, two genera, *Chaetocauda* and *Dryomys*, one species apiece, are found in China.

GENUS *CHAETOCAUDA* (monotypic)

四川毛尾睡鼠属 Sichuanmaowei Shuishu Shu

Chinese Dormouse *Chaetocauda sichuanensis*

四川毛尾睡鼠 Sichuanmaowei Shuishu—**Distinctive Characteristics:** HB 90–91; T 92–102; HF 18–19; E 17–19; GLS 26–27; Wt 24–36 g. Dorsal surface light reddish brown; venter, inner limbs, and feet are white. Dark chestnut around the large eyes; vibrissae long (up to 31 mm). Tail round (not flattened as in the Forest Dormouse); the tail tip is covered with dense hairs forming a club shape. **Distribution:** N Sichuan. Endemic. **Natural History:** Occurs in subalpine forest with mixed coniferous and broadleaf trees. Constructs nests in trees generally at a height of 3–3.5 m; nest diameter is 12 cm. Diet consists of green plants. Nocturnal. Breeds in May and produces litters of four young. **Conservation Status:** China RL—EN A1c; B1ab(iii). IUCN RL—DD.

GENUS *DRYOMYS*—Dormice

睡鼠属 Shuishu Shu—睡鼠 Shuishu
One of the three species of *Dryomys* occurs in China.

Forest Dormouse *Dryomys nitedula*

林睡鼠 Lin Shuishu—**Distinctive Characteristics:**
HB 85–120; T 75–115; HF 19–24; E 13–19; GLS 25–28; Wt 36–61 g. Dorsal pelage gray brown; a distinct dark blackish patch extends from the region around the eye and below the ear anteriorly, but not to the end of the nose; tail flat and covered with long light brown hair; ears rounded and short; feet naked. **Distribution:** NW Xinjiang; extending across Central Asia to as far west as Switzerland. **Natural History:** Lives in broadleaf forests and mixed conifers but prefers oak. Constructs nests, with an entrance on one side, lined with moss, feathers, and hair, in tree holes or niches in trees. In winter may make underground nests, in which it hibernates. Primarily nocturnal; an excellent climber. Diet consists of nuts, seeds, and fruit, but also may include insects and larvae; stores food. Utters a variety of vocalizations: soft melodic calls, clicks, snarling, hissing, and whistling sounds when excited or threatened. Litter size is small (generally three or four young, but as many as seven). Two litters are produced in a breeding season that extends throughout summer. **Conservation Status:** China RL—EN A2c + 3c. IUCN RL—LC.

FAMILY CASTORIDAE

GENUS *CASTOR*—Beavers

河狸科 Heli Ke; 河狸属 Heli Shu—河狸 Heli
Beavers are very large rodents adapted to aquatic habitats. Guard hairs dense; ears with valves; tail large and flat, ovate, covered with large scales; hind feet possess complete webs, fourth toe with double nails; forefeet small, armed with robust claws. Incisors robust and deeply pigmented, modified for cutting branches and stripping tree bark. Dental formula: 1.0.1.3/1.0.1.3 = 20. The single genus occurs in aquatic habitats throughout the Holarctic. Of two species, one occurs in China.

Eurasian Beaver *Castor fiber*

河狸 He Li—**Distinctive Characteristics:** HB 60–100 cm; T length 215–300, breadth 102–127; HF 160–170; E 35–40; GLS 125–151; Wt 17–30 kg. There is

essentially no sexual dimorphism in size. Head round, limbs short; each foot possesses five toes; hairs long, whole body brown, feet black; hind foot webs complete (fig. 4), tail large, flat, and ovate; adapted to aquatic life; anal gland present, enlarged in males. **Distribution:** N Xinjiang; extending across N Eurasia. **Natural History:** Inhabits rivers and lakes, where it makes dams and creates ponds, although in Xinjiang it frequently uses underground nests in lieu of building dams. These dams, ranging between 5 and 30 m in length, regulate water levels and stream flows. Lodges are dug into banks or constructed in ponds by piling branches held together by mud; entrances to lodges are through an underwater passage. Has a strictly herbivorous diet consisting of aquatic plants, tubers, and trees (preferring willows and aspen). Beavers are social animals, living in small family groups. They communicate by slapping their tail on the water surface, whistling, or through deposits from their scent glands. In Xinjiang, normally 1–2 km separate lodges. Sexual maturity is reached in three years (occasionally two); gestation is 103–108 days; and litter size ranges from one to six (normally two or three). One litter is born annually. **Conservation Status:** The beaver's thick, waterproof fur was formerly considered precious, leading to heavy exploitation. The Chinese subspecies of the Eurasian Beaver (*C. f. birulai*) is one of the rarest and least-known aquatic mammals in China. In the 1970s it was believed that only 100 animals remained in fewer than 20 family groups. Cur-

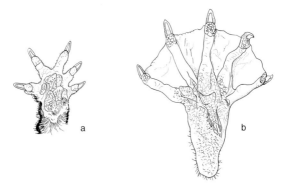

Figure 4. Feet of the Eurasian Beaver showing the large webbed hind foot (a = front foot; b = hind foot).

rently, only one substantial population is known, at the Buergan River Beaver Reserve along the Xinjiang-Mongolian border—a narrow strip 50 km long and only 500 m wide. Here the population is estimated to be only 500 animals, and only 700 may live in all of China. Firewood gathering has depleted much of the forest on which the beavers need to subsist; heavy grazing pressure has further reduced vegetation needed by beavers. China RL—EN A1bcd. China Key List— I. IUCN RL—LC.

FAMILY DIPODIDAE—Jerboas, Birch Mice, and Jumping Mice

跳鼠科 Tiaoshu Ke—跳鼠 Tiaoshu
This family comprises a variety of long-tailed, primarily saltatorial rodents, and many of the morphological specializations within the family are related to this form of locomotion. The family is composed of six subfamilies, all of which occur in China (Allactaginae, Cardiocraniinae, Dipodinae, Euchoreutinae, Sicistinae, Zapodinae). All forms hibernate seasonally. Jerboas possess numerous convergent adaptations with the New World family Heteromyidae. Dental formula: $1.0.0–1.3/1.0.0.3 = 16–18$.

SUBFAMILY ALLACTAGINAE—Four- and Five-toed Jerboas, Fat-tailed Jerboas

五趾跳鼠亚科 Wuzhitiaoshu Yake—五趾跳鼠 Wuzhitiaoshu
The largest jerboas, with long ears that when turned forward extend beyond the tip of the nose in most species; eyes large. Hind limbs three or four times longer than forelimbs, and the hind foot with five toes (fig. 5); the three central metatarsals are fused into a cannon bone, and the outer two toes are vestigial (they do not touch the ground, and their tips do not reach the base of the three middle toes). The tail is long and slender, far longer than the head and body; long hairs on the tip of the tail mostly grow laterally, forming a compressed, white and black tuft of hairs. Contains three genera, two of which occur in China.

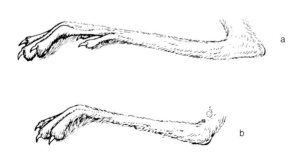

Figure 5. Comparison of the toe pattern of a five-toed jerboa (*Allactaga sibirica*; a) and a three-toed jerboa (*Dipus sagitta*; b).

GENUS *ALLACTAGA*—Four- and Five-toed Jerboas

五趾跳鼠属 Wuzhitiaoshu Shu—五趾跳鼠 Wuzhitiaoshu
Typical jerboas. Genus occurs throughout N and E Eurasia; 11 species, five of
which occur in China.

Balikun Jerboa *Allactaga balikunica*

游跳鼠 You Tiaoshu—**Distinctive Characteristics:**
HB 115–132; T 165–190; HF 57–61; E 31–36; GLS
30–33; Wt 65–80 g. Dorsum yellow, brown, and
gray, with black stripes; base of hairs gray, middle
of hairs yellow, and tips dark brown. Darker coloration on rump, and sides tending toward grayish
white. Venter, forelegs, and insides of hind legs pure
white, while the back of foot is sandy yellowish
gray. Tail with weakly developed tuft of darker hairs, base of ventral side without
white hairs. **Distribution:** Balikun region, Xinjiang; extending into Mongolia.
Natural History: Occupies rocky sandy areas with sparse vegetation. Diet consists of green leaves, grass seeds, roots, shoots, and insects. Lives alone in burrows. Is a good jumper. Nocturnal. Reproduction has been reported in May;
some indication that it may breed twice per year; litter size one to three young.
Conservation Status: China RL—LC. IUCN RL—LC.

Gobi Jerboa *Allactaga bullata*

巨泡五趾跳鼠 Jupaowuzhi
Tiaoshu—**Distinctive Charac-
teristics:** HB 115–145; T 165–200; HF 56–62; E 31–38; GLS 30–35; Wt 80–93 g.
Similar to *A. siberica* in color; pelage light, the entire dorsal pelage as well as the
outer sides of the thighs grayish buff; ventral surface, forearms, hind limbs, and
upper lip pure white to the roots of the hairs; there is a prominent hip stripe on
the outside posterior half of the thigh. Overall color lighter and slightly more
reddish than that of *A. balikunica*. Tail has well-developed tuft of hairs; base of
ventral surface of tuft white, black portion of inner surface with a white median
longitudinal stripe, the distal 20 mm of tail pure white (in *A. balikunica* the
broad white median line is replaced by a narrow black line at the basal part of
the tuft). **Distribution:** N China; extending into Mongolia. **Natural History:**
Occupies open sandy desert characterized by saltworts, ephedra, and desert
bushes. Lives alone in relatively simple unplugged burrows that extend up to 60

cm in length. Burrows contain well-defined nest chambers without bedding. Burrows are readily visible, due to the contrast of light sand against a background substrate of dark gravel. Considered one of the most "desert loving" of the Gobi rodents. Eats green vegetation, roots, seeds, and insects (grasshoppers and beetles). Nocturnal. Breeds once or twice each year between May and August; litter size one to three young. **Conservation Status:** China RL—LC. IUCN RL—LC.

Small Five-Toed Jerboa *Allactaga elater*

小五趾跳鼠 Xiaowuzhi Tiaoshu—**Distinctive Characteristics:** HB 90–115; T 144–185; HF 46–55; E 29–39; GLS 25–29; Wt 54–73 g (male); 44–59 g (female). Small size, but has long tail, large ears, and large hind feet. Dorsum dark to dusky gray; sides a light dusty yellow; distinct white hip stripe. Neck, chest, and belly snow white. Long vibrissae. The dark portion of the tail tuft is black, and the tip pure white. A whitish line divides the tail tuft along the medial surface to the tip of the tuft in most specimens. Hind feet with five well-developed toes that are widely separated and sport comb-like structures. Front feet are significantly smaller, and claws are markedly shorter than in *A. sibirica*. The long ears nearly close to form a tube near the base. **Distribution:** N Xinjiang; species extends across Iranian Plateau and to the Caucasus. **Natural History:** Occupies deserts and semidesert habitats, shunning sandy expanses and preferring clay and gravel substrates or desert grasslands. Never found in areas of dense vegetation, it does commonly occur in areas sparsely vegetated with wormwood (*Artemisia maritima*). Constructs burrows that can be shallow or up to 60 cm deep; burrows are always plugged, and very little dirt is piled at the entrance, so they are difficult to locate. Burrows may extend up to 138 cm in length, and a spherical nest chamber is centrally located. May occupy up to four different types of burrows: winter, summer, reproduction, and temporary. May dig burrows in hard ground with the aid of their incisors. Solitary. While primarily nocturnal, can be seen foraging several hours before sunset and after sunrise. Diet consists of underground roots and stems, as well as leaves, seeds, and insects. Can jump up to 2.4 m in a single hop. Reproductive season extends from April to July; females may produce one to three litters of two to eight young during this period. First litters average 4.5 young; second litters, 3.7 young. Males and some females attain sexual maturity at three to three and a half months of age. **Conservation Status:** China RL—LC. IUCN RL—LC.

Great Jerboa *Allactaga major*

大五趾跳鼠 Dawuzhi Tiaoshu—**Distinctive Characteristics:** HB 180–263; T 230–308; HF 80–98; E 50–64; GLS 41–47; Wt 280–420 g. Largest Chinese jerboa; has soft silky fur. Dorsal surface brown-gray with a tinge of cinnamon to sandy yellow-gray; sides lighter and yellower. Dramatic white band extends across hip. Ventrally, pure white from throat to chest and belly. Tail with conspicuous white tuft at the end. **Distribution:** N Xinjiang; extending into W Kazakhstan, S Russia, and Ukraine. **Natural History:** Occupies deserts, semidesert, and steppe habitats with firm soil (density increases as soil becomes firmer and more open). Primarily nocturnal, but frequently crepuscular. Can leap at extremely high speeds (40–50 km/h). Solitary. Occupies four different types of burrow: permanent summer burrows (up to 2 m deep, no obvious soil mounds on surface, females with a nest chamber); temporary summer burrows occupied during the day; temporary summer burrows occupied at night; and winter burrows (100–250 cm deep). Diet consists of seeds and tulip bulbs. Two to three litters of three to six young produced each year. **Conservation Status:** China RL—LC. IUCN RL—LC.

Mongolian Five-Toed Jerboa *Allactaga sibirica*

五趾跳鼠 Wuzhi Tiaoshu—**Distinctive Characteristics:** HB 130–170; T 180–230; HF 67–76; E 41–57; GLS 36–47; Wt 82–140 g. Dorsal pelage variable, mostly dark pale brown with dusty ripples, or sandy yellow; ventral pelage white; outer thigh with a large white stripe; tip of the muzzle and back of the nose dark brown; ears as long as the head; tail pale russet, tip of tail well furred and white, with a broad and distinctive black band; first toe longer than fifth toe. **Distribution:** Desert regions of N China; extending from Central Asia, across Mongolia and S Russia into the Baikal region. **Natural History:** Found in open gravelly and clay desert habitats, as well as mountain and desert grasslands (avoids mountainous country). Solitary and nocturnal, although it may be crepuscular in spring and autumn. Reported to jump in bounds up to 2 m long. Its permanent burrows are less complex than those of *A. major*. Burrows extend approximately 5 m in length at a depth of 35–65 cm and have one to three openings. Hibernates from September to April in soft nests constructed in its burrow. Temporary burrows, in contrast, are shorter (60–120 cm long) and shallower (20–30 cm deep). In spring it is reported to live primarily off of bulbs of *Gagea uniflora*, although it is also reported to be the most insectivorous of jerboas, eating insects, locusts, and beetles. It also includes leaves, stems, and seeds in its diet. Breeding begins in April or May, and one or two litters may be born in an extended breeding season. Litters normally consist of two to five young, although litters of eight or nine have been reported. **Conservation Status:** China RL—LC. IUCN RL—LC.

GENUS *PYGERETMUS*—Fat-tailed Jerboas

肥尾跳鼠属 Feiweitiaoshu Shu—肥尾跳鼠 Feiweitiaoshu

Compared to jerboas in the genus *Allactaga*, fat-tailed jerboas have shorter ears and lack a premolar. Dental formula: 1.0.0.3/1.0.0.3 = 16. Of three species in the genus, all confined to Central Asia, only one is present in China.

Dwarf Fat-Tailed Jerboa *Pygeretmus pumilio*

小地兔 Xiao Ditu—**Distinctive Characteristics:** HB 90–125; T 121–185; HF 47–52; E 20–30; GLS 24–28; Wt 27–65 g. Pelage similar to *Allactaga sibirica* in color, but much more variable; tail tuft not as prominent, the black portion narrow when viewed from the sides, white tip narrow (only 10–15 mm). Broad white stripe across the hip. **Distribution:** NW China; extending into Mongolia and west across Central Asia to NE Iran. **Natural History:** Inhabits clay and gravel deserts and semideserts, preferring hollows and dry ancient riverbeds. Tends to be associated with succulent vegetation, primarily of the family Chenopodiaceae. Diet is primarily herbivorous and in summer primarily consists of succulents. Stores fat in its tail as a reserve during times of food scarcity. Individuals occupy separate but extensively overlapping home ranges. Day burrows consist of single narrow tunnels (100–180 cm long and 60–75 cm deep). These burrows may have one or two entrances, which are plugged and inconspicuous when viewed from above. Additionally, animals utilize from three to five shelter burrows (25–45 cm deep) during their nightly activities; entrances are conspicuous and not plugged. Two to three litters with two to five young are produced each year. **Conservation Status:** China RL—LC. IUCN RL—LC.

SUBFAMILY CARDIOCRANIINAE—Dwarf Jerboas

心颅跳鼠亚科 Xinlutiaoshu Yake—心颅跳鼠 Xinlutiaoshu

Small jerboas with small tubular ears and tails without tufted hairs. Possess one small upper premolar. Hind feet are elongated but show no sign of fusion of the metatarsals as in other jerboa subfamilies. Subfamily comprises two genera and seven species distributed across Asia; three species representing both genera occur in China.

GENUS *CARDIOCRANIUS* (monotypic)

五趾心颅跳鼠属 Wuzhixinlutiaoshu Shu

Five-Toed Pygmy Jerboa *Cardiocranius paradoxus*

五趾心颅跳鼠 Wuzhixinlu Tiaoshu—**Distinctive Characteristics:** HB 45–60; T 59–78; HF 22–27; E 5–6; GLS 21–25; Wt 7–12 g. Large head with small eyes; ears short and tubular; base of tail may have a thickened fat layer. Dorsum dusky grayish buff to ochraceous; ventral pelage pure white; narrow rusty-yellow stripes present between dorsum and venter. The fifth (outermost) toe is about 4 mm shorter than the fourth toe, and the innermost toe is vestigial; soles of hind feet with a bristly pad of stiff hairs. Metatarsals not aligned for jumping, as in most other jerboas. Front of incisors has a longitudinal groove. **Distribution:** N China; extending into Mongolia, Tuva, and E Kazakhstan. **Natural History:** Inhabits burrows in rocky desert or sand hills, generally occupying those initially dug by other species. Nocturnal. Possesses obvious body fat deposits in summer, when tail may reach a diameter of 8 mm. Diet primarily seeds and grains. Reproduces once each year. Ecology poorly known. **Conservation Status:** China RL—LC. IUCN RL—DD.

GENUS *SALPINGOTUS*—Three-toed Pygmy Jerboas

三趾心颅跳鼠属 Sanzhixinlutiaoshu Shu—三趾心颅跳鼠 Sanzhixinlutiaoshu Small jerboas with large heads; hind limbs with three toes and soles with highly developed long brushes. Of six species found throughout Central Asia, two occur in China.

Thick-Tailed Pygmy Jerboa *Salpingotus crassicauda*

肥尾心颅跳鼠 Feiweixinlu Tiaoshu—**Distinctive Characteristics:** HB 41–54; T 93–105; HF 20–23; E 6–10; GLS 23–24; Wt 10–14 g. Dorsal pelage light sandy yellow; ventral pelage white. Nearly a quarter of the base of the tail greatly inflated; tail wholly covered with short hairs, longer at the tip, but not formed into a tuft. Hind feet small, with a thick, brushlike pad beneath the hind toes. **Distribution:** NW China; extending into S and SW Mongolia and E Kazakhstan. **Natural History:** Occupies sandy areas with stabilized vegetation. Inhabits two distinct types of burrow: simple and temporary, and composite and permanent (extending up to 3 m in length with plugged entrances). Prefers insects without a hard exoskeleton, seeds, and green vegetation in its diet. May breed only in spring, producing an average litter size of 2.7 young. Ecology poorly known. **Conservation Status:** China RL—LC. IUCN RL—DD.

Koslov's Pygmy Jerboa *Salpingotus kozlovi*

三趾心颅跳鼠 Sanzhixinlu Tiaoshu—**Distinctive Characteristics:** HB 43–56; T 110–126; HF 24–27; E 9–12; GLS 22–28; Wt 7–12 g. Dorsal pelage silky, sandy colored with scattered gray; head less gray than dorsum; base of dorsal pelage light yellowish gray; sides light; ventral pelage white to pale yellowish. Tail covered with scattered long hairs, its tip with long hairs formed into a tuft; pad of stiff hairs under hind foot. **Distribution:** NW China; extending into S and SE Mongolia. **Natural History:** Lives in sandy areas, generally those overgrown with tamarisk and saxaul. Diet consists of green vegetation and seeds; also eats insects. Nocturnal, but sometimes also crepuscular. Reproduces in April–May; litter size three to five young. Ecology poorly known. **Conservation Status:** China RL—LC. IUCN RL—LC.

SUBFAMILY DIPODINAE—Three-toed Jerboas

跳鼠亚科 Tiaoshu Yake—跳鼠 Tiaoshu

Medium to small jerboas; ears short, when turned forward reach just to the eyes. Hind limbs with three toes resulting from the fusion of the three central metatarsals into a cannon bone and the loss of digits one and five (fig. 5); soles with well-developed brush. Tail slender and longer than head and body, with tufted hairs, except in *Stylodipus* (tail hairs arranged feather-like). Occurs in deserts and grasslands from Europe, Africa, and Asia within the Palaearctic realm. Of four genera, two occur in China.

GENUS *DIPUS* (monotypic)

三趾跳鼠属 Sanzhitiaoshu Shu

Northern Three-Toed Jerboa *Dipus sagitta*

三趾跳鼠 Sanzhi Tiaoshu—**Distinctive Characteristics:** HB 101–155; T 145–190; HF 52–67; E 13–24; GLS 30–36; Wt 56–117 g. Pelage sandy brown to

rusty brown dorsally; white ventrally; a distinct white stripe originates at the tail and extends forward over the hip. Hind feet with long white hairs, only three toes (central three metatarsals have fused to form a cannon bone; fig. 5), and a stiff brush of hairs forms a pad beneath the toes. Tail tuft has a white tip extending beyond a black band. **Distribution:** Across arid regions of N China; extending into Iran and the Caucasus and east into NE Manchuria. **Natural History:** Inhabits high sandy deserts and semidesert, generally between 1,000 and 1,300 m but as high as 3,000 m (in the Altai Mountains). Solitary, and occupies three burrow types: permanent summer burrows (1–5 m long, 50–150 cm deep); temporary summer burrows; and hibernation burrows. Permanent burrows can contain three to five chambers. Burrows are sealed during the day and sometimes marked with a distinctive pyramid of sand; wind may blow this sand away and the entrance may become difficult to locate. Normally bounds 10–15 cm; however, when agitated may jump 120–140 cm. Nocturnal. Eats seeds, leaves, roots, and even insects. Hibernates for long periods, normally from November to March. Mating season peaks from March to May, during which time females produce two or three litters of two to eight (generally three or four) young; gestation lasts 25–30 days. **Conservation Status:** China RL—LC. IUCN RL—LC.

GENUS *STYLODIPUS*—Three-toed Jerboas

羽尾跳鼠属 Yuweitiaoshu Shu—羽尾跳鼠 Yuweitiaoshu

Black or brown hairs on hind toes and sides of soles shorter than in *Dipus*. Tail tip lacks tuft of black and white hairs; hairs on distal half of tail arranged gradually longer along side axis in a feather-like formation; terminal hairs dark and without white tip. Ears short; white spots behind ears. The three species in the genus are restricted to Central Asia; two species occur in China.

Andrews' Three-Toed Jerboa *Stylodipus andrewsi*

蒙古羽尾跳鼠 Mengguyuwei Tiaoshu—**Distinctive Characteristics:** HB 113–130; T 136–150; HF 50–59; E 16–18; GLS 31–34; Wt 60 g. Dorsum straw gray; crown gray with whitish spots present over the eye and a characteristic white spot behind the ear. A white stripe runs across the hip, and the entire venter is pure

white. The tail is thick with
a layer of fat and covered
with straw-gray hairs that
gradually increase in
length toward the distal
end, forming a flat
"feather"; the distal 30 mm
of the tail is black. Of the
three digits, the middle one is the longest; the sole of the hind foot is hairy,
with a brushlike pad beneath the toes. Differs from *S. telum* in having upper
premolars. **Distribution:** N China; extending into Mongolia. **Natural History:** Inhabits semidesert, grassy beach, and grassland habitats, and even
enters coniferous and shrub forests. Diet consists of green vegetation and
seeds. Nocturnal. Breeds once each year; litter size two to four young. Ecology poorly known. **Conservation Status:** China RL—LC. IUCN RL—LC.

Thick-Tailed Three-Toed Jerboa *Stylodipus telum*

羽尾跳鼠 Yuwei Tiaoshu—**Distinctive Characteristics:** HB 104–133; T 140–
165; HF 50–54; E 15–21; GLS 30–33; Wt 70–90 g. In summer, dorsum light
grayish yellow; this background is conspicuously darkened by black flecks
created by guard hairs with completely black-gray tips; sides light straw and
also conspicuously darkened by small blackish-gray flecks; a white stripe
extends across the hip; top of head dull and dark colored. **Distribution:** N
Xinjiang; extending into Kazakhstan, Uzbekistan, Turkmenistan, E Ukraine,
and to the N Caucasus. **Natural History:** Found in desert and mountainous
grassland, where it is not exclusively confined to sandy areas, preferring clay
substrate to shifting sands. Lives in association with saltbush and *Artemisia*,
also extending its range into pine forests. Does not hop like most jerboas;
rather its gait more closely resembles that of a gerbil. Solitary and nocturnal.
Occupies a permanent burrow (100–270 cm long; 20–120 cm deep) with multiple entrances, each sealed with a plug. Home ranges of males and females
equivalent; those of the same sex do not overlap, while those of males and
females overlap considerably. Shelter burrows are often used by several individuals. Diet consists of seeds, bulbs, and green vegetation; does not construct
food caches. Breeds twice each year, with peaks in the spring and autumn; litter size two to four young. **Conservation Status:** China RL—LC.
IUCN RL—LC.

SUBFAMILY EUCHOREUTINAE

GENUS *EUCHOREUTES* (monotypic)

长耳跳鼠亚科 Chang'ertiaoshu Yake; 长耳跳鼠属 Chang'ertiaoshu Shu

Long-Eared Jerboa *Euchoreutes naso*

长耳跳鼠 Chang'er
Tiaoshu—**Distinctive Characteristics:** HB 80–95; T 144–185; HF 41–49; E 37–47; GLS 29–31; Wt 24–38 g. This subfamily is represented by a single, unmistakable species, set apart by its large ears. Medium in size compared with other members of the family. Dorsum sandy yellow, with base of hairs gray; sides and ventral pelage wholly white. Head long and slender, rostrum pointed, eyes small, vibrissae long (normally longer than half of HB length). Central three metatarsals partially fused, with the middle toe slightly longer than adjacent toes and the two lateral toes short. Tuft of long hairs on tip of tail well developed but growing all around shaft of tail rather than forming a flat "flag" as in true jerboas; tail white with a black band set back from the white tip. **Distribution:** Across arid regions of NW China; extending northward into Mongolia. **Natural History:** An inhabitant of sandy desert regions; usually found in sand hills on the edge of desert oases or in sandy valleys with sparse vegetation. Diet is primarily green plants, but may also contain insects and lizards. Breeds in early spring; litter size two to six young. **Conservation Status:** China RL—LC. IUCN RL—LC.

SUBFAMILY SICISTINAE

GENUS *SICISTA*—Birch Mice

蹶鼠亚科 Jueshu Yake; 蹶鼠属 Jueshu Shu—蹶鼠 Jueshu
This subfamily contains a single genus. Species have a small, mouselike form and a long and semiprehensile tail. Although they do not possess the specialized long legs or feet found throughout the Dipodidae, they still move about primarily by jumping. They also readily climb vegetation using their outer toes to grasp limbs and curling their tails around branches for support. The 13 species are distributed in forests and meadows across the N Palaearctic; four species are found in China.

Long-Tailed Birch Mouse *Sicista caudata*

长尾蹶鼠 Changwei Jueshu—**Distinctive Characteristics:** HB 59–67; T 96–115; HF 16–18; E 13; GLS 19–21; Wt 8 g. Dorsally relatively light grayish brown with a tinge of yellow; along the line of the spine sparse black- or brown-tipped hairs. Ventrally a dirty whitish with yellowish tinge. Long tail uniform pale yellowish gray. **Distribution:** Heilongjiang and Jilin; extending to Sakhalin Island, Russia. **Natural History:** Occupies coniferous and mixed broadleaf forests. This species is poorly known. **Conservation Status:** China RL—DD. IUCN RL—DD.

Chinese Birch Mouse *Sicista concolor*

蹶鼠 Jue Shu—**Distinctive Characteristics:** HB 51–76; T 86–109; HF 17–18; E 11–14; GLS 19–20; Wt 5–8 g. Dorsum dark russet, sprinkled with black hairs; no black longitudinal stripe along spine. Ventral pelage gray-white. Tail very long and same color as back, underside lighter. Back and front feet with short white hair; soles bare. Upper incisors orange (and grooved), while lower incisors are white. **Distribution:** C China; extending south into India. **Natural History:** Occupies temperate forest edge, shrub, and grassland habitats. Constructs a neatly woven ball of grass as a nest, located in crevices or bushes. Diet consists of green vegetation, berries, and seeds. Nocturnal; hibernates in underground burrows. Vocalization a high-pitched whistle. Believed to produce a single litter of three to six young annually. **Conservation Status:** China RL—NT. IUCN RL—LC.

Southern Birch Mouse *Sicista subtilis*

草原蹶鼠 Caoyuan Jueshu—**Distinctive Characteristics:** HB 59–73; T 79–84; HF 14–17; E 11–15; GLS 18–21; Wt 12–13 g. Dorsally deep grayish straw brown to pale gray with yellowish-straw tinge; longitudinal black stripe extends down middle of spine from head to base of tail (more conspicuous on back than on head); yellowish straw-gray bands lie adjacent to stripe on either side. Whitish ventrally, with intermittent grayish or slightly strawish tinge; tail brownish gray dorsally, whitish underneath. **Distribution:** N Xinjiang; extending into Kazakhstan, Russia, and to E Austria. **Natural History:** Occupies grassland steppe, extending into semidesert regions. Can be found in birch woods dominated by grassy meadows. Primarily nocturnal, although it can be found active at any time of day or night. Diet consists of green vegetation and insects. Poorly known. **Conservation Status:** China RL—NA. IUCN RL—LC.

Tian Shan Birch Mouse *Sicista tianshanica*

天山蹶鼠 Tianshan Jueshu—**Distinctive Characteristics:** HB 67–73; T 99–114; HF 16–19; E 11–15; GLS 18–21; Wt 9–14 g. Pelage uniformly colored, lacking black spinal stripe; dorsally yellowish straw gray; flanks lighter with more straw hues. Ventrally dull whitish gray with a light tinge of straw. Chin and throat white. **Distribution:** N Xinjiang; extending into Kazakhstan. **Natural History:** Found in forested regions, in rocks of meadows at 2,500–3,000 m. Primarily nocturnal but can also be seen active during the day. Its main shelter type is holes in rotten stumps. A single litter of three to six young is produced. **Conservation Status:** China RL—LC. IUCN RL—LC.

SUBFAMILY ZAPODINAE

GENUS *EOZAPUS*—Jumping Mice

林跳鼠亚科 Lintiaoshu Yake; 林跳鼠属 Lintiaoshu Shu— 林跳鼠 Lintiaoshu
The subfamily Zapodinae comprises three genera and five species, most of which are distributed widely across North America. The only Asian form is the monotypic genus *Eozapus*, which is endemic to China. The Zapodinae all have long hind limbs, modified for saltatorial locomotion, and long tails.

Chinese Jumping Mouse *Eozapus setchuanus*

四川林跳鼠 Sichuan Lintiaoshu—**Distinctive Characteristics:** HB 70–100; T 115–144; HF 26–31; E 11–15; GLS 21–24; Wt 15–20 g. Ochraceous tawny dorsally, with a darker and sharply defined dorsal area from the forehead to the tail; sides pale reddish brown. Ventrally white, but with an evident pale brown

5-mm-wide longitudinal stripe in southern forms, whereas in the north characterized by a wholly white belly with no ventral stripe. The tail is long and thinly haired, distinctly bicolored with dusky above and pure white below; tip white. **Distribution:** C China. Endemic. **Natural History:** Found at high elevations in mountainous regions, where it primarily occupies shrub-steppe or meadow habitats, although it may be found in spruce forests. Diet primarily consists of green plants. **Conservation Status:** China RL—VU A1c. IUCN RL—LC.

FAMILY PLATACANTHOMYIDAE

GENUS *TYPHLOMYS*—Spiny Dormice

刺山鼠科 Cishanshu Ke; 猪尾鼠属 Zhuweishu Shu—猪尾鼠 Zhuweishu
This is a small and unique family, currently composed of only two genera (*Platacanthomys* and *Typhlomys*) and three species (only one of which is found in China). These rodents closely resemble dormice (family Gliridae), with which they have frequently been aligned. They may be distinguished from the dormice, however, by their number of teeth (dental formula: 1.0.0.3/1.0.0.3 = 16; compared with 20 for glirids), and their distinctive tail (the distal two-thirds of the tail is covered with long hairs and resembles a bottlebrush). The fifth digit on the front foot sports a rudimentary thumb with a nail.

Chinese Pygmy Dormouse *Typhlomys cinereus*

猪尾鼠 Zhuwei Shu—**Distinctive Characteristics:** HB 67–90; T 100–138; HF 19–23; E 14–17; GLS 21–25; Wt 15–32 g. Mouselike, with prominent, nearly naked ears. The long hairy tail has rings of scales closest to the body, while the long hairs on the distal two-thirds end in a white, brushlike tuft. Vibrissae long and white. The short pelage is uniformly dark mouse gray dorsally, while the ventral surface is grayish, the hairs tipped with white. **Distribution:** C and SE China. Endemic. **Natural History:** Occupies subtropical forests at elevations of 360–1,570 m. A burrowing form, it subsists on a diet of leaves, stems, fruits, and seeds. Little is known of its reproduction. Although it possesses four pairs of mammae, reported litter sizes are small, ranging from two to four. **Conservation Status:** China RL—LC. IUCN RL—LC.

FAMILY SPALACIDAE—Bamboo Rats and Zokors

鼹形鼠科 Yanxingshu Ke—鼹形鼠 Yanxingshu
This family comprises rodents that are all fossorial or subterranean, and each is characterized by specific and extreme morphological, physiological, and behavioral specializations associated with this way of life. Currently the Spalacidae is composed of four subfamilies (Myospalacinae, Rhizomyinae, Spalacinae, Tachyoryctinae), the first two of which occur in China. Dental formula: 1.0.0.3/1.0.0.3 = 16.

SUBFAMILY MYOSPALACINAE—Zokors

鼢鼠亚科 Fenshu Yake—鼢鼠 Fenshu
Stocky medium-sized rodents with a conical tail, the length of which is 25% or less of HB length. The pelage is soft and thick, covering the eyes and vestigial pinnae (in the species accounts no ear lengths are given, as these are rarely measured). Front feet are strongly built, with recurved digits—the center three claws being three times or more the length of hind claws. The Myospalacinae is divided into two genera, *Eospalax* and *Myospalax*, both found in China.

GENUS *EOSPALAX*—Zokors

中华鼢鼠属 Zhonghua Fenshu Shu—鼢鼠 Fenshu
These zokors have consistently been clustered together because of their many similarities, in addition to their morphological adaptations to a fossorial way of life. *Eospalax* contains only three species, all confined to China.

Chinese Zokor *Eospalax fontanierii*

中华鼢鼠 Zhonghua Fenshu—**Distinctive Characteristics:** HB 155–245; T 40–62; HF 25–38; GLS 41–49; Wt 150–620 g. Dorsal pelage a dark rust; grayish-black base of hairs usually not concealed. Ventral pelage grayish black with reddish hair tips; a prominent white blaze on the forehead; tail nearly naked. **Distribution:** Broadly distributed in C to NE China. Endemic. **Natural History:** Occupies steppe grasslands. Fossorial; constructs an elaborate burrow system with characteristic domes of loose dirt piled near entrances. Burrows may extend up to 100 m in length and contain large food-storage areas (34 × 18 × 23 cm; holding 2.4–4.5 kg of vegetation; the largest stores may reach 30 kg). Food-finding tunnels range 8–13 cm below the surface, while pathway tunnels may reach a depth of 25–48 cm; the greatest burrow depths reach 180–240 cm. Primarily eats roots and stems. Often considered a pest, although recent analyses have highlighted the important role that the Chinese Zokor plays in the ecosystem. As ecosystem engineers these rodents increase local environmental heterogeneity at the landscape level, aid in the formation, aeration, and mixing of soil, and enhance infiltration of water into the soil, thus curtailing erosion. They are also a major link in the food chain, and their loss (should populations be poisoned) leads to a cascading loss of many other species. Reproduction begins in early spring, and one to three litters of one to seven young (generally two or three) are produced. **Conservation Status:** China RL—LC. IUCN RL—LC.

Rothschild's Zokor *Eospalax rothschildi*

罗氏鼢鼠 Luoshi Fenshu—**Distinctive Characteristics:** HB 149–172; T 29–37; HF 23–31; GLS 33–44; Wt 164–440 g. Dorsal pelage grayish brown, with red-tipped hairs and a white blaze above the head in some specimens. Tail is hairy and bicolored, grayish yellow above and white beneath. Ventral pelage light grayish brown. Compared with those of other zokors, the claws are relatively slender and light. **Distribution:** C China. Endemic. **Natural History:** Occupies forest, scrub, and grassland habitat; may occur in cropland. Generally found between 1,000 and 3,000 m in elevation. Favors soft soil, in which it constructs complicated burrows. Diet is broad, including grasses, roots, and occasionally crops. Reproduction begins in April; one litter of between one and five young produced annually. **Conservation Status:** China RL—LC. IUCN RL—LC.

Smith's Zokor *Eospalax smithii*

斯氏鼢鼠 Sishi Fenshu—**Distinctive Characteristics:** HB 162–255; T 34–39; HF 25–33; GLS 42–51; Wt 180–460 g. Dorsal pelage dark brown, hairs minutely tipped with cinnamon; back of head dark gray to velvety black; dark brown around ears; long black and white vibrissae. May sport a white blaze on forehead. Ventral pelage grayish brown washed with cinnamon. **Distribution:** C China. Endemic. **Natural History:** Primarily lives in steppe and open fields, grasslands, and occasionally cropland. Prefers wet soft soil in which it constructs complicated burrows with separate living and storage areas. Diet consists primarily of grasses. Two litters are produced between May and September (with a breeding peak in June–July). Litter size two to four, with as many as eight young. **Conservation Status:** China RL—NT. IUCN RL—LC.

GENUS *MYOSPALAX*—Zokors

鼢鼠属 Fenshu Shu—鼢鼠 Fenshu

Myospalax forms a distinctive grouping of zokors marked by features of their skull. There are three species within *Myospalax*, two of which extend into China, and one of which (*M. myospalax*) occurs close to the Xinjiang border and may eventually be included in the Chinese mammal fauna.

Steppe Zokor *Myospalax aspalax*

草原鼢鼠 Caoyuan Fenshu—**Distinctive Characteristics:** HB 140–233; T 48–69; HF 28–36; GLS 38–48; Wt 225–422 g. Dorsum grayish yellow tinged with light brown; base of dorsal pelage gray; lip white; forehead sometimes with white spots; ventral pelage grayish white; tail and upper side of hind feet covered with short white hairs. **Distribution:** NE China; extending north into Russia and Mongolia. **Natural History:** Found in rich, dark, soft soil habitats on open steppe or farmland. Spacing between burrow entrances 1–3 m; diameter of the mound of soil demarcating burrows is 50–70 cm. Burrows reach a depth of 30–50 cm but may extend to 2 m deep in winter. Diet normally consists of underground roots. Breeds in May–June, with young from a single litter of two to five young appearing in July. **Conservation Status:** China RL—LC. IUCN RL—LC.

North China Zokor *Myospalax psilurus*

东北鼢鼠 Dongbei Fenshu—**Distinctive Characteristics:** HB 200–270; T 35–55; HF 25–37; GLS 43–52; Wt 185–400 g. Dorsal pelage reddish gray; cheeks and forehead ashy fawn; there is a small white blaze on the back of the head; tail and hind feet nearly naked, with only sparse white bristles. Ventral pelage gray. **Distribution:** C and NE China; extending to Mongolia and Russia (Amur region). **Natural History:** Occupies grasslands and agricultural fields at low elevations (but some populations may extend up to 1,400 m). Males and females live separately in extensive and complicated burrows that may extend as long as 40 m. Mounds of dirt outside of entrances may extend 40–59 cm in diameter and reach a height of 8–15 cm. Normal tunnels are 10 cm in diameter and run 10–50 cm below the surface. However, these zokors construct two or three special burrows to store food that reach depths of 90 cm; more than 350 g of food may be stored in each compartment. Their diet primarily consists of roots but may include insects. One litter of two to five young is produced in the April–June reproductive season. **Conservation Status:** China RL—LC. IUCN RL—LC.

SUBFAMILY RHIZOMYINAE—Bamboo Rats

竹鼠亚科 Zhushu Yake—竹鼠 Zhushu
Bamboo rats are solidly built animals with clear adaptations to fossorial life and a diet of bamboo shoots. Their short tail is sparsely haired and lacks scales, covered, instead, with soft wrinkled skin. Ear pinnae small. Dental formula: 1.0.0.3/1.0.0.3 = 16. The Rhizomyinae is divided into two genera, *Cannomys* and *Rhizomys*, both of which occur in China.

GENUS *CANNOMYS* (monotypic)

小竹鼠属 Xiaozhushu Shu

Lesser Bamboo Rat *Cannomys badius*

小竹鼠 Xiao Zhushu—**Distinctive Characteristics:** HB 175–215; T 54–67; HF 27–32; E 5–11; GLS 44–53; Wt 210–340 g (Chinese specimens appear to be smaller than those in other parts of the species' range). Dorsally red-brown to grayish brown, with soft dense pelage. Occasionally has white bands on the top of the head and on the throat. Ventral pelage lighter and less thick. Tail sparsely haired. **Distribution:** E Yunnan; extending into E Nepal, N India, Bhutan, SE Bangladesh, Myanmar, Thailand, Laos, Cambodia, and NW Vietnam. **Natural History:** Lives primarily in bamboo thickets in mountainous areas in the tropical-subtropical zone (300–950 m elevation); can occur in brush and other broadleaf vegetation. Excavates extensive burrows (tunnels may reach 58 m in length and 60 cm in depth) with a spacious sleeping chamber. Burrows are normally plugged when occupied. Emerges in the evening to feed on young roots and shoots, primarily of bamboo. Reaches sexual maturity at one year of age and produces litters of two to five young. Gestation is 40–43 days, and the naked young are slow to develop; weaning occurs at about eight weeks. **Conservation Status:** China RL—NA. IUCN RL—LC.

GENUS *RHIZOMYS*—Bamboo Rats

竹鼠属 Zhushu Shu—竹鼠 Zhushu
This genus comprises three large stocky burrowing rodents, all of which are found in China. The tails are short and naked, and the short ears protrude above the fur.

Hoary Bamboo Rat *Rhizomys pruinosus*

银星竹鼠 Yinxing Zhushu—**Distinctive Characteristics:** HB 240–345; T 90–130; HF 40–50; E 13–20; GLS 56–71; Wt 1,500–2,500 g. Pelage grayish brown to chocolate brown, darker dorsally than on the belly; interspersed dorsal guard hairs are white at the tip, yielding a grizzled appearance; tail nearly hairless. **Distribution:** Widespread throughout S China; extending to NE India, E Myanmar, Thailand, Laos, Cambodia, Vietnam, and N Malay Peninsula. **Natural History:** Lives in bamboo thickets or bunch beard grass, generally at low elevations. When sympatric with *R. sinensis*, *R. pruinosis* normally lives lower than 1,000 m, while *R. sinensis* is found higher. Lives alone in relatively simple burrows with a single entrance marked with a mound, tunnel, nest (12 × 32 cm), toilet, and predator escape hole. Nests are lined with grass and bamboo. Comes out to feed at night, primarily on roots and stems of bamboo and beard grass, although roots of other plants are occasionally harvested. Has been reported to breed year-round, but peak reproductive seasons are November–December and March–June. During breeding, males relocate to the burrow system of a female. Following a 22-day gestation, females produce litters of one to five altricial young. Weaning occurs 56–78 days following birth. **Conservation Status:** China RL—LC. IUCN RL—LC.

Chinese Bamboo Rat *Rhizomys sinensis*

中华竹鼠 Zhonghua Zhushu—**Distinctive Characteristics:** HB 216–380; T 50–96; HF 38–60; E 15–19; GLS 58–87; Wt 1,875–1,950 g. Fur soft, dorsum and sides brownish gray, darker on forehead and side of face. Ventral pelage sparsely haired. **Distribution:** C and SE China; extending into N Myanmar and Vietnam. **Natural History:** Occupies bamboo thickets, generally at high elevations, but may also occupy pine forests. Burrows are constructed in soft soils in which individuals live a solitary existence (except to mate). Each home range is marked by four to seven external mounds of dirt marking the plugged entrances, each of which may be 50–80 cm in diameter and 20–40 cm high. Burrows may extend up to 45 m in length and to depths of 20–30 cm below the surface. A den (20–25 cm diameter) is lined with bamboo leaves, and all burrow systems have an escape tunnel. Most burrows are occupied for about a year, after which the occupant shifts to a new site because of depletion of food resources. The diet consists primarily of roots and shoots of bamboo; most foraging occurs on the surface. Litters of two to four (but as many as eight) can be produced in all seasons (reproduction peaking in spring). Young are naked at birth and not weaned until three months of age. **Conservation Status:** China RL—LC. IUCN RL—LC.

Large Bamboo Rat *Rhizomys sumatrensis*

大竹鼠 Da Zhushu—**Distinctive Characteristics:** HB 381–480; T 141–192; HF 50–68; E 25–28; GLS 80–88; Wt 2,150–4,000 g. Dorsal pelage light brown with long, coarse guard hairs, giving a shaggy appearance; hair tips very sharp; crown and cheeks reddish; darker hairs form a triangle on the forehead; tail long and naked, with a pink tip; feet large, with sturdy, long claws. Ventral pelage slightly lighter than dorsum and sparsely haired so that belly skin is visible. Two posterior sole pads joined. **Distribution:** S Yunnan; extending to Myanmar, Vietnam, Cambodia, Laos, Thailand, Malay Peninsula, and Sumatra. **Natural History:** Lives in bamboo thickets in areas of soft soil. Its solitary burrows are shorter than those of other bamboo rats, reaching a length of 9 m and dug to a depth of 1 m. Large mounds mark the one to six burrow entrances. Emerges at night, when it may climb bamboo plants. Diet primarily bamboo, although it may eat other roots or cultivated plants. Known to grind its molars noisily and to utter harsh grunts. Reproductive activity is biseasonal (February–April; August–October). Litters of three to five young are born after a 22-day gestation in an underground nest. Life span is four years. **Conservation Status:** China RL—NA. IUCN RL—LC.

FAMILY CRICETIDAE—Cricetid Rodents

仓鼠科 Cangshu Ke— 仓鼠 Cangshu
A very large family of rodents with six subfamilies, two of which occur in China: the Arvicolinae (voles, lemmings, and water voles) and the Cricetinae (hamsters).

SUBFAMILY ARVICOLINAE—Voles, Lemmings, Water Voles

平亚科 Ping Yake—鼠平类 Pinglei
A diverse group of primarily herbivorous rodents including voles and lemmings.
Most are terrestrial and make elaborate runways through vegetation or just
below the surface of the ground. One species occurring in China is strictly fossorial (*Ellobius tancrei*), and one is amphibious (*Arvicola amphibius*). Nests are
made underground or in rocky crevices and other sheltered places. These
rodents are active year-round, day and night. Nearly all subfamily members are
stocky in build and have short limbs, a short tail, and reduced ears and eyes. Of
28 genera of Arvicolinae, 15 can be found in China.

GENUS *ALTICOLA*—Mountain Voles

高山鼠平属 Gaoshanping Shu—高山鼠平 Gaoshanping
Pale grayish-brown voles of open, rocky mountain habitats. Of 12 species, six
occur in China.

Silver Mountain Vole *Alticola argentatus*

银色高山鼠平 Yinse Gaoshanping—**Distinctive Characteristics:** HB 94–115; T
30–33; HF 18–20; E 14–15; GLS 24.5–27; Wt 25–40 g. Dorsal pelage usually
some shade of straw brown with grayish mixtures. The dorsal pelage color pales
along the sides and gradually blends into the grayish-white ventral pelage.
Unlike *A. baraskhin* and *A. semicanus*, the ventral pelage of this species lacks
reddish tones. Tail about one-third HB length and covered in white or pale
brown hairs. The upper surface of the tail may be slightly browner than the
underside, but it is never distinctly bicolored. Dorsal surfaces of hands and feet
white or grayish white. **Distribution:** N Xinjiang and Gansu; extending southwest through E Kazakhstan, Kyrgyzstan, and Tajikistan to NW India, NW Pakistan, and N Afghanistan. **Natural History:** Lives among boulders and eroding
rocky outcrops in alpine grasslands and shrublands at elevations between 1,500
and 3,500 m. Diurnal and strictly herbivorous. Eats green grass when available
and dried grass through winter. Tunnels under rocks and in rocky crevices,
where it builds a spherical nest about 20–25 cm in diameter. Cuts and dries
plants on sunny rocks during the day and drags the hay into the nest for the
night. Emits a high-pitched piping sound. Breeds twice each year, usually
between April and August. Average litter size four or five young. **Conservation
Status:** China RL—LC. IUCN RL—LC.

Gobi Altai Mountain Vole *Alticola barakshin*

阿尔泰高山䶄 Aertai Gaoshanping—**Distinctive Characteristics:** HB 100–125; T 18–26; HF 17–21; E 15–19; GLS 27–30; Wt 31–40 g. Dorsal pelage variable in color, but usually brownish gray with some dull reddish tones on the upper back and sides. Ventral pelage grayish white with a pale orange wash. Tail very short and indistinctly bicolored, pale brown above and white below. Dorsal surfaces of hands and feet white or grayish white. **Distribution:** One record from E Xinjiang. Occurs at low to middle elevations throughout the Gobi and Mongol Altai of S Mongolia and the Tuva region of Russia. **Natural History:** Reported from rocky, brush-covered hill slopes where it seems to favor stands of juniper. Herbivorous. A female captured in June was lactating and had six placental scars. **Conservation Status:** China RL—NA. IUCN RL—LC.

Large-Eared Mountain Vole *Alticola macrotis*

大耳高山䶄 Da'er Gaoshanping—**Distinctive Characteristics:** HB 100–125; T 21–29; HF 15–17; E 13–16; GLS 25.5–28.0; Wt 36–40 g. Dorsal pelage dark gray-brown with scattered long black hairs. Ventral pelage white. Tail short and distinctly bicolored, dark brown above, white below. **Distribution:** N Xinjiang (Tarbagatai and Altai mountains); extending eastward through S Siberia to the vicinity of Lake Baikal. **Natural History:** Lives in conifer forest and mixed deciduous-coniferous forest on rocky mountain slopes. **Conservation Status:** China RL—LC. IUCN RL—LC.

Mongolian Mountain Vole *Alticola semicanus*

半白高山䶄 Banbai Gaoshanping—**Distinctive Characteristics:** HB 104–140; T 24–35; HF 19–23; E 15–21; GLS 27–31. A large mountain vole. Dorsal pelage buffy gray with scattered black hairs. Ventral pelage buffy white and sharply demarcated from the dorsal pelage. There is often a yellowish-red stripe at the border between the dorsal and ventral pelage. Tail covered with white hairs and in stark contrast with the rather dark color of the dorsal pelage. **Distribution:** E Nei Mongol; extending to Mongolia and adjacent parts of S Russia. **Natural History:** Inhabits rocky meadow outcrops. Mainly nocturnal, but also active at times during the day. Strictly herbivorous. Lives under rocks and boulders, leaving large quantities of banana-shaped droppings near the entrances to its hole. **Conservation Status:** China RL—LC. IUCN RL—LC.

Stoliczka's Mountain Vole *Alticola stoliczkanus*

斯氏高山䶄 Sishi Gaoshan-ping—**Distinctive Characteristics:** HB 100–121; T 14–24; HF 20–23; GLS 25–28. Dorsal pelage pale brownish gray, often with a hint of reddish brown and sharply demarcated from the pale grayish-white ventral pelage. Tail very short and covered in pure white hairs. **Distribution:** Tibetan Plateau; extending into N India and Nepal. **Natural History:** Inhabits arid and semiarid grassland and scrubland between the upper limits of coniferous forest and the edge of the snow line. Diurnal. Eats grass and alpine herbs. Breeds twice each year between April and August. Litter size four or five. **Conservation Status:** China RL—LC. IUCN RL—LC.

Flat-Headed Mountain Vole *Alticola strelzowi*

扁颅高山䶄 Bianlu Gaoshanping—**Distinctive Characteristics:** HB 104–135; T 33–47; HF 19–22; E 14.5–26; GLS 25–30. Dorsal pelage variable but generally grayish brown. Ventral pelage grayish white. Tail relatively long for the genus, usually white but sometimes with a faint brownish tinge on the dorsal surface. Dorsal surfaces of hands and feet white. **Distribution:** N Xinjiang; extending from Kazakhstan to NW Mongolia. **Natural History:** Inhabits rocky slopes and eroding outcrops with narrow cavities and crevices. Constructs piles of stone and debris at the entrance to its crevice. Diurnal. Eats grass stems and seeds. Stores vegetation in crevices for consumption through winter. There are at least three litters per breeding season, and specimens with 7–11 embryos have been reported. **Conservation Status:** China RL—LC. IUCN RL—LC.

GENUS *ARVICOLA*—Water Voles

水䶄属 Shuping Shu—水䶄 Shuping
A very large, brown semiaquatic vole. Of three species of *Arvicola*, only one is found in China.

Eurasian Water Vole *Arvicola amphibius*

水𪕦 Shui Ping—**Distinctive Characteristics:** HB
145–185; T 90–110; HF 28–32; E 14–15; GLS 34–42; Wt 130–270 g. A large
semiaquatic vole. Dorsal pelage thickly furred, variable in color, but usually
some shade of dark brown with long black guard hairs scattered throughout. Pelage color somewhat paler brown on the cheeks and along the sides of the body
and blending into the buffy-brown ventral pelage. Tail entirely dark brown and
covered in short, stiff hairs. Hands and feet bear long claws and are dark brown
on dorsal surfaces. Flank glands, measuring about 20 × 10 mm, are most conspicuous in males. **Distribution:** N Xinjiang; extending across the Palearctic.
Natural History: Inhabits moist meadows, weedy riverbanks and lakeshores,
and upriver swamps. May also occur in irrigated farmland and villages. May be
active at any time, but is most active at dawn and dusk. Feeds primarily on succulent vegetation, but also consumes some insects, mollusks, and small fish.
Lives in complex burrows that are usually not deeper than 1 m. Males mark territories with flank gland secretions. Reproduction occurs during the warmer
months of the year and may begin as early as February in mild years. Gestation
period is 21 days. Females produce two to four litters per year. Average litter size
is between four and six young. **Conservation Status:** China RL—LC. IUCN
RL—LC.

GENUS *CARYOMYS*—Montane Forest Voles

绒𪕦属 Rongping Shu—绒𪕦 Rongping
Small, dark brown voles similar to *Eothenomys*, and once included as a subgenus
within it, but now regarded a distinct genus. Females have only four mammae
(two inguinal pairs). The two species of *Caryomys* are endemic to China.

Eva's Vole *Caryomys eva*

洮州绒鼠 Taozhou Rongshu—**Distinctive Characteristics:** HB 83–100; T
46–60; HF 15–18; E 10.5–13; GLS 21–24.5. Dorsal pelage dark reddish brown.
Ventral pelage dark gray with buff-brown tips. Tail less than half HB length, dark

brown above, paler brown below, but not distinctly bicolored. Dorsal surfaces of hands and feet dark brown. **Distribution:** C China. Endemic. **Natural History:** Mountain forests, and particularly damp, mossy forest at elevations between about 2,600 and 4,000 m. Appears to fill the ecological niche of *Eothenomys* at higher elevations. Feeds on seeds, buds, young leaves, bark, and grass. **Conservation Status:** China RL—LC. IUCN RL—LC.

Inez's Vole *Caryomys inez*

苛岚绒鼠 Kelan Rongshu—
Distinctive Characteristics: HB 87–94; T 32–42; HF 15–16; E 10–12; GLS 23–24. Dorsal pelage uniform dull buff brown. Ventral pelage pale buff. Tail more than half HB length, bicolored, dark brown above, paler brown below. Dorsal surfaces of hands and feet brown. Ears small, only slightly projecting above the fur. **Distribution:** C China. Endemic. **Natural History:** Inhabits overgrown wooded gullies and ravines between 500 and 2,000 m elevation, where it burrows in loose soil. Reproduction occurs from March to October. One female was reported to have two embryos. **Conservation Status:** China RL—LC. IUCN RL—LC.

GENUS *ELLOBIUS*—Mole Voles

鼹形田鼠属 Yanxingtianshu Shu—鼹形田鼠 Yanxingtianshu
A fossorial form highly specialized for subterranean life. Fur short and velvety; small eyes; ears vestigial. The long, white incisors protrude outside of the mouth. Of five species of *Ellobius*, only one occurs in China.

Eastern Mole Vole *Ellobius tancrei*

鼹形田鼠 Yanxing Tianshu—
Distinctive Characteristics:
HB 95–131; T 8–20; HF 19–24; E 4; GLS 24–36; Wt 30–88 g. A fossorial vole highly adapted to life underground. Dorsal pelage soft, velvety, and highly variable in coloration from dark grayish brown to pale sandy brown. Ventral pelage

ranges from dark grayish brown to nearly pure white. Face and top of head have a distinctive dark brown patch between the eyes and ears. Tail short and covered in gray-based sandy-brown hairs but with a short tuft of grayish-white hairs at the tip. Hands and feet covered in white hairs and somewhat broadened but otherwise not much specialized for digging and having very small claws. Ear pinnae reduced to an inconspicuous fleshy ridge about 4 mm high. **Distribution:** NW and NC China; extending westward into E Turkmenistan, Uzbekistan, and E Kazakhstan. **Natural History:** Inhabits steppes, semideserts, and grasslands, especially in moist valleys and near the banks of lakes and streams. Sometimes found in oasis farmlands. Feeds on the underground parts of plants and especially starch bulbs and tubers. A fossorial "head-lift digger," it uses its incisors and skull to loosen and shovel dirt. Lives in a complex burrow system including food storage and nest chambers. Long burrow passages are 5–6 cm in diameter and usually lie at depths between 10 and 40 cm, while nest and food storage chambers descend to depths of 50–70 cm. Active day and night but spends little time outside burrows during the day. At night, however, may range quite far from burrows. Extremely timid, it may emit a birdlike chirp when frightened. Reproduction typically occurs between April and September. Males and females reach reproductive maturity at about 90 days. Gestation period is about 26 days, and females have their first litter at about five months of age and may have as many as six or seven litters of three to four or five to seven, depending on environmental conditions. Offspring remain in their underground nest until they are weaned at about 60 days of age. The interval between litters is 34–36 days. **Conservation Status:** China RL—LC.

GENUS *EOLAGURUS*—Steppe Voles

东方兔尾鼠属 Dongfangtuweishu Shu—东方兔尾鼠 Dongfangtuweishu
Pale sandy yellow, short-tailed voles of desert steppes. Similar to *Lagurus* but distinguished by larger size and the absence of a mid-dorsal stripe in the adult pelage. There are two species of *Eolagurus*, and they both occur in China.

Yellow Steppe Vole *Eolagurus luteus*

黄兔尾鼠 Huang Tuwei-
shu—**Distinctive Characteristics:** HB 105–195; T 12–22; HF 19–21; E 5–9; GLS 28–32. Dorsal pelage pale sandy brown, occasionally with darker tinges on the back of the head and around the eyes. Sides pale sandy yellow, blending into the pale yellow ventral pelage (venter pure white in *E. przewalskii*). Dorsal surfaces and soles of hands and feet furred yellow-brown. First digit of forelimb with a small, pointed claw

(large and obtuse claw in *E. przewalskii*). Juveniles may exhibit a faint mid-dorsal stripe, but this is absent in adults. **Distribution:** N Xinjiang; extending from E Kazakhstan to W Mongolia. **Natural History:** Inhabits dry steppes and semideserts. In spring and summer occurs at lower elevations, where it will remain until the grass is all dried, at which time it will move up to higher elevations to feed on montane grass through winter. Diurnal. Feeds on roots, tubers, and seeds in the vicinity of holes, emerging for only very short periods of time. Once the food around the hole has been depleted, will move on to a new hole or dig a new one. Reproduction occurs in the summer months; produces at least three litters of about six to nine young per litter. The young are sexually mature within three to four weeks. Population sizes and the extent of the distribution of the species may fluctuate greatly from year to year. In years of abundance the species may be distributed across all of N Xinjiang, reaching densities of 1,000–3,000 per hectare. When populations crash, however, the species is rare and restricted to just a few localities with very favorable conditions. Disease transmission is a problem during high population years. **Conservation Status:** China RL—LC. IUCN RL—LC.

Przewalski's Steppe Vole *Eolagurus przewalskii*

普氏兔尾鼠 Pushi Tuweishu—**Distinctive Characteristics:** HB 125–130; T 11–15; HF 19–22; E 7. Dorsal pelage pale sandy brown; sides brighter yellow and blending into the generally pure white ventral pelage, although there may occasionally be some gray-based hairs on the middle of the chest and abdomen. Tail very short, buff above, white below. Feet, including the soles, well covered with pure white fur and a fringe of somewhat stiffened hairs along their outer margins. First digit of forelimb with a large, obtuse claw (small and pointed in *E. luteus*). **Distribution:** N China; extending through Mongolia. **Natural History:** Inhabits montane meadows and riverbanks. Diurnal, feeds on grass, roots, tubers, and seeds. Burrows are complex, with three to seven openings and as many as three storage chambers, and three nests per burrow system. Excavated burrow systems also have one to three enlarged chambers in addition to the usual nests and storage areas. Reproduction occurs between May and August; females give birth to about three litters of three to eight young each. **Conservation Status:** China RL—LC. IUCN RL—LC.

GENUS *EOTHENOMYS*—Chinese Voles

绒鼠属 Rongshu Shu—绒鼠 Rongshu
Dark-colored forest voles; pelage often has a vague brassy sheen. The genus can be divided into two species groups: the *melanogaster* group (*cachinus*, *melanogaster*, *miletus*) and the *chinensis* group (*chinensis*, *wardi*, *proditor*, *custos*, *olitor*).

Females have only four mammae (two inguinal pairs). All of the eight known species of *Eothenomys* are found in China.

Kachin Chinese Vole *Eothenomys cachinus*

克钦绒鼠 Keqin Rongshu—**Distinctive Characteristics:** HB 108; T 56; HF 19; E 15; GLS 26.5. A large-bodied member of the *melanogaster* species group. Dorsal pelage somewhat tawny brown. Ventral pelage grayish with a pale buff to ochraceous wash. Tail relatively long, much longer than in any other member of the *melanogaster* species group (but shorter than in *E. chinensis*). Similar to *E. miletus* but geographically isolated. **Distribution:** Yunnan west of Salween River valley; extending to adjacent NE Myanmar. **Natural History:** Known from dense montane forest between 2,300 and 3,200 m, where it seems to favor steep slopes and stream banks. **Conservation Status:** China RL—LC. IUCN RL—LC.

Sichuan Chinese Vole *Eothenomys chinensis*

中华绒鼠 Zhonghua Rongshu—**Distinctive Characteristics:** HB 110–125; T 63–76; HF 19–24; E 12–15. A large-bodied member of the *chinensis* species group. The tail is more than half of HB length, the longest of all the *Eothenomys*. Dorsal pelage grayish brown. Ventral pelage slate gray and with a characteristic pinkish-buff wash in the center of the abdomen. Tail dark brown above, slightly paler below. Dorsal surfaces of the hands and feet grayish brown. **Distribution:** Known only from the vicinity of Mount Emei, Sichuan. Endemic. **Natural History:** Recorded between 1,500 and 3,000 m. **Conservation Status:** China RL—LC. IUCN RL—LC.

Southwest Chinese Vole *Eothenomys custos*

西南绒鼠 Xi'nan Rongshu—**Distinctive Characteristics:** HB 81–105; T 35–59; HF 16.5–20; E 12–14. A member of the *chinensis* species group, similar to *E. chinensis* and

E. wardi, but averaging smaller and with a shorter tail. Dorsal pelage dark brown. Ventral pelage grayish. Tail bicolored, dark brown above, whitish below. Dorsal surfaces of hands and feet dark brown with a few pale hairs. **Distribution:** NW Yunnan, S Sichuan. Endemic. **Natural History:** Inhabits montane forests between 2,500 and 4,800 m, where it is especially common along stream banks. Also found in scrub, bamboo, and open and rocky meadows. Reproduction occurs from early summer to late fall. **Conservation Status:** China RL—LC. IUCN RL—LC.

Père David's Chinese Vole *Eothenomys melanogaster*

黑腹绒鼠 Heifu Rongshu—**Distinctive Characteristics:** HB 87–108; T 21–42; HF 15–17; E 10–12. A small-bodied member of the *melanogaster* group. Dorsal pelage dark brown, often very nearly black. Ventral pelage slate gray, sometimes washed with buff or brown. Tail short to medium in length, dark brown above, paler below. Individuals from Sichuan and Yunnan average smaller than those from E China. **Distribution:** Central S and SE China, including Taiwan; extends into Myanmar and Vietnam. **Natural History:** Common in pine-rhododendron forest between 700 and 3,000 m. Breeds in February–March, and then again in September–October, with populations reaching peaks in May–June and September–October. Average home range for males is 417 m²; for females, 469 m². Home ranges of same-sex individuals overlap, indicating no territoriality in the species. **Conservation Status:** China RL—LC. IUCN RL—LC.

Yunnan Chinese Vole *Eothenomys miletus*

大绒鼠 Da Rongshu—**Distinctive Characteristics:** HB 110–120; T 40–50; HF 18–21; E 12–15. The largest member of the *melanogaster* species group. Dorsal pelage soft, long, and thick; rich, dark reddish brown, blending into the blue-gray ventral pelage. Occurs together with *E. melanogaster* over much of its range, but *E. miletus* is usually larger. May also be confused with *E. cachinus*. **Distribution:** S China. Endemic. **Natural History:** Occurs in montane forests. **Conservation Status:** China RL—LC. IUCN RL—LC.

Black-Eared Chinese Vole *Eothenomys olitor*

昭通绒鼠 Zhaotong Rongshu—**Distinctive Characteristics:** HB 80–92; T 29–39; HF 14–17; E 9–11. The smallest member of the *chinensis* group and the

smallest of all *Eothenomys*. Similar to *E. melanogaster*, but smaller. Dorsal pelage dark brown to nearly black. Ventral pelage slate gray. Tail and feet dark brown. **Distribution:** S China. Endemic. **Natural History:** Known from montane habitats between 1,800 and 3,350 m. **Conservation Status:** China RL—LC. IUCN RL—LC.

Yulong Chinese Vole *Eothenomys proditor*

玉龙绒鼠 Yulong Rongshu—**Distinctive Characteristics:** HB 105–115; T 26–34; HF 17–20; E 12–13. A large member of the *chinensis* species group. Dorsal pelage dark brown over the back, reddish brown over the rump, blending along the sides into the slate-gray ventral pelage. Tail dark brown above, paler below, feet dark brown. **Distribution:** Restricted to the border region between Sichuan and Yunnan. Endemic. **Natural History:** Inhabits meadows and rocky areas between 2,500 and 4,200 m. Reproductive activity occurs from spring to fall. **Conservation Status:** China RL—VU D2.

Ward's Chinese Vole *Eothenomys wardi*

德钦绒鼠 Deqin Rongshu—**Distinctive Characteristics:** HB 101–107; T 59–66; HF 19–20; E 14–15. A member of the *chinensis* species group and somewhat similar to *E. chinensis*, but much smaller and with a shorter tail and shorter hind feet. **Distribution:** NW Yunnan in the Mekong and Salween river valleys. Endemic. **Natural History:** Stream banks in forest, open and rocky meadows between 2,400–4,250 m. Reproduction from early summer to late fall. **Conservation Status:** China RL—LC. IUCN RL—NT.

GENUS *LAGURUS* (monotypic)

兔尾鼠属 Tuweishu Shu

Steppe Vole *Lagurus lagurus*

草原兔尾鼠 Caoyuan Tuweishu—**Distinctive Characteristics:** HB 80–120; T 7–19; HF 15; E 5. Dorsal pelage pale grayish buff with a distinctive blackish stripe extending along the midline of the back. Ventral pelage buffy white. Tail short and colored like the dorsal pelage. The dorsal and much of the ventral surfaces of the hands and feet are covered with buffy-gray fur. Females have four pairs of mammae. **Distribution:** NW Xinjiang; extending into Mongolia and through Kazakhstan to Ukraine. **Natural History:** Inhabits rocky steppes and semideserts up to 2,800 m. May also occur in grasslands, agricultural areas, and along the edges of roads and canals, but generally avoids areas with brushy undergrowth. Feeds on green grasses and legumes in warmer months, roots and tubers through winter. Diurnal, but most active in early morning and late evening. Constructs a system of burrows extending to about 90 cm below the surface and with two to three entrances. A spherical grass-lined nest chamber is situated about halfway down the burrow system. Males and females live together in the same burrow until the appearance of young, at which time the males move to a nearby burrow. Reproduction occurs from April until October, with a peak in summer months. Estrous cycle is seven days, gestation 20 days. Females may have as many as six litters per year. Litter size usually varies from four to eight, depending on precipitation levels. Young reach sexual maturity at four to six weeks, and population densities may reach 30–50 per hectare. **Conservation Status:** China RL—LC. IUCN RL—LC.

GENUS *LASIOPODOMYS*—Brandt's Voles

毛足田鼠属 Maozutianshu Shu—毛足田鼠 Maozutianshu

Voles modified for a semifossorial life: tail very short, ears shortened, barely projecting above fur, foreclaws slightly enlarged. All three species of the genus occur in China.

Brandt's Vole *Lasiopodomys brandtii*

布氏田鼠 Bushi Tianshu—
Distinctive Characteris-
tics: HB 110–130; T 22–30; HF 18–24; E 9–12; GLS 25–30; Wt 55–84 g. A very distinctive pale vole with a short tail. Dorsal pelage pale buffy yellow or sand colored with admixtures of black hairs. Sides of face below ear lack mixtures of black hairs and appear brighter yellow. The color of the dorsal pelage blends along the sides into the buffy-gray ventral pelage. Tail monocolored, pale sandy

brown. Dorsal surfaces of hands and feet covered in pale buffy-white fur; claws on all digits of hands and feet long and sharp. **Distribution:** NE China; extending into Mongolia and Russia. **Natural History:** Inhabits dry grasslands to elevations of about 2,000 m. Strictly herbivorous, eating the green grasses around its burrows through the warmer months and storing dried grass in nest chambers for winter. Strictly diurnal, it emerges from its burrows only after the sun has become sufficiently warm and bright. Lives in large colonies and constructs both simple and complex burrows at depths of 14–24 cm. Entrances to burrows are 3–5 cm across and are surrounded by conspicuous mounds of dirt. Simple burrows have two to five exit holes and dirt mounds about 4 cm high and 10–25 cm across; these lack storerooms and nest chambers and are usually occupied by a single young vole. Complex burrows have 4–12 exit holes and dirt mounds 6–12 cm high and 40–80 cm across; they may have as many as two nests and four storage chambers, usually occupied by older voles. Overall, complex burrows are 10–30 m long and cover an area of 8–23 m². Emits a high-pitched, sharp trill warning whistle when danger is sensed. Reproduction occurs from mid-March to September, yielding four or five litters of six to eight young each; however, under favorable conditions there may be as many as 12–15 young per litter. **Conservation Status:** This species has been considered an agricultural pest and subjected to widespread poisoning campaigns. China RL—LC. IUCN RL—LC.

Smokey Vole *Lasiopodomys fuscus*

青海田鼠 Qinghai Tianshu—**Distinctive Characteristics:** HB 110–150; T 22–31; HF 18–22; E 14–19; GLS 26–32; Wt 30–58 g. Dorsal pelage grayish brown and rather sharply demarcated along the sides from the gray-buff ventral pelage. Tail bicolored, brown above, buff below. Dorsal surfaces of hands and feet grayish buff. Readily distinguished from the other two species in the genus by the rather sharp demarcation between dorsal and ventral pelage. **Distribution:** S Qinghai. Endemic. **Natural History:** Inhabits moist meadows in high mountain grasslands between 3,700 and 4,800 m. **Conservation Status:** China RL—LC. IUCN RL—LC.

Mandarin Vole *Lasiopodomys mandarinus*

棕色田鼠 Zongse Tianshu—
Distinctive Characteristics: HB 97–113; T 20–27; HF 15–18; E 7–12; GLS 24–26. Dorsal pelage ranges from pale reddish brown (chestnut) to dark grayish brown. Ventral pelage ranges from light buff-brown to dark gray-brown. On

paler specimens the tail is a uniform buff color, but on dark specimens the tail is bicolored, grayish brown above and buff below; the dorsal surfaces of the hands and feet likewise range from buff to grayish brown. Paler-colored individuals of this species may be difficult to distinguish from *L. brandtii*. **Distribution:** NE and C China; extending into Mongolia, Russia, and Korea. **Natural History:** Inhabits rocky mountain steppe up to 3,000 m. Usually found away from woods but near water sources. Especially common in dense brush along the banks of lakes, rivers, and streams. Feeds on the underground parts of plants. Highly social and lives in extended family groups. Members occupy a common burrow to which they remain strongly attached. In summer groups consist of one breeding male for every one to two breeding females, plus the young of one to three generations. Total number of individuals per burrow averages 8.7, but ranges between 3 and 22. Reproduction occurs between March and August, yielding litters of two to four young. **Conservation Status:** China RL—LC. IUCN RL—LC.

GENUS *MICROTUS*—Voles

田鼠属 Tianshu Shu— 田鼠 Tianshu

Typical voles not especially modified for subterranean life. Females have four pairs of mammae. Of 62 species, 12 occur in China.

Field Vole *Microtus agrestis*

黑田鼠 Hei Tianshu—**Distinctive Characteristics:** HB 109; T 44; HF 18.5; E 13; GLS 26–28. Dorsal pelage dark grayish brown. Hairs of ventral pelage gray-based with buff-gray tips. Tail bicolored, brownish black above, white below. Dorsal surfaces of feet grayish white; hind feet have six plantar pads. Winter pelage brighter, more ochraceous. **Distribution:** N Xinjiang; ranging across the Palaearctic from W Europe to Lake Baikal, Siberia. **Natural History:** Inhabits moist and densely vegetated meadows, lakeshores, and river edges. Uncommon in agricultural areas. Herbivorous and prefers green grass when available but also consumes stored roots, bulbs, and bark through the winter. Active at all times, but most active in early morning and late evening. Digs a short burrow approximately 20–30 cm in length and leading to a small, round, grass-lined nest measuring 35–38 cm long and 23–27 cm high. Leading from the nest chamber are several short exit tunnels and one or two passages 5–10 cm long leading to small food storage chambers. Burrows are usually dug under some form of cover such as root masses, bushes, stumps, or piles of twigs. Alarm call consists of a staccato *tucktucktucktucktuck*. Females reach sexual maturity after 40 days of age, males after 45 days; females are polyestrous, with a postpartum estrus cycle and a 21-day gestation period. Reproduction occurs from April to September, with females having two to four litters of about three offspring each, but ranging anywhere between one and seven depending on conditions. Populations fluctuate over a cycle of three to four years. In high population years females outnumber males five to one; however, during population lows the percentage of females to males is roughly equal. Young are born naked and blind; by day 4 some hairs are visible, and by day 6 there is a juvenile coat of gray-black hairs. Eyes open by day 9 or 10; by day 11 they begin feeding for themselves, and weaning occurs at day 14. **Conservation Status:** China RL—LC. IUCN RL—LC.

Common Vole *Microtus arvalis*

普通田鼠 Putong Tianshu—**Distinctive Characteristics:** HB 102–132; T 32–40; HF 14–19; E 14–15; GLS 27–29.5. Dorsal pelage from light buffy brown to dark brownish gray; hairs of ventral pelage gray-based with buffy-gray tips. Tail bicolored, brownish black above, white below; tail with a slight terminal tuft. Dorsal surfaces of hands and feet drab brown, with silvery-white hairs; hind feet have six plantar pads. **Distribution:** NE China; extending westward through Europe. **Natural History:** Lives in a wide variety of open habitats including moist meadows, forest steppe, moist forest, and sometimes agricultural areas. Eats a variety of green plants supplemented with seeds and insects in summer and roots and bark through winter. Active at all times, but more so when dark. Groups of related individuals inhabit one nest—a grass-lined chamber about 10–20 cm in diameter at a depth of up to 20–30 cm. Four to six exit burrows extend from the nest chamber, and from smaller chambers for food storage and special latrine rooms for the accumulation of excrement. May also dig temporary burrows in the area surrounding the nesting burrow, and the entire surface outside the nest is marked by trails. Makes use of special feeding stations where it is less visible to predators. When populations reach high levels and when an area's resources are depleted, will migrate to outlying areas. Alarm call consists of a high-pitched single syllable. A fecund species; females are capable of breeding as early as two weeks following birth. Gestation lasts 19–21 days, with females producing about seven litters of five offspring yearly, but ranging between 1 and 13 offspring depending on conditions. Under favorable conditions reproduction may continue through the winter months, albeit at lower rates. **Conservation Status:** China RL—LC. IUCN RL—LC.

Clarke's Vole *Microtus clarkei*

克氏田鼠 Keshi Tianshu—**Distinctive Characteristics:** HB 114–134; T 62–67; HF 19–21; E 12–15. Externally very similar to *M. fortis*, but with the dorsal pelage less yellow and more of a warm reddish brown; hairs of ventral pelage dark gray with silver tips. Tail brown above, dirty white below. Dorsal surfaces of hands and feet dirty white; soles of hind foot have only five plantar pads instead of the usual six for the genus. **Distribution:** SW China; extending to N Myanmar. **Natural History:** Known from coniferous forests and alpine meadows at elevations between 3,400 and 4,290 m. **Conservation Status:** China RL—LC. IUCN RL—LC.

Reed Vole *Microtus fortis*

东方田鼠 Dongfang Tianshu—**Distinctive Characteristics:** HB 120–139; T 48–67; HF 22–25; E 13–15. A large and relatively long-tailed species of *Microtus*. Dorsal pelage dark reddish brown; sides somewhat buff brown and blending into the grayish ventral pelage. Tail bicolored, dark brown above, whitish below. Dorsal surfaces of hands and feet light brown; hind feet have only five plantar pads (but a rudimentary sixth pad may sometimes be present). **Distribution:** Widespread throughout E China; extending into Russia and Korea. **Natural History:** Common to wet environments, especially lakeshores, riverbanks, and streams surrounded by heavy vegetation. Although favoring waterside habitats, these voles may invade adjacent agricultural areas and undeveloped lands when overcrowded or forced out by rising water levels in spring and early summer. However, these migrations never exceed 5 km, and with the subsidence of water levels the voles will return to their favored lakeshore and riverbank habitats. The species is also known to inhabit marshy parts of steppe and forests to elevations of about 2,000 m. There are distinct seasonal changes in diet. During the growing season feeds predominantly on grass stems and leaves. During the fall begins to store grasses and grain for use through winter, at which time may also feed on roots, bark, and the pith of reeds; however, at all times leaves appear to represent the most favored parts of plants. Active day and night, is slow moving on land but an excellent swimmer. These voles dig burrows of varying extent and to varying depths depending on the local conditions. In well-drained soils burrows are dug to a depth of about 10–15 cm and overall length of 120–150 cm. Passages branching from the main corridor may lead to dead ends, storage rooms, or nest chambers, and there are numerous escape tunnels to the surface throughout. Under heavy cover or in very wet areas burrows may be shallower and may even take the form of open ruts on the ground's surface. In damp areas, such as along overgrown riverbanks and lakeshores, these voles will construct a large, spherical

(25–30 cm diameter) nest above ground. Often found right next to the water, five or six nests sometimes occur in close proximity, with obvious paths leading to the nests. Reproduction occurs from April to November with up to six litters of five offspring per litter in favorable years. Gestation lasts about 20 days, and the interval between litters is 40–45 days. Females reach sexual maturity by three and a half to four months of age; males mature a little later. **Conservation Status:** China RL—LC. IUCN RL—LC.

Narrow-Headed Vole *Microtus gregalis*

狭颅田鼠 Xialu Tianshu—**Distinctive Characteristics:** HB 89–122; T 21–32; HF 15–18; E 9–12; GLS 25–27. Dorsal pelage pale yellow-buff, lighter along the sides and blending into the grayish-buff ventral pelage. In winter the dorsal pelage is a brighter ochraceous red. Tail may be monocolored yellow-buff or bicolored dark brown above and yellow-buff below. Dorsal surfaces of hands and feet brownish white. **Distribution:** NW and NE China; widely distributed throughout the Palearctic. **Natural History:** Inhabits dry steppe and grassy meadows at elevations up to about 4,000 m. Consumes both the exposed and underground parts of a variety of plants but prefers legumes and cereals. Active at all times but especially toward evening and at night. Lives in complex burrows at depths of 10–25 cm. One burrow may have as many as 10 or more openings as well as up to five nest chambers and storage chambers. The vole's narrow cranium is apparently an adaptation to life in narrow burrows and cracks in frozen ground. Reproduction occurs during the warmer months. About five litters are produced per season; the number of young per litter varies through the year. The first litter of the season usually consists of only two young, but litters of seven to nine offspring per litter are more common. Litters of up to 12 offspring have been recorded. **Conservation Status:** China RL—LC. IUCN RL—LC.

Kazakhstan Vole *Microtus ilaeus*

伊犁田鼠 Yili Tianshu—**Distinctive Characteristics:** HB 100–127; T 32–48; HF 17–20; E 12; GLS 29. Dorsal pelage pale grayish brown. Ventral pelage buffy gray. Tail pale brown above, white below. Dorsal surfaces of hands and feet white. **Distribution:** Tian Shan of N Xinjiang; extending west to Uzbekistan. **Natural History:** Inhabits forest, forest steppe, and scrub meadow. **Conservation Status:** China RL—LC. IUCN RL—LC.

Taiwan Vole *Microtus kikuchii*

台灣田鼠 Taiwan Tianshu—**Distinctive Characteristics:** HB 95–120; T 68–85; HF 20–25; E 12–15; GLS 27.8–30.5. Dorsal pelage warm reddish brown; sides somewhat brighter, almost fulvous brown, and blending into the grayish-orange ventral pelage. Tail rather long for the genus, bicolored, dark brown above, whitish below. Dorsal surfaces of hands and feet light brown to nearly white. **Distribution:** Taiwan. Endemic. **Natural History:** Inhabits highland forest. **Conservation Status:** China RL—LC. IUCN RL—NT.

Lacustrine Vole *Microtus limnophilus*

经营田鼠 Jingying Tianshu—**Distinctive Characteristics:** HB 88–118; T 32–44; HF 20–21; E 13–14; GLS 26–28. Similar to and often confused with *M. oeconomus*. Dorsal pelage distinctly yellow; individual hairs gray at the base, pale buff terminally. Hairs of ventral pelage gray-based with white tips, imparting an overall bluish-gray effect. Tail bicolored, buffy brown above, white below. Dorsal surfaces of hands and feet buffy white. Females have four pairs of mammae: two pectoral pairs, two abdominal pairs. **Distribution:** C China. Limits of geographic range uncertain; a likely endemic. **Natural History:** Saline desert and alpine meadows. May reach high numbers on the Tibetan Plateau. **Conservation Status:** China RL—LC. IUCN RL—LC.

Maximowicz's Vole *Microtus maximowiczii*

莫氏田鼠 Moshi Tianshu—**Distinctive Characteristics:** HB 116–155; T 37–60; HF 18–22; E 12–16.6. A large vole resembling *M. oeconomus* externally. Dorsal pelage dark blackish brown with ochraceous specks; paler brown along the sides, gradually blending into the dark grayish-white ventral pelage. Tail monocolored dark brown or bicolored, brown above, white below. Dorsal surfaces of hands and feet brownish white; hind foot has six plantar pads. **Distribution:** NE China;

extending into Mongolia and S Russia. **Natural History:** Occupies densely vegetated mountain foothills and riverbanks. Especially active in early morning and late evening. Digs burrows in dense vegetation, leaving obvious heaps of discarded soil around the entrance to its burrow in mounds 50–100 cm across and 15–20 cm high. The passage to the burrow is only 20–30 cm long and leads directly to a round, 35-cm-diameter nest chamber that is about 25 cm high. Constructs special food storage chambers, which it fills with roots and bulbs before winter. Reproduction little known; females with seven and nine embryos have been reported. **Conservation Status:** China RL—LC. IUCN RL—LC.

Mongolian Vole *Microtus mongolicus*

蒙古田鼠 Menggu Tianshu—**Distinctive Characteristics:** HB 119–132; T 28–38; HF 17–19; E 13–14. Dorsal pelage dark reddish brown, sides lighter and blending into the gray ventral pelage. Tail distinctly bicolored, dark brown above, buff below. Dorsal surfaces of hands and feet with mixtures of brown and silvery-white hairs. **Distribution:** NE China; extending into Mongolia and Russia. **Natural History:** Little known. **Conservation Status:** China RL—LC. IUCN RL—LC.

Root Vole *Microtus oeconomus*

根田鼠 Gen Tianshu—**Distinctive Characteristics:** HB 102–122; T 32–49; HF 16–18; E 12–16; GLS 29–32. Dorsal pelage reddish brown. Ventral pelage yellowish brown; tail bicolored, dark brown above, white below. Dorsal surfaces of feet silvery; hind foot has six plantar pads. **Distribution:** N Xinjiang and N Nei Mongol; ranging across the Holarctic. **Natural History:** Inhabits dense vegetation along the edges of lakes, streams, and marshes. Swims well and is most active late in the day and at night. Digs its burrow into the bases of vegetation clumps, and tunnel systems are often extensive. Feeds on succulent grasses. Litter size large, ranging from 2 to 11 young. Produces multiple (two to five) litters per year, and young reach sexual maturity at six weeks of age. **Conservation Status:** China RL—LC. IUCN RL—LC.

Social Vole *Microtus socialis*

社田鼠 She Tianshu—**Distinctive Characteristics:** HB 92–100; T 20–25; HF 17–18. A small, light-colored vole with a very short tail. Dorsal pelage pale buffy brown; sides paler and yellower. Ventral hairs gray-based with pale buff tips. Tail indistinctly bicolored, buffy brown above, somewhat paler buff below. Dorsal

surfaces of feet buffy white; hind foot has five plantar pads. **Distribution:** NW Xinjiang; extending across the Palaearctic. **Natural History:** Found in scattered clumps of grass. Diurnal, lives in burrows, and feeds on succulent grasses. **Conservation Status:** China RL—LC. IUCN RL—LC.

GENUS *MYODES*—Red-backed Voles

红背鼠属 Hongbeishu Shu—红背鼠 Hongbeishu
Most species have a reddish dorsal pelage. Of 12 species of *Myodes*, four occur in China.

Tian Shan Red-Backed Vole *Myodes centralis*

灰棕背䶄 Huizongbei Ping—**Distinctive Characteristics:** HB 85–112; T 35–59; HF 17–19; E 14. Dorsal pelage generally dark brown with only a hint of red, but varying from light brown on top of the head to dark grayish brown over the rump. Sides of face and body grayish brown with a slight yellow tinge, blending into the buffy-gray underparts. Tail bicolored, dark brown above, white below. Distinguished from other species of *Myodes* occurring in China by the lack of a conspicuously reddish dorsal pelage. **Distribution:** NW Xinjiang (Tian Shan); extending westward into Kazakhstan and Kyrgyzstan. **Natural History:** Occurs in montane forest. Eats grain and to a lesser extent grassy vegetation. **Conservation Status:** China RL—LC. IUCN RL—LC.

Gray Red-Backed Vole *Myodes rufocanus*

棕背䶄 Zongbei Ping—
Distinctive Characteristics: HB 100–122; T 27–35; HF 17–20; E 15–19. Dorsal pelage rich reddish brown from crown to rump; sides of face and flanks distinctly and contrastingly gray, sometimes with a slight mixture of buffy hairs where the gray sides meet the reddish back. Hairs of ventral pelage gray-based

with buffy-white tips, appearing grayish overall. Tail blackish brown above, grayish white below. Dorsal surfaces of the hands and feet pale grayish brown. The winter pelage is considerably brighter and more yellowish dorsally and whiter ventrally. **Distribution:** NW and NE China; extending across Mongolia and the Palearctic. **Natural History:** Inhabits forests and woodlands. Commonly found among fallen trees and in dense underbrush. Eats green leaves, shoots, and to a lesser extent seeds. Active day and night, but primarily nocturnal. Breeding season generally April–October, with breeding peaks in spring and fall (warmer climates) or summer (cooler climates). Most breeding females give birth to two to four litters per season. Gestation 18–19 days, litter size four to seven, newborns weigh about 2 g and are weaned after about 17 days; sexual maturity attained between 30 and 60 days. **Conservation Status:** China RL—LC. IUCN RL—LC.

Northern Red-Backed Vole *Myodes rutilus*

红背䶄 Hongbei Ping—**Distinctive Characteristics:** HB 95–100; T 25–27; HF 18–20; E 14–19. Dorsal pelage deep reddish brown from crown to rump; muzzle, sides of face, and flanks ochraceous brown; hairs of ventral pelage gray-based with white tips, appearing grayish overall. Tail well furred, reddish brown above, pale buff below. Dorsal surfaces of hands and feet brownish white. Winter pelage brighter and yellower. Superficially similar to *M. rufocanus*, with which it is often sympatric, but *M. rutilus* is smaller and more richly colored. **Distribution:** NW and NE China; ranging across Mongolia and the Holarctic from N Scandinavia to NE Canada. **Natural History:** Inhabits forests and woodlands, where it is more commonly found among fallen trees and in dense underbrush. Eats green vegetation and shoots and to a lesser extent seeds. Active day and night but primarily nocturnal. Make burrows either in the ground (generally under tree roots, stones, or shrubs) or in tree holes or the forks of limbs. Nests comprise moss or grass clippings. Known to make a variety of vocalizations, including chattering, squeaking, and barking. Females reach sexual maturity at four months of age, and gestation is short (17–20 days). Two or three litters of 1–11 young are produced annually. **Conservation Status:** China RL—LC. IUCN RL—LC.

Shanxi Red-Backed Vole *Myodes shanseius*

山西绒鼠 Shanxi Rongshu—**Distinctive Characteristics:** HB 105–106; T 25–30; HF 20–21; E 13–15. Similar to *M. rufocanus* (and sometimes regarded a subspecies), but with the reddish area of the back tending to be less rufous, and with the sides more ochraceous gray and lacking the contrastingly grayish sides so characteristic of *M. rufo-*

canus. Dorsal pelage dull reddish brown; hairs on the sides gray-based with pale ochraceous tips. Ventral hairs gray-based with buff tips, pelage appearing grayish buff overall. Tail brown above, whitish below. Dorsal surfaces of hands and feet brownish white. **Distribution:** C China. Endemic. **Natural History:** Inhabits forests and woodlands. Eats green vegetation, shoots, and to a lesser extent seeds. Primarily nocturnal. **Conservation Status:** China RL—LC. IUCN RL—LC.

GENUS *MYOPUS* (monotypic)

林旅鼠属 Linlüshu Shu

Wood Lemming *Myopus schisticolor*

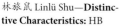

林旅鼠 Linlü Shu—**Distinctive Characteristics:** HB 75–100; T 14–15; HF 16–17; E 11–14; GLS 25–28. Red-backed, gray-sided lemming of coniferous taiga forest. Small, thickset, and bearing soft, dense fur. May be confused with red-backed voles (*Myodes*). Overall a dull slate-gray lemming with a narrow wash of reddish-brown hairs extending from the top of the head and along the upper back. This wash of reddish-brown fur increases in intensity and in the extent to which it covers the dorsal pelage, such that the lower back and rump are almost entirely bright reddish brown. The sides of the muzzle, face, and body are a dull slate gray, the individual hairs dull slate gray with silver-gray tips. Entirely black hairs are scattered throughout the dorsal pelage. Ventral pelage slate gray, similar in overall appearance to the coloration along the sides but somewhat lighter. Dorsal surfaces of the feet grayish brown; pads naked. Tail moderately haired, grayish brown above, pale gray below. **Distribution:** Extreme NE China; ranging across the entire coniferous taiga zone from Scandinavia to Kamchatka Peninsula. **Natural History:** Inhabits taiga forest, where it primarily lives in moss habitats. Constructs its burrows and runways in moss, and moss makes up the majority of its diet. Nocturnal. Breeding occurs primarily during summer, and litters of one to six young are produced at 25-day intervals. Sexual maturity occurs at one month of age. **Conservation Status:** Rare in collections, but may be the dominant small mammal species in NE Siberia. China RL—LC. IUCN RL—LC.

GENUS *NEODON*—Mountain Voles

松田鼠属 Songtianshu Shu
Similar to *Microtus*. Females have four pairs of mammae. All four species occur in China.

Forrest's Mountain Vole *Neodon forresti*

云南松田鼠 Yunnan Songtianshu—**Distinctive Characteristics:** HB 100–134; T 36–43; HF 17–20; E 13–15. A large species of *Neodon*. Similar to *N. irene*, but larger and with a longer, darker brown pelage. Dorsal pelage dark brown; ventral pelage gray washed with grayish white. Tail bicolored, brown above, white below. Dorsal surfaces of hands and feet grayish white. **Distribution:** NW Yunnan and adjacent N Myanmar. **Natural History:** Rocky alpine meadows between 3,350 and 3,650 m. **Conservation Status:** China RL—VU D2. IUCN RL—DD.

Irene's Mountain Vole *Neodon irene*

高原松田鼠 Gaoyuan Songtianshu—**Distinctive Characteristics:** HB 80–108; T 22–40; HF 15–19; E 11–13. Dorsal pelage dark grayish brown, somewhat brighter ochraceous brown along the sides, and blending into the dark gray ventral pelage. Tail bicolored, brownish above, whitish below; dorsal surfaces of hands and feet brownish white. **Distribution:** High mountains of C China. Endemic. **Natural History:** Alpine meadows and shrubby mountainsides. A female specimen collected in August had three nearly mature embryos. **Conservation Status:** China RL—LC. IUCN RL—LC.

Juniper Mountain Vole *Neodon juldaschi*

帕米尔松田鼠 Pami'er Songtianshu—**Distinctive Characteristics:** HB 83–105; T 29–39; HF 15–17; E 11–14. Dorsal pelage pale brown; ventral pelage grayish brown. Tail bicolored, pale brown above, silvery-white below. **Distribution:** Far W China; extending into Pakistan, NE Afghanistan, E Tajikistan, and SW Kyrgyzstan. **Natural History:** Inhabits montane steppe above 3,000 m. Herbivorous; known to make winter stores. **Conservation Status:** China RL—LC. IUCN RL—LC.

Sikkim Mountain Vole *Neodon sikimensis*

锡金松田鼠 Xijin Songtianshu—**Distinctive Characteristics:** HB 97–119; T 30–52; HF 17–22; E 11–16. A dark brown vole, very similar to *N. irene.* **Distribution:** S Xizang; extending through the Himalayas of Nepal, NE India, and Bhutan. **Natural History:** Inhabits alpine meadows and dense vegetation growing at the edges of rhododendron and coniferous forest between 2,100 and 3,700 m. Eats green vegetation and seeds to a lesser extent. Pregnant females reported with two or three embryos. **Conservation Status:** China RL—LC. IUCN RL—LC.

GENUS *PHAIOMYS* (monotypic)

白尾松田鼠属 Baiwei Songtianshu Shu

Blyth's Mountain Vole *Phaiomys leucurus*

白尾松田鼠 Baiwei Songtianshu—**Distinctive Characteristics:** HB 98–128; T 26–35; HF 16–19; E 10–13. Dorsal pelage pale yellowish brown, paler along the sides and blending into the yellowish-gray ventral pelage. Tail a monocolored yellowish brown. Dorsal surfaces of hands and feet pale yellowish white. Adaptations to a semifossorial life include short ears and elongated claws. **Distribution:** Tibetan Plateau; extending south along the Himalayan massif to NW India. **Natural History:** High-elevation grassy habitats, especially along watercourses. Strictly herbivorous. Lives in colonies; digs deep burrows, especially in the banks of streams and lakes. The uterus of one specimen contained seven embryos. **Conservation Status:** China RL—LC. IUCN RL—LC.

GENUS *PROEDROMYS* (monotypic)

沟牙田鼠属 Gouyatianshu Shu

Duke of Bedford's Vole *Proedromys bedfordi*

沟牙田鼠 Gouya Tianshu—**Distinctive Characteristics:** HB 75–100; T 14–15; HF 16–17; E 11–14; GLS 25–28. Dorsal pelage with long, dull brown hairs, ventral pelage grayish white. Tail well haired, brown above and dull white below. Hands and feet dull white. **Distribution:** Recent specimens known from only two localities in S Gansu and N Sichuan.

Endemic. **Natural History:** Mountain forests; the two known specimens were collected at 2,440 and 2,550 m. **Conservation Status:** China RL—VU D2. IUCN RL—VU B1ab(iii).

GENUS *VOLEMYS*—Voles

川田鼠属 Chuantianshu Shu—川田鼠 Chuantianshu
Similar to *Microtus*, but distinguished by cranial characteristics and long tail relative to HB length. Both of the two known species occur in China.

Sichuan Vole *Volemys millicens*

四川田鼠 Sichuan Tianshu—**Distinctive Characteristics:** HB 83–95; T 46–53; HF 18–18.5; E 14; GLS 23.7–24.7. Dorsal pelage dark brown. Ventral pelage grayish. Tail grayish brown above, white below. Dorsal surfaces of hands and feet white. Similar to *V. musseri* but smaller. **Distribution:** Known from six specimens from the type locality in the mountains of NW Sichuan. Endemic. **Natural History:** Known from forests above 4,000 m. **Conservation Status:** China RL—VU A1ac. IUCN RL—DD.

Marie's Vole *Volemys musseri*

马瑟川田鼠 Masechuan Tianshu—**Distinctive Characteristics:** HB 90–129; T 47–70; HF 18–23; GLS 24.5–27.5. Dorsal pelage dark brown. Ventral pelage dark gray with a pale buff wash. Tail bicolored, dark brown above, buff white below. Dorsal surfaces of hands and feet buffy. Similar to *V. millicens* but larger. **Distribution:** W Sichuan (Qionglai Shan range, 2,318–3,660 m). Endemic. **Natural History:** Collected from rocks and cliffs in alpine meadows. **Conservation Status:** China RL—DD. IUCN RL—DD.

SUBFAMILY CRICETINAE—Hamsters

仓鼠亚科 Cangshu Yake—仓鼠 Cangshu
Form stout; tail short, the greatest length not more than HB length; body covered with dense hairs; with large internal cheek pouches; pinnae short and

densely furred. Dental formula: 1.0.0.3/1.0.0.3 = 16. Of seven genera of Criceti-nae, six occur in China.

GENUS *ALLOCRICETULUS*—Hamsters

短尾仓鼠属 Duanweicangshu Shu—短尾仓鼠 Duanweicangshu
Allocricetulus has been included frequently within *Cricetulus*, although in some respects it appears more similar to *Cricetus*. Both species of *Allocricetulus* occur in China.

Mongolian Hamster *Allocricetulus curtatus*

无斑短尾仓鼠 Wuban Duanweicangshu—**Distinctive Characteristics:** HB 85–130; T 18–25; HF 14–20; E 11–17; GLS 27–33; Wt 30–70 g. Tail short, near or slightly longer than hind foot; tail appears conical, as basal hairs grow out long and nearly reach the tail tip. All dorsal surfaces a pale buffy gray, almost light cinnamon; ventrally white, extending up the sides and including thighs, fore-arms, and cheeks; no dark patch on chest. **Distribution:** N China; extending into Mongolia. **Natural History:** An obligate species of sand-dune habitats in grass-lands or semidesert. Eats seeds and sometimes insects. Constructs very simple, short burrows with only a few entrances; caches seeds in burrows to eat over winter. Active in early evening and at night. Reproduction begins in April, and two or three litters of four to nine young are produced each year. **Conservation Status:** China RL—LC. IUCN RL—LC.

Eversman's Hamster *Allocricetulus eversmanni*

短尾仓鼠 Duanwei Cangshu—**Distinctive Char-acteristics:** HB 93–115; T 17–28; HF 15–18; E 12–16; GLS 30–33; Wt 36–60 g. Size medium; tail very short, near or slightly longer than hind foot. Dorsal pelage sandy ochre or brown, hairs dark gray at base, darker than in *A. curtatus*. Sides and ventral pelage grayish white, hairs white at tip and light gray at base; white below neck and on under-side of hind feet and tail. A prominent dark patch is found on the chest. Long hairs grow out to cover most of tail. **Distribution:** N Xinjiang; extending into Kazakhstan. **Natural History:** Occurs in grasslands and semidesert habitats, but also known to occur in woody areas. Eats vegetation, seeds, insects, and a variety of small vertebrates (lizards, nestling birds, young squirrels, etc.). Nocturnal. Constructs a simple burrow system that goes straight down (or slightly slanting) to a maximum depth of 30 cm. There is a nest at the end of the burrow, and often branches radiate from the burrow at that point. Often can be found living in burrows constructed by other mammals. Solitary and aggressive. Reproduction begins in April, and two or three litters of four to six young are produced; reproduction can also take place in winter. **Conservation Status:** China RL—LC. IUCN RL—LC.

GENUS *CANSUMYS* (monotypic)

甘肃仓鼠属 Ganshucangshu Shu

Gansu Hamster *Cansumys canus*

甘肃仓鼠 Gansu Cangshu—**Distinctive Characteristics:** HB 100–170; T 77–111; HF 17–24; E 15–23; GLS 32–40; Wt 61–120 g. Dorsal pelage thick and dense, a hoary-gray color. Possesses a conspicuous white patch on the cheek and at the base of the ears; white under the neck; ears dark brown outside and black inside. Feet delicate; long toes on forefeet; claws white; one digit of hind foot short and flattened (almost nail-like). Tail shaggy at the base; distal half white. Significantly smaller than *Tscherskia triton*. **Distribution:** C China. Endemic. **Natural History:** Poorly known. It is found in mountainous habitats, generally between 1,000 and 1,400 m elevation. Occupies deciduous forests. Originally described as an arboreal form (unlike other hamsters); this contention is supported by its morphology—the delicate feet and nail-like claw, coupled with the shaggy pelage (especially the tail). In spite of its arboreal habits, it can be found on the ground, even nesting in rocks. Nocturnal, and primarily active in spring and summer. Diet consists of leaves and even grasses. Litter size is six to eight. **Conservation Status:** China RL—LC. IUCN RL—LC.

GENUS *CRICETULUS*—True Hamsters

仓鼠属 Cangshu Shu— 仓鼠 Cangshu
Mouselike in appearance, but with short tail. Feet white and sparsely haired (fig. 6); ears long and delicate. White-bellied, and with a slender skull. All eight species of *Cricetulus* live in China.

Figure 6. Comparison of the feet of dwarf hamsters of the genus *Cricetulus* (naked or sparsely haired; a) and genus *Phodopus* (generously haired; b).

Ladak Hamster *Cricetulus alticola*

高山仓鼠 Gaoshan Cangshu—**Distinctive Characteristics:** HB 80–98; T 36–42; HF 15–18; E 13–16; GLS 25–28; Wt 22–48 g. Dorsal pelage grayish yellow-brown. There are no spots on the back, and the boundary between the dorsal and ventral pelage is indistinct, more like a wavy line along the side; thigh gray. Tail short, light brown on top and white underneath. **Distribution:** Far E China; extending into W Nepal and India (Kashmir and Ladakh). **Natural History:** Occupies coniferous and birch forests to desert steppe, shrubland, swampy meadow, and highland meadow—obviously a very broad niche. Normally found at elevations ranging from 3,100 to 5,200 m. Primarily nocturnal but can also be active during the day. Diet consists of grass seed, grains, and insects. Reproduction occurs from May to August, with a peak in June and July. Littter size ranges from 5 to 10 young (7 or 8 being most common). **Conservation Status:** China RL—LC. IUCN RL—LC.

Striped Dwarf Hamster *Cricetulus barabensis*

黑线仓鼠 Heixian Cangshu—**Distinctive Characteristics:** HB 72–116; T 15–26; HF 13–19; E 14–17; GLS 22–28; Wt 20–35 g. Size small, tail averages about 30% length of HB. Dorsal pelage light grayish brown, with a faint black longitudinal stripe along the midline; ears blackish and rimmed with white edge. Ventral pelage gray, the hairs tipped with white. **Distribution:** C to NE China; extending into Russia, Mongolia, and Korea. **Natural History:** Inhabits arid country, although it adapts to and is commonly found in croplands. Occupies a simple burrow system with two or three entrances; the circular opening has a diameter of 2–3 cm. The burrow runs to 1 m in length at a depth of 10–50 cm, and four or five branches end in nest or food storage areas. Nests are lined with grass. About four to five individuals (a maximum of eight) occupy each burrow. Most active in the first half of the night. Diet consists of grains and legumes, and these seeds are stored in caches. Hibernates over winter, emerging in February–March. Reproduction peaks in March and April, and again in autumn. May breed two to five times each year, producing large litters (range 1–10; average 6 or 7). **Conservation Status:** China RL—LC. IUCN RL—LC.

Kam Dwarf Hamster *Cricetulus kamensis*

康藏仓鼠 Kangzang Cangshu—**Distinctive Characteristics:** HB 88–112; T 51–64; HF 17–18; E 16–18; GLS 27–29; Wt 20–40 g. Dorsal pelage dark brown-

ish gray, but may have black spots or streaks on the back; ventral pelage grayish white, the hairs dark at base, white at tip. Tail has dark narrow stripe above, is wholly white below and at tip, and is thick and covered with long guard hairs. Sides of body have wavelike appearance formed by contrasting colors of dorsal and ventral pelage; black coloration extends down upper part of hind leg. **Distribution:** W China. Endemic. **Natural History:** Lives in high mountain grasslands, shrubby marshes, and open steppe at high elevations (3,300–4,100 m). Active day and night. Eats grains, grass seeds, and insects. Constructs a simple burrow

50 cm deep, where it stores grain on which to feed during winter. Reproduces from May to August, primarily during June and July. Litter size ranges from 5 to 10, normally 7 or 8. **Conservation Status:** China RL—LC. IUCN RL—LC.

Lama Dwarf Hamster *Cricetulus lama*

藏南仓鼠 Zangnan Cangshu—**Distinctive Characteristics:** HB 86–103; T 40–50; HF 15–18; E 14–18; GLS 26–28; Wt 24–39 g. Pelage light, similar to that of *C. kamensis* but without any dark dorsal fur; not as striking as *kamensis*. No black on upper thigh, as in *kamensis*. Tail shorter than *kamensis*, averaging less than half of HB length, and bicolored, dark on top and white underneath. The white fur on the side is shorter and grayer than in *kamensis*, and there is no wavy line on the side. **Distribution:** Xizang. Endemic. **Natural History:** Believed to be similar to that of *kamensis*. **Conservation Status:** China RL—LC. IUCN RL—LC.

Long-Tailed Dwarf Hamster *Cricetulus longicaudatus*

长尾仓鼠 Changwei Cangshu—**Distinctive Characteristics:** HB 80–135; T 35–48; HF 15–21; E 15–20; GLS 25–31; Wt 15–50 g. Size small, near *C. barabensis* or slightly larger. Dorsal color sandy yellow or dark brownish gray; ventral pelage grayish white, with hairs grayish black at base, white at tip; sides of body have a nearly horizontal sharp line formed by contrasting colors of dorsal and ventral pelage. Tail slender, long, obviously longer than hind foot, about 33% length of HB or even longer; dark on top and white underneath. Backs of feet pure white; ears dark with white rim. **Distribution:** N China; extending to Kazakhstan and Russia. **Natural History:** Inhabits desert country to shrubland to forests and alpine meadows. It occupies shallow burrows often constructed under rocks that extend horizontally beneath the surface. Constructs food stores and grass-lined nests. Sometimes occupies burrows built by other small mammals. Eats vegetation and insects. Nocturnal. At least two litters of four to nine young are produced each year, beginning in March or April. **Conservation Status:** China RL—LC. IUCN RL—LC.

Gray Dwarf Hamster *Cricetulus migratorius*

灰仓鼠 Hui Cangshu—**Distinctive Characteristics:** HB 85–120; T 23–39; HF 15–18; E 15–21; GLS 22–31; Wt 31–58 g. Size medium; tail about 30% length of HB and fully furred; ears large. Dorsal pelage sandy brownish gray; ventral pelage sometimes has gray-based hairs, the rest of the hairs white. **Distribution:** NW China; extending to Mongolia, Kazakhstan, Russia, Central Asia, Middle East, and SE Europe. **Natural History:** Lives in desert and semidesert habitats, extending into grasslands and alpine meadows. Constructs a burrow system that runs as deep as 1.5 m with several food storage and nesting chambers. Nocturnal or crepuscular; does not hibernate. Eats seeds, green vegetation, and insects. Produces up to three litters of 1–13 young (average 6 or 7) each year following a 19-day gestation period. **Conservation Status:** China RL—LC. IUCN RL—LC.

Sokolov's Dwarf Hamster *Cricetulus sokolovi*

索氏仓鼠 Suoshi Cangshu—**Distinctive Characteristics:** HB 77–114; T 18–32; HF 13–18; E 13–19; GLS 23–26. Dorsal pelage gray with a brownish-yellow or walnut hue; lighter in tone than in some forms of *C. barabensis*. There is an evident dark stripe that runs down the dorsal midline from the nape of the neck to the base of the tail; this stripe is most prominent in young animals and gradually fades to a shadow in the oldest animals. Ventrally a light gray, with a distinct separation between the dorsal and ventral pelage. Ears are the same color as the dorsum, but with a dark brown spot in the middle of the ear. Tail is similarly colored on top as the dorsum, but lighter underneath, without a sharp separation in color. Feet are white, and the toes tend to curl up (that is, the feet are not flat). **Distribution:** Nei Mongol; extending into Mongolia. **Natural History:** Lives in shrubby habitat in sandy areas. Burrows are normally constructed under desert shrubs. Reproduction begins in mid-May, and two or three litters of four to nine young may be produced annually. **Conservation Status:** China RL—DD. IUCN RL—LC.

Tibetan Dwarf Hamster *Cricetulus tibetanus*

藏仓鼠 Zang Cangshu—**Distinctive Characteristics:** HB 103; T 30–37; HF 17–18; E 15–16; GLS 23.5–25.4. Dorsal pelage a nearly uniform ochraceous, fading to a lighter sandy color toward the forehead, cheek, and neck. Ears are a contrasting dusky brown, with a narrow edge of white on the tips and a small tuft of white at their base. Tail is bicolored, pure white below and dusky on top. Ventral area white, as are the backs of the feet. **Distribution:** Qinghai and Xizang. Endemic. **Natural History:** Believed to be similar to that of *C. kamensis*. **Conservation Status:** China RL—DD. IUCN RL—LC.

GENUS *CRICETUS* (monotypic)

原仓鼠属 Yuancangshu Shu

Black-Bellied Hamster *Cricetus cricetus*

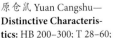

原仓鼠 Yuan Cangshu—**Distinctive Characteristics:** HB 200–300; T 28–60; HF 28–36; E 22–32; GLS 44–52; Wt 290–425 g. Largest species in the Cricetinae; form stout; tail short, equal to or longer than hind foot; sole of each foot hairy posteriorly and naked anteriorly; cheek pouch present. Dorsal pelage brown; ventral pelage uniform black; head and sides of body with three or four conspicuous light spots. Four pairs of mammae. **Distribution:** N Xinjiang; extending to Russia, Kazakhstan, and across Europe to Belgium. **Natural History:** Lives in dry grassland to forest meadow habitats, generally at low elevation. Constructs an elaborate burrow system up to 2 m in depth, containing multiple entrances (5–10) and chambers for nesting and food storage (in summer these are 30–60 cm deep). Hibernates; nocturnal or crepuscular. Diet consists of seeds and tubers; food caches may be extensive, with a total weight of up to 65 kg. Large litters of 3–15 are born following a 20-day gestation; multiple litters can be produced each year beginning in spring. Young may mature and breed in their summer of birth. **Conservation Status:** China RL—NT. IUCN RL—LC.

GENUS *PHODOPUS*–Dwarf Hamsters

毛足鼠属 Maozushu Shu—毛足鼠 Maozushu
Form short, feet broad and short; entire sole and lower side of toes densely covered with white hairs, no foot pads visible (fig. 6); tail very short, not longer than hind foot; large internal cheek pouches. Females have four pairs of mammae. Two of the three species of *Phodopus* occur in China.

Campbell's Hamster *Phodopus campbelli*

坎氏毛足鼠 Kanshi Maozushu—**Distinctive Characteristics:** HB 76–105; T 4–14; HF 12–18; E 13–15; GLS 22–26; Wt 23 g. Size small; dorsal pelage dark gray, tinged with pale brown, with a black mid-dorsal stripe from the nape of the neck to the base of the tail; ventral pelage gray at base, white at tip; colors on the sides intergrade, yielding a wavelike pattern on the lateral pelage. Tail extremely short; soles of feet covered with white hairs. **Distribution:** Across N China; extending to Russia, Mongolia, Kazakhstan. **Natural History:** Occurs in grasslands, semidesert, and desert; more likely to be found living on soils with a firmer substrate than *P. roborovskii*. Burrows (with four to six vertical entrances) lead to a nest chamber as deep as 1 m (but normally shallower) and food caches of seeds. May occupy burrows of *Meriones* (gerbils) rather than digging their own. Diet primarily seeds, but is known to consume insects. Nocturnal or crepuscular; does not hibernate. Breeds from April to October, producing three or four litters of four to eight young following a 20–22 day gestation period. Juveniles may become reproductively active in their first year. **Conservation Status:** China RL—LC. IUCN RL—LC.

Desert Hamster *Phodopus roborovskii*

小毛足鼠 Xiao Maozushu—
Distinctive Characteristics:
HB 61–102; T 6–11; HF
9–12; E 10–13; GLS 19–23;
Wt 10–20 g. Slightly smaller than *P. campbelli*; HB length generally <90 mm.
Dorsal pelage light sandy brown, dark gray at base. The ventral surface is white,
along with the mouth area, limbs, and foot surfaces. The different colors of dorsal and ventral pelage do not intergrade but form a distinct line along the sides.
The thickly covered tail is also pure white. **Distribution:** Across N China;
extending to Mongolia, Russia, and Kazakhstan. **Natural History:** Occurs in
sandy deserts and grasslands; avoids areas with clay soil or those overgrown with
shrubby vegetation. Burrows with a single opening (4 cm diameter) are dug
between sand dunes or at their edge. Burrows extend 90 cm deep and contain a
single nest and two or three food caches. Eats seeds (often filling its cheek
pouches); also known to consume green vegetation and insects. Nocturnal; does
not hibernate. Reproduces from March to September (or even later). Up to four
litters ranging from three to nine young are born following a 20-day gestation.
Young of the year may become reproductively active. **Conservation Status:**
China RL—LC. IUCN RL—LC.

GENUS *TSCHERSKIA* (monotypic)

大仓鼠属 Dacangshu Shu

Greater Long-Tailed Hamster *Tscherskia triton*

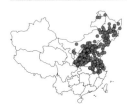

大仓鼠 Da Cangshu—**Distinctive Characteristics:**
HB 142–220; T 69–106; HF 20–25; E 17–24; GLS 36–42; Wt 92–241 g. Larger
than largest species of *Cricetulus*; tail long, about half HB length. Dorsal pelage
pale brownish gray; ventral hairs gray at base, white at tip. Tail dark brown to tip;
long hair at the base only. **Distribution:** C to NE China; extending to E Russia,

Korea. **Natural History:** Generally found in open xeric areas where it constructs deep vertical burrows in which it caches vast quantities of seed in a large storage chamber. Occasionally known to harvest leaves. Primarily nocturnal, although can be seen active during the day. Life expectancy about one year (tends to waste away following breeding). Reproductive season May to August, but extending to September in some areas. Breeds two or three times and generally produces litters of 8–10 young. **Conservation Status:** Has been considered an agricultural pest. China RL—LC. IUCN RL—LC.

FAMILY MURIDAE—Old World Rats and Mice

鼠科 Shu Ke—鼠类 Shulei

The Muridae, with 730 species, is the largest family of mammals. Morphological and molecular data clearly differentiate the Muridae into five subfamilies, two of which occur in China.

SUBFAMILY GERBILLINAE—Gerbils

沙鼠亚科 Shashu Yake—沙鼠 Shashu

Form ratlike, but tending toward saltatorial habits and less obviously specialized than jerboas; hind foot has slight tendency toward elongation, tail very long, hair cover dense. Habits typically sand dwelling and burrowing. Occurs in the Palaearctic realm and Africa. Of 16 genera currently known, three are found in China, mainly occurring in NW and N China.

GENUS *BRACHIONES* (monotypic)

短耳沙鼠属 Duan'ershashu Shu

Przewalski's Gerbil *Brachiones przewalskii*

短耳沙鼠 Duan'er Shashu—**Distinctive Characteristics:** HB 67–103; T 56–78; HF 22–24; E 6–9; GLS 24–29; Wt 12–42 g. Size small, ears short, body hairs short; forelimbs with well-developed claws, slightly adapted to subterranean living habits; hind soles completely covered with hairs. Dorsal pelage sandy or light grayish; ventral pelage wholly white. Tail light colored and pointed. **Distribution:** Arid lands of NW China. Endemic. **Natural History:** Prefers semipermanent sand dunes overgrown with shrubs or close to wooded areas. Burrow system is quite simple compared with that of most gerbils; the opening is about 4.5 cm in diameter, and the tunnels run no deeper than 60 cm. Przewalski's gerbil characteristically occurs at lower density than other gerbils. **Conservation Status:** China RL—LC. IUCN RL—LC.

GENUS *MERIONES*—Gerbils

沙鼠属 Shashu Shu—沙鼠 Shashu

Form ratlike; ears somewhat enlarged in size; tail long, near HB length, covered with longer hairs; hind limbs and hind feet slightly elongate, soles mostly covered with hairs, naked near ankles; claws on forefeet somewhat elongate. The 17 species of *Meriones* occur in Central and SW Asia and N Africa; five species live in China.

Cheng's Gerbil *Meriones chengi*

郑氏沙鼠 Zhengshi Shashu—**Distinctive Characteristics:** HB 131–150; T 88–117; HF 31–34; E 17; GLS 36–38. Medium-sized gerbil. Dorsal pelage dark brown, darker than in *M. meridianus*, grayish black at base; ventral pelage wholly white, with light gray base of hairs at middle. Soles of all feet covered with hairs; a narrow naked stripe near ankles; hind feet with black claws. Tail length about three-quarters of HB length; tail pale brown both above and below and terminally tufted. **Distribution:** E Xinjiang (Turpan Basin). Endemic. **Natural History:** Inhabits mountainous regions and semidesert or xeric grasslands, normally above 1,000 m elevation. A highly social species, it constructs many burrows, characteristically at the bases of shrubs. **Conservation Status:** China RL—LC. IUCN RL—LC.

Libyan Gerbil *Meriones libycus*

红尾沙鼠 Hongwei Shashu—**Distinctive Characteristics:** HB 100–180; T 108–180; HF 31–38; E 11–22; GLS 36–42; Wt 56–155 g. Tail as long as HB; hind soles only partly covered with hairs, so have naked area; claws dark. Dorsal pelage grayish brown, darker than in *M. meridianus*; hairs of ventral pelage white at tip, gray at base; tail with pale brown hairs, but distal one-third portion nut brown or black. **Distribution:** NW China; extending west to Middle East (Saudi Arabia, Jordan, Iraq, Syria, Iran, Afghanistan) and to N Africa (Egypt). **Natural History:** Occupies desert habitat, generally in areas with stabilized dunes. Becomes most abundant in unflooded river plains. Frequently occupies the burrows of *Rhombomys* in areas of sympatry. Where it constructs its own burrows, they are less complicated than those of *Rhombomys*, while being more complicated than those of most other gerbils. Between 10 and 60 burrow entrances may characterize a territory. Burrows consist of two layers: the upper one is utilized for food storage, and the deeper one (1–1.5 m below the surface) holds the nest chamber. This species often lives socially in burrow systems, occurring in smaller dispersed groups during summer, but forming larger groups (25–30 individuals) in winter. Highly mobile, frequently changing burrows or even migrating should forage conditions deteriorate. It is usually diurnal but can be seen active at any time of day or night. Diet consists primarily of seeds, and burrow caches may weigh up to 10 kg. Reproductively active year-round, except during the hottest summer months. Multiple litters of five to six young are produced each year. **Conservation Status:** China RL—LC. IUCN RL—LC.

Mid-Day Gerbil *Meriones meridianus*

子午沙鼠 Ziwu Shashu—**Distinctive Characteristics:** HB 95–134; T 84–120; HF 25–34; E 10–19; GLS 31–36; Wt 30–60 g. Medium in size; tail length similar to HB length; hind feet covered with dense hairs, soles with no naked portion, claws white. Dorsal pelage light grayish yellow, drab brown, or dark brown, hairs grayish black at base; ventral pelage wholly white except pale brown narrow stripe at chest; tail dark pale brown to bright ochraceous above, slightly lighter below. **Distribution:** Northern C China to NW China; extending to Mongolia, Afghanistan, Iran, and the Caucasus region. **Natural History:** Most desert-adapted of all gerbils. Occupies sandy terrain with different degrees of soil stabilization, preferring brushy habitats characterized by thorn scrub under which it constructs its burrows. Primarily nocturnal (in contrast with *M. unguiculatus*); it is only active during the day in winter (it is unclear how it was given the common name Mid-day Gerbil). Colonial. Burrows are dug under roots of plants and may be simple to fairly complicated. Winter burrows extend to a depth of 2 m or more, and their length ranges up to 4 m. Diet consists mainly of seeds and fruits of desert plants, although it is also known to consume leafy vegetation. Stores are small, usually less than 800 g. Reproduction is spread out over the year, although the intensity drops off during summer and during November and December. Litter size ranges from 1 to 12, averaging about 6 young. **Conservation Status:** China RL—LC. IUCN RL—LC.

Tamarisk Gerbil *Meriones tamariscinus*

柽柳沙鼠 Chengliu Shashu—
Distinctive Characteristics:
HB 135–190; T 115–150; HF 32–39;
E 15–21; GLS 36–44; Wt 60–180 g. Size
large; dorsal pelage rusty brown; ventral
pelage wholly white; tail sharply bicolored, dark brown above, white below. Soles of hind feet have long dark brown spots and are entirely covered with hairs; claws nearly white. **Distribution:** NW China; extending into Kazakhstan and across Central Asia to N Caucasus. **Natural History:** Occupies desert and semi-desert, where its preferred habitat is grass and bush-covered sandy areas. Highest densities are in dry river courses, but it can also occupy saline marshes, areas avoided by other gerbils. Maximum population densities are less than those of other gerbils, normally ranging from 20 to 30 per hectare. Burrows are dug under tree roots and bushes and normally consist of only two to four entrances. Burrows can extend up to 6 m in length. Nests of plant stems and bird feathers are constructed at depths of 50 cm (summer) to 250 cm (winter). Primarily nocturnal. These gerbils are wide ranging and have been known to move up to 1.5 km. Their diet consists of green parts of plants, although they also eat fruits, insects, and even small rodents. Their food caches may weigh up to 4.5 kg. Reproduction can occur year-round, although reproductive activity is diminished in winter. Litter size ranges from one to eight (usually four or five). **Conservation Status:** China RL—LC. IUCN RL—LC.

Mongolian Gerbil *Meriones unguiculatus*

长爪沙鼠 Changzhua
Shashu—**Distinctive Characteristics:** HB 97–132; T 85–106; HF 24–32; E 13–15; GLS 30–36. Size slightly smaller than other gerbils; tail shorter than HB, 70–90% of HB length. Soles of hind feet entirely covered with hairs; claws grayish black. Ear pinnae exposed; dorsal pelage grayish brown; hairs of ventral pel-

age gray at base, white at tip, presenting dull white appearance, different from other species in China; tail sharply bicolored, dark grayish brown above, pale brown below, with black tuft of hairs at extremity. **Distribution:** NE China; extending into Mongolia and Russia. **Natural History:** Lives in semidesert, sandy steppe, or grassland habitat; not found in mountainous terrain. Can occur in areas with compact soils. Active during both day and night, although primarily diurnal during winter. Density is quite variable over its range, but it can occur at extremely high densities under some conditions. Colonial; its normal social unit is the family group. Families live together and mutually defend their burrow system, and all members contribute to gathering food stores (which can weigh as much as 20 kg). Burrow structure is not complicated. Burrows can extend 5–6 m in length and have nest chambers situated at 45 cm in depth (summer) or 150 cm in depth (winter). Diet consists of seeds and greens, but it also consumes fruits of desert plants. Peak reproduction extends from February until September; litter size 2–11 (average about 6). **Conservation Status:** China RL—LC. IUCN RL—LC.

GENUS *RHOMBOMYS* (monotypic)

大沙鼠属 Dashashu Shu

Great Gerbil *Rhombomys opimus*

大沙鼠 Da Shashu—**Distinctive Characteristics:** HB 150–185; T 130–160; HF 36–47; E 12–19; GLS 39–45; Wt 169–275 g. Size large; tail length near or somewhat less than HB length. Dorsal pelage ochraceous tinged with light grayish, the color most vivid over the rump and lighter over the shoulders; ventral pelage dull white; chin white; tail rusty brown both above and below, sprinkled with black long hairs near extremity; ears well furred. **Distribution:** NW China; extending to Mongolia, Kazakhstan, Afghanistan, Iran, and Pakistan. **Natural History:** Occupies desert to semidesert habitat and is most successful in dry riverbeds dominated by shrubby vegetation. Diurnal; most active at dawn. Constructs large entrance holes to a very elaborate burrow system that consists of long, deep tunnels and nest and food storage chambers. In winter the nest chambers may be as deep as 2.5 m. The continuous occupancy of these burrows, coupled with the ongoing removal of soil, yields large depressions up to a meter deep and many meters in diameter. Feeds on succulent bushes (such as *Salsola*). Vegetation is often stored underground, but occasionally haypiles are constructed on the surface that range in size from 2 to 3 m in diameter and up to 1 m in height. Foraging can radically alter the local vegetative landscape, and in some situations the species is considered a pest and controlled. These animals live in family groups, and multiple families (up to three) may occupy a single burrow system, although these families may remain behaviorally intolerant of each other. A family may also occupy multiple burrow systems. When predators are sighted, repetitive alarm calls are uttered, coupled with foot-drumming. Highly mobile; may migrate distances of up to 10 km. Reproduction is possible year-round, although the intensity diminishes in summer. Litter size ranges from 1 to 14 (usually 4–7). **Conservation Status:** China RL—LC. IUCN RL—LC.

SUBFAMILY MURINAE—Murine Rodents

鼠亚科 Shu Yake—鼠类 Shulei
A subfamily of 126 genera and 561 species confined to Australia and the Old World (excepting introductions), where they range throughout much of Europe, Africa, and Asia. Seventeen genera of murine rodents, or typical rats and mice, occur in China.

GENUS *APODEMUS*—Field Mice

姬鼠属 Jishu Shu—姬鼠 Jishu
Small, soft-furred mice of open grassy fields, croplands, woods, and forest edges. Dorsal pelage usually yellowish brown to reddish brown. One species has a mid-dorsal stripe. Ventral pelage white or grayish white. Tail more or less equal to or slightly shorter than HB length and bicolored, dark brown above and pale below. Dorsal surfaces of hands and feet pale brownish white. Females usually have four pairs of mammae, but one species occurring in China (*A. latronum*) has only three pairs. Of 20 species, eight occur in China.

Striped Field Mouse *Apodemus agrarius*

黑线姬鼠 Heixian Jishu—**Distinctive Characteristics:** HB 80–113; T 72–115; HF 19–22; E 12–15; GLS 24–28; Wt 29–38 g. Dorsal pelage yellowish brown to pale reddish brown and often with a thin, blackish-brown mid-dorsal stripe, but this is less distinct among individuals from the southern part of the range and may be little more than a faint mid-dorsal darkening; pelage becoming somewhat brighter yellow-brown along the sides. Ventral pelage grayish white and fairly well demarcated from the dorsal pelage but not forming a sharp line. Tail approximately equal to or shorter than HB length, dark brown above, paler below. Ears not differing in color from the surrounding parts of head and shoulders. Females have four pairs of mammae (two pectoral pairs, two abdominal pairs). **Distribution:** W Yunnan to N Heilongjiang and Taiwan, with a disjunctive population in NW Xinjiang; extending into Siberia and Korea. **Natural History:** Occurs in agricultural areas, grassy and open woodland habitats, usually below 1,000 m. Eats seeds and some insects. Diurnal. Reproduction occurs between March and November, with peaks between April and May and from July through October. Litter size ranges from 1 to 10, averaging 5 or 6. **Conservation Status:** China RL—LC. IUCN RL—LC.

Chevrier's Field Mouse *Apodemus chevrieri*

高山姬鼠 Gaoshan Jishu—**Distinctive Characteristics:** HB 88–110; T 83–105; HF 22–25; E 14–16; GLS 26–30. Closely related to and very much resembling *A. agrarius*, but distinguished by larger size and complete absence of a mid-dorsal stripe. **Distribution:** C China. Endemic. **Natural History:** Occurs in agricultural areas, grassy fields, and open woodland habitats between 1,800 and 2,300 m. Eats seeds primarily, but also consumes insects. Diurnal. **Conservation Status:** China RL—LC. IUCN RL—LC.

South China Field Mouse *Apodemus draco*

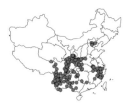

中华姬鼠 Zhonghua Jishu—**Distinctive Characteristics:** HB 87–106; T 80–102; HF 20–23; E 15–17; GLS 24–28. Dorsal pelage pale reddish brown and becoming somewhat brighter yellow-brown along the sides. Ventral pelage grayish white, fairly well demarcated from dorsal pelage but not forming a sharp line. Tail equal to or slightly longer than HB length, dark brown above, paler below. Ears dark blackish brown, much darker than the surrounding parts of the heads and shoulders. Females have four pairs of mammae (two pectoral pairs, two abdominal pairs). **Distribution:** E Xizang and Yunnan extending east to Fujian and northeast to Hebei; extending to Myanmar and NE India. **Natural History:** Inhabits wooded areas up to about 3,000 m. Approximate home range for adult males 4,000–5,000 m², for females 2,200–2,600 m². **Conservation Status:** China RL—LC. IUCN RL—LC.

Large-Eared Field Mouse *Apodemus latronum*

大耳姬鼠 Da'er Jishu—**Distinctive Characteristics:** HB 92–107; T 100–120; HF 25–27; E 18–21; GLS 28–30. Dorsal pelage dark brown, becoming somewhat brighter reddish brown along the sides. Ventral pelage grayish white, indistinctly demarcated from dorsal pelage. Tail approximately equal to HB length, dark brown above, paler below. Ears dark blackish brown, much darker than the surrounding parts of the heads and shoulders. Females have three pairs of mammae (one pectoral pair, two abdominal pairs). Similar to *A. draco*, and some authors consider it a subspecies of that taxon, but *A. latronum* is larger, has longer ears and hind feet, and is further distinguished as being the only China species with just three pairs of mammae. **Distribution:** C China; extending to N Myanmar. **Natural History:** Occurs in alpine forests and adjacent meadows from about 2,700 to 4,000 m. **Conservation Status:** China RL—LC. IUCN RL—LC.

Himalayan Field Mouse *Apodemus pallipes*

帕氏姬鼠 Paishi Jishu—**Distinctive Characteristics:** HB 72–110; T 70–110; HF 19–22; E 14–18; GLS 27–28.5. Dorsal pelage ranges from pale buffy brown to drab brownish gray. Ventral pelage grayish white and fairly well demarcated from the dorsal pelage. Tail approximately equal to or slightly longer than HB length; bicolored, brown above, whitish below. Dorsal surfaces of hands and feet pale buffy brown. Similar to *A. uralensis* but larger and with a paler dorsum and more white on the underparts. **Distribution:** Range in China marginal, restricted to W Xizang; distribution centered in the Pamir Mountains in Central Asia and extending into the Hindu Kush and Himalayas. **Natural History:** Occurs in coniferous and rhododendron forests at elevations ranging from 1,465 to 3,965 m, with most records from above 2,440 m. **Conservation Status:** China RL—LC. IUCN RL—LC.

Korean Field Mouse *Apodemus peninsulae*

大林姬鼠 Dalin Jishu—**Distinctive Characteristics:** HB 80–118; T 75–103; HF 21–23; E 14–17; GLS 25–29. Dorsal pelage pale reddish brown, becoming somewhat paler yellow-brown along the sides. Ventral pelage grayish white, fairly well demarcated from the dorsal pelage but not forming a distinct line. Tail approximately equal to or somewhat shorter than HB length. Ears not differing in color from the surrounding parts of head and shoulders. Females have four pairs of mammae (two pectoral pairs, two abdominal pairs). **Distribution:** Throughout much of China excepting the xeric western regions and the eastern lowlands; extending to S Siberia and Korea. **Natural History:** Favors brushy growth and woodlands. **Conservation Status:** China RL—LC. IUCN RL—LC.

Taiwan Field Mouse *Apodemus semotus*

台湾姬鼠Taiwan Jishu—**Distinctive Characteristics:** HB 82.5–100; T 100–119; HF 23–25.5; E 15–17; GLS 29; Wt 18.5–39 g. Very similar to *A. draco* of the mainland. The only other species of *Apodemus* occurring on Taiwan is *A. agrarius*, which has a faint mid-dorsal stripe and occurs at elevations below 1,000 m. **Distribution:** Taiwan. Endemic. **Natural History:** A habitat generalist reported from grassland, broadleaf and coniferous forests, bamboo, and subalpine shrub from 1,800 to 3,200 m. Favors microhabitats with dense ground cover but is sometimes captured in houses. Capable of breeding year-round, but there are two peak breeding seasons: April–May and September–October. Breeding is most frequent in the fall. Mean litter size about 3.5 (range 2–6). **Conservation Status:** China RL—LC. IUCN RL—LC.

Herb Field Mouse *Apodemus uralensis*

小眼姬鼠 Xiaoyan Jishu—**Distinctive Characteristics:** HB 85–102; T 83–97; HF 18–22; E 14–16; GLS 23.5–25. Dorsal pelage pale sandy brown to pale reddish brown. Ventral pelage sharply demarcated, white but with the grayish underfur showing through. Tail bicolored, brown above and white below. Dorsal surfaces of hands and feet white. **Distribution:** NW China; extending to C Europe. **Natural History:** Forest edges and open areas bordering forests. **Conservation Status:** China RL—LC. IUCN RL—LC.

GENUS *BANDICOTA*—Bandicoot Rats

板齿鼠属 Banchishu Shu—板齿鼠 Banchishu
Large, shaggy burrowing rats. The dorsal pelage ranges from pale grayish brown to almost black and is marked with numerous black guard hairs projecting above the fur along the midline of the back; the ventral pelage is usually grayish white. Scantily haired tail thick and more or less equal to HB length. Bandicoot rats are often found in association with human-degraded habitats and are especially common near water. They are similar to the Brown Rat (*Rattus norvegicus*). Of three species of bandicoots, only one is found in China.

Greater Bandicoot Rat *Bandicota indica*

板齿鼠 Banchi Shu—**Distinctive Characteristics:** HB 188–328; T 190–280; HF 46–60; E 25–33; GLS 48.6–63.6; Wt 500–1,000 g. A very large, coarse-haired rat. Dorsal pelage shaggy, dark blackish brown, with long, coarse black guard hairs along the midline of the back; sides brownish gray. Ventral pelage dark brownish gray. Tail thickened, somewhat shorter than HB length, monocolored dark brown to almost black, and covered in short, stiff bristles. Dorsal surfaces of hands and feet dark blackish brown, but the claws are pale brown and strongly developed for digging. Females have six pairs of mammae (one pectoral pair, two postaxillary pairs, one abdominal pair, two inguinal pairs). **Distribution:** S China, including Taiwan; extending throughout mainland S and SE Asia and Sri Lanka. Introduced to Java and parts of the Malay Peninsula. **Natural History:** A synanthropic species occurring in fields, villages, and cities, it prefers to be near water and is especially common in lowland rice fields. Feeds on mollusks, crabs, fish, fruits, tubers, rice, sugar cane, and other crops. Insects, earthworms, and leaves make up a small part of the diet. Nocturnal. Constructs elaborate burrows in stream banks, paddy dikes, and at the edges of fields. Spends the day in its burrow, emerging after dusk to feed throughout the night. Often searches for prey near water but returns to a particular feeding place to consume it. Typical litter size between five and seven. Offspring sexually mature at 170 days. Many authors have described this species as being particularly ferocious when captured. **Conservation Status:** China RL—LC. IUCN RL—LC.

GENUS *BERYLMYS*—White-toothed Rats

硕鼠属 Shuoshu Shu—硕鼠 Shuoshu
Large rats with a short and crisp, iron-gray-colored dorsal pelage, which is sharply demarcated from the pure white ventral pelage. Females have four or five pairs of mammae. All four species of *Berylmys* occur in China.

Berdmore's White-Toothed Rat *Berylmys berdmorei*

大炮硕鼠 Dapao Shuoshu—**Distinctive Characteristics:** HB 175–255; T 134–192; HF 36–46; E 23–29; GLS 42; Wt 118–235. Dorsal pelage iron gray. Ventral pelage pure white. Tail shorter than HB length, entirely dark brown above from base to tip, underside of tail ranges from solid brown to mottled grayish white speckled with black. Dorsal surfaces of hands and feet grayish white. Females have five pairs of mammae (one pectoral pair, two postaxillary pairs, two inguinal pairs). **Distribution:** S Yunnan (Xishuangbanna); extending from S Myanmar to S Vietnam. **Natural History:** Inhabits forests from near sea level to at least 1,400 m, but most common in upland areas, where it is reported to favor swampy areas. Occasionally an agricultural pest, but generally avoids human habitations. Terrestrial and nocturnal; spends the day in its burrow. **Conservation Status:** China RL—NA. IUCN RL—LC.

Bowers' White-Toothed Rat *Berylmys bowersi*

青毛硕鼠 Qingmao Shuoshu—**Distinctive Characteristics:** HB 236–285; T 249–292; HF 48–61; E 32–36; GLS 52–58.5; Wt up to 420 g. The largest species of *Berylmys*. Dorsal pelage dull brownish gray. Ventral pelage pure white. Tail slightly longer than HB length, usually entirely dark brown with a white tip, rarely monocolored brown. Dorsal surfaces of hands and feet dark brown, but digits and sides of feet white. Females have only four pairs of mammae (one pectoral pair, one postaxillary pair, two inguinal pairs). **Distribution:** S China; extending from NE India to Vietnam and south to the Malay Peninsula and N Sumatra. **Natural History:** Nocturnal and predominantly terrestrial, although a capable climber. Spends the day in its burrow. Most common in primary forest between 1,000 and 1,600 m, but may also occur in secondary forest and scrub. Primarily a forest rat, but also found in cultivated fields and scrub along the margins of forest. Largely vegetarian, mostly eating fruits and vegetables but also some insects and land mollusks. Digs a large burrow among rocks, holes in fallen logs, along forest streams and paths, and at the base of trees. Typical litter size two to five. **Conservation Status:** China RL—LC. IUCN RL—LC.

Mackenzie's White-Toothed Rat *Berylmys mackenziei*

白齿家鼠 Baichi Jiashu—**Distinctive Characteristics:** HB 233–272; T 248–262; HF 50–61; E 27–31; GLS 50.5–57.7; Wt 265 g. Similar to *B. bowersi*, but smaller and with white more or less covering the distal half of the tail; dorsal surfaces of the hind feet dark brown, but digits and sides of feet white; hands white, without a blaze of brown hairs on the dorsal surface; and females have five pairs of mammae (one pectoral pair, two postaxillary pairs, two inguinal pairs). **Distribution:** Known from a single specimen collected in C Sichuan (Mount Emei); otherwise known from NE India to S Vietnam. **Natural History:** A highland species; the only specimen known from China was collected at 2,000 m. **Conservation Status:** China RL—VU D2. IUCN RL—DD.

Manipur White-Toothed Rat *Berylmys manipulus*

小泡硕鼠 Xiaopao Shuoshu—**Distinctive Charac-teristics:** HB 135–185; T 140–187; HF 33–40; E 23–25; GLS 36.2–42.7. Similar to *B. berdmorei*, but smaller—the smallest species in the genus. Tail equal to or slightly longer than HB length, and with the distal half to third entirely white; dorsal surfaces of hands and feet white. Five pairs of mammae (one pectoral pair, two postaxillary pairs, two inguinal pairs). **Distribution:** Range in China restricted to Yunnan west of Salween River; extending from NE India to N Myanmar. **Natural History:** Oak-scrub forest and upland rain forests to at least 1,800 m. Avoids agricultural areas and human habitations. Eats plants, insects, and earthworms. Terrestrial, burrow dweller. **Conservation Status:** China RL—NA. IUCN RL—DD.

GENUS *CHIROMYSCUS* (monotypic)

费氏树鼠属—Feishishushu Shu

Indochinese Chiromyscus *Chiromyscus chiropus*

费氏树鼠 Feishishushu—**Distinctive Characteris-tics:** HB 138–160; T 200–233; HF 27–29; E 19–20; GLS 38.6. A monotypic genus similar to *Niviventer*, but with a nail instead of a claw on the first digit of each hind foot. Dorsal pelage orange-brown and with an ochraceous lateral line along the margin with the ventral pelage. Ventral pelage sharply demarcated, creamy white. Tail bicolored, brown above, whitish below. Broad dark brown rings encircle each eye. **Distribution:** S Yunnan (Xishuangbanna); extending from Myanmar to Vietnam. **Natural History:** An arboreal species favoring deciduous forest. **Conservation Status:** China RL—DD. IUCN RL—LC.

GENUS *CHIROPODOMYS*—Tree Mice

笔尾树鼠属 Biweishushu Shu—笔尾树鼠 Biweishushu
Small arboreal mice with short, broad face; soft, woolly fur; and a long, tufted tail. The first digit of each hand is short and bears a broad nail; the first digit of each foot has a thick fleshy pad and an embedded nail. Of six species of *Chiropodomys*, one occurs in China.

Indomalayan Tree Mouse *Chiropodomys gliroides*

笔尾树鼠 Biwei Shushu—**Distinctive Characteristics:** HB 81–101; T 105–134; HF 18–22; E 16–20; GLS 23.5–26; Wt 20–33 g. A small arboreal mouse with a short rostrum and large eyes surrounded by a dark ring of black fur. Dorsal pelage soft and fluffy, pale reddish brown; whiskers very long and extending well

beyond the ears when laid flat. Ventral pelage pure creamy white, sharply demarcated from dorsal pelage. Tail grayish brown and with a tuft of longer hairs at the tip (hairs ca. 3.5 mm). Dorsal surfaces of hands white, feet white with a brown blaze; first digit of foot bears a flattened nail and is opposable. Females have two pairs of inguinal mammae. **Distribution:** S China, including Hainan Island; extending from NE India to Vietnam and south to Bali. **Natural History:** Inhabits primary and secondary forest from near sea level to ca. 2,600 m. Primarily herbivorous, but the composition of its diet is not completely known. Nocturnal and arboreal, but sometimes descends to the ground. Nests in hollow parts of trees. Uses woody lianas as runways through dense understory vegetation. The species seems to be more common in forest with an understory of bamboo, but also occurs in areas completely devoid of bamboo. Litter size averages two. Polyestrus, with each estrous period lasting about one day and an estrous cycle lasting a minimum of seven days; gestation approximately 20 days. There is apparently no restricted breeding season, and pregnancies occur throughout the year. **Conservation Status:** China RL—VU A2c + 3c. IUCN RL—LC.

GENUS *DACNOMYS* (monotypic)

大齿鼠属 Dachishu Shu

Millard's Dacnomys *Dacnomys millardi*

大齿鼠 Dachi Shu—**Distinctive Characteristics:** HB 228–290; T 308–335; HF 50–56; E 25–29; GLS 60. A giant, long-tailed rat similar in size to *Leopoldamys*, but with the demarcation between the dorsal and ventral pelage not as sharp. Pelage short and thin, dark grayish brown flecked with buff dorsally, becoming paler along the sides and blending into the pale brownish-white ventral pelage; the individual hairs of the ventral pelage are grayish brown at the base with dull creamy-white tips, except on the throat, axillary, and inguinal regions, where the hairs are pure creamy white to their bases; tail unicolored brown, sparsely haired; dorsal surfaces of hands and feet pale brown, with white digits; eight mammae (one pectoral pair, one postaxillary pair, two inguinal pairs). **Distribution:** Yunnan; extending from E Nepal to NW Vietnam. **Natural History:** Inhabits highland forests above 1,000 m. **Conservation Status:** China RL—NT. IUCN RL—DD.

GENUS *HADROMYS*—Hadromys

壮鼠属 Zhuangshu Shu—壮鼠 Zhuangshu
Large, stout-bodied rats with soft, thick, grayish-brown fur and large rounded
ears. Of two *Hadromys* species, one occurs in China.

Yunnan Hadromys *Hadromys yunnanensis*

云南壮鼠 Yunnan Zhuangshu—**Distinctive Characteristics:** HB 123–140; T 114–132; HF 24–27; E
15–20; GLS 32–33; Wt 41–77 g. Fur soft and dense; dorsal pelage dark grayish
brown sprinkled with black and either yellow or white, becoming reddish over
the back and rump and with a yellow-ochre patch on the cheek. Ventral pelage
pure white. Tail shorter than HB length; dorsal surface of tail brown, underside
white. Hands and feet long and slender; four pairs of mammae (one pectoral
pair, one postaxillary pair, two inguinal pairs). **Distribution:** Known only from
Ruili County, W Yunnan. Endemic. **Natural History:** Terrestrial. Occurs
between 970 and 1,300 m elevation. **Conservation Status:** China RL—VU D2.
IUCN RL—DD.

GENUS *HAPALOMYS*—Marmoset Rats

猬鼠属 Rongshu Shu—猬鼠 Rongshu
Arboreal rats with a long, soft pelage and a long tail ending in a tuft of hairs. The
big toe is opposable and bears a flat nail instead of a claw. The ears are conspicuously fringed with very long, fine hairs. Females have four pairs of mammae.
Only one of two species of *Hapalomys* occurs in China.

Lesser Marmoset Rat *Hapalomys delacouri*

小猬鼠 Xiao Rongshu—**Distinctive Characteristics:** HB 123–136; T 140–160; HF 22–24; E 14–15;
GLS 32–34. Dorsal pelage ochraceous brown, hairs long and soft. Ventral pelage
pure white, sharply demarcated from dorsal pelage; tail slightly longer than HB
length, pale brown near the base, darker brown toward the tip, ending in short
tuft of hair approximately 6 mm long. Ears conspicuously fringed with very long,
fine hairs that are more than twice the length of the pinnae; vibrissae long,

extending to the shoulders when laid back against the body; four pairs of mammae (one pectoral, one postaxillary, two inguinal); hands and feet short and broad; the thumb is fully opposable and bears a nail instead of a claw. **Distribution:** S China, including Hainan Island; extending to N Laos and Vietnam. **Natural History:** Highly arboreal and probably restricted to bamboo habitats between 1,200 and 1,500 m. **Conservation Status:** China RL—EN A1bc. IUCN RL—VU A4c.

GENUS *LEOPOLDAMYS*—Leopoldamys

长尾大鼠属 Changweidashu Shu—长尾大鼠 Changweidashu
Large, long-tailed rats with short, sleek fur. Dorsal pelage brown to grayish brown. Ventral pelage pure white and sharply demarcated. Tail indistinctly bicolored, dark brown above, creamy white below. Dorsal surfaces of hands and feet brownish white. One of four species of *Leopoldamys* lives in China.

Edward's Leopoldamys *Leopoldamys edwardsi*

小泡巨鼠 Xiaopao Jushu—
Distinctive Characteristics: HB 210–290; T 264–315; HF 42–58; E 28–32; GLS 54–58; Wt 230–480 g. Very large rats with a long tail, long ears, and fairly short, sleek fur. Dorsal pelage brown to grayish brown. Ventral pelage pure white and sharply demarcated. Tail indistinctly bicolored, dark brown above, creamy white below. Dorsal surfaces of hands and feet brownish white. **Distribution:** C and SE China, including Hainan Island; extending west to India and south to Indochina, Myanmar, and Thailand. **Natural History:** Inhabits lowland and montane forests. Omnivorous. Primarily nocturnal and terrestrial but will climb short distances for food. **Conservation Status:** China RL—LC. IUCN RL—LC.

GENUS *MAXOMYS*—Maxomys

刺鼠属 Chishu Shu—刺鼠 Chishu
Medium-sized, short-furred, reddish-orange forest rats. The dorsal pelage is usually spinous in the Chinese species, bright orange-red, and sharply demarcated from the creamy-white ventral pelage. Tail about as long as HB length; the base is brown above, but the tip is entirely white. Hind foot long and slender. Of 17 species of *Maxomys*, only one occurs in China.

Indomalayan Maxomys *Maxomys surifer*

红刺鼠 Hong Cishu—**Distinctive Characteristics:** HB 160–226; T 160–227; HF 40–47; E 24–28; GLS 43.3–47; Wt 90–230 g. Dorsal pelage bright reddish orange with admixtures of black guard hairs, becoming paler along the sides and form-

ing a sharp line of demarcation with the pure white ventral pelage. Hind foot nearly five times as long as it is wide, with small, smooth plantar pads. Females have four pairs of mammae (one pectoral pair, one postaxillary pair, two inguinal pairs). **Distribution:** S Yunnan (Xishuangbanna); extending across Indochina, Thailand, and Myanmar. **Natural History:** Cursorial rats adapted for life on trop-

ical rain-forest floors. Lives in burrows on the forest floor. Nocturnal and omnivorous, feeding on roots, fallen fruits, insects, and small vertebrates. Litter size typically ranges between two and five. **Conservation Status:** China RL—LC. IUCN RL—LC.

GENUS *MICROMYS* (monotypic)

巢鼠属 Chaoshu Shu

Harvest Mouse *Micromys minutus*

巢鼠 Chao Shu—**Distinctive Characteristics:** HB 55–68; T 54–79; HF 14–16; E 10; GLS <20 mm; Wt 5–7 g. Tiny field mouse of the Palaearctic realm. The dorsal pelage is reddish brown above; ventral hairs gray-based with dull white tips. The tail is prehensile, allowing it to climb easily through tall grassy vegetation. Tail bicolored, dark brown above, slightly paler below. Head short and rounded, with a very short muzzle. Hind foot with a claw on the first digit (in *Vandeleuria* there is a nail). Females have four pairs of mammae. **Distribution:** NW, NE, C, and S China; extending across the Palaearctic. **Natural History:** Inhabits tall grass fields, rice fields, bamboo stands, and other weedy areas. Eats seeds, green vegetation, and some insects. Active day or night. Constructs a special nest during the breeding season consisting of a tightly woven ball of plant fibers suspended on tall stems about 100–130 cm above the ground and about 60–130 mm in diameter. Typical litter sizes range between five and nine. Home range approximately 400 m^2 for males, 350 m^2 for females. **Conservation Status:** China RL—LC. IUCN RL—LC.

GENUS *MUS*—Old World Mice

小鼠属 Xiaoshu Shu—小鼠 Xiaoshu

Small terrestrial mice including both wild and synanthropic species. Of the 38 species currently allocated to the genus, only four occur in China (not including *Mus musculus*, the introduced house mouse). The fur of Chinese species may be soft or stiff and ranges from dark gray to pale yellowish brown dorsally, and dark gray to white ventrally. Females have five pairs of mammae (one pectoral, two postaxillary, two inguinal). Most of the species occurring in China are to some extent associated with human-modified habitats, being most common in rice fields and scrubby habitats around villages.

Ryukyu Mouse *Mus caroli*

琉球小家鼠 Liuqiu Xiaojiashu—**Distinctive Characteristics:** HB 72–95; T 75–95; HF 15–19; E 12–14; GLS 19–20.5; Wt 11.5–19.5. Dorsal pelage grayish brown, fur rather stiff. Ventral pelage grayish white. Tail equal to or slightly shorter than HB length, sharply bicolored, dark brown above, paler below. Dorsal surfaces of hands and feet pale brown. Upper incisors dark orange. Similar to *M. cervicolor*, but with a longer tail that is sharply bicolored. **Distribution:** S China including Hainan Island, Hong Kong, and Taiwan; extending south to Vietnam, Cambodia, Laos, and Thailand. **Natural History:** Common in and around rice fields, grassy areas, scrub, and secondary growth. Burrows are typically constructed in rice-paddy dikes and usually have two entrances leading to a central chamber. Burrow entrances are left open and are usually marked by small mounds of freshly dug soil. The species is primarily nocturnal, but it is not unusual for individuals to emerge from their burrows for brief periods during the day. **Conservation Status:** China RL—LC. IUCN RL—LC.

Fawn-Colored Mouse *Mus cervicolor*

仔鹿小鼠 Zilu Xiaoshu—**Distinctive Characteristics:** HB 70–95; T 50–70; HF 14–19; E 13–15; GLS 20.5–24.5; Wt 8–17.5 g. Dorsal pelage very soft and orange-brown to brownish gray. Ventral pelage creamy white, the hairs with pale gray bases. Tail shorter than HB and distinctly bicolored, dark brown above and white below. Dorsal surfaces of hands and feet white. Similar to *M. caroli*, with which it is often sympatric, but distinguished by its smaller size and shorter tail. **Distribution:** Known from only two localities in Yunnan; extending from N India and Nepal east through Myanmar, Laos, Cambodia, and N Vietnam. **Natural History:** Occurs in secondary growth, grass, brush, rice fields, and other agricultural areas. **Conservation Status:** China RL—NA. IUCN RL—LC.

Cook's Mouse *Mus cookii*

丛林小鼠 Conglin Xiaoshu—**Distinctive Characteristics:** HB 77–96; T 83–91; HF 19.5; E 15; GLS 24–25; Wt 16.5–23. Dorsal pelage dark grayish brown, with a stiff texture. Ventral pelage grayish white. Tail shorter than HB length, brown above, paler below. Dorsal surfaces of hands and feet grayish white. Upper inci-

sors pale orange. Resembles *M. caroli*, but larger, with paler orange upper incisors and without a sharply bicolored tail. **Distribution:** Yunnan, west of the Salween River; extending from Nepal to Myanmar and south to Thailand, Laos, and Vietnam. **Natural History:** Reported from upland rice fields and other disturbed habitats. **Conservation Status:** China RL—NA. IUCN RL—LC.

Indochinese Shrewlike Mouse *Mus pahari*

锡金小鼠 Xijin Xiaoshu—**Distinctive Characteristics:** HB 75–105; T 70–100; HF 21–23; E 15–17; GLS 24–26; Wt 21–24 g. A long-nosed, shrewlike mouse with small eyes and short ears. Dorsal pelage dark blue-gray, spiny in adults; ventral pelage silver gray. Tail equal to or slightly shorter than HB, bicolored, dark brown above, white below. Dorsal surfaces of hands and feet white. **Distribution:** S China; extending from NE India through N Myanmar to Thailand, Laos, Vietnam, and Cambodia. **Natural History:** Little known; builds a grass nest but does not burrow. Strictly nocturnal and terrestrial. Feeds on insects. **Conservation Status:** China RL—LC. IUCN RL—LC.

GENUS *NESOKIA*—Short-tailed Bandicoot Rats

地鼠属 Dishu Shu—地鼠 Dishu

Short-tailed, burrowing rats similar to *Bandicota*, but with larger hands, longer claws, and more forward-projecting upper incisors that are only slightly pigmented or completely white. Females have four pairs of mammae. One of the two species of *Nesokia* is distributed in China.

Short-Tailed Bandicoot Rat *Nesokia indica*

印度地鼠 Yindu Dishu—**Distinctive Characteristics:** HB 150–194; T 110–129; HF 23–37; E 16–22; GLS 36–42; Wt 137–203 g. A stocky rat with a broad head, short snout, and short, rounded ears. The incisor teeth are very broad, and the lower set is wider than the upper set. Dorsal pelage thick and shaggy, grayish brown, with orange across the shoulders. Ventral pelage pale gray. Tail very short and thinly furred. Females have four pairs of mammae (one pectoral pair, one abdominal pair, and two inguinal pairs). **Distribution:** NW China; extending to NE Egypt through the Arabian Peninsula. **Natural History:** Inhabits mountainous areas, where it is especially common in agricultural areas. A highly fossorial species, it digs extensive burrows in firm, damp soil using its large teeth; feeds on underground bulbs and succulent grass roots. Adults are solitary and aggressive and rarely emerge above ground. Reproduction occurs throughout the year, but litter size is low and probably close to four young per litter. **Conservation Status:** China RL—LC. IUCN RL—LC.

GENUS *NIVIVENTER*—Niviventer

白腹鼠属 Baifushu Shu—白腹鼠 Baifushu
Medium-sized rats having a yellowish-brown to reddish-brown or brownish-gray, spinous dorsal pelage and a sharply demarcated creamy-white ventral pelage. The tail is about the same length as HB or somewhat longer and may be monocolored or bicolored. Females have four pairs of mammae. Of 17 species of *Niviventer*, 10 occur in China.

Anderson's Niviventer *Niviventer andersoni*

安氏白腹鼠 Anshi Baifushu—**Distinctive Characteristics:** HB 150–198; T 194–269; HF 31–40; E 22–28; GLS 39–46. Dorsal pelage long and soft; dark grayish brown with mixtures of black hairs mid-dorsally; brighter ochraceous brown along sides of cheeks, neck, and body. Ventral pelage creamy white and sharply demarcated from the dorsal pelage. There is a contrastingly blackish area extending from the base of the vibrissae back to and around the eye and partway to the base of the ear. Tail longer than HB; bicolored, dark brown above but becoming progressively paler toward the tip so that the terminal third is white. The underside of the tail is pale brownish white. There is a slight tuft of longer hairs at the tip of the tail. Dorsal surfaces of hands and feet usually dark brown, but digits and sides of the feet are whitish. Resembles *N. excelsior*, with which it is sympatric, but distinguished by its darker dorsal pelage and larger size. **Distribution:** Along the eastern edge of the Tibetan Plateau. Endemic. **Natural History:** Little known. Inhabits high montane forest at elevations between approximately 2,000 and 3,000 m. **Conservation Status:** China RL—LC. IUCN RL—LC.

Brahman Niviventer *Niviventer brahma*

梵鼠 Fan Shu—**Distinctive Characteristics:** HB 136–155; T 201–237; HF 31–34; E 20–25; GLS 35.8–38.1. A beautiful *Niviventer* with long, soft, thick fur. Dorsal pelage bright orange-brown to yellow-brown with mixtures of very long black guard hairs; face with dark blackish-brown patches extending from the tip of the nose to just behind the ears. The bright fulvous-orange sides are sharply demarcated from the gray-based white ventral pelage, and there is usually a streak or patch of buff-brown fur along the midline of the chest. Tail long, about 1.5 times HB length, and more or less uniform brown in color; the underside is usually slightly paler brown, but the tail is never distinctly bicolored. Tail tipped with a little brush of hair; dorsal surfaces of hands and feet brownish gray, with pale brown fingers and toes. Females have three pairs of mammae (one postaxillary pair, one abdominal pair, and one inguinal pair). **Distribution:** Yunnan west of Salween River (NW Gaoligong Mountains); extending to NE India and N Myanmar. **Natural History:** Inhabits cool, damp, high-elevation forests. Terrestrial. **Conservation Status:** China RL—VU D2. IUCN RL—LC.

Confucian Niviventer *Niviventer confucianus*

北社鼠 Bei Sheshu—**Distinctive Characteristics:** HB 116–173; T 154–255; HF 28–35; E 21–25; GLS 31.5–38, rarely up to 43. Dorsal pelage may be soft or spiny, ranging in color from reddish brown to dull brownish gray with an area of brighter ochraceous brown along the sides. Ventral pelage pale yellowish white, sharply demarcated from the dorsal pelage. There is sometimes a buffy spot on the center of the chest. Tail only slightly longer than head and body, dark brown above, whitish below; tip completely white. Sometimes difficult to distinguish from *N. fulvescens*; where the two species occur together, *N. confucianus* is usually darker. **Distribution:** Common throughout the highlands of S, C, and E China; extending to N Myanmar, NW Thailand, and NW Vietnam. **Natural History:** An abundant species occurring in all kinds of habitats from primary forest to cultivated land. **Conservation Status:** China RL—LC. IUCN RL—LC.

Spiny Taiwan Niviventer *Niviventer coninga*

台湾白腹鼠 Taiwan Baifushu—**Distinctive Characteristics:** HB 140–205; T 174–262; HF 30–37; E 22–29; GLS 39–49; Wt 108–176 g. A large-bodied species with a reddish-brown to yellow-brown, spiny pelage. Ventral pelage creamy white. Tail slightly shorter than HB, bicolored, dark brown above, paler below. Similar to *N. culturatus*, but larger. **Distribution:** Taiwan. Endemic. **Natural History:** Found in broadleaf forest, forest edge, and scrub growth; restricted to elevations below 2,000 m. **Conservation Status:** China RL—LC. IUCN RL—LC.

Soft-Furred Taiwan Niviventer *Niviventer culturatus*

台湾社鼠 Taiwan Sheshu—**Distinctive Characteristics:** HB 130–150; T 170–200; HF 29–35; E 23–25; GLS 37–39. Dorsal pelage dark grayish brown, sharply demarcated from the creamy-white ventral pelage. Tail bicolored, brown above,

creamy white below; the terminal portion is entirely white. Dorsal surfaces of hands and feet brown, but the digits and sides are white. Face rather grayish, but with dark patches in front of and just behind the eyes. **Distribution:** Taiwan. Endemic. **Natural History:** Favors primary hemlock forests but may also be found in secondary habitats. Normally restricted to highlands between 2,000 and 3,000 m in elevation. Usually found in association with large logs on the forest floor. **Conservation Status:** China RL—LC. IUCN RL—NT.

Smoke-Bellied Niviventer *Niviventer eha*

灰腹鼠 Hui Fushu—**Distinctive Characteristics:** HB 112–130; T 165–195; HF 28–31; E 17–19; GLS 29–33. A small *Niviventer* with a long tail (ca. 1.5 times HB length). Dorsal pelage long, soft, and fluffy, without spines, dull brownish orange in color, sides somewhat brighter orange; individual hairs of ventral pelage gray-based with dull grayish-white tips, giving the ventral pelage an overall grayish-white or "smoky" appearance; ears dark brown and with conspicuous brownish-black tuft of hair at the front base of each. There may also be an indistinctly marked extension of brown fur from the eye-ring to the vibrissae, but this patch does not extend as far as the nose. Tail long, brownish black above, slightly paler below but not distinctly bicolored; the hairs of the tail increase in length distally to form a small brush at the tip. Hind feet long and slender, their dorsal surfaces dark brown; fingers and toes are brownish white. Females have three pairs of mammae: one postaxillary pair, one abdominal pair, and one inguinal pair. **Distribution:** S Xizang and Yunnan; extending to Nepal, NE India, and N Myanmar. **Natural History:** Inhabits cool, damp temperate forests characterized by conifers and rhododendrons. Elevational range approximately 2,500–3,300 m. Eats insects and especially larvae mostly but also some fruits and starchy roots. Predominantly terrestrial. **Conservation Status:** China RL—LC. IUCN RL—LC.

Sichuan Niviventer *Niviventer excelsior*

川西白腹鼠 Chuanxi Baifushu—**Distinctive Characteristics:** HB 127–175; T 190–213; HF 31–33; E 22–27; GLS 38.1–41.3. A large species of

Niviventer similar to *N. andersoni* but a little smaller. Dorsal pelage dull grayish brown, a somewhat richer orange-brown along the sides and sharply demarcated from the pure white ventral pelage. Tail longer than HB, bicolored, dark brown above, pale brownish white below; the terminal portion (a half to a quarter) is entirely white and tufted. Dorsal surfaces of hands and feet brown; fingers and toes brownish white. There is a faint dark brown patch extending forward from the eye to the base of the vibrissae. **Distribution:** SW China. Endemic. **Natural History:** Little known beyond the fact that it inhabits high-elevation montane forests. **Conservation Status:** China RL—LC. IUCN RL—LC.

Indomalayan Niviventer *Niviventer fulvescens*

针毛鼠 Zhenmao Shu—**Distinctive Characteristics:** HB 131–172; T 160–221; HF 30–34; E 17–23; GLS 32–40; Wt 60–135 g. Dorsal pelage highly variable even within populations, ranging from dull ochraceous brown to bright fulvous orange. Ventral pelage yellowish white and sharply demarcated. Tail averages slightly longer than HB and is usually bicolored, dark brown above and whitish along the entire length of the underside. Occasionally, individuals will have a monocolored brown tail. **Distribution:** Widely distributed throughout S China, including Hainan Island; extending from N Pakistan to Indochina and south to Sumatra, Java, and Bali. **Natural History:** A common rat favoring all kinds of forest habitats, but also occurring in scrub, bamboo, and agricultural areas near forest. Predominantly terrestrial, but may climb vines. Omnivorous, it feeds on seeds, berries, insects, and probably some green vegetation. **Conservation Status:** China RL—LC. IUCN RL—LC.

Indochinese Arboreal Niviventer *Niviventer langbianis*

南洋鼠 Nanyang Shu—**Distinctive Characteristics:** HB 131–162; T 154–199; HF 29–33; E 19–22; GLS 33–40; Wt 58–98 g. Dorsal pelage yellowish brown to reddish brown, with dark brown spines and with an indistinct fringe of buffy hairs at the sharply demarcated border of the dorsal and ventral pelage. Ventral pelage white. Tail monocolored brown. Dorsal surfaces of hands and feet pale brown to white, sometimes with a dark brown patch. **Distribution:** Reported from a single marginal locality in Yunnan; extending throughout Indochina, Thailand, Myanmar, and NE India. **Natural History:** Occurs in evergreen forests, where it is usually spottily distributed, being fairly common in some forests and seemingly absent from similar habitats within its range. The species is primarily arboreal, although it is sometimes trapped on the ground. **Conservation Status:** China RL—NA. IUCN RL—LC.

Indochinese Mountain Niviventer *Niviventer tenaster*

缅甸山鼠 Miandian Shanshu—**Distinctive Characteristics:** HB 120–189; T 174–234; HF 32–35; E 23–26; GLS 37–42; Wt 53–140 g. Dorsal pelage yellowish brown interspersed with dark brown spines. Ventral pelage white and sharply demarcated. Dorsal surface of the tail brown but often with a mottled white tip; ventral surface of tail paler brown but not sharply demarcated. Ears conspicuously large for the genus. **Distribution:** Hainan Island; extending from Myanmar through Thailand and Laos to Vietnam and south to Cambodia. **Natural History:** Montane forest. **Conservation Status:** China RL—DD. IUCN RL—LC.

GENUS *RATTUS*—Old World Rats

家鼠属 Jiashu Shu—家鼠 Jiashu

A diverse genus of Old World rats perhaps best known for its human-commensal species. The pelage may be soft or coarse and ranges in color through shades of gray, red, yellow, orange, brown, and black. The ventral pelage may be white or gray. *Rattus* species are omnivorous, eating a wide variety of plants and animals, and highly adaptable. Of 66 species of *Rattus*, seven occur in China.

Indochinese Forest Rat *Rattus andamanensis*

黑缘齿鼠 Heiyuan Chishu—**Distinctive Characteristics:** HB 128–185, T 172–222, HF 32–36, E 20–25, GLS 40–43; Wt 125–155. A large *Rattus* with a long, thick pelage. Dorsal pelage varying shades of brown with mixtures of pale-brown-tipped and black-tipped hairs and with conspicuous long black guard hairs along much of the midline of the back. Other species of *Rattus* may have long black guard hairs in the dorsal pelage, but these tend to be restricted to the rump. Ventral pelage sharply demarcated from the dorsal pelage, hairs pure creamy white or rarely with small spots of grayish-based hairs. Tail much longer than HB and a uniform dark brown. Dorsal surfaces of the feet dark brown. Six pairs of mammae: three pectoral and three inguinal. **Distribution:** S China, including Hainan Island; extending into Indochina, Thailand, Myanmar, and NE India. **Natural History:** Most often found in agricultural areas, scrub, and around houses. **Conservation Status:** China RL—LC. IUCN RL—LC.

Pacific Rat *Rattus exulans*

缅鼠 Mian Shu—**Distinctive Characteristics:** HB 91–140; T 105–160; HF 22–23; E 15–17.5; GLS 28–33; Wt 43–55 g. A small species with a grayish-brown dorsal pelage and pale gray ventral pelage. Tail slightly longer than HB and

monocolored dark brown. Females have four pairs of mammae (one pectoral pair, one postaxillary pair, two inguinal pairs). **Distribution:** Widespread throughout SE Asia, but range in China restricted to Taiwan and Yongxing Island of Xisha archipelago, South China Sea. **Natural History:** Closely associated with human habitations, only rarely found far from villages. It is highly arboreal, climbing through brush, low trees, and on the walls and roofs of houses. Constructs a nest in roof thatch or elevated about 20 cm above the ground in dense grass. **Conservation Status:** China RL—DD. IUCN RL—LC.

Losea Rat *Rattus losea*

黄毛鼠 Huangmao Shu—**Distinctive Characteristics:** HB 120–185; T 128–175; HF 24–32; E 18–21; GLS 33–40; Wt 22–90 g. A relatively small-sized species of *Rattus* with a soft, dense pelage lacking obvious spines. Dorsal pelage varying shades of dull gray-brown with mixtures of pale-brown-tipped and black-tipped hairs, becoming somewhat paler along the sides and blending into the gray-based buffy-brown ventral pelage without a clear line of demarcation. The inguinal region and underside of the chin are often pure white. Tail approximately equal to HB length or somewhat shorter, monocolored brown or only very slightly paler brown below. Dorsal surfaces of the hands and feet brown. Females have five pairs of mammae (one pectoral pair, one abdominal pair, three inguinal pairs). **Distribution:** SE China, including Hainan Island and Taiwan; extending into Indochina and Thailand. **Natural History:** Inhabits grass, scrub, mangroves, cultivated fields, and other human-modified areas from sea level up to about 1,000 m. Terrestrial. Studies in Vietnam suggest that population sizes may fluctuate in relation to the availability of field crops. **Conservation Status:** China RL—LC. IUCN RL—LC.

White-Footed Indochinese Rat *Rattus nitidus*

大足鼠 Dazu Shu—**Distinctive Characteristics:** HB 148–180; T 135–206; HF 32–36; E 21; GLS 34–44; Wt 114–136 g. A medium-sized species of *Rattus* with a short, thick pelage. Dorsal pelage varying shades of brown but generally dark grayish brown with mixtures of pale-brown-tipped and black-tipped hairs, becoming somewhat paler gray along the sides and blending into the dull grayish color of the ventral pelage. Tail approximately equal to HB length, mono-colored brown or slightly paler brown on the underside. Dorsal surfaces of hands and feet a lustrous pearly white. Females have six pairs of mammae (one pectoral pair, two postaxillary pairs, one abdominal pair, two inguinal pairs). **Distribution:** Widespread across C and SE China, including Hainan Island; extending across mainland SE Asia from N India through Nepal, Bhutan, Myanmar, and N Thailand to Vietnam. **Natural History:** Occupies disturbed habitats along the courses of streams and rivers; however, in areas where agricultural habitats and villages are not overrun with the introduced *R. rattus*, this species will readily occupy these habitats as well. The species is a major agricultural pest in China, infesting all kinds of agricultural areas including rice, wheat, corn, and potato fields. Terrestrial and active day and night. Breeding occurs between March and November, with peaks in March–April and August–September. Litter size ranges from 4 to 15 but averages about 8, with females producing two or three litters per year. **Conservation Status:** China RL—LC. IUCN RL—LC.

Brown Rat *Rattus norvegicus*

褐家鼠 He Jiashu—**Distinctive Characteristics:** HB 205–260; T 190–250; HF 38–50; E 19–26; GLS 45–55; Wt 230–500 g (rarely up to 1 kg). A large *Rattus*. Dorsal pelage varying shades of brown with mixtures of pale-brown-tipped and black-tipped hairs, becoming somewhat paler along the sides and blending into the gray ventral pelage without a clear line of demarcation. Some pure white hairs may be present in the axillary region. Tail always shorter than HB, indistinctly bicolored, dark brown above, grayish white below. Dorsal surfaces of feet white, sometimes with a pearly luster not unlike that of *R. nitidus*. Females have six pairs of mammae (one pectoral pair, two postaxillary pairs, one abdominal pair, two inguinal pairs). **Distribution:** Original distribution comprised N China, SE Siberia, and Japan, but the species has been since introduced worldwide. **Natural History:** In China the species is more common in colder climates at higher latitudes. At southern latitudes it is restricted to habitats modified by humans and especially in association with water (sewers, ports, and warehouses). Terrestrial and an excellent swimmer. **Conservation Status:** China RL—LC. IUCN RL—LC.

Himalayan Rat *Rattus pyctoris*

拟家鼠 Ni Jiashu—**Distinctive Characteristics:** HB 140–165; T 135–178; HF 32–34; E 20–25. A small-sized species of *Rattus* with dense, shaggy fur. Dorsal pelage dull grayish brown, paler along the sides. Hairs of ventral pelage buffy white, but patches of gray-based hairs sometimes present on the chest or throat. Tail approximately equal to HB length or somewhat longer, dark brown above, paler brown below, especially near the base of the tail. Dorsal surfaces of feet dusky white, lacking the pearly luster seen in *R. nitidus* and *R. norvegicus*. Females have six pairs of mammae. **Distribution:** SW China; extending westward to SE Kazakhstan and Iran. **Natural History:** A montane species generally occurring at elevations above 1,200 m to approximately 4,250 m. **Conservation Status:** China RL—LC. IUCN RL—LC.

Oriental House Rat *Rattus tanezumi*

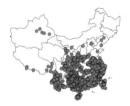

黄胸鼠 Huangxiong Shu—**Distinctive Characteristics:** HB 105–215; T 120–230; HF 26–35; E 17–23; GLS 38–44. A medium-sized species of *Rattus* with a short, coarse pelage. Dorsal pelage varying shades of brown with mixtures of pale-brown-tipped and black-tipped hairs; hairs of ventral pelage gray-based with buffy-white tips; ventral pelage not sharply demarcated from dorsal pelage. Tail longer than HB, monocolored brown or slightly paler along the underside near the base. Feet whitish on the sides and on the fingers and toes but with distinctive dark grayish-brown patches in the center. **Distribution:** Widespread in SE China, including Hainan Island and Taiwan; range extending from E Afghanistan to NE India, Korea, and Indochina south to Isthmus of Kra, but the species has been widely introduced throughout Asia. **Natural History:** Most commonly found in and around villages and agricultural areas, where it is equally at home on the ground or climbing through the rafters of houses. **Conservation Status:** China RL—LC. IUCN RL—LC.

GENUS *VANDELEURIA*—Vandeleuria

长尾攀鼠属 Changweipanshu Shu—长尾攀鼠 Changweipanshu
Small orange climbing mice with a long tail and with the first and fifth digits of both the hands and feet partially opposable and lacking claws. One of three species of *Vandeleuria* occurs in China.

Indomalayan Vandeleuria *Vandeleuria oleracea*

长尾攀鼠 Changwei Panshu—**Distinctive Characteristics:** HB 61–90; T 92–110; HF 17–18; E 11–16; GLS 19–22.6. Dorsal pelage dull rusty brown to bright reddish brown. Ventral pelage pure creamy white. Tail uniform brown

and very long, averaging 1.5 times HB length and appearing naked. The first and fifth digits of the hands and feet are shorter than the third and fourth and bear a flattened nail. Females have four pairs of mammae (two thoracic pairs and two inguinal pairs). **Distribution:** Yunnan; extending to India, Sri Lanka, Nepal, Myanmar, Thailand, Vietnam, and probably south throughout Indochina. **Natural History:** Arboreal and strictly nocturnal. Eats fruits, buds, and flowers. A very agile denizen of thick vegetation, it occurs in understory trees, shrubs, and dense grassy vegetation, and even in piles of brush. Builds a grass nest along slender branches several meters above the ground. Litter size three to six. **Conservation Status:** China RL—VU A1c. IUCN RL—LC.

GENUS *VERNAYA* (monotypic)

滇攀鼠属 Dianpanshu Shu

Vernay's Climbing Mouse *Vernaya fulva*

滇攀鼠 Dian Panshu—**Distinctive Characteristics:** HB 58–75; T 120–133; HF 18–18.5; E 17; GLS 20–22.3. A small arboreal mouse with an exceptionally long tail about twice HB length. Externally similar to *Vandeleuria*, but with a much longer tail and with pointed claws on all digits except the thumb. Dorsal pelage rich orange-brown, brighter fulvous along the sides. Hairs of ventral pelage gray-based with white tips, but only the white shows, so the ventral pelage appears pale buffy white. Tail dark brown above, slightly paler below, but not distinctly bicolored. **Distribution:** C China; extending into N Myanmar. **Natural History:** Arboreal. Specimens collected between 2,100 and 2,700 m elevation. **Conservation Status:** China RL—EN A1c. IUCN RL—LC.

FAMILY HISTRICIDAE—Old World Porcupines

豪猪科 Haozhu Ke—豪猪 Haozhu

Form stout, whole body covered with round or flat quills; tail also has quills or stiff hairs; fore and hind feet have five digits without long claws. Dental formula: 1.0.1.3/1.0.1.3 = 20. Occurs widely throughout the Indo-Malayan realm, S Palaearctric realm, and most portions of Africa. The family comprises three genera, of which two occur in China.

GENUS *ATHERURUS*—Brush-tailed Porcupines

帚尾豪猪属 Zhouweihaozhu Shu—帚尾豪猪 Zhouweihaozhu
Size small, body long, limbs stout, ears short and round; extremity of tail covered with white tufted quills, posterior portion of quills possess many "beaded" knobs; quills on dorsum flat, grooved above; quills on belly soft and fine. Distribution disrupted; occurs in both Indo-Malayan and African realms. Of two species, only one occurs in China.

Asiatic Brush-Tailed Porcupine *Atherurus macrourus*

帚尾豪猪 Zhouwei Haozhu—**Distinctive Characteristics:** HB 345–525; T 139–228; HF 64–75; E 30–36; GLS 83–120; Wt 2–4 kg. A small porcupine with a long, scaly tail that ends in a brush of white bristles over 20 cm in length. Quills grooved. Has two pairs of mammae, placed laterally. **Distribution:** Central S China; extending to India, Myanmar, Thailand, Laos, Vietnam, Malaysia, and Sumatra. **Natural History:** Found in dense forests where it constructs and occupies burrows. These burrows may connect and hold up to three individuals. May favor rocky areas. Nocturnal and generally terrestrial but known to climb trees. Diet consists of roots, tubers, and green plants. One (sometimes two) precocial young born following a 100–110 day gestation. Two litters may be produced per year. Young leave the nest after about one week, the time it takes for their quills to harden. **Conservation Status:** China RL—VU A2cd + 3cd. IUCN RL—LC.

GENUS *HYSTRIX*—Old World Porcupines

豪猪属 Haozhu Shu—豪猪 Haozhu
Form larger and stouter than *Atherurus*; tail short, less than 115 mm; sides and chest have flat quills; quills on hindquarters and tail round. Occurs broadly in S Europe, S Asia, and N Africa. Consists of eight species, one of which occurs in China.

Malayan Porcupine *Hystrix brachyura*

豪猪 Hao Zhu—**Distinctive Characteristics:** HB 558–735; T 80–115; HF 75–93; E 25–38; GLS 131–146; Wt 10–18 kg. Heavyset porcupine with very small eyes and ears. In median area between frontal and anterior dorsum, quills have light brown base and white upper portion, forming white stripes; neck possesses a white stripe; body dark brown;

quills on dorsum square at anterior portion and round at posterior portion, base and tip of quills white, middle part brown. Tail bears peculiar tubular quills with hollow tip that extend 20–30 cm in length; these rattle when tail is shaken. Has three pairs of mammae, placed laterally. **Distribution:** Broadly distributed across SE China, including Hainan Island; extending into Nepal, India (Sikkim and Assam), Myanmar, Thailand, Indochina, Malaysia, Sumatra, Borneo. **Natural History:** Occupies forests and open fields, where large burrows are dug into banks and under rocks. These burrows may be occupied by family groups that emerge at night and forage together along well-defined runways. Diet consists of roots, tubers, bark, vegetation, and fallen fruit. Although these porcupines do not "throw" their quills, when in danger they can forcefully hurl themselves backward and drive their quills into the enemy.

When alarmed they rattle the tail quills, snort, and stomp their feet. Following a gestation of about 110 days, two (sometimes three) precocial young are born. Two litters may be produced per year. **Conservation Status:** China RL—VU A2cd + 3cd. IUCN RL—LC.

ORDER LAGOMORPHA—Pikas, Rabbits, and Hares

兔形目 Tuxing Mu—鼠兔类 Shutu Lei, 兔类 Tulei
The most characteristic feature separating lagomorphs from rodents is the presence of a second, peg-like upper incisor that sits behind the large anterior incisor. Dental formula: 2.0.3.2–3/1.0.2.3 = 26–28, with a long postincisor diastema. Lagomorph means "hare-shaped"—thus signifying a characteristic posture (more pronounced in leporids than pikas). They generally have large hind feet, large ears, and small tails. Produce two types of fecal pellets (round, hard and viscous, soft, dark), and engage in coprophagy of the soft feces. Lagomorphs are found worldwide, with the exception of Australia, Oceania, and S South America, although they have been widely introduced into these regions. Includes two families, Ochotonidae and Leporidae, both represented in China.

FAMILY OCHOTONIDAE

GENUS *OCHOTONA*—Pikas

鼠兔科 Shutu Ke; 鼠兔属 Shutu Shu—鼠兔 Shutu
Small, with an egg-shaped form and soft, dense pelage; ears short and round; tail concealed (and usually not included in standard measurements); forefeet (with five digits) shorter than hind feet (four digits). Dental formula: 2.0.3.2/1.0.2.3 = 26. Pikas are diurnal, nonhibernating generalized herbivores. Some species occur in rock and talus environments; these generally are long-lived, occur in low-density populations with low turnover, and have low reproductive rates. Other species construct burrows and live in meadow or steppe environments; these usually

live at high densities with high turnover, are short-lived, and have high reproductive rates. The Ochotonidae apparently originated in Asia. Currently there are 28 species of pika, all in a single genus, *Ochotona*. Two species occur in the mountains of W North America, the remainder in Asia. China is home to 22 species of pika, the most of any country; 10 of these are endemic to China.

Alpine Pika *Ochotona alpina*

高山鼠兔 Gaoshan Shutu—**Distinctive Characteristics:** HB 152–235; HF 26–35; E 17–26; GLS 41–54; Wt 226–360 g. A large pika, although some Chinese forms are smaller than those outside of China. In summer, dorsal pelage dark or cinnamon brown; flanks have a rust-red tinge. Underneath light brown or light whitish yellow. In winter, dorsal pelage pale grayish brown, head and anterior dorsum tinged with yellow. **Distribution:** NW and NE China; extending into Kazakhstan, Russia, and Mongolia. **Natural History:** Inhabits rocky regions and crevices in forested regions at elevations greater than 2,000 m; may occupy old moss-covered scree or lacunae under tree roots. A generalized herbivore; may feed on mosses, pine nuts, and branches of trees. Constructs large haypiles (up to 30 kg/ha of vegetation may be cached). Lives in family territories (an adult pair and their young) at low density (10–12/ha). Frequently vocalizes (songs or long calls given by males during mating season, territorial calls, alarm calls). Produces two litters averaging three young. **Conservation Status:** China RL—LC. IUCN RL—LC.

Silver Pika *Ochotona argentata*

宁夏鼠兔 Ningxia Shutu—**Distinctive Characteristics:** HB 208–235; HF 31–35; E 22–25; GLS 48–52; Wt 176–236 g. In winter, the dorsum is a striking silvery color, the hairs being a pale steel gray with fine black tips. Feet white above and grayish below. Ventral pelage white, tinged with buffy. Summer pelage is bright rusty red, similar to that of *O. rutila* and *O. macrotis*. **Distribution:** Known only from the Helan Shan in Ningxia, where its range is extremely restricted to a 2 × 1.5 km ridge-top area. Endemic. **Natural History:** A rock-dwelling pika found in forested areas. It currently is only known to occupy mine tailings and also may be found living inside mines as far as 20 m from the entrance. A generalized herbivore, it constructs a typical pika haypile. Relatively unvocal in comparison with *O. pallasi* and *O. alpina*. **Conservation Status:** Its habitat has been greatly impacted within its restricted distributional range. China RL—VU D2. IUCN RL—CR B1ab(i,ii) + B2ab(i,ii).

Gansu Pika *Ochotona cansus*

间颅鼠兔 Jianlu Shutu—**Distinctive Characteristics:** HB 116–165; HF 22–29; E 14–24; GLS 33–39; Wt 50–99 g. In summer, dorsal pelage dark russet, tea brown, or dark brown to dull grayish buff (there is considerable variation through out

the geographic range); a light stripe from the chest to abdomen is somewhat inconspicuous. Ventral pelage light white, generally tinged with buffy. Winter pelage is uniformly grayish russet. **Distribution:** Highlands of C China. Endemic. **Natural History:** Occupies open areas within shrublands adjoining alpine meadow, primarily inhabiting the *Potentilla fruticosa* and *Caragana jubata* zone at 2,700–3,800 m. Constructs simple burrows with few openings. A generalized herbivore. Lives in family groups composed of an adult pair and their young in a communal burrow system. Mating system monogamous. Most behavioral interactions affiliative and expressed among family members. Four distinct vocalizations are given: male-only long calls (or songs), short calls (territorial and antipredator function), whines, and trills. May spend twice as much time surface active as *O. curzoniae*. Produces three litters of up to six young. **Conservation Status:** China RL—LC. IUCN RL—LC; but two isolated subspecies (*O. c. morosa* in Shaanxi and *O. c. sorella* in Shanxi and Ningqu) may be threatened.

Plateau Pika *Ochotona curzoniae*

高原鼠兔 Gaoyuan Shutu—**Distinctive Characteristics:** HB 140–192; HF 28–37; E 18–26; GLS 39–44; Wt 130–195 g. In summer, dorsal pelage sandy brown or dark sandy russet; ventral pelage sandy yellow or grayish white; dorsal side of ears rust colored with white margin. In winter, dorsal pelage light, sandy yellow or yellowish white, softer and longer than summer pelage. The nose has a blackish tip, with the same color extending to and ringing the lips. Feet have hairy soles; long, black claws on fore and hind feet. **Distribution:** Tibetan Plateau; extending into N Nepal and N India. **Natural History:** Lives in burrows in open alpine meadow, meadow steppe, or desert steppe at high elevations (3,000–5,000 m). Strictly herbivorous; may store vegetation during late summer to use as food over winter. Highly social; lives in well-defined and defended family burrow system territories. Family groups are composed of either an adult pair (monogamy), a male with multiple females (polygyny), or multiple males and female(s) (polyandry), along with their young from sequential litters born during the breeding season. Affiliative social interactions (such as allo-grooming, nose rubbing, sitting side-by-side) are expressed frequently within family groups, primarily among siblings of all ages and their father. They utter six different calls: the long call (or song) given only by adult males during the mating season; the soft and repetitive short call given mostly by adult females when predators have been sighted; and whines, trills, muffles, and transition calls given primarily by young animals. Young tend to remain in their family burrow system throughout their summer of birth, and dispersal—when it occurs—is normally only a short distance. The population density of the Plateau Pika increases throughout the summer with the addition of each weaned litter to family groups and may approach over 300 animals per hectare. Rate of mortality during winter is high, leading to a dispersal shuffle in early spring of surviving animals into the variable mating systems on individual family burrow system territories. Three to five litters of two to eight young are born during the summer. **Conservation Status:** The high density of Plateau Pikas and the burrows that they construct make this a keystone species in the Tibetan alpine meadow ecosystem. Nearly all predators rely on pikas for food, and their burrows serve as nesting habitat for a variety of birds and lizards. The burrowing activity also decreases erosion (allowing the soil to absorb more water during the heavy monsoon rains) and increases the rate of nutrient cycling on the meadows. Nevertheless, this species has been labeled as a pest species and poisoned over much of its geographic range in recent years. China RL—LC. IUCN RL—LC.

Daurian Pika *Ochotona dauurica*

达乌尔鼠兔 Dawu'er Shutu—
Distinctive Characteristics: HB 150–200; HF 27–33; E 16–26; GLS 39–45; Wt 110–150 g. Summer pelage yellowish brown to straw gray dorsally; ventral surface whitish with a buffy collar that continues posteriorly onto the chest. Winter pelage uniformly a pale sandy yellow, grayish russet, or sandy brown. Ears have a clear white margin; dorsal side of ears blackish brown (no rust-colored patch as in *O. curzoniae*). Pads at the ends of the toes are concealed in dense hair of the sole (unlike the exposed toes of *O. pallasi*). **Distribution:** Gobi Desert south to northern (xeric) reaches of the Tibetan Plateau; also extends north through the Gobi Desert of Mongolia and Russia. **Natural History:** Occupies desert grassland, often selecting low-lying fertile areas, where populations may be subject to flooding. Inhabits burrows. A generalized herbivore; gathers large haypiles that attract both domestic and wild ungulates as a food source. Ecology very similar to that of *O. curzoniae*. Lives in territorial family groups of breeding adults and young of the year; family burrow systems may possess as many as 15–20 entrances. Populations can reach high, but fluctuating, densities. Very social, with amicable behaviors including allo-grooming, sitting in contact, huddling, and boxing. Three discrete vocalizations (long call—primarily uttered by males—short calls, and trills). Several large lit-

ters (of up to 11 young) are produced each season. **Conservation Status:** Considered an agricultural pest and often poisoned, yet is a keystone species for biodiversity throughout its range. China RL—LC. IUCN RL—LC.

Chinese Red Pika *Ochotona erythrotis*

红耳鼠兔 Hong'er Shutu—**Distinctive Characteristics:** HB 181–285; HF 32–42; E 32–39; GLS 48–51; Wt 184–352 g. One of the flashiest pikas—in summer, dorsal pelage bright rusty red throughout, in contrast with the pure white belly, chin, legs, and feet. The large red ears are thin and sparsely furred. In winter the species becomes a drab pale gray dorsally and ventrally, although the ears retain their reddish coloration. **Distribution:** Northeastern edge of the Tibetan Plateau. Endemic. **Natural History:** Inhabits rock faces and crags; found commonly along the Huang He. May live in adobe walls. Primarily found above 2,000 m. Generalized herbivore; stores vegetation for the winter. Constructs simple burrows that extend only 1–2 m in length; has not been reported to be vocal. Produces two litters of three to seven young between May and August. **Conservation Status:** China RL—LC. IUCN RL—LC.

Forrest's Pika *Ochotona forresti*

灰颈鼠兔 Huijing Shutu—**Distinctive Characteristics:** HB 155–185; HF 27–30; E 18–23; GLS 37–41; Wt 110–148 g. In summer both dorsal and ventral pelage blackish brown or dark reddish brown; dark gray spots form behind each ear—in some forming a dorsal collar and extending onto the face, but the forehead remains brown; dorsal side of ears light chestnut with well-defined white edge. Winter pelage grayish brown dorsally, only slightly lighter ventrally. Fore claws significantly longer than in *O. thibetana*; feet dull white. **Distribution:** NW Yunnan and SE Xizang; extending into NW Myanmar, NE India, and Bhutan. In this guide, Forrest's Pika includes the Gaoligong Pika (*O. gaoligonensis*) and the Black Pika (*O. nigritia*) which were considered independent species in *A Guide to the Mammals of China*; these are sympatric color variants of Forrest's Pika. **Natural History:** Inhabits broadleaf and coniferous forests, and shrub thickets at high elevations (2,600–4,400 m) along the E Himalayan massif. Very little is known about this species. It is thought to be a burrowing pika and a generalized herbivore. **Conservation Status:** China RL—NT. IUCN RL—LC.

Glover's Pika *Ochotona gloveri*

川西鼠兔 Chuanxi Shutu—**Distinctive Characteristics:** HB 160–220; HF 31–36; E 31–39; GLS 43–53; Wt 140–300 g. Summer pelage tea brown, grayish brown, grayish russet, or grayish brown dorsally; head from rostrum to forehead orange or pale brown (in some forms tip of nose is orange-rufous and light gray patches are above eyes, like a mask; in others, cheek dark gray and rostrum smoky yellow); venter and upper side of feet grayish white, dull gray, or white; large, thinly haired ears light chestnut, orange-brown, or orange. Winter pelage similar to summer pelage but slightly lighter in color. **Distribution:** Eastern third of Tibetan Plateau. Endemic. **Natural History:** Inhabits talus and rocky clefts at high elevations (3,500–4,200 m), but it may also occur as low as 1,700 m in Sichuan. Can be found living commensally in adobe walls of villages and lamaseries. A generalized herbivore; constructs prominent haypile. Appears to be a typical rock-dwelling pika. Few details known of its biology. **Conservation Status:** China RL—LC. IUCN RL—LC.

Himalayan Pika *Ochotona himalayana*

喜马拉雅鼠兔 Ximalaya Shutu—**Distinctive Characteristics:** HB 140–186; HF 28–32; E 26–30; GLS 41–45; Wt 120–175 g. Dorsal pelage dark tea brown; dorsal side of neck and shoulders tinged with rufous-brown or dark brown spots; buffy spots present behind ears, white margin of ears obscure; ventral pelage grayish yellow; upper side of feet grayish yellow or tinged with white. **Distribution:** Lives along northern flank of Himalayas. Endemic. **Natural History:** Occupies rocky habitats (cracks in walls, precipices, and talus) along coniferous forest margins at high elevations (2,400–4,200 m). Generalized herbivore. Active primarily at dawn and dusk. Litter size ranges from three to four. A poorly known pika. **Conservation Status:** China RL—LC. IUCN RL—LC.

Tsing-Ling Pika *Ochotona huangensis*

黄河鼠兔 Huanghe Shutu—**Distinctive Characteristics:** HB 125–176; HF 23–32; E 16–24; GLS 36–41; Wt 52–108 g. Summer pelage dark brown or chestnut, dorsum tinged with conspicuous black; throat collar very pale buffy, extend-

ing as a short buffy median line to the lower chest; ears with white margin; ventral pelage drab or light ochraceous. Winter pelage mostly grayish. **Distribution:** Mountains of C China. Endemic. **Natural History:** Inhabits montane mix of conifers and broadleaf trees, birch forest, coniferous forest, and shrub meadow, occasionally grasslands, usually at elevations of less than 2,700 m (but may extend up to 4,000 m). Generalized herbivore. Constructs complicated burrows and is believed to adopt most of the normal life-history suite characteristics of burrowing pikas; otherwise poorly known. **Conservation Status:** China RL—LC. IUCN RL—LC.

Northern Pika *Ochotona hyperborea*

东北鼠兔 Dongbei Shutu—**Distinctive Characteristics:** HB 150–204; HF 22–33; E 17–22; GLS 38–43; Wt 122–190 g. In summer, dorsal pelage bright russet with some darkening from black hairs in the middle of the back; sides and belly lighter; ears grayish with a narrow white rim; in subspecies *O. h. coreana* (found in Jilin), rostrum bears black stripes above. In winter, pelage grayer, with a mixture of pale ochraceous and black dorsally and dull whitish clay ventrally. **Distribution:** NE China; extending from the Ural Mountains, Russia, to Hokkaido, Japan (widest distribution of any pika). **Natural History:** A characteristic rockdwelling pika, although it may also occupy crevices under fallen logs and in moss banks, sometimes in the shadow of forest; some populations may occur as low as 1,000 m. A generalized herbivore; known to construct a large haypile. Adult male-female pairs defend large territories on which they are sedentary; territories are large, thus population density is low. Social contact between the male and female is limited. Young disperse to fill vacancies in nearby territories. Vocalizations are loud and sharp; a long call (or song) is given by adult males, both genders utter the short call used to advertise territory occupancy and as an antipredator warning. Generally two litters with three or four young are produced each summer, although characteristically only one litter will be weaned successfully. **Conservation Status:** China RL—LC. IUCN RL—LC.

Ili Pika *Ochotona iliensis*

伊犁鼠兔 Yili Shutu—**Distinctive Characteristics:** HB 203–204; HF 42–43; E 36–37; GLS 45–48; Wt 217–250 g. A large pika; brightly colored with large rusty-red spots on the forehead and crown as well as on the sides of the neck; dorsally gray; ears well furred and edges lined with rufous. **Distribution:** Inhabits a restricted geographic range in two spurs of the Tian Shan (Xinjiang). Endemic. **Natural History:** Prefers slightly sloping rock walls containing gaps or holes, where it makes its den; generally occurs between 2,800 and 4,000 m. Generalized herbivore;

stores vegetation in haypiles.
A nonvocal pika. Individually
territorial and lives at low
population density; social
interactions uncommon.
While normally diurnal, also
can be active at night. Litter
size unknown, but assumed
small; apparently only one or
two litters born each breeding
season. **Conservation Status:** Population declining and highly fragmented. Surveys in 2002 and 2003 failed
to find any Ili Pikas in over 50% of the
localities where they had been recorded a
decade earlier. China RL—EN A2abc; C2a(i). IUCN RL—EN A2abc; C2a(i).

Koslov's Pika *Ochotona koslowi*

柯氏鼠兔 Keshi Shutu—**Distinctive Characteristics:** HB
220–240; HF 38–42; E 16–20; GLS
40–47; Wt 150–180 g. In summer, dorsum ochraceous pink; dorsal side of ears
yellowish white or buffy, with white margin; ventral pelage yellowish white or grayish white. Pelage long and thick. In winter, pelage slightly lighter, a yellowish
white. **Distribution:** Kunlun Mountains near the junction of Qinghai, Xizang,
and Xinjiang. Endemic. **Natural History:** Constructs burrows in smooth, sandy
soils in basins or mountain valleys at high elevations (4,200–4,800 m). Vegetative
habitat throughout its range characterized as high-cold grassland type (Moorcroft sedge, *Carex moocroftii*; purple flower needlegrass, *Stipa purpurea*). Generalized herbivore. Favored plants include falcate crazyweed (*Oxytropis falcate*),
rock jasmine (*Androsace acrolasia*), and creeping false tamarisk (*Myricaria
prostrata*). Behavior typical of burrowing pikas; lives in communal family groups.
Burrows are generally shallow (extending to a depth of only 30–40 cm). Lives in
colonies at high density (burrow density 44–152 per ha). Females possess four
pairs of mammae; the first pair anterior to the forelimbs. Limited data available
on reproduction, but litters of four to eight have been recorded. **Conservation
Status:** Following its original description, nearly 100 years passed before it was
rediscovered. China RL—EN B1ab(i,ii,iii). IUCN RL—EN B1ab(i,ii,iii).

Ladak Pika *Ochotona ladacensis*

拉达克鼠兔 Ladake Shutu—**Distinctive Charac-teristics:** HB 180–229; HF 34–40; E 24–33; GLS 47–51; Wt 190–288 g. In summer, dorsal pelage sandy yellowish brown, head with brown, pale brown, or reddish-brown spots; dorsal side of ear light brown or orange-brown; underparts gray or light yellowish white. In winter dorsal pelage ochraceous. **Distribution:** Along northern and western edge of the Tibetan Plateau (primarily Kunlun Mountains); extending into Kashmir. **Natural History:** A burrowing pika that occupies barren (normally xeric) alpine valleys in high mountains (4,200–5,400 m). Digs huge holes under gravel, beside shrubs, or in meadows. Generalized herbivore. May feed on roots of cushion plants in winter; its long incisors may be an adaptation for this foraging niche. Vocal, social, and lives in family groups with well-defined territories. Poorly known species. **Conservation Status:** China RL—LC. IUCN RL—LC.

Large-Eared Pika *Ochotona macrotis*

大耳鼠兔 Da'er Shutu—**Distinctive Characteristics:** HB 150–204; HF 30–33; E 27–36; GLS 34–45; Wt 142–190 g. Summer pelage pale brownish gray with an ochre tinge; head and shoulders with smoky-yellow or brown spots (S Xizang form without any brown spots); ventral pelage white to grayish white; feet white with toe pads exposed. In winter, dorsal pelage pale gray with smoky-yellow highlights. Ears more thickly furred inside than in *O. roylei*. **Distribution:** Found in high mountain ranges across W China; distributional range includes where these mountains (Tian Shan, Pamir, Hindu Kush, Himalayas) extend outside of China. **Natural History:** Inhabits rocky landscapes at high elevations (up to 6,400 m); where sympatric with *O. roylei*, it occupies the higher elevational range. Generalized herbivore. May not store vegetation in a haypile like some pika species. Lives at low density in territories occupied by a pair of breeding adults and their young. Long-lived. Development of vocal behavior weak; occasional alarm or territorial calls uttered. Usually two small litters, averaging three young, produced per year. **Conservation Status:** China RL—LC. IUCN RL—LC.

Muli Pika *Ochotona muliensis*

木里鼠兔 Muli Shutu—**Distinctive Characteristics:** HB 222; HF 35; E 30–35; GLS 50–51; Wt 235 g. In summer, dorsum grayish brown (brighter and grayer than in *O. gloveri*); rostrum and eye regions tinged with buffy; dorsal side of ears chestnut or orange-red; light spots behind ear and around tail region; chin, venter, and inguinal region grayish white; upper side of feet grayish white. **Distribution:** SW Sichuan. Endemic. **Natural History:** Inhabits grassy slopes and rocky clefts at the margins of dense coniferous forests at high elevation (3,600 m). Generalized herbivore. Poorly known pika. **Conservation Status:** China RL—VU D2. IUCN RL—DD.

Nubra Pika *Ochotona nubrica*

奴布拉鼠兔 Nubula Shutu—**Distinctive Characteristics:** HB 140–184; HF 27–35; E 21–27; GLS 37–43; Wt 96–135 g. Dorsum gray to brownish red with black hairs interspersed throughout the coat (the pelage is less saturated in the west and darkens toward the east; overall pelage less saturated than in *O. thibetana*); base of all hairs charcoal black; flanks straw gray; ventral surface dull white to yellowish; ear patches dull buffy whitish, ears blackish behind with white edges; feet brownish gray. **Distribution:** Xizang; extending south into the Himalayas (Ladakh, Nepal). **Natural History:** Found in alpine desert habitat at 3,000–4,500 m, where it constructs burrows in shrubby habitat (*Caragana, Salix, Lonicera*). Generalized herbivore. Social; lives in well-defined family group territories. Biology poorly known. **Conservation Status:** China RL—LC. IUCN RL—LC.

Pallas's Pika *Ochotona pallasi*

蒙古鼠兔 Menggu Shutu—**Distinctive Characteristics:** HB 160–220; HF 27–36; E 18–23; GLS 42–50; Wt 174–254 g. In summer, dorsal pelage sandy yellow or sandy yellowish brown; sides of neck below ears with brown or reddish-brown spots; ventral pelage dull gray or tinged with yellowish; upper side of feet creamy yellow, and toe pads bare and black (in contrast with the heavily furred feet of sympatric *O. dauurica*). In winter, dorsum light gray or grayish yellow; underparts grayish white. **Distribution:** Distributed discontinuously in the N Gobi Desert region; extending into Mongolia, Kazakhstan, and Russia. **Natural History:** Appears intermediate between obligate rock-dwelling and burrowing species of pika. It inhabits desert steppe and montane grassland, living in rocky clefts or burrowing (burrows are characterized by many entrances). Generalized herbivores; construct large haypiles. Populations may have variable densities—some reaching 100 per hectare. They are relatively long-lived (up to four years of age). Mating system polygynous, and aggressive encounters between neighboring adult males are frequent. Within a family territory, adult males and females interact rarely and construct separate haypiles. Vocal, with considerable variation among forms; populations in NE Xinjiang do not utter the long call that is characteristic of many pika species. In late summer, they collect stones that they use to close burrow entrances before the onset of winter. Many large litters (1–12 young) produced each season. Young may mature and breed in summer of birth. Gestation is 25 days. **Conservation Status:** China RL—LC. IUCN RL—LC; although two isolated subspecies (*O. p. hamica* of E Xinjiang and *O. p. sunidica* of N Nei Mongol) are considered threatened.

Royle's Pika *Ochotona roylei*

灰鼠兔 Hui Shutu—**Distinctive Characteristics:** HB 155–204; HF 25–34; E 26–32; GLS 41–46; Wt 130–180 g. Summer dorsal pelage iron gray, dark gray, or dark grayish brown; head, front, and shoulders with pale brown or reddish highlights ranging to bright chestnut; dorsal side of ear dark grayish brown, and hairs in ear short and sparse (compared to the heavily furred ears of *O. macrotis*); ventral summer pelage light white, grayish white, or dark gray; upper side of foot white or dull white, sometimes tinged with buffy. In winter, ventral pelage lighter, gray. **Distribution:** Mountainous regions of S Xizang; extending west along Himalayan massif to Kashmir. **Natural History:** Inhabits talus areas in humid hilly country characterized by rhododendrons, deodar, or spruce forests. Generally found at lower elevations (3,500–4,500 m) than *O. macrotis*. May invade rockwall huts of local people. Generalized herbivore. Caching behavior less well developed than in most pikas, but more likely to construct haypiles than *O. macrotis*. Lives in family territories composed of an adult male, adult female, and their offspring. Highly vocal, although most calls uttered are faint and difficult to hear. Can give a piercing whistle, however. Generally active at dawn and dusk. One to two litters averaging three young are produced. **Conservation Status:** China RL—LC. IUCN RL—LC.

Turkestan Red Pika *Ochotona rutila*

红鼠兔 Hong Shutu—**Distinctive Characteristics:** HB 196–230; HF 36–39; E 27–29; GLS 46–53; Wt 220–320 g. In summer, dorsal pelage bright reddish brown; dorsal side of ears grayish black; neck behind ears with white spots sometimes forming a yellowish-white collar; venter ochraceous or white but with a rusty-red transverse stripe on the chest. In winter, dorsum pale brown and ventral pelage light ochraceous or white. **Distribution:** Mountains of W Xinjiang; species occurs mostly outside of China, where it is found sporadically in the mountains of Central Asia. **Natural History:** A rock-dwelling pika that prefers the cover of large boulders at moderate elevations (normally not found higher than 3,000 m).

Generalized herbivore. Caches vegetation in haypiles like most pikas; most foraging occurs within talus rather than far from the talus-vegetation edge. Lives at low density on large family territories composed of an adult pair and their young (during the reproductive season). Most affiliative social interactions are among family members, and some (but not all) juveniles overwinter with their parents. In fall, male and female partners rarely interact, even while continuing to share the same territory. The Turkestan Red Pika is silent compared with most pikas; it has no song, no typical alarm call, and vocalizations are not used for communication among family members. Normally two litters averaging about four young are produced each season. Young do not become reproductively active in their summer of birth. **Conservation Status:** China RL—LC. IUCN RL—LC.

Moupin Pika *Ochotona thibetana*

藏鼠兔 Zang Shutu—**Distinctive Characteristics:**
HB 140–180; HF 24–32; E 17–23; GLS 36–42; Wt 72–136 g. In summer, dorsal pelage tea brown, reddish brown, dark brown, or sandy brown; a well-marked buffy collar extends across the coat and continues down the midline of the belly; otherwise ventral pelage dull gray, dull grayish yellow, ochraceous, and white; ears dark brown, their edge narrowly bordered in white; soles of feet moderately furred. In winter, dorsal coat buffy to dull brown. Larger than *O. cansus*, although still a small form. **Distribution:** Primarily mountains of E Tibetan Plateau and along Himalayan massif; extending to N Myanmar, Bhutan, and Sikkim (India). **Natural History:** A burrowing pika that characteristically inhabits rhododendron and bamboo forests at moderate elevations (can be found as low as 1,800 m) to high-elevation subalpine forests. Can occupy rocky areas under forest cover. Generalized herbivore. Stores vegetation in haypiles. A social, burrowing pika. Can be active at night. Litter size one to five. **Conservation Status:** China RL—LC. IUCN RL—LC.

Thomas's Pika *Ochotona thomasi*

狭颅鼠兔 Xialu Shutu—**Distinctive Characteristics:** HB 105–165; HF 22–29; E 17–22; GLS 33–37; Wt 45–110 g. In summer, dorsal pelage russet; underparts light white or tinged with yellow. In winter, dorsum mouse gray, the hairs with conspicuously black tips. **Distribution:** C China. Endemic. **Natural History:** Inhabits hilly shrub forest (rhododendron, *Salix, Caragana jubata, Potentilla fruticosa*) at elevations of 3,400–4,020 m. Generalized herbivore. Not well known; ecology believed to be similar to that of *O. cansus*. **Conservation Status:** China RL—NT. IUCN RL—LC.

FAMILY LEPORIDAE—Rabbits and Hares

兔科 Tu Ke—兔类 Tulei
Medium-sized, "hare-shaped," nonhibernating generalized herbivores. Ears long; short tail. Four digits on each foot, but first digit tends to be reduced on both forefoot and hind foot. Dental formula (usually): 2.0.3.3/1.0.2.3 = 28. Found worldwide, except Australia, Oceania, and S South America, areas to which leporids have been successfully introduced. The family is comprised of 11 genera, many of them monotypic and threatened with extinction; 61 species overall. Only *Lepus*, the true hares and the most successful of leporids, is represented in China.

GENUS *LEPUS*—Hares

兔属 Tu Shu—兔类 Tulei
Of the leporids, *Lepus* are the largest forms and have the longest ears and very long hind feet. Young are precocial at birth. Of 32 species of hares, 10 occur in China, two of which are endemic.

Yunnan Hare *Lepus comus*

云南兔 Yunnan Tu—**Distinctive Characteristics:** HB 322–480; T 95–110; HF 98–130; E 97–135; GLS 84–95; Wt 1,800–2,500 g. A medium-sized hare. Dorsal fur soft, long, and flat; dorsal pelage grayish pale brown or dark gray. Posterior portion of hip vaguely gray, and an ochraceous buff extends on the flanks, forelegs, and to the outer side of the hind legs. A whitish band extends from the muzzle to the base of the ear, including an arch over the eye. Top of ears black, inside of ears pale gray. Tail brownish above and without a distinct stripe, light gray tinged with yellow below. Ventral pelage white. **Distribution:** Central S China; also recorded in N Myanmar. **Natural History:** Inhabits montane meadows and shrubs at middle elevations (1,300–3,200 m); prefers warm and wet habitats; may move into forest edges or open forests. Diet consists of forbs and shrubs. There are reports that each adult has three burrows, and that those of males are smaller, shallower, and straighter than those of females. They are active during the day but primarily forage at night. Breeding normally begins in April, with the first of two or three litters appearing in May. Litter size one to four young (generally two). **Conservation Status:** China RL—NT. IUCN RL—LC.

Korean Hare *Lepus coreanus*

高丽兔 Gaoli Tu—**Distinctive Characteristics:** HB 425–490; T 60–75; HF 108–122; E 73–79; GLS 82–86; Wt 1,700 g. Medium-sized hare with thick pelage. Dorsal fur grayish yellow with brown hair tips; head same color as back. Tail light brown on top and at tip. Underneath, pure white. **Distribution:** Widespread in Korean Peninsula, extending north into S Jilin. **Natural History:** Apparently known in China from a single specimen, but is common throughout the Korean Peninsula, where it occupies lowland and mountainous habitats. **Conservation Status:** Common in neighboring Korea. China RL—LC. IUCN RL—LC.

Hainan Hare *Lepus hainanus*

海南兔 Hainan Tu—**Distinctive Characteristics:** HB 350–394; T 45–70; HF 76–96; E 76–98; GLS 73–84; Wt 1,250–1,750 g. A small hare. Pelage soft, brightly colored; dorsal pelage pale brown tinged with chestnut brown and black; sides of body mixed with pale brown and brownish white; chin and ventral pelage pure white; tail with brownish-black stripes above, white below; feet pale brown with white marks; a whitish ring circles the eye and extends back toward the base of the ear and anteriorly toward the muzzle. Winter pelage brighter than summer pelage. **Distribution:** Hainan Island; greatest density in the northwestern and southwestern parts of the island. Endemic. **Natural History:** Inhabits shrub forest and short grasslands in the low-lying plains; does not live in the mountains. A shy animal. Primarily active before midnight, with activity level dropping after midnight; occasionally seen active during the day. It has never been observed burrowing. **Conservation Status:** Extirpated from much of its former range, most likely due to habitat destruction and unsustainable harvesting. China RL—VU A2cd + A3cd; B1ab(iii). China Key List—II. IUCN RL—VU A2ac + A3cd; B1ab(iii).

Manchurian Hare *Lepus mandshuricus*

东北兔 Dongbei Tu—**Distinctive Characteristics:** HB 410–540; T 50–80; HF 110–145; E 75–118; GLS 79–89; Wt 1,400–2,600 g. Pelage soft, long, and thick. Dorsal pelage grayish black to blackish brown to rust brown; breast, flanks, and legs cinnamon; ears ochraceous; neck dull rust brown. Belly whitish, and tail blackish brown above, dull white below. In winter appears lighter, with some individuals ash gray. Frequently includes melanistic (black) individuals, and these have been misidentified and assigned as *L. melainus*. **Distribution:** NE China; extending into Russia and perhaps North Korea. **Natural History:** Mainly inhabits coniferous and broadleaf forests, particularly where tall Mongolian oaks occur with an undergrowth of Manchurian hazelnuts, at elevations between 300 and 900 m. Does not like open valleys or grasslands, and shies away from human habitation. Is replaced by *L. tolai* in areas cleared of forest, and can be sympatric with *L. timidus*. Feeds on bark and twigs of willow, linden, maple, apple, birch, and elm, as well as various shrubs, herbs, and fallen fruit. Appears to represent the Old World equivalent of the Snowshoe Hare (*L. americanus*) in North America. A very shy animal, it is presumably solitary. Does not bed down in lairs in the open; rather it settles in holes in tree trunks. Nocturnal, but also active at dawn. Litter size small, usually only one or two and occasionally as large as five. Breeding begins in April, with young first appearing in May. **Conservation Status:** China RL—LC. IUCN RL—LC.

Woolly Hare *Lepus oiostolus*

高原兔 Gaoyuan Tu—**Distinctive Characteristics:** HB 400–580; T 65–125; HF 102–140; E 105–155; GLS 84–100; Wt 2,000–4,250 g. A stocky hare. Pelage thick and soft; tips of hairs mostly curved so that dorsal pelage is wavelike and curly. Ears largest among the Chinese hares; dark at tips. Dorsal pelage sandy yellow, light pale brown, dark yellowish brown, or tea brown; hip with a large silvery-gray, dull gray, lead-gray, or brownish-gray spot, obviously different from the color of the dorsal pelage. Bushy tail white above, except for a brown-gray narrow stripe on the dorsal surface, and white below. There is a whitish ring around the eye. Muzzle elongated and narrow. **Distribution:** Across central and western highlands of China; extending into Ladakh, Nepal, and Sikkim (India). **Natural History:** Found primarily in upland grasslands of various types, montane meadow, shrub meadow, and alpine cold desert, generally at elevations above 3,000 m to as high as 5,300 m. Southeastern populations inhabit montane coniferous and broadleaf mixed forests. Primarily eats grasses and herbaceous plants. Shy and solitary, although it may be seen foraging in small groups during the mating season. Activity is usually confined to a restricted area, where the same individual can be seen night after night. While primarily nocturnal, this hare can be seen active during the day. Will rest in quiet, low areas exposed to the sun but sheltered from the wind during the day. Molts only once per year. Breeding begins in April and produces two litters of four to six young. **Conservation Status:** China RL—LC. IUCN RL—LC.

Chinese Hare *Lepus sinensis*

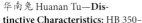

华南兔 Huanan Tu—**Distinctive Characteristics:** HB 350–450; T 40–57; HF 81–111; E 60–82; GLS 67–93; Wt 1,025–1,938 g. A small hare with short ears. Overall, the animal has a rather uniform but rich color, with short, straight, and sometimes coarse fur. Dorsum and head sandy pale brown, dark pale brown, or grayish yellow, often with chestnut or rufous tones; tail color same chestnut-rufous as the back. Underside ochraceous buff, not contrasting sharply with the back. Tips of the ears have black triangular markings; a ring is present around the eyes. Winter pelage yellowish mixed with black-tipped hairs. **Distribution:** SE China, including Taiwan; extends into N Vietnam. **Natural History:** Lives in open-edge grassland habitat and scrubby vegetation in hill country. Can occur at up to 4,000–5,000 m in bamboo. Eats leafy plants, other green shoots, and twigs. Does not dig its own burrow, rather utilizes those made by other animals. Occupied burrows usually have a smooth opening, and pellets are piled outside the entrance. Nocturnal, although can be seen active during the day. Females breed from April until August, giving birth within their burrows. Litter size averages three precocial young. **Conservation Status:** China RL—LC. IUCN RL—LC.

Desert Hare *Lepus tibetanus*

藏兔 Zang Tu—**Distinctive Characteristics:** HB 401–480; T 87–109; HF 109–135; E 81–110; GLS 84–92; Wt 1,625–2,500 g. A slender-bodied hare with a relatively small head. Dorsal pelage sandy yellow or drab tinged with blackish; hip grayish, and outside of hind leg and forefeet white; ears wide, with tufted hairs anteriorly, tip of ear black-brown; tail with black-brown dorsal stripes; eye surrounded by light ring. Underparts pale yellow to white. In winter, pelage thick and a grayer sandy-brown color. **Distribution:** Across NW China; extending into S Siberia and west into Pakistan and Afghanistan. **Natural History:** Occupies desert, semidesert, and steppe, where it is found in grassland or shrubby habitats on the slopes of riverbanks; does not occupy alpine grasslands, although it may extend into the subalpine belt (3,500–4,000 m). Eats herbaceous plants, seeds, berries, roots, and twigs. Mainly active at dusk but can also be seen during the day. Does not construct its own burrow. Breeds up to three times each year; litter size 3–10. **Conservation Status:** China RL—LC. IUCN RL—LC.

Mountain Hare *Lepus timidus*

雪兔 Xue Tu—**Distinctive Characteristics:** HB 452–620; T 50–75; HF 135–165; E 80–110; GLS 87–106; Wt 2,140–2,700 g. Large hare. Pelage straight and coarse; ears short, obviously shorter than hind feet; tail short and usually all white in summer and winter. Summer pelage brown, pale brown, or ochraceous pale brown; dorsal hairs light brown or dull gray above, light grayish white below; winter pelage wholly white except for black-tipped ears. Has four pairs of mammae. **Distribution:** NW and NE China; extends across Palearctic from Scandinavia to E Siberia and Hokkaido (Japan). **Natural History:** Inhabits coniferous forest of subarctic zone, in particular grass habitats in open pine, birch, and juniper forests or along rivers. Eats twigs, buds, and bark of birch, juniper, poplar, and willow; also palatable berries, grasses, and clovers when available. Tends to forage in a fixed area. Is more social than other hares and often gathers to feed in the same place in groups of 20–100. May live in pairs. Nocturnal, yet may show increased daylight activity in summer when nights are short. Life span may extend 8–10 years. Molts twice per year; the spring molt is quite extended. May burrow 1–2 m into hillsides or lie in a shallow depression under vegetation for cover. In winter may burrow into the snow to a depth of 100–120 cm. Mating begins in early spring, and first litters normally appear in May. Produces one or two litters of three to six precoital young. Gestation is about 50 days. **Conservation Status:** China RL—LC. China Key List—II. IUCN RL—LC.

summer coat

winter coat

Tolai Hare *Lepus tolai*

托氏兔 Tuoshi Tu—**Distinctive Characteristics:** HB 400–590; T 72–110; HF 110–127; E 83–120; GLS 80–88; Wt 1,650–2,650 g. Coloration is variable across

the species range in China. Dorsal pelage is sandy yellow, pale brown, dusty yellow, or sandy gray, interspersed with dark brown and laurel-red stripes; hip grayish to ochraceous (southern forms); tail with broad black or blackish-brown stripe above, wholly white below and at sides; eye surrounded by a grayish-white area (ochraceous in southern forms) tending back to the base of the ear and forward toward the muzzle; tips of ears black. Ventral pelage pure white. **Distribution:** NW, C, and NE China; extends from Central Asia across S Siberia and Mongolia. **Natural History:** Occupies grasslands and forest meadows (never true forests); prefers tall grass or shrubby areas for the cover they provide. Generally found at lower elevations (600–900 m). Eats grass, roots, and herbaceous plants. Nocturnal. Does not burrow (except to give birth) but creates a shallow depression using its front paws for resting; the depth of these depressions is shallower during hot weather and deeper when it is cold and windy. It may remain motionless and hide in the depression for as long as possible before running from approaching danger. Utilizes fixed (and restricted) routes while foraging. Reproduces two or three times each year; litter size two to six young. **Conservation Status:** China RL—LC. IUCN RL—LC.

Yarkand Hare *Lepus yarkandensis*

塔里木兔 Talimu Tu—**Distinctive Characteristics:** HB 285–430; T 55–86; HF 90–110; E 90–110; GLS 76–88; Wt 1,100–1,900 g. Somewhat small; pelage short and straight; dorsal pelage sandy brown interspersed with many grayish-black stripes; ears relatively long, tips not black; tail light smoke gray or similar to dorsal pelage, white or creamy yellowish white along the sides and below. Ventral pelage wholly white. Winter pelage lighter, light sandy brown above. **Distribution:** Xinjiang. Endemic. **Natural History:** Inhabits internal basins and various desert sites, largely in tamarisk and poplar forests along the margins of rivers. Frequently uses reed vegetation along rivers for cover. Active from dawn until midmorning, then again in the late afternoon; may also forage at night. Hides in shallow depressions under vegetation during the day. Utilizes traditional routes while foraging, and these routes can be as long as 1–2 km. Significant genetic subdivision occurs among isolated populations throughout the Tarim Basin. Breeding begins in February and may extend seven or eight months; two or three litters of two to five young produced annually. **Conservation Status:** While locally common, may be of conservation concern because of habitat patchiness, habitat loss, and unsustainable harvest. China RL—VU A1cd. China Key List—II. IUCN RL—NT.

ORDER ERINACEOMORPHA

FAMILY ERINACEIDAE—Hedgehogs and Gymnures

猬目 Wei Mu; 猬科 Wei Ke—刺猬 Ciwei
Although previously included in the order Insectivora along with the moles and shrews, the hedgehogs and gymnures are now thought to represent a separate, distantly related clade—the Erinaceomorpha, represented by a single family, the Erinaceidae. The fore and hind limbs possess five toes (but some genera outside China have four toes); eyes and ears are well developed; habits are terrestrial. The hedgehogs belong to the subfamily Erinaceinae and are most easily recognized by a dorsal covering of protective quills. The gymnures, subfamily Galericinae, lack quills but have the ability to secrete an offensive scent for protection. The family Erinaceidae is found throughout Asia, Europe, and Africa. Both subfamilies, Erinaceinae and Galericinae, are represented in China.

SUBFAMILY ERINACEINAE—Hedgehogs

猬亚科 Ciwei Yake—刺猬 Ciwei
Dorsal surface covered in a distinctive coat of stiff spines; nose elongated; neck and tail short, and posture crouched, giving these animals a distinctly compact appearance. The Erinaceinae comprises five genera and 16 species; of these, three genera and four species occur in China.

GENUS *ERINACEUS*—Eurasian Hedgehogs

刺猬属 Ciwei Shu—刺猬 Ciwei
Dorsal surface covered with sharp, stiff, smooth quills, hind feet have well-developed first digit (big toe); ears short, not longer than quills on top of head. Dental formula: 3.1.3.3/2.1.2.3 = 36. Broadly distributed in Europe and Asia. Of four species of *Erinaceus*, one occurs in China.

Amur Hedgehog *Erinaceus amurensis*

东北刺猬 Dongbei Ciwei—**Description:** HB 158–287; T 17–42; HF 34–54; E 16–26; GLS 47–58; Wt 600–1,000 g. Head, dorsum, and sides covered with long, pointed spines; tail very short. Ventral hair consistently light, and face usually light. Quills on dorsum have two kinds of coloration: one is wholly white; the other has white or yellowish-brown basal and terminal bands and a brown or dark brown middle band, producing an overall light brownish-gray dorsal color, including limbs and sides. Spines on top of head separated by a narrow bare space. **Distribution:** C and E China; extending to Russia and Korea. **Natural History:** Occupies a variety of habitats, including villages and city parks, all kinds of croplands, deciduous forests and shrublands, mesic steppes, woodland steppes, montane terrain, lower-level coniferous forests, and subalpine habitats. It does not live in dark taiga forests in N Manchuria. Nocturnal. Forages on ground-dwelling invertebrates, especially fly larvae. Hibernates in winter, entering torpor in October and emerging in spring. There are one or two litters per year, with four to six young per litter. **Conservation Status:** China RL—LC. IUCN RL—LC.

GENUS *HEMIECHINUS*—Desert Hedgehogs

大耳猬属 Da'erwei Shu—大耳猬 Da'erwei
Size small; ears large, clearly projecting above the surrounding spines; ventral pelage soft; surface of spines faintly grooved; hind feet with first digits small. Distributed from N Africa eastward through the Near East and Central Asia to Mongolia, N and W China, and southward to Pakistan and NW India. Of two species of *Hemiechinus*, one lives in China.

Long-Eared Hedgehog *Hemiechinus auritus*

大耳猬 Da'er Wei—**Description:** HB 170–230; T 18–28; HF 32–39; E 31–40; GLS 44–48; Wt 280–500 g. Size small; ears large and pale, projecting above quills. Dorsum sandy beige; forehead, cheeks, and upper part of head pale rusty; ventral pelage soft and fine; surface on spines faintly grooved. **Distribution:** NW

China; extending to Mongolia, Ukraine, Libya, and W Pakistan. **Natural History:** Inhabits semiarid steppes and shrublands throughout its broad geographic range but is less tolerant of true desert conditions. It also occurs in croplands of various sorts. It feeds mainly on insects and other invertebrates, but frogs, snakes, lizards, and small mammals are also taken, as well as both wild and cultivated fruits, such as melons. Nocturnal. It digs its own burrows with its long-clawed forefeet in many substrates (sand, clay, rocky) as daytime refuges, in which a single litter of four to seven young is born during the warm season. By October, these hedgehogs retire to their burrows and hibernate until the coming of spring. May fall prey to small carnivores such as foxes and to raptors such as the Eurasian Eagle Owl. **Conservation Status:** China RL—NT. IUCN RL—LC.

GENUS *MESECHINUS*—Steppe Hedgehogs

林猬属 Linwei Shu—刺猬 Ciwei
Ears equal in length to quills or slightly longer; the first toe on hind foot is small; none of the dorsal quills are nearly wholly white. Both species of *Mesechinus* occur in China.

Daurian Hedgehog *Mesechinus dauuricus*

达乌尔猬 Da'wu'er Wei—
Description: HB 175–250; T 14–15; E 25–29; GLS 52; Wt 500 g. Size slightly larger than *Erinaceus* and *Hemiechinus*. Ears projecting above spines on head; no wholly white spines among darker ones. Dorsal pelage rather coarse; surface of spines not grooved, but covered with small papillae, 3–5 mm at the end; penis spines long and slender, some with hooks; dorsum light brown. Dental formula: 3.1.3.3/2.1.2.3 = 36. **Distribution:** C and NE China; extending to Mongolia and Russia (Amur Basin). **Natural History:** Inhabits grassland habitat in the dry steppe zone. Diet includes small mammals, lizards, and insects. Hibernates. Produces litters of three to seven young in late spring to early summer. **Conservation Status:** China RL—VU A2cd. IUCN RL—LC.

Hugh's Hedgehog *Mesechinus hughi*

林猬 Lin Wei—**Description:** HB 155–200. Ears shorter than spines; spines and pelage dark; white ring present at tip of darker spines. Pelage on spineless area coarser than in *M. dauuricus*, darker brown; spines smooth. **Distribution:** C China. Endemic. **Natural History:** A very poorly known species, and very rare in museum collections. The species occurs in sympatry with *Erinaceus amurensis* in the Chingling mountains in Shaanxi, where both inhabit low-elevation coniferous forest and subalpine habitats. **Conservation Status:** China RL—VU A2cd. IUCN RL—LC.

SUBFAMILY GALERICINAE—Gymnures

毛猬亚科 Maowei Yake—毛猬 Maowei
Pelage without stiff spines. Most forms appear small and shrewlike. Tail nearly bare. Galericinae contains five genera, of which three occur in China.

GENUS *HYLOMYS*—Gymnures

毛猬属 Maowei Shu—毛猬 Maowei
Appearance shrewlike to ratlike, but size variable; rostrum sharp, ears well developed, tail short; pelage on the body surface hairy. Of three species of *Hylomys*, one occurs in China.

Short-Tailed Gymnure *Hylomys suillus*

毛猬 Maowei—**Description:** HB 120–150; T 19; HF 23–25; E 12–15; GLS 31–33. Appearance ratlike, slightly stouter; rostrum pointed. Dorsal hairs rusty black; ventral pelage buffy, lighter than dorsal; dorsum sometimes shows faint black lines. Two pairs of mammae, one pair inguinal, one pair thoracic. Tail short, subequal to hind foot length and shorter than in other species of *Hylomys*, about 10–15% of HB length. Ears short, about 10% of HB length. Distinguished from rodents of similar size and shape in lacking paired, curving, chisel-shaped teeth at front of mouth; have instead paired, nearly straight, conical incisor teeth at front of mouth, separated by a distinct space. Dental formula: 3.1.4.3/3.1.4.3 = 44. **Distribution:** SE Yunnan; extending through Indochina and peninsular Malaysia. **Natural History:** Appears to be confined to hill and mountain forests with dense understory and ground litter. Reported to form runways and burrows but may climb up into shrubs, perhaps foraging for fruits such as *Ficus* and *Melastoma*. However, its main foods are obtained from ground litter and the soil: arthropods, snails, and earthworms. A pregnant female with two embryos was caught in late February at an elevation of 500 m. Others report litter sizes of three to six, and elevational ranges up to 3,500 m. Litter size and breeding season probably vary with season and elevation. **Conservation Status:** China RL—VU B1ab(i,ii,iii). IUCN RL—LC.

GENUS *NEOHYLOMYS* (monotypic)

海南新毛猬属 Hainanxin Maowei Shu

Hainan Gymnure *Neohylomys hainanensis*

海南新毛猬 Hainanxin Maowei—**Description:** HB 132–147; T 36–43; HF 24–29; E 17–22; GLS 33–36; Wt 52–70 g. Tail longer than in *Hylomys suillus*; tail about 30% of HB length, evidently longer than hind feet. Form hedgehog-like, slightly stouter, rostrum pointed; first upper canine somewhat enlarged. Dental formula: 3.1.4.3/3.1.3.3 = 42, but variable. Hairs mouse gray, lighter than in *H. suillus*, tinged with yellowish brown; black lines on anterior midback faintly present. **Distribution:** Hainan Island. Endemic. **Natural History:** Described as "vole-like" and known to construct burrows. Occupies tropical rain forest and subtropical forest. Very poorly known. **Conservation Status:** China RL—EN B1ab(i,ii,iii) (as *Hylomys*). IUCN RL—EN B1ab(iii).

GENUS *NEOTETRACUS* (monotypic)

駒猬属 Qu Wei Shu

Shrew Gymnure *Neotetracus sinensis*

駒猬 Qu Wei—**Description:** HB 91–125; T 56–78; HF 21–36; E 14–18; GLS 27–32. Shrewlike in appearance; tail longer than in either of the other two gymnures, about 50% of HB length; ears long, about 15% of HB length. Dorsum a dull olive brown; ventral pelage gray, tinged with light yellow. Rostrum short, postorbital process robust and projecting. Dental formula: 3.1.3.3/3.1.3.3 = 40. **Distribution:** Central S China; extending to Myanmar, Vietnam. **Natural History:** This species inhabits subtropical evergreen forest at higher elevations

(1,500–2,700 m) than *Hylomys suillus*. These forms appear to be allopatric to parapatric in distribution. They are probably ground foragers that subsist on forest-floor invertebrates (ants, caterpillars, earthworms) and vegetable matter. The species utilizes runways and burrows along moss- and fern-covered banks and under logs, rocks, or any other good cover. **Conservation Status:** China RL—LC. IUCN RL—LC.

ORDER SORICOMORPHA—Shrews and Moles

駒鼱目 Qujing Mu—駒鼱 Qujing
Shrews and moles were formerly included in the order Insectivora, along with tenrecs, golden moles, solenodons, and hedgehogs, but recent evidence suggests this to be a paraphyletic clade. Taxa previously united within an all-inclusive Insectivora are now generally regarded as constituting three orders in two clades: an African clade including the tenrecs and golden moles (order Afrosoricida), and a Holarctic clade including the hedgehogs and gymnures (order Erinaceomorpha) and the shrews, moles, and allies (order Soricomorpha). The Soricomorpha comprises four families—Nesophontidae, Solenodontidae, Soricidae, and Talpidae; the latter two are represented in China. Shrews and moles are rarely observed in the wild, and most of what is known of their natural history comes from trapping data.

FAMILY SORICIDAE—Shrews

駒鼱科 Qujing Ke—駒鼱 Qujing
Size small, many smaller than most mice; pelage fine and thick; head and rostrum pointed; body and limbs slender, and claws very small; a few aquatic species have fringes of hairs or webs on toes; eyes small; ears short but visible. Lateral scent glands present. Mainly insectivorous, terrestrial, and plantigrade, but some develop arboreal, semiaquatic, or semisubterranean habits. Shrews have high metabolic rates and are active both day and night. Of three subfamilies, two occur in China: Soricinae and Crocidurinae.

SUBFAMILY CROCIDURINAE—Crocidurine Shrews

麝鼱亞科 Shequ Yake—麝鼱 Shequ
The Crocidurinae are distributed in Asia, Europe, and Africa. Of nine genera, two occur in China.

GENUS *CROCIDURA*—White-toothed Shrews

麝鼱屬 Shequ Shu—麝鼱 Shequ
Size typical of Soricidae. Distributed in Asia, Africa, and Europe; most species concentrated in tropical and subtropical zones; a few species occur in N Europe. Of the 172 species of *Crocidura*, 11 are known from China. Many species of *Crocidura* are very similar in external morphology, differing mainly in body size and relative length of tail, and the hairiness of the tail. Identification of these forms is

difficult in the hand, and some currently recognized species probably represent complexes of more than one species.

Asian Gray Shrew *Crocidura attenuata*

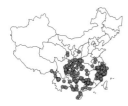

灰麝鼩 Hui Shequ—**Distinctive Characteristics:** HB 66–89; T 41–60; HF 13–16; E 7–13; GLS 19–22; Wt 6–12 g. Tail relatively short (usually 60–70% of HB length); hind foot usually less than 16 mm. Dorsal pelage smoky brown to dark grayish black, gradually merging into dark gray on venter; summer pelage darker; tail dark brown above and lighter below, but the contrast is not strong. Throughout its range it is often the most commonly captured shrew. **Distribution:** Widespread in C and SE China; extending to India (Assam, Sikkim), Nepal, Bhutan, Myanmar, Thailand, Vietnam, peninsular Malaysia. **Natural History:** A common shrew found in all kinds of habitats: lowland rain forest, bamboo forest, herbaceous vegetation, scrub, and montane forest, to elevations approaching 3,000 m. Little is known about breeding in this species, but litter sizes of four and five have been noted. **Conservation Status:** China RL—LC. IUCN RL—LC.

Southeast Asian Shrew *Crocidura fuliginosa*

长尾大麝鼩 Changweida Shequ—**Distinctive Characteristics:** HB 79–105; T 62–89; HF 15–19; E 10; GLS 22–25; Wt 13 g. A very large, long-tailed shrew; tail usually more than 80% of HB length, at its longest about 90% of HB length. Dorsal pelage smoky brown to dark grayish black, gradually merging into dark gray on the venter; tail dark brown above and lighter below, but the contrast is not strong. **Distribution:** C and S China; extending to N India, Myanmar, peninsular Malaysia, and Vietnam. **Natural History:** This species tends to be found below 3,000 m and appears to be restricted to river valleys and foothills. **Conservation Status:** China RL—LC. IUCN RL—LC.

Gmelin's Shrew *Crocidura gmelini*

北小麝鼩 Beixiao Shequ—**Distinctive Characteristics:** HB 52–72; T 25–42; HF 11–14; GLS 17–18. Nearly as small as *C. shantungensis*, but ventral pelage lighter gray and tail often shorter. **Distribution:** NW Xinjiang; extending through Mongolia, Kazakhstan, Uzbekistan, Afghanistan, Pakistan,

Turkmenistan, Iran, and to Israel. **Natural History:** Adapted to arid habitats, including salt-grass plains and sand dunes; tamarisk shrubs growing on low sandy mounds; and ecotones between tamarisk and salt grass. Also inhabits thick riparian vegetation along the Yarkand River and arid, grassy steppe environments. **Conservation Status:** China RL—VU B1ab(i,ii,iii). IUCN RL—LC.

Indochinese Shrew *Crocidura indochinensis*

南小麝鼩 Nanxiao Shequ—**Distinctive Characteristics:** HB 66; T 47–50; HF 12–13; E 9–11; GLS 17–18. Similar to *C. wuchihensis*, but larger. **Distribution:** S China; extending to Myanmar, N. Thailand, and Vietnam. **Natural History:** Inhabits montane forests from 1,200 to 2,400 m. **Conservation Status:** China RL—VU A3c; B1ab(i,ii,iii) (as *C. horsfieldii*). IUCN RL—LC.

Ussuri White-Toothed Shrew *Crocidura lasiura*

大麝鼩 Da Shequ—**Distinctive Characteristics:** HB 68–104; T 28–47; HF 15–23. A large shrew; dorsal pelage long and dense, blackish to dark brown merging into brownish gray on lateral surface; venter slate gray; tail thick and nearly monocolored. Size largest and tail relatively the shortest in this genus; tail about 45% of HB length. **Distribution:** NE China; a Palaearctic species restricted to NE Asia. **Natural History:** Occupies broadleaf forest, forest glades, bogs, dry meadows, and shrubby thickets along the banks of rivers and lakes; also in agricultural fields and roadside verges overgrown with sagebrush. Nutrition is based on animal foods. Its diet is predominantly insects and other invertebrates, and small vertebrate animals. Females may produce litters containing as many as 10 embryos, and it is believed that they reproduce throughout the spring–summer period. **Conservation Status:** China RL—VU B1ab(i,ii,iii). IUCN RL—LC.

Chinese White-Toothed Shrew *Crocidura rapax*

华南中麝鼩 Huananzhong Shequ—**Distinctive Characteristics:** HB 56–70; T 38–47; HF 11–13; GLS 17.4–18.3. Similar in general form to *C. vorax*, but dorsal pelage much darker brown, and ventral pelage nearly as dark but grayish brown; tail not bicolored, dark brown over entire length, or nearly so; long sensory hairs sparse, restricted to basal third of tail. **Distribution:** S China, including Hainan Island and Taiwan; extending to India and other bordering countries. **Natural History:** Information lacking. **Conservation Status:** China RL—LC. IUCN RL—DD.

Asian Lesser White-Toothed Shrew *Crocidura shantungensis*

山东小麝鼩 Shandong Xiaoshequ—**Distinctive Characteristics:** HB 51–65; T 35–43; HF 10–13; GLS 15.5–17. Smallest white-toothed shrew in Eurasia; similar in size to *C. wuchihensis*, but has lighter pelage than that species and is distributed farther to the north; tail very short, less than 70% of HB length, and broad at base, tapering to tip, and bearing a scattering of long sensory hairs. **Distribution:** Widely distributed from C to E and NE China, including Taiwan; extending to E Russia and Korea. **Natural History:** With such an extensive range, this species has been recorded in a wide variety of habitats. In the western section of its distribution, it is found in semidesert grasslands, while farther to the north it occupies steppe biotopes and the southern fringe of coniferous forest and mixed broadleaf forest. In the south-central portion of its range it occurs in montane forests, while along the southeastern edge it occupies the heavily agricultural Yangtze River valley. **Conservation Status:** China RL—LC. IUCN RL—LC.

Siberian Shrew *Crocidura sibirica*

西伯利亚麝鼩 Xiboliya Shequ—**Distinctive Characteristics:** HB 58–80; T 30–39; HF 10–13; GLS 18–20; Wt 50–96 g. Size medium, but tail quite short, usually less than half of HB length; tail uniformly colored dark brown; color of pelage lighter than that of other white-toothed shrews: dorsum dark brownish gray; venter whitish gray, sharply delineated. **Distribution:** NW China; extending to Mongolia and Central Asia. **Natural History:** Found in a variety of habitats within its rather limited range, due to the range of elevations it occupies. These habitats include montane coniferous forest, streamside meadows with thickets of willow and birch and aspen groves, dark taiga with ground cover of diverse herbaceous plants, swampy lakeshores and flooded meadows, and creek valleys. Known to occupy mole tunnels. Principal diet insects; stomach contents have contained a variety of beetles and orthopterans. **Conservation Status:** China RL—VU A3c; B1ab(i,ii,iii) + 2ab(i,ii,iii). IUCN RL—LC.

Taiwanese Gray Shrew *Crocidura tanakae*

台湾麝鼩 Taiwan Shequ—**Distinctive Characteristics:** HB 70–86; T 47–62; HF 12–14.5; E 8–10; GLS 20–22. Very similar to *C. attenuata*. **Distribution:** Taiwan. Endemic. **Natural History:** A common species occurring in grassland, secondary forest, bamboo thickets, and pastures from sea level to 2,200 m. Females with one or two embryos have been found in March and August, and with two or three embryos in February. **Conservation Status:** China RL–LC. IUCN RL—LC.

Voracious shrew *Crocidura vorax*

西南中麝鼩 Xinanzhong Shequ—**Distinctive Characteristics:** HB 54–90; T 41–51; HF 11–14; GLS 18.8. Dorsum light grayish brown; venter gray and only slightly lighter than the dorsal surface. Similar to *C. rapax*, but larger and much paler in both dorsal and ventral coloration. Individual dorsal hairs are tricolored, and there is a pale band toward the tips of the individual hairs that give the pelage its paler look. Tail distinctly bicolored. **Distribution:** Central S China; extending to India, Thailand, Laos, and Vietnam. **Natural History:** A highland species. The holotype was captured in timberline forest on Ssu Shan (Snow Mountain) at 4,000 m. Poorly known. **Conservation Status:** China RL—VU B1ab(i,ii,iii) + 2ab(i,ii,iii). IUCN RL—LC.

Wuchi Shrew *Crocidura wuchihensis*

五指山麝鼩 Wuzhishan Shequ—**Distinctive Characteristics:** HB 55–65; T 35–42; HF 10–13; E 6–9; GLS 15–17; Wt 3.5–6 g. Dorsal pelage dark grayish brown, individual hairs slate gray at base but brownish near their ends and sometimes tipped with silvery gray; ventral pelage somewhat grayer; dorsal surfaces of hands and feet whitish, with brown pigmentation evident laterally; tail brown, with long bristles along the proximal half. Similar to *C. indochinensis*. **Distribution:** Hainan Island and perhaps Yunnan; extending to Vietnam and Laos. **Natural History:** Little known; specimens have been captured in forests between 1,300 and 1,500 m. **Conservation Status:** China RL—VU A3c; B1ab(i,ii,iii) (as *C. horsefieldii*). IUCN RL—DD.

GENUS *SUNCUS*—Musk Shrews

臭鼩属 Chouqu Shu— 臭鼩 Chouqu
Either larger or smaller than typical size of Soricidae; white teeth. Distributed in Old World tropical and subtropical zones. Of 18 species of *Suncus*, two are reported from China.

Etruscan Shrew *Suncus etruscus*

小臭鼩 Xiao Chouqu—**Distinctive Characteristics:** HB 43–53; T 20–31; HF 6–9; E 4.5–6; GLS 13–14; Wt 2–3 g. This species is the smallest of the known mammals in China. Dorsal pelage dark grayish brown, ventral pelage pale gray; fur short, velvety; tail bicolored, darker above. **Distribution:** SW Yunnan (known only from Gengma County); extending throughout Indochina, India, and Sri Lanka, across Central Asia, to Europe and N Africa. **Natural History:** Poorly known in China. Observations from throughout its range indicate that it occupies open grasslands, scrub, and deciduous woodlands where it occurs under logs and rocks or in similar crevices. It also frequents human habitations. Diet consists of small insects, such as termites. **Conservation Status:** China RL—CR B1ab(i,iii) + 2ab(i,ii,iii). IUCN RL—LC.

Asian House Shrew *Suncus murinus*

臭鼩 Chouqu—**Distinctive Characteristics:** HB 119–147; T 60–85; HF 19–22; GLS 30. Largest shrew in China. Snout long, with profuse, soft vibrissae; ear naked, prominently "crumpled" in appearance; fur short, dense, and velvety, usually ash gray in color, but darker morphs are sometimes seen. Body pelage varies from blackish to brownish to light bluish gray dorsally, with underparts slightly paler; tail long and heavy, with long, coarse hairs thinly scattered along its length; scent glands on the flanks are surrounded by stiff hairs pointing inward, most prominent in the breeding season. **Distribution:** C and SE China, including Hainan Island and Taiwan; extending to Japan, continental and peninsular Indo-Malayan region, Myanmar, Bhutan, Nepal, Sri Lanka, India, Pakistan, and Afghanistan. **Natural History:** Commensal forms of this species are usually found in or near human habitation, in grain storehouses, and in cultivated fields. Wild forms, in contrast, occupy sparse vegetation, both shrubs and forest, often far from a significant human presence. They seem to favor moist habitats, being especially abundant in swamps and around ponds. House shrews are omnivorous, eating seeds and fruit as well as insects and other invertebrates. They occasionally attack large frogs and snakes (up to 46 cm length), but they concentrate on insects such as crickets, cockroaches, and dipterans (taken in flight). There are two breeding seasons per year, the first premonsoonal and the second toward the end of the monsoon (roughly April–June and August–October). Litter size is one to five, averaging three or four young. Young are weaned in about three weeks but remain with the mother for another two to three weeks, moving about by "caravaning." **Conservation Status:** China RL—LC. IUCN RL—LC.

SUBFAMILY SORICINAE—Red-toothed Shrews

鼩鼱亚科 Qujing Yake—鼩 Qujing
The Soricinae is distributed mainly in Asia, Europe, and North America. The Soricinae can be divided into six tribes, four of which are represented in China. In all, there are 12 genera and 148 species; nine genera and 39 species occur in China.

GENUS *ANOUROSOREX*—Mole Shrews

短尾鼩属 Duanweiqu Shu—短尾鼩 Duanwei Qu
This genus is the only one of the Soricinae that is fully adapted to a life underground, although *Blarinella* and *Soriculus nigrescens* and *Sorex unguiculatus* are partially so. Rostrum blunt and projecting; forefeet with well-developed claws; tail very short, shorter than hind feet; tail with no hair but covered with scales; eyes and external ears very reduced; ear pinnae hidden in pelage. Mainly distributed in SE Asia. Of four species, two occur in China.

Chinese Mole Shrew *Anourosorex squamipes*

短尾鼩 Duanwei Qu—
Distinctive Characteristics:
HB 74–110; T 8–19; HF 11–16; E 0; GLS 23–26. Body fur dense and lax; color dark grayish brown, uniform dorsally and laterally, ventral surface only slightly lighter; tail extremely short and thin; forefeet have somewhat lengthened claws. **Distribution:** Central S China; extending to N Vietnam, Thailand, Myanmar, Bhutan, E India. **Natural History:** A fossorial species found at intermediate elevations (1,200–3,000 m) in montane forests of various kinds. Tunnels in friable soils, but probably forages on the ground surface under leaf litter. **Conservation Status:** China RL—LC. IUCN RL—LC.

Taiwanese Mole Shrew *Anourosorex yamashinai*

台灣短尾鼩 Taiwanduanwei Qu—**Distinctive Characteristics:** HB 50–98; T 7–13; HF 13–16; E 0; GLS 23–26. Similar to *A. squamipes*, but separable based on its smaller body size and shorter tail, as well as range. **Distribution:** Taiwan. Endemic. **Natural History:** Ranges from 300 m to more than 3,000 m in the mountains, including subtropical forests through mixed deciduous to coniferous and above timberline to alpine tundra. It is most abundant in deciduous forests between 1,500 and 2,500 m but has also been captured in agricultural fields, riparian woodlands, and dwarf bamboo. **Conservation Status:** China RL—NE. IUCN RL—LC.

GENUS *BLARINELLA*—Asiatic Short-tailed Shrews

川鼩属 Chuanqu Shu—川鼩 Chuanqu
Size fairly large for shrews; tail relatively short, about half HB length; external ears vestigial; forefeet with strong claws. The shrews of this genus are among the few species adapted to an underground digging life in the subfamily Soricinae. The genus contains three species, all occurring in China.

Indochinese Short-Tailed Shrew *Blarinella griselda*

甘肅川鼩 Gansu Chuanqu—**Distinctive Characteristics:** HB 52–79; T 31–42; HF 8–14; E 6; GLS 19–21; Wt 8 g. Size medium; color of venter slightly lighter than dorsum, which is dark gray-brown with lighter grayish highlights; tail lighter than dorsum; dorsal surfaces of hands and feet brownish. **Distribution:** Arc from S Gansu to SW Yunnan; extending to N Vietnam. **Natural History:** Specimens from Vietnam were collected in bamboo forest between 1,500 and 1,700 m elevation. **Conservation Status:** China RL—LC. IUCN RL—LC.

Asiatic Short-Tailed Shrew *Blarinella quadraticauda*

黑齒鼩鼱 Heichi Qujing—**Distinctive Characteristics:** HB 65–81; T 40–60; HF 13–16; GLS 20–22. Size relatively large; dorsal and ventral fur uniform dark brown without any gray-brown highlights; tail color and dorsal surfaces of hands and feet as dark as or darker than the dorsal pelage. Of the three species of *Blarinella*, *quadraticauda* is the largest and has the longest tail. **Distribution:** Sichuan. Endemic. **Natural History:** Most commonly found in riparian growth along streams in montane coniferous forest and upward to the alpine zone, but may also occur in secondary forest away from streams. Semifossorial; burrows through leaf litter or grassy ground cover when foraging for invertebrates. **Conservation Status:** China RL—NT. IUCN RL—NT.

Burmese Short-Tailed Shrew *Blarinella wardi*

云南川駒 Yunnan Chuanqu—**Distinctive Characteristics:** HB 60–69; T 32–43; HF 10–13; GLS 18–20. Smallest of the Asian short-tailed shrews; dorsal fur uniformly dark brown, as in *quadraticauda*, but venter visibly lighter, grayish. Feet whitish, while the other two *Blarinella* species have dark feet. **Distribution:** W Yunnan; extending into Myanmar. **Natural History:** Temperate forests, including openings and edges, between 1,600 and 3,000 m elevation; forages in cool, damp ground cover. **Conservation Status:** China RL—NT. IUCN RL—LC.

GENUS *CHIMARROGALE*—Oriental Water Shrews

水駒属 Shuiqu Shu—水駒 Shuiqu
A large shrew adapted to aquatic life. Guard hairs slender and soft; rump has long and slender hairs; tail length less than HB length; hind feet with a fringe of stiff hairs along sides of toes. Occurs throughout mainland East Asia; includes six species, two of which occur in China.

Himalayan Water Shrew *Chimarrogale himalayica*

喜马拉雅水駒 Ximalaya Shuiqu—**Distinctive Characteristics:** HB 115–132; T 79–112; HF 17–30; E 0; GLS 25–28; Wt 23–56 g. In Taiwan only: HB 109–130, T 80–101, HF 23–26. Pelage blackish brown; ventral surface somewhat lighter, not sharply differentiated laterally; whole body, especially dorsum and rump, have scattered coarse white hairs; fringe of whitish hairs along margin of fore and hind feet and toes; tail long, fringe of white mid-ventral hairs along basal third to half of tail. Cusps of teeth unpigmented. **Distribution:** Widespread throughout C to SE China, including Taiwan; extending through SE Asia to Indochina. **Natural History:** Inhabits clear streams flowing through evergreen forest from 250 to 2,000 m elevation. Reported to feed on both fish and aquatic insects. **Conservation Status:** China RL—LC. IUCN RL—LC.

Chinese Water Shrew *Chimarrogale styani*

斯氏水駒 Sishi Shuiqu—**Distinctive Characteristics:** HB 96–108; T 61–85; HF 20–23; GLS 23–25. Similar to the Himalayan Water Shrew, but slightly smaller, and dorsal pelage darker, almost black, and sharply delineated from the wholly white ventral surface. **Distribution:** C China; extending to N Myanmar. **Natural History:** Occurs in high-elevation areas between 1,700 and 3,500 m, where it is found in or adjacent to cool mountain streams. Very little is known about this species, but it is likely to be elevationally allopatric with *C. himalayica*, although they are geographically sympatric. **Conservation Status:** China RL—NT. IUCN RL—LC.

GENUS *CHODSIGOA*—Asiatic Shrews

亚洲駒属 Yazhouqu Shu—洲駒 Yazhouqu
Originally named as a subgenus of *Soriculus*. The cusps of the teeth are tipped with red and the tail is rather thin. Known from China and countries bordering it to the south. There are eight known species, seven of which occur in China.

De Winton's Shrew *Chodsigoa hypsibia*

川西长尾駒 Chuanxi Changweiqu—**Distinctive Characteristics:** HB 73–99; T 60–80; HF 15–18; GLS 19–22. Dorsal pelage brownish gray; ventral pelage more brownish; tail indistinctly bicolored, grayish above and whitish below, usually shorter than HB; dorsal surfaces of hands and feet whitish. **Distribution:** C China. Endemic. **Natural History:** Occurs in montane regions where the natural geography is very complicated and marked with high mountains, deep valleys, and highly diversified, elevationally zoned vegetation. With the exception of the isolated Eastern Tombs population in Hebei (elevation 300 m), normally occupies mid- and high-montane areas at elevations of 1,200–3,500 m. **Conservation Status:** China RL—LC. IUCN RL—LC.

Lamulate Shrew *Chodsigoa lamula*

甘肃长尾鼩 Gansu Changweiqu—**Distinctive Characteristics:** HB 54–75; T 43–66; HF 11–16; GLS 17–19. Very similar to *C. hypsibia*, but smaller. **Distribution:** C China. Endemic. **Natural History:** Poorly known. Apparently it lives in montane forests at high elevations (ca. 3,000 m). **Conservation Status:** China RL—LC. IUCN RL—LC.

Lowe's Shrew *Chodsigoa parca*

云南缺齿鼩 Yunnan Quechiqu—**Distinctive Characteristics:** HB 68–84; T 74–108; HF 15–20; E 8–10; GLS 19–21; Wt 7–9.5 g. Dorsal pelage slate gray with brownish tinges; ventral pelage similarly colored but slightly lighter; tail longer than HB and distinctly bicolored, brown above and creamy white below; dorsal surfaces of hands and feet appear creamy white with a faint brownish tinge. **Distribution:** Central S China; extending to N Myanmar, Thailand, Vietnam. **Natural History:** Specimens collected from near the China border in Vietnam were from montane bamboo forests between 1,500–2,000 m elevation, and in W Yunnan they have been recorded at up to 3,000 m. **Conservation Status:** China RL—NT (as *Soriculus parca*). IUCN RL—LC.

Pygmy Red-Toothed Shrew *Chodsigoa parva*

滇北长尾鼩 Dianbei Changweiqu—**Distinctive Characteristics:** Not available. **Distribution:** Known only from the type locality in the Likiang range, W Yunnan. Possibly endemic. **Natural History:** Poorly known. Specimens have been collected around 3,000 m elevation. **Conservation Status:** China RL—NE. IUCN RL—LC.

Salenski's Shrew *Chodsigoa salenskii*

大长尾鼩 Da Changweiqu—**Distinctive Characteristics:** HB 78; T 110; HF 22; GLS 25. Very similar to *C. smithii*, but larger skull. **Distribution:** Guizhou and Sichuan. Endemic. **Natural History:** Unknown. **Conservation Status:** China RL—EN A2c; D2 (as *Soriculus salenskii*). IUCN RL—DD.

Smith's Shrew *Chodsigoa smithii*

缺齿鼩 Quechi Qu—**Distinctive Characteristics:**
HB 72–96; T 92–108; HF 16–19; GLS 21–23. Dorsal
pelage dark grayish brown; underside somewhat
lighter; tail pale brown above, white below; dorsal surfaces of hands and feet
brownish white. Similar to *C. salenskii* and *C. parca* but intermediate in size
between these two. **Distribution:** C China. Endemic. **Natural History:** Poorly
known. Most specimens have come from forested mountains at high elevations
(over 3,000 m). Their morphology, long tail, and large hind feet suggest that they
may be more agile climbers than some other members of the subgenus. Widely
sympatric with *C. hypsibia*. **Conservation Status:** China RL—VU B1ab(i,ii,iii) +
2ab(i,ii,iii) (as *Soriculus smithii*). IUCN RL—LC.

Lesser Taiwanese Shrew *Chodsigoa sodalis*

阿里山长尾鼩 Alishan Changweiqu—**Distinctive
Characteristics:** HB 65–71; T 64–73; HF 13–15; Wt
4.2–5.6 g. A small, slender form; body covered with
long (4–5 mm) hairs. Dorsal pelage dark gray-
brown, gradually blending into dark gray venter;
winter pelage without a distinct boundary between
the dorsal and ventral coloration; tail dark olive
brown above and below, about the same length as
HB, fore and hind feet relatively large and covered with short whitish hairs. **Distribution:** Taiwan. Endemic. **Natural History:** This species was recently rediscovered in broadleaf forest at 1,560 m. **Conservation Status:** China RL—EN
C2a(i,ii) (as *Soriculus sodalis*). China RL—DD.

GENUS *EPISORICULUS*—Long-tailed Asiatic Shrews

长尾亚洲鼩属 Changweiyazhouqu Shu—长尾亚洲鼩 Changweiyazhouqu
Once included as a subgenus within *Soriculus*, members of *Episoriculus* are distinguished by having a longer tail and shorter claws. All four species of *Episoriculus* occur in China.

Hodgson's Red-Toothed Shrew *Episoriculus caudatus*

长尾鼩鼱 Changwei Qujing—**Distinctive Characteristics:** HB 58–74; T 48–69; HF 12–16; GLS
17–19. Dorsal pelage cinnamon brown with faint
gray tinges; ventral pelage paler; tail about equal to
or shorter than HB length and either monocolored
or bicolored, brown above, whitish below; dorsal
surfaces of hands and feet whitish with scattered

brown hairs in center. **Distribution:** SW China; extending to India (Kashmir) and N Myanmar. **Natural History:** This shrew is widespread at middle elevations, above 2,200 m, frequenting dense oak-rhododendron forest and, higher up, subalpine and alpine meadows. It is also common at the edge of rhododendron and coniferous forests and is attracted to riparian habitats with rich ground litter or to rocky ground supporting grasses and mosses. It is frequently found near human habitation and cultivated fields. There are two breeding seasons; litters of five or six young are produced during April–June, and litters ranging from three to five are born during the August–October period. **Conservation Status:** China RL—LC. IUCN RL—LC.

Taiwanese Red-Toothed Shrew *Episoriculus fumidus*

台灣長尾鼩鼱 Taiwanchangwei Qujing—**Distinctive Characteristics:** HB 53–71; T 37–52; HF 11–14.5; GLS 18–19. Dorsal pelage brownish above, with a sharp transition to the grayish venter; tail relatively short, less than HB length, dark above, light below. **Distribution:** Taiwan. Endemic. **Natural History:** Prefers dense ground cover in both broadleaf and coniferous forest, and subalpine shrublands in high mountains of C Taiwan, between 1,560 and 2,438 m elevation. It is active both day and night. The breeding season is between March and June, the dry season in Taiwan. Mean litter size is 3.4 young (range 2–4). Whether more than one breeding season occurs per year has not been determined. The species is sympatric with *Chodsigoa sodalis* at Tsuifeng (2,300 m) and on Ali Shan (2,438 m). **Conservation Status:** China RL—NT (as *Soriculus fumidus*). IUCN RL—LC.

Long-Tailed Red-Toothed Shrew *Episoriculus leucops*

印度長尾鼩 Yindu Changweiqu—**Distinctive Characteristics:** HB 53–81; T 58–83; HF 12–19; GLS 18–21. Size large; pelage uniformly dark blackish brown to slate gray, both dorsally and ventrally; tail only slightly longer than HB length. Body structure of this species shows fossorial adaptations. **Distribution:** SW China; extending along E Himalayas from C Nepal eastward to Bhutan, India (Sikkim, Assam), N Myanmar, N Vietnam. **Natural History:** Favors moist conifer, rhododendron, and broadleaf deciduous forests at elevations between 3,000 and 3,500 m. It can also be found in moist stands of dwarf bamboo, shrubs, and grasses, and is known to inhabit villages and cultivated fields. It is sympatric with the smaller *E. caudatus*. Diet consists of earthworms. It may produce litters of six young. **Conservation Status:** China RL—LC. IUCN RL—LC.

Long-Tailed Mountain Shrew *Episoriculus macrurus*

缅甸长尾鼩 Miandian Changweiqu—**Distinctive Characteristics:** HB 47–73; T 76–101; HF 14–18; GLS 17–19. Pelage light gray. HB length moderate, but tail very long, usually more than 1.5 times length of HB; hind feet large. **Distribution:** SW China; extending to Nepal, India, Myanmar, and Vietnam. **Natural History:** Semiarboreal habits, as its morphology suggests (long tail, large hind feet). Primarily occupies temperate broadleaf evergreen forests to lower rhododendron forests, where it is adapted to a life on the ground in closed evergreen forests with scanty undergrowth. Occasionally found in bushes near water. It is sympatric with *E. caudatus*. **Conservation Status:** China RL—LC. IUCN RL—LC.

GENUS *NECTOGALE* (monotypic)

蹼足鼩属 Puzuqu Shu—蹼足鼩 Puzuqu

Elegant Water Shrew *Nectogale elegans*

蹼麝鼩 Pu Shequ—**Distinctive Characteristics:** HB 90–115; T 100–104; HF 25–27; GLS 25–27. Of all the Soricidae, this shrew is most adapted to aquatic life, in terms of body conformation: external ear pinnae valvate; middle and sides of tail have fringes of stiff, short hairs, which, because of their different lengths, change the cross section of the tail from quadrangular at the base to triangular and, finally, flat at the tip; feet fully webbed, fringe of stiff hairs along sides of toes. Dorsal pelage dark slaty gray, with scattered white-tipped hairs, especially on the rump; dorsum sharply demarcated from the grayish-white sides and venter; feet dark above and fringed with stiff white hairs. Size similar to that of *Chimarrogale himalayica*, but tail longer, and feet larger. The webbed feet and uniquely haired tail make this species unmistakable. **Distribution:** SW China; extending to Nepal, India (Sikkim), Bhutan, N Myanmar. **Natural History:** Only fully aquatic shrew in China. Active during the day, and may be observed foraging for aquatic invertebrates and small fish in rapidly flowing streams in mountainous regions. One foraging technique is for the shrew to work its way upstream at the water's edge, exploring under rocks, sticks, and stream-bank vegetation for some tens of meters, and then to swim out into swift water, where it allows itself to float downstream and seems to forage in this deeper water, diving down periodically. **Conservation Status:** China RL—NT. IUCN RL—LC.

GENUS *NEOMYS*—Water Shrews

水鼩鼱属 Shuiqujing Shu—水鼩鼱 Shui Qujing
Semiaquatic; hind feet and undersurface of tail have fringes of silvery hair; cusps of teeth heavily pigmented. Of three species, one occurs in China.

Eurasian Water Shrew *Neomys fodiens*

水鼩鼱 Shui Qujing—**Distinctive Characteristics:** HB 69–94; T 44–80; HF 17–21; Wt 8–26 g. Sharply bicolored pelage, dark brown above, grayish buff on sides and belly; mid-ventral line of silvery hairs on tail; short, silvery hairs fringe digits of fore and hind limbs. Tail long, more than half of HB length; ears and eyes small, covered in hairs; feet large, toes edged with fringes of long, stiff hairs. **Distribution:** NE and NW China; extending from Europe (British Isles) across Asia to North Korea and Sakhalin Island, Russia. **Natural History:** Generally lives close to water and seems to prefer less turbid, fast-flowing streams; mostly found in forests, but may also visit woodlands, grasslands, or even alpine heaths; has been found at up to 2,500 m in the European Alps. Forages both on the ground surface and below, in tunnels that it excavates or remodels from those of moles. The tunnel system may have several entrances, either under ground litter or underwater. It feeds on insect larvae of many kinds, mollusks, crustaceans, small fish and amphibians, earthworms, and terrestrial insects such as beetles. Whether it feeds on small mammals is uncertain, but submaxillary glands secrete venom that in other shrew species enables the shrew to immobilize a small rodent. The breeding season is in the spring and summer months, and the litter size averages 6 young (range 3–15); two litters per year may be produced, depending on favorable weather. **Conservation Status:** China RL—VU D2. IUCN RL—LC.

GENUS *SOREX*—Holarctic Shrews

鼩鼱属 Qujing Shu—鼩鼱 Qujing
Size small; greatest body mass less than 16 g; length of hind foot less than 18 mm; GLS less than 23.3 mm; dorsum color generally grayish to reddish brown, darker mid-dorsally; venter usually paler; head long and rostrum pointed; teeth red; tail nearly half of HB length; limbs slender; both forefeet and hind feet with five toes. This is the most common genus of Soricinae and is widely distributed in N Asia, Europe, and North America. Of 77 *Sorex*, 18 occur in China.

Tian Shan Shrew *Sorex asper*

天山鼩鼱 Tianshan Qujing—**Distinctive Characteristics:** HB 55–77; T 32–47; HF 10–14; GLS 19–20; Wt 5–12 g. Medium-large size. Once thought to be a subspecies of *S. araneus*, the common shrew of N Europe; very similar to *S. excelsus* and *S. tundrensis*. **Distribution:** NW Xinjiang; extending to Kazakhstan. **Natural History:** Probably an alpine specialist; inhabits spruce forests, moist alpine meadows, and stands of shrubs and reeds, generally at elevations of 2,000–3,000 m. It favors cluttered places with a thick layer of friable litter. Active throughout the year, generally during twilight and night, but it is occasionally encountered during the day. Its diet is diverse but is predominantly composed of insects. Breeding begins at the end of March or early in April. At this time the testes of males enlarge to 6 mm. They remain in this condition to the end of July and then regress to their original dimensions, 1–2 mm. Litter size is 1–8 (average 5.3). Independent young are first noticed in early July. **Conservation Status:** China RL—NA. IUCN RL—LC.

Lesser Striped Shrew *Sorex bedfordiae*

小纹背鼩鼱 Xiaowenbei Qujing—**Distinctive Characteristics:** HB 50–72; T 48–66; HF 11–15; GLS 17–19. A black mid-dorsal stripe runs from the base of the neck to the base of the tail in most individuals (less conspicuous than that of *S. cylindricauda*); both dorsal and ventral pelages are dark brown, almost monotone or the venter is slightly lighter. Compared with *S. cylindricauda*, body size distinctly smaller, and proportion of tail length to HB length longer. **Distribution:** C China; extending to Myanmar and Nepal. **Natural History:** Occurs between 2,135 and 4,270 m (higher, on average, than *S. cylindricauda*). It lives in the ground litter and forages on insects. It shares this niche with its congener *S. minutus*, but the two appear to be allopatric in distribution. In addition, *Soriculus nigrescens* and *Episoriculus caudatus* are taken in association with *S. bedfordiae*. **Conservation Status:** China RL—NT. IUCN RL—LC.

Laxmann's Shrew *Sorex caecutiens*

中鼩鼱 Zhong Qujing—**Distinctive Characteristics:** HB 52–65; T 30–38; HF 11–13. Rostrum long and narrow; no light stripe on side. Size relatively small; tail length more than half of HB length, usually 65% or more. Overlaps with *S. tundrensis* in distribution; the two species are relatively difficult to distinguish. **Distribution:** NW and NE China;

extending from E Europe across Asia to Korea, Sakhalin Island (Russia), and Japan. **Natural History:** A boreally adapted species that inhabits the Eurasian portion of the circumpolar taiga zone. It is widespread in both lowland and montane taiga forest and also ventures onto adjacent tundra. It is partial to damp ground that supports berry bushes and small trees, and extends along the shores of swamps and streams in moorlands. Feeds mainly on insects, especially beetles, a few spiders, millipedes, and earthworms, and also conifer seeds.

Breeding season is June to August, and up to four litters may be produced in that time. Litter size ranges from 2 to 11, with a mean of 7 to 8. **Conservation Status:** China RL—NT. IUCN RL—LC.

Gansu Shrew *Sorex cansulus*

甘肃驹鼩 Gansu Qujing—**Distinctive Characteristics:** HB 62–64; T 38–43; HF 12. Once thought to be a subspecies of *S. caecutiens*. Small *Sorex*; dorsal pelage dust colored to grayish brown; sides buffy; ventral pelage hazel; forefeet and hind feet white-brown; dorsum of tail dark brown, venter of tail slightly lighter. **Distribution:** Restricted distribution in C China. Endemic. **Natural History:** Rare and poorly known. Specimens have been found at high elevations (2,600–3,000 m). **Conservation Status:** China RL—VU D2. IUCN RL—DD.

Stripe-Backed Shrew *Sorex cylindricauda*

纹背驹鼩 Wenbei Qujing—**Distinctive Characteristics:** HB 67–77; T 55–62; HF 15–16; GLS 17–21. Dorsal pelage cinnamon brown; venter dark gray-brown, nearly as dark as dorsum. Conformation similar to that of *S. caecutiens* but larger; conspicuous dark stripe running down spine from neck to rump; tail about equal to HB length or slightly shorter (about 80%). **Distribution:** C China. Endemic. **Natural History:** Since this species has consistently been confused with *S. bedfordiae*, it is not possible to separate statements made about the biology of "*cylindricauda*" except to note that its habitat must include montane forests that surround the type locality, Moupin, Sichuan. **Conservation Status:** China RL—LC. IUCN RL—LC.

Large-Toothed Siberian Shrew *Sorex daphaenodon*

栗齿駒鼱 Lichi Qujing—**Distinctive Characteristics:** HB 48–76; T 25–39; HF 10–13. Pelage dark brown dorsally and lighter gray-brown ventrally, separated by a distinct line; soles of feet dark brown; reddish-brown pigment of teeth much more extensive and deeper in color than in other species of *Sorex*; teeth more massive than those of other large shrews. Size larger than *S. caecutiens*; tail about half of HB length. **Distribution:** NE China; extending across Asia from Sakhalin Island (Russia) to Kazakhstan and the Ural Mountains. **Natural History:** Occupies mixed forest (conifer and broadleaf types) over much of its range, and may also occupy birch groves in wooded steppe. Diet consists of earthworms, spiders, millipedes, and insects (lepidoptera, orthoptera, including crickets, diptera, and a variety of beetles). Breeding occurs in the summer months, and pregnant females are encountered in June–August. Litter size ranges from four to nine (average seven). Males with enlarged gonads have been recorded from June to the middle of September. Preyed on by nocturnal and diurnal birds of prey and mammalian carnivores (Sable, Siberian Weasel, Ermine). **Conservation Status:** China RL—DD. IUCN RL—LC.

Chinese Highland Shrew *Sorex excelsus*

云南駒鼱 Yunnan Qujing—**Distinctive Characteristics:** HB 60–73; T 44–51; HF 13–16; GLS 18–20; Wt 5–10 g. Brown back, buff sides, and gray belly (the dorsal and ventral colors differentiated distinctly); tail sharply bicolored, brown above, white below; feet white to silvery gray. Size medium; once thought to be subspecies of *S. araneus*; very similar to *S. asper*, *S. cansulus*, and *S. tundrensis*. **Distribution:** SW China; possibly extending into Nepal. **Natural History:** Occurs in alpine and montane forest regions up to 4,000 m elevation. In S Qinghai it has been captured along small streams with shrubby banks and moist litter on the soil surface. **Conservation Status:** China RL—VU B1ab(i,ii,iii) + 2ab(i,ii,iii); C1. IUCN RL—LC.

Slender Shrew *Sorex gracillimus*

细駒鼱 Xi Qujing—**Distinctive Characteristics:** HB 48–52; T 37–43; HF 10–11; GLS <17. A very small shrew that closely resembles *S. minimus*, but the head is shaded with an olive-green tint. Tail is long and furred, with a terminal dark

tassel. **Distribution:** NE China; extending to NE Asia (Hokkaido, Japan, Sakhalin, Russia, North Korea). **Natural History:** Primarily occupies coniferous forest habitat in mountainous areas. Also occurs in riparian willows, tall-grass sections of buckwheat, and large bamboo stands. Maximum densities are attained in mixed coniferous-broadleaf forests and riparian willows. It avoids fields and meadows. Density is higher in secondary woodland than in deep, continuous taiga. Diet primarily consists of invertebrates living in the surface litter and upper soil horizon. Breeding occurs between May and October. Litter size one to eight (average five to six). **Conservation Status:** China RL—NA. IUCN RL—LC.

Taiga Shrew *Sorex isodon*

远东鼩鼱 Yuandong Qujing—**Distinctive Characteristics:** HB 65–83; T 40–48; HF 13–15; GLS 19–21. Once thought to be subspecies of *S. araneus* or *S. sinalis*, *S. isodon* is somewhat smaller, with a relatively shorter tail and shorter rostrum. Size large; ventral pelage hazel to dark brownish gray, slightly lighter than dorsal pelage; these gradually blend laterally. **Distribution:** NE China; extending across Eurasia from Scandinavia to the Pacific (Kamchatka Peninsula and Sakhalin Island, Russia, and Korea). **Natural History:** Occupies low-lying evergreen-forested country. Its very large range overlaps three other large *Sorex*: *araneus*, *roboratus*, and *unguiculatus*, the last two also occurring in China. The ability of *isodon* to coexist with these two potential competitors is attributed to its specialized diet of fly larvae and pupae. **Conservation Status:** China RL—NA. IUCN RL—LC.

Eurasian Least Shrew *Sorex minutissimus*

姬鼩鼱 Ji Qujing—**Distinctive Characteristics:** HB 39–55; T 20–35; HF 7–11; GLS 12.4–14.2; Wt 1.4–2.9 g. By far the smallest soricid shrew found in China. Similar in size to *Suncus etruscus*, from which it can be separated on the basis of tooth pigmentation. Pelage somewhat tricolored, brownish dorsally, and lighter gray ventrally, separated by brownish-gray flanks. **Distribution:** Central S and NE China; extending from Scandinavia to E Siberia, South Korea, and the islands of Sakhalin (Russia) and Hokkaido (Japan). **Natural History:** Poorly known because it is so hard to capture and observe. Apparently ranges across a wide variety of habitats, evidenced by the large geographic range it occupies. It avoids open tundra, preferring taiga forests. **Conservation Status:** China RL—LC. IUCN RL—LC.

Eurasian Pygmy Shrew *Sorex minutus*

小駒鼩 Xiao Qujing—**Distinctive Characteristics:** HB 46–52; T 35–36; HF 10–11; GLS 15–17. Dorsal pelage medium brown, contrasting with gray-white venter; tail relatively thick and hairy. **Distribution:** NW Xinjiang; extending from Europe to Lake Baikal, Russia. **Natural History:** Poorly known. Apparently it occupies coniferous forests, although it may also occur in rocky habitats at high elevation. It lives on a diet of arthropods and beetles. **Conservation Status:** China RL—NA. IUCN RL—LC.

Ussuri Shrew *Sorex mirabilis*

大駒鼩 Da Qujing—**Distinctive Characteristics:** HB 74–97; T 63–73; HF 16–18; Wt 11–14 g. The largest species of *Sorex*; dorsal hair iron gray, not distinct from gray ventral surface. **Distribution:** NE China; extending to Korea and E Russia. **Natural History:** A poorly known and rarely encountered species. Apparently its preferred habitat consists of primary broadleaf and coniferous-broadleaf forest. Here it inhabits valleys and the slopes of hills. Demonstrates a higher level of activity than other red-toothed shrews. Apparently this activity is related to the lesser nutritional value of its primary foodstuffs—earthworms, other invertebrates, and the flesh of rodents. It consumes 214.2% of its body weight daily. Breeding occurs once a year, with young beginning to appear in traps only at the end of August. In favorable years two litters are possible. Young first become sexually mature in the following warm season. **Conservation Status:** China RL—VU B1ab(i,iii); D2. IUCN RL—DD.

Kashmir Pygmy Shrew *Sorex planiceps*

克什米尔駒鼩 Keshimi'er Qujing—**Distinctive Characteristics:** HB 57–75; T 37–48; HF 10–14. Dorsal pelage is brown, shading gradually into grayish on the venter. Feet are light, and tail is bicolored, brown on top and light gray to white below. **Distribution:** Far W China; extending to N Pakistan and India (Kashmir). **Natural History:** Lives in coniferous forest and alpine rocky habitats (up to 3,600 m) that may be covered with snow for up to eight months of the year. Presumably lives on various species of arthropods, including woodlice and beetles. **Conservation Status:** China RL—DD. IUCN RL—LC.

Flat-Skulled Shrew *Sorex roboratus*

扁颅鼩鼱 Bianlu Qujing—**Distinctive Characteristics:** HB 58–87; T 31–43; HF 12–15.5; GLS 20–22. Dorsal pelage very dark brown, sides lighter, ventral pelage buffy gray. Tail sharply bicolored, dark brown above, pale below. **Distribution:** Xinjiang (Altai Mountains); extending from N Mongolia west to the Ob River. **Natural History:** Inhabits tundra and northern taiga. **Conservation Status:** China RL—NE. IUCN RL—LC.

Chinese Shrew *Sorex sinalis*

陕西鼩鼱 Shaanxi Qujing—**Distinctive Characteristics:** HB 64–85; T 49–68; HF 13–17; GLS 20–22. A large, long-tailed shrew; pelage uniformly gray-brown to drab brown, both dorsally and ventrally; once thought to be a subspecies of *S. araneus*; similar to *S. isodon*; ventral pelage hazel, only slightly lighter than dorsum. **Distribution:** C China. Endemic. **Natural History:** Occupies rocky, mossy mountaintop habitat at elevations ranging from 2,700 to 3,000 m. It coexists with another large shrew, *S. cylindricauda*. **Conservation Status:** China RL—VU A2c; D2. IUCN RL—DD.

Tibetan Shrew *Sorex thibetanus*

藏鼩鼱 Zang Qujing—**Distinctive Characteristics:** HB 51–64; T 32–54; HF 12–13; GLS 16–18. Once thought to be subspecies of *S. minutus*, but size is larger. **Distribution:** C China. Endemic. **Natural History:** Unknown. **Conservation Status:** China RL—LC. IUCN RL—DD.

Tundra Shrew *Sorex tundrensis*

苔原鼩鼱 Taiyuan Qujing—**Distinctive Characteristics:** HB 60–85; T 22–36; Wt 5–10 g. Summer pelage is tricolored, dark brown above, pale gray-brown on the sides, and pale gray on the underside. Winter pelage bicolored, dark brown above, pale gray below. **Distribution:** NE and NW China; extending across the Bering Strait into

Alaska and N Canada. **Natural History:** Inhabits dense vegetation of grasses and shrubs. **Conservation Status:** China RL—NE. IUCN RL—LC.

Long-Clawed Shrew *Sorex unguiculatus*

长爪駒鼩 Changzhao Qujing—**Distinctive Characteristics:** HB 70–91; T 41–51; HF 12–14; GLS 19–21; Wt 6–10 g. Size large. Pelage color dark brown, both dorsally and ventrally, but venter slightly paler and grayer than dorsum. Forefeet broad, with claws more than 3 mm long, much longer than claws on hind feet. **Distribution:** NE China; extending to E Russia and Hokkaido Island (Japan). **Natural History:** Very common in grasslands and open fields of plains or low mountains. In some parts of its range, it occupies bamboo groves or riparian willows. Burrows with its strong, broad forefeet and enlarged claws. Forages in tunnels and in litter on surface. Main foods are earthworms, insects, centipedes, and snails. Its distribution is connected to thick stands of coniferous and mixed pine-broadleaf forest. It is sympatric with *S. caecutiens* and *S. isodon*, to which it is often subordinate. Reproduction occurs during the warm season; litter size ranges from one to seven. **Conservation Status:** China RL—NE. IUCN RL—LC.

GENUS *SORICULUS* (monotypic)

长尾駒鼩属 Changweiqujing Shu

Himalayan Shrew *Soriculus nigrescens*

大爪长尾駒 Dazhua Changweiqu—**Distinctive Characteristics:** HB 70–94; T 32–48; HF 12–17; GLS 20–23; Wt 17.5–25.5 g. Pelage dust colored; forefeet and claws enlarged, larger than hind feet; tail short, not more than three-quarters of HB length. Cusps of teeth dark red-brown. **Distribution:** SW China; extending to Nepal, Bhutan, and India (Assam). **Natural History:** Common in three of the elevational zones in the Himalayas, in ascending order: mixed deciduous-coniferous forest, conifer-rhododendron forest, and above timberline, the alpine zone. Insects (beetles, flies, bees) and especially earthworms constitute the primary foods. Is partially adapted to a life underground. Has a primary (June–July) and a secondary (August–October) breeding season. Average litter size in spring is 6 and in autumn is 4.5; overall, litter sizes range from 3 to 9. Young males born in spring may mature rapidly, attaining breeding condition toward the end of their first summer. Young are born into a nest formed of dry grasses and other fiber, about 12–15 cm in diameter, placed under stones. **Conservation Status:** China RL—NA. IUCN RL—LC.

FAMILY TALPIDAE—Moles and Shrew Moles

鼹科 Yan Ke—鼹类 Yan Lei

Moles are highly adapted for fossorial life, or in some cases semiaquatic life, having a cylindrical body, pointed rostrum, and enlarged, outward-turned forefeet with thick, sharp claws for digging through loose soil. The eyes are minute and hidden in the pelage, and there is a complete absence of external ears. The fur is soft and lustrous; almost all of the hairs are the same length and will lie in any direction. Shrew moles comprise a lineage basal to moles and, while having a mole-like skull and dentition, retain a more shrewlike external appearance (feet not enlarged for digging, external ears present) and have a more ambulatory lifestyle. Habits terrestrial, mostly subterranean; some are aquatic; feeding habits insectivorous or polyphagous. Species from all three subfamilies (Scalopinae, Talpinae, and Uropsilinae) occur in China.

SUBFAMILY SCALOPINAE—American Moles

美洲鼹亚科 Meizhouyan Yake—美洲鼹 Meizhouyan

The subfamily Scalopinae comprises seven species from five genera. Most occur in North America, but one monotypic genus is endemic to C China.

GENUS *SCAPANULUS* (monotypic)

甘肃鼹属 Gansuyan Shu

Gansu Mole *Scapanulus oweni*

甘肃鼹 Gansu Yan—**Distinctive Characteristics:** HB 108–136; T 37–41; HF 14–20; E 0; GLS 27–32. Form mole-like, but readily distinguished from all other Chinese talpids by the first toe of the hind foot, which is set outward at a slight angle to the remaining toes and is stouter and more sharply curved than in other moles. Pelage drab brownish gray; tail about twice the length of the hind foot, stout and densely haired. Only *Scaptonyx fusicaudus* has a tail that measures longer relative to hind foot, but that species is smaller, and the Gansu Mole is distinguished by the characters described above. Dental formula: 2.1.3.3/2.1.3.3 = 36. **Distribution:** C China. Endemic. **Natural History:** Occupies mossy undergrowth of montane fir forest, thus a habitat similar to that of *Scaptonyx*. However, *Scapanulus* is significantly larger than *Scaptonyx*, and it may excavate larger, deeper tunnel systems and differ in foraging modes, since the two species are geographically sympatric over a wide area. **Conservation Status:** China RL—VU A1bc. IUCN RL—LC.

SUBFAMILY TALPINAE—True Moles

鼹亚科 Yan Yake—鼹类 Yanlei
The subfamily Talpinae comprises a group of predominantly Old World moles and desmans but also includes one North American form. Most are modified for burrowing, although the desmans (*Desmana*), a group not occurring in China, are aquatic. Of all the moles occurring in China, all but one (the Gansu Mole) belong to the Talpinae. The subfamily comprises 11 genera and 28 species; of these, five genera and 10 species are found in China.

GENUS *EUROSCAPTOR*—Oriental Moles

东方鼹属 Dongfangyan Shu—东方鼹 Dongfangyan
Euroscaptor is sometimes considered a subgenus of the European genus *Talpa*. The species-level taxonomy of the group is still uncertain, with most species known from very few specimens. Dental formula: 3.1.4.3/3.1.4.3 = 44. Five of six species of *Euroscaptor* occur in China.

Greater Chinese Mole *Euroscaptor grandis*

巨鼹 Ju Yan—**Distinctive Characteristics:** HB 150; T 10; HF 18; E 0; GLS 37. Size very large, much larger than the sympatric *E. longirostris*. Pelage dark brown, not black, as in *E. longirostris*. Tail short and swollen at the end and sparsely covered with long brown hairs. **Distribution:** C Sichuan, W Yunnan; probably extending into adjacent Myanmar, but not yet recorded from this area. Endemic. **Natural History:** Occupies forest habitat. **Conservation Status:** China RL—VU B1ab(i,ii,iii).

Kloss's Mole *Euroscaptor klossi*

克氏鼹 Keshi Yan—**Distinctive Characteristics:** HB 123–138; T 11–16.5; HF 16; E 0; GLS 30–32. Pelage dark blackish brown. Tail about as long as the hind foot. Similar to *E. micrura*, but with a longer tail. **Distribution:** S Yunnan; extending to Thailand, Laos, and peninsular Malaysia. **Natural History:** Occupies forest habitat. **Conservation Status:** China RL—NA. IUCN RL—LC.

Long-Nosed Mole *Euroscaptor longirostris*

长吻鼹 Changwen Yan—**Distinctive Characteristics:** HB 90–145; T 11–25; HF 14–23; E 0; GLS 30–33. Body dark gray to black, sometimes with slightly brownish tinge; tail sparsely haired except toward the tip, where white hairs may be up to 12.5 mm long. Rostrum longer and narrower than in any of the larger moles in China. **Distribution:** Widely distributed in S China; apparently extending into NW Vietnam. **Natural History:** Thought to be a montane species, ranging between 1,800 and 2,900 m in elevation. Occupies mesic mossy habitat in alpine birch forests. This species also co-occurs widely with another

small, blackish mole, *Mogera insularis*, in S China. Poorly known. **Conservation Status:** China RL—VU A1acd. IUCN RL—LC.

Himalayan Mole *Euroscaptor micrura*

短尾鼹 Duanwei Yan—**Distinctive Characteristics:** HB 128–135; T 5–9; HF 15–16; E 0; GLS 30–34; Wt 44–72. Similar to *E. klossi*, but with a shorter, club-shaped tail. **Distribution:** W Yunnan; extending to E Himalayas and peninsular Malaysia. **Natural History:** Occupies forest habitat, where it usually uses surface tunnels. Does not construct large mounds or dig deeply into the ground. **Conservation Status:** China RL—NA. IUCN RL—LC.

Small-Toothed Mole *Euroscaptor parvidens*

小齿鼹 Xiaochi Yan—**Distinctive Characteristics:** HB 140; T 6; HF 18; E 0; GLS 34. Similar to *E. klossi* and *E. micrura* in external appearance. **Distribution:** S Yunnan; extending to Vietnam. **Natural History:** Little known; the holotype was collected near a stream at 800 m elevation. **Conservation Status:** China RL—NA. IUCN RL—DD.

GENUS *MOGERA*—East Asian Moles

缺齿鼹属 Quechiyan Shu—缺齿鼹 Quechiyan
Size small or very large; HB length varies in individuals, longest about 220 mm, shortest less than 100 mm. Dental formula: 3.1.4.3/3.0.4.3 = 42. Tail thickset. The five species of *Mogera* range widely across E Asia; two species occur in China.

Insular Mole *Mogera insularis*

华南缺齿鼹 Huanan Quechiyan—**Distinctive Characteristics:** HB 87–137; T 3–14; HF 5–18; E 0; GLS 27–33. Size very small; pelage slate black both dorsally and ventrally, except for whitish hairs scattered on feet and tip of tail. The only species of mole to occur on Taiwan and Hainan; however, in S China, it occurs with *Euroscaptor longirostris*, another small, dark-colored mole. Externally, *M. insularis* has a shorter, broader rostrum than *E. longirostris*, and the enlarged claws of its forefeet are narrower than the broad claws of *E. longirostris*. **Distribution:** S China, including Hainan Island and Taiwan. Endemic. **Natural History:** Common in the hill country of S China, as well as in high mountains. **Conservation Status:** China RL—NT. IUCN RL—LC.

Large Mole *Mogera robusta*

大缺齿鼹 Da Quechiyan—**Distinctive Characteristics:** HB 170–220; T 19–23; HF 22–24; E 0; GLS 37–48. By far the largest mole in China. Hairs on dorsum brownish mixed with gray, with metallic sheen; anterior portion of nose paler and yellower; ventral pelage has shiny silvery-yellow hue and on chest a weakly defined pale gray region; feet and claws yellow. Tail relatively short but well haired; forefeet very large, with long, thick claws. **Distribution:** NE China; extending into Russia and Korea. **Natural History:** Habitat is montane woodland, forest, grassland, and farmland. Rarely found on steep slopes with rocky soils. Little else is known about its biology. **Conservation Status:** China RL—NT. IUCN RL—LC.

GENUS *PARASCAPTOR* (monotypic)

白尾鼹属 Baiweiyan Shu

White-Tailed Mole *Parascaptor leucura*

白尾鼹 Baiwei Yan—**Distinctive Characteristics:** HB 100–112; T 10–15; HF 15–16; E 0; GLS 27–30. Pelage dark blackish brown; tail very short and club-shaped, usually with white hairs. Dental formula: 3.1.3.3/3.1.4.3 = 42. **Distribution:** Yunnan and Sichuan; extending to Myanmar and India (Assam). **Natural History:** Inhabits montane forests and scrub-grassland between 1,000 and 3,000 m. **Conservation Status:** China RL—LC. IUCN RL—LC.

GENUS *SCAPTOCHIRUS* (monotypic)

麝鼹属 Sheyan Shu

Short-Faced Mole *Scaptochirus moschatus*

麝鼹 She Yan—**Distinctive Characteristics:** HB 100–126; T 14–23; HF 15–19; E 0; GLS 30–36. A medium-sized mole. Pelage clear grayish brown; paler around mouth and forearms. Tail slender, usually subequal in length to hind foot, sparsely covered with hairs and with a small tuft at the tip. Dental formula: 3.1.3.3./3.1.3.3 = 40. **Distribution:** C to NE China. Endemic. **Natural History:** Occupies the cold, dry northeastern quadrant of China and is adapted to arid conditions to a much greater extent than other moles. These include sandy grasslands and meadows, loess regions, and even the borders of deserts, such as the Ordos. The scarcity of earthworms, a staple of mole diet in most mesic regions, has resulted in the Short-faced Mole feeding on larvae of beetles and other arthropods. **Conservation Status:** China RL—NT. IUCN RL—LC.

GENUS *SCAPTONYX* (monotypic)

长尾鼩鼹属 Changweiquyan Shu

Long-Tailed Mole *Scaptonyx fusicaudus*

长尾鼩鼹 Changwei Quyan—**Distinctive Characteristics:** HB 72–90; T 26–45; HF 17; E 0; GLS 23; Wt 12 g. Small, long-tailed mole; the pelage is dark gray-brown, both dorsally and ventrally, with scattered white hairs; tail surface covered with black hairs. Dental formula: 3.1.4.3/2.1.4.3 = 42. **Distribution:** C China; extending to Myanmar and N Vietnam. **Natural History:** Although small, like *Uropsilus*, this is a true mole and is apparently fully fossorial. It appears to be restricted to high elevations (2,000–4,100 m), in montane coniferous forests with damp, friable soils. Here it digs shallow burrows, recognizable because of their small diameter compared to those of other larger Chinese moles. *Scaptonyx* is geographically sympatric with all four species of *Uropsilus*, but this is not surprising, since the former forages below the soil surface, while the latter seek food on the surface in leaf litter. **Conservation Status:** China RL—NT. IUCN RL—LC.

SUBFAMILY UROPSILINAE

鼩鼹亚科 Quyan Yake
The subfamily Uropsilinae contains a single genus, *Uropsilus*, found in China.

GENUS *UROPSILUS*—Shrew Moles

鼩鼹属 Quyan Shu—鼩鼹 Quyan
A basal lineage within the Talpidae that differs from other talpids in having a shrewlike external form not modified for burrowing. Fur long and directed backwards, not short and velvety as in moles; snout long and thin; external ear present; forefeet small, not broadened for digging; tail long. The natural history of shrew moles is very poorly known. All seem to have similar habits, foraging on the ground surface among leaf litter for small invertebrates. They may form faint trails along the surface, where ground cover is sparse, but apparently do not burrow into the soil. All four species of *Uropsilus* are found in China.

Anderson's Shrew Mole *Uropsilus andersoni*

峨眉鼩鼹 Emei Quyan—**Distinctive Characteristics:** HB 65–83; T 59–72; HF 14–17.5; GLS 21–22. This species is darker than its congeners. **Distribution:** Known only from Mount Emei and adjacent small area. Endemic. **Natural History:** Presumed similar to its congeners, but very little is known. **Conservation Status:** China RL—EN B2ab(i,ii,iii); C2a(i,ii). IUCN RL—DD.

Gracile Shrew Mole *Uropsilus gracilis*

长吻鼩鼹 Changwen Quyan—**Distinctive Characteristics:** HB 69–84; T 67–78; HF 15–18; GLS 22–23. Similar to *U. investigator*, but pelage lighter in color. **Distribution:** SW China; extending to N Myanmar. **Natural History:** Inhabits mixed deciduous-coniferous forests, usually above the rhododendron zone and up to timberline (3,000–4,000 m, depending on topographic conditions). Unlike its congeners, it occupies alpine tundra habitats, at least in the Likiang range. **Conservation Status:** China RL—LC. IUCN RL—LC.

Inquisitive Shrew Mole *Uropsilus investigator*

怒江鼩鼹 Nujiang Quyan—**Distinctive Characteristics:** HB 67–83; T 54–75; HF 13–16; GLS 20–22. Very similar to *U. gracilis* and once regarded as a subspecies within it, *U. investigator* is distinguished by its darker, almost black pelage color. **Distribution:** NW Yunnan. Endemic. **Natu-**

ral History: Occurs in open alpine meadows or perhaps fir forests at high elevations (3,600–4,600 m). **Conservation Status:** China RL—EN C2a(i,ii); D. IUCN RL—DD.

Chinese Shrew Mole *Uropsilus soricipes*

鼩鼹 Qu Yan—**Distinctive Characteristics:** HB 66–80; T 50–69; HF 14–17; GLS 20–21.5. Dorsum dark brown; ventral surface dark slate gray; back of feet same color as upper tail and dorsum. **Distribution:** C China. Endemic. **Natural History:** Very poorly known. *U. soricipes* is geographically sympatric with *U. gracilis* in the vicinity of Wenchuan, Sichuan, but is segregated elevationally; *U. soricipes* is found below 2,200 m, while *U. gracilis* is found higher, above 3,000 m. **Conservation Status:** China RL—VU A1c. IUCN RL—LC.

ORDER CHIROPTERA—Bats

翼手目 Yishou Mu—蝙蝠 Bianfu
The order Chiroptera contains the only mammals capable of true flight. Characters include specialized forelimbs; phalanges especially elongated; radii longer than humeri; ulnae reduced; patagium between phalanges linked with hind legs; and hind legs and tail also linked by uropatagium that usually possesses cartilagenous calcaria, which function as stays. Most species are insectivorous, although a few species are frugivorous. Bats are nocturnal and possess highly developed ears. For most species the flight path and prey capture completely depend on emitting and retrieving ultrasonic vocalizations, but Pteropodidae rely on vision.

The order is distributed throughout both Eastern and Western hemispheres except in polar regions. Most forms are found in tropical and temperate zones, with diversity inversely related to latitude. Relationships of higher categories are sufficiently unclear to argue against recognition of traditional suborders Megachiroptera (including the single family Pteropodidae) and Microchiroptera (all remaining families). Of 18 families, seven occur in China.

FAMILY PTEROPODIDAE—Old World Fruit Bats

狐蝠科 Hufu Ke—狐蝠 Hufu
Size medium to very large; tragus absent; ear edges form a complete ring; second digit free, with three phalanges and usually with claw; tail reduced or absent. Distributed in tropical and subtropical zones of the Eastern Hemisphere; range extends eastward to Australia but not to New Zealand; of 42 genera, six occur in China.

GENUS *CYNOPTERUS*—Short-nosed Fruit Bats

犬蝠属 Quanfu Shu—犬蝠 Quanfu

Size medium; forearm length 54–92 mm; nostrils noticeable and nearly proboscis-like; upper lip with deep vertical grooves in middle; second digit with developed claws; tail short but conspicuous, distal half separated from uropatagium; calcar short, length about equal to breadth of hind foot; ears with pale edges. Dental formula: 2.1.3.1/2.1.3.2 = 30. Widely distributed in tropical and subtropical zones of Indo-Malayan realm. Of seven species, two occur in China.

Lesser Short-Nosed Fruit Bat *Cynopterus brachyotis*

短耳犬蝠 Duan'er Quanfu—**Distinctive Characteristics:** HB 70–84; T 9–12; HF 13–15; E 13–18; FA 54–72; GLS 27–31. Externally quite similar to *C. sphinx*, with which it has been confused in the past, but slightly smaller and paler in color; ears shorter, about 13–18 mm. Fur color ranges from light grayish through dark or bright brown; breeding adults may have orange or yellow area on throat and shoulders; basal third of ear hairy, margins pale or whitish; fingers whitish in contrast to dark brown wing membranes. **Distribution:** Guangdong; extending to the Indian subcontinent and through S Malayan region. **Natural History:** Little is known from China, but some information is available from other areas. Common in both secondary forests and agricultural areas, this bat is also taken in small villages. Normally roosts in pairs or small colonies in the foliage but may also use dimly lighted regions of caves. Feeds on fruit, nectar, and pollen of at least 10 families of plants. Marked animals moved from 0.2 to 1.3 km, and recaptures suggested a population density of 0.2–0.3 animals per hectare. Females appear to be polyestrous and are thought to produce a single young twice per year. The gestation period is three and a half to four months, and lactation lasts six to eight weeks. Documented longevity is five years in the wild and is likely considerably more than that. **Conservation Status:** China RL—VU B1ab(i,ii,iii). IUCN RL—LC.

Greater Short-Nosed Fruit Bat *Cynopterus sphinx*

犬蝠 Quanfu—**Distinctive Characteristics:** HB 80–90; T 7–12; HF 16–19; E 18–21; FA 66–83; GLS 30–38. Size medium; wingspan averages 380 mm; dorsal hair olive brown; body sides reddish brown; ventral surface rusty yellow to greenish brown; female pelage distinctly paler; ears with pale edges. **Distribution:** S China from Xizang to Fujian; extending from Indian subcontinent across SE Asia. **Natural History:** Primarily an inhabitant of lowland forested regions and agricultural areas. Feeds on a variety of fruits, flowers, and even leaves. In doing so, it is likely to be an important pollinator and seed disperser of various plants. Plucks small fruits without landing, and carries them to feeding roosts a short distance away. Shuttles back and forth between fruiting trees and feeding roosts several times per night. Roosts are most often in the foliage, and it is known to modify leaves, stems, and clusters of fruit into "tents" that serve as shelters. Colonies are usually small, and composition within roosts suggests a harem structure, with males defending roosts containing various numbers of females and young. The reproductive system is one of bimodal polyestry, with females undergoing postpartum estrus, and producing a single young twice per year. The gestation period is 115–125 days. The young weigh about 11 g at birth and grow rapidly to about 25 g by the time they are weaned at about one month. Adult dimensions are attained by about two months of age. **Conservation Status:** China RL—NT. IUCN RL—LC.

GENUS *EONYCTERIS*—Dawn Bats

大长舌果蝠属 Dachangsheguofu Shu—大长舌果蝠 Dachangsheguofu
Tongue long and pointed, quite extensible; second digit without claws; metacarpals of fifth digit much shorter than those of third; tail length about equal to hind foot length (with claw); size medium or small; forearm length 60–80 mm. Dental formula: 2.1.3.2/2.1.3.3 = 34. Distributed in the Indo-Malayan realm. Of three species, only one occurs in China.

Lesser Dawn Bat *Eonycteris spelaea*

长舌果蝠 Changsheguofu—
Distinctive Characteristics: HB 80–130; T 11–23; HF 17–24; E 17–24; FA 61–73; GLS 35–37. Compound hairs (from glandular areas) short and thick; dorsal hair dark brown or blackish brown; ventral surface paler and taupe colored; anal glands well developed; third molar in upper jaw tiny. **Distribution:** S China; extending from Indian subcontinent to Malaysia and Indonesian archipelago. **Natural History:** Roosts primarily in caves, making them

vulnerable to disturbance. Colonies of tens of thousands have been reported from areas outside China. Found commonly in disturbed and agricultural areas, although they do occur in primary forest as well. These are nectar-feeding bats and have adapted to using the flowers of many important agricultural and orchard crops. They are particularly abundant in banana plantations. Known to travel up to 38 km to reach feeding areas. Females become sexually mature at six months, but males mature later, at one year or more of age. Reproductive cycle in China unknown, but reported to breed asynchronously and aseasonally in India. **Conservation Status:** China RL—VU A1acd; B1ab(i,ii,iii). IUCN RL—LC.

GENUS *MACROGLOSSUS*—Long-nosed Fruit Bats

小长舌果蝠属 Xiaochangsheguofu Shu—小长舌果蝠 Xiaochangsheguofu
Third and fifth metacarpals subequal in size. Dental formula: 2.1.3.2/2.1.3.3 = 34. Distributed from Myanmar to the Solomon Islands and N Australia. One of two species is found in China.

Greater Long-Nosed Fruit Bat *Macroglossus sobrinus*

安氏长舌果蝠 Anshi Changsheguofu—**Distinctive Characteristics:** HB 70–89; T 0–6; HF 10–18; E 14–19; FA 38–52; GLS 28–29. Rostrum elongated and slender, clearly adapted for nectar feeding. Ears medium-sized, brown, with small antitragus and narrow, rounded tips. Pelage soft and fine, uniformly clay brown dorsally and buffy brown ventrally. Forearms and inner part of wing membranes haired, as are the upper surface of the tibiae and interfemoral membrane. Wing membranes insert at base of fourth toe; calcar reduced. **Distribution:** S Yunnan; extending to Myanmar, NE India, S Laos, C and S Thailand, and Vietnam. **Natural History:** Nothing known for China. Elsewhere known to occur in evergreen forest at up to about 2,000 m in montane and lowland forests, and in mangrove swamps. They have been found roosting in palm trees in small groups of 5–10 individuals. May roost outside of buildings in NE India. Feed on nectar and pollen of wild bananas and other plants. Home ranges are thought to be small, with typical movements of 1–2 km per night. They may breed year-round, but few data are available. **Conservation Status:** China RL—NA. IUCN RL—LC.

GENUS *PTEROPUS*—Flying Foxes

狐蝠属 Hufu Shu—狐蝠 Hufu
Size largest in the Chiroptera; forearm length more than 90 mm; second digit with well-developed claw (fig. 7); hind foot with well-developed calcar; tail absent; uropatagium rather narrow; rostrum elongated. Dental formula: 2.1.3.2/2.1.3.3 = 34. Distributed in Indo-Malayan realm, eastward to Australia; of 65 species, four are reported from China.

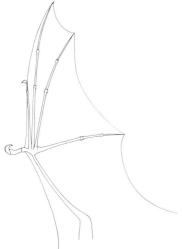

Figure 7. Wing of a flying fox (*Pteropus*) showing the second digit with a well-developed claw and an enlarged thumb.

Ryukyu Flying Fox *Pteropus dasymallus*

琉球狐蝠 Liuqiu Hufu— **Distinctive Characteristics:** HB 186–227; HF 40–55; E 20–28; FA 124–141; GLS 60–65. Size smaller than *P. giganteus*; upper part of tibia with hairs; entire body with long, compound hairs, giving fur an almost woolly aspect; color reddish brown, with yellowish-white nape. **Distribution:** Taiwan; extending to Ryukyu and Philippine islands. **Natural History:** Poorly known. Hunted for food in the past, populations have been reduced to the point that the species is considered endangered. **Conservation Status:** China RL—EN A1acd; B1ab(i,ii,iii). CITES—II. IUCN RL—NT.

Indian Flying Fox *Pteropus giganteus*

大狐蝠 Dahu Fu—**Distinctive Characteristics:** HB 198–300; HF 43–58; E 33–45; FA 152–186; GLS 63–78. Size very large; forearm length 186 mm on Chinese specimens; ear long and sharp; breadth of uropatagium 28 mm; head and dorsal hair dark taupe; shoulder and nape rusty brown, separated from dorsal color by a black stripe; chin, throat, and upper chest blackish brown; venter paler than dorsum. **Distribution:** E Qinghai; extending across the Indo-Malayan realm. **Natural History:** Nothing known from China. In other areas, this species forms large, conspicuous colonies in the canopy of large forest trees. Feeds on a wide variety of fruits, including some orchard crops. Females are monestrous and bear a single young after a gestation period of 140–150 days. **Conservation Status:** China RL—NA. CITES—II. IUCN RL—LC.

Lyle's Flying Fox *Pteropus lylei*

泰国狐蝠 Taiguo Hufu—**Distinctive Characteristics:** HB 200–250; HF 40–45; E 35–39; FA 145–160; GLS 61–67. Medium-sized flying fox, with dark brown rostrum becoming paler between the ears, yellowish mantle, and black dorsum and wings. Ventrally, the chin is dark, throat varies from yellowish to reddish, and venter is black. Fur on mantle somewhat softer than other areas. Nostrils separated by deep groove, rendering them almost tubular in appearance. **Distribution:** Yunnan; extending to Cambodia, Thailand, and Vietnam. **Natural History:** Nothing known from China. In other areas, it is known to form large colonies in trees that can become stripped of leaves by the bats' activity. It is thought to be a pest of some fruit crops. **Conservation Status:** China RL—NA. CITES—II. IUCN RL—VU A4cd.

Large Flying Fox *Pteropus vampyrus*

马来大狐蝠 Malaida Hufu—**Distinctive Characteristics:** HB 259–340; HF 44–65; E 28–57; FA 190–210; GLS 75–87. Externally similar to *P. giganteus*, but larger. Also, the venter tends to be darker than that of *P. giganteus*. Throat dark russet brown; chest and abdomen blackish brown, with occasional paler hair tips. **Distribution:** Shaanxi (Xi'an); extending to Myanmar, Indonesia, Malaysia, Philippines, and Vietnam. **Natural History:** Nothing known from China. Forms large colonies in forest canopy, including primary and secondary forest, agroecosystems, and mangroves along the coast. Reported to feed on a wide variety of fruits, and may fly 10–20 km from roosts to foraging sites. Heavily hunted in some areas, where its large size makes it a useful food item. Ranges from sea level up to 1,300 m. Females give birth to a single young, varying seasonally depending on location. Young remain with mothers for two or three months, and the life span may exceed 15 years. **Conservation Status:** China RL—NA. CITES—II. IUCN RL—NT.

GENUS *ROUSETTUS*—Rousette Fruit Bats

果蝠属 Guofu Shu— 果蝠 Guofu
Size medium; length of forearm 73–103 mm; second digit with claw; has tail and calcar. Dental formula: 2.1.3.2/2.1.3.3 = 34. Distributed in Africa and S Asia, to Indonesian islands. Two of nine species are found in China.

Geoffroy's Rousette *Rousettus amplexicaudatus*

抱尾果蝠 Baowei Guofu—**Distinctive Characteristics:** HB 105–115; T 15–17; HF 20–23; E 18–20; FA 79–87; GLS 35–40. Slightly smaller than *R. leschenaultii*, but with considerable overlap in size. *R. amplexicaudatus* is darker in color than *R. leschenaultii* and tends to be a uniform dull grayish brown. The underparts are gray-brown, the neck is pale gray, and the wings are uniformly dark brown. The ears tend to be a bit narrower (12–13 mm) than those of *R. leschenaultii* (14–15 mm). **Distribution:** Yunnan; extending to Cambodia, Thailand, Myanmar, and Laos; Malay Peninsula through Indonesia, Java, and Bali; Philippines; New Guinea; and Bismarck archipelago to Solomon Islands. **Natural History:** Occurs from sea level up to 2,200 m elevation. Roosts are known from caves, rock crevices, and old tombs. May travel long distances each night in search of appropriate fruit. Use a primitive form of echolocation while foraging. Gestation is thought to be about 15 weeks, and lactation about three months. **Conservation Status:** China RL—NA. IUCN RL—LC.

Leschenault's Rousette *Rousettus leschenaultii*

棕果蝠 Zong Guofu—**Distinctive Characteristics:** HB 95–120; T 10–18; HF 19–24; E 18–24; FA 80–99; GLS 34–40. Medium-sized species, with first digit 23–31 mm and second phalanx of third digit 41–51 mm; dorsal hair uniformly dark brown; nape and ventral surface relatively pale grayish brown. **Distribution:** Across S China, including Hainan Island; extending to Sri Lanka, Pakistan, Vietnam, and Malay Peninsula, plus Sumatra, Java, Bali, and Mentawai Islands (Indonesia). **Natural History:** Generally found in forested areas, where it roosts in colonies of up to 2,000 individuals in caves and man-made structures. Colonies may shift depending on food availability. Roosts containing both sexes are known, as are male-only and female-only colonies. The breeding system appears to be bimodal polyestry, with the females having postpartum estrus after the birth of a single young twice each year. Lactation lasts about two months, and females become sexually mature at about five months, in time to participate in the second breeding cycle of their birth year. Both sexes reach full adult size after one year, and males become sexually mature at about 15 months. **Conservation Status:** China RL—LC. IUCN RL—LC.

GENUS *SPHAERIAS* (monotypic)

球果蝠属 Qiuguofu Shu

Blanford's Fruit Bat *Sphaerias blanfordi*

布氏球果蝠 Bushi Qiu-guofu—**Distinctive Characteristics:** HB 80–90; HF 11–12; E 16–20; FA 50–61; GLS 27–28. Body dull grayish brown; pelage long and dense; fur extends onto tibia and underside of forearm; anterior margin of ears edged in white; antitragus small and triangular; tail absent; interfemoral membrane very narrow, with no calcar; wing membrane inserts on distal half of first phalanx of outer toe; uropatagium reduced. Dental formula: 2.1.3.1/2.1.3.2 = 30. **Distribution:** E Xizang and Yunnan; extending to N India and Bhutan through Myanmar, N Thailand, and Vietnam. **Natural History:** Very poorly known but thought to be most common in lower montane forests. **Conservation Status:** China RL—EN B1ab(i,ii,iii) + 2ab(i,ii,iii). IUCN RL—LC.

FAMILY RHINOLOPHIDAE

GENUS *RHINOLOPHUS*—Horseshoe Bats

菊头蝠科 Jutoufu Ke; 菊头蝠属 Jutoufu Shu— 菊头蝠 Jutoufu
Ears wide and long, without tragus; rostrum with complicated, leaflike skin outgrowth—the nose leaf. Skin surrounding nostrils expanded into three parts: lower part horseshoe-shaped, covering the upper lip and surrounding the nostrils, with a notch in the center; above the nostrils it forms a pointed, erect lancet, attached at the base; between the horseshoe and the lancet is the sella, flattened from side to side and attached at the base by various folds and ridges. First toe with only two phalanges, others each with three; second digit of forelimb with metacarpal bone only, lacking phalanx; third digit with two phalanges. Distributed widely in the Eastern Hemisphere; east to Philippines, New Guinea, and NE Australia; mainly occurs in tropical and temperate zones. Dental formula: 1.1.2.3/2.1.3.3 = 32. Of 77 species of *Rhinolophus*, 20 are known to occur in China.

Intermediate Horseshoe Bat *Rhinolophus affinis*

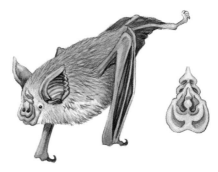

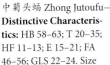

中菊头蝠 Zhong Jutoufu—**Distinctive Characteristics:** HB 58–63; T 20–35; HF 11–13; E 15–21; FA 46–56; GLS 22–24. Size smaller than that of *R. ferrumequinum*; tibia length 20–25 mm; tail length about 1.5 times that of tibia; wing membrane long; fourth and fifth metacarpal bones about equal in length, both slightly longer than third; horseshoe lobe of nose leaf large, accessory lobe very reduced; sellar leaf slightly fiddle-like, its lateral margins a little sunken; conjoined leaf low and round; apical lobe cuneal; hair color brown or taupe, ventral surface slightly paler. **Distribution:** Widely dispersed across SE China, including Hainan Island; extending widely in the Indo-Malayan realm. **Natural History:** Found both in wet western highlands and in more tropical eastern lowlands. Occurs from sea level up to at least 2,000 m, and roosts in caves. Roosts contain both sexes, with little or no spatial segregation. Forages near ground level, as evidenced by frequent capture in mist nets. Echolocation frequencies from 73 to 80 kHz have been recorded. Reproductive habits unknown in China, but there is some indication of bimodal polyestry from other areas. Females bear only a single young at a time. **Conservation Status:** China RL—NT. IUCN RL—LC.

Little Japanese Horseshoe Bat *Rhinolophus cornutus*

角菊头蝠 Jiao Jutoufu—**Distinctive Characteristics:** HB 38–44; T 17–27; HF 7–8; E 16–19; FA 38–41; GLS 16. Size very small; tibia long, around 16.2–17.4 mm; tail distinctly longer than tibia; ears very large, wing membrane not very prolonged; middle rictus of horseshoe lobe without small mammillary process; sellar leaf wide, tending to be narrow from basal part to upper section; conjoined leaf in sharp triangle form, higher than the top level of sellar leaf; pelage color blackish brown, basal portion of hairs off-white. **Distribution:** Widely distributed across SE China, including Hainan Island; extending to Japan and the Ryukyu Islands. It is likely that *R. cornutus* is restricted to Japan, and that the Chinese records actually pertain to *R. pusillus*. **Natural History:** Occur in caves or rock crevices; this species is not common in houses. A variety of moth wings have been found beneath their roosts. **Conservation Status:** China RL—NT; IUCN RL—LC.

Greater Horseshoe Bat *Rhinolophus ferrumequinum*

马铁菊头蝠 Matie Jutoufu—**Distinctive Characteristics:** HB 56–79; T 25–44; HF 10–14; E 18–29; FA 53–64; GLS 21–25. Size large; length of tibia 23–26.6 mm; wing membrane long; metacarpal bones of third, fourth, and fifth digits increasing in length gradually; horseshoe lobe of nose leaf very wide, its accessory lobe small and inconspicuous; lateral margins of sellar leaf sunken and slightly fiddle-shaped; conjoined leaf low and round; tip of apical lobe sharp, long, and narrow; only a medium-sized vertical groove left in underlip, two lateral grooves have disappeared; pelage color smoky gray-brown. **Distribution:** Occurs throughout C and E China; extending across the Palaearctic realm. **Natural History:** This is the most northerly species in the genus, and it occupies a wide range of habitats. It is active year-round in southern parts of the range but hibernates during the northern winters. Adult bats forage up to 2–3 km from the roost each night, feeding on beetles and a variety of other insects. Like other hibernators, they have a long life span and have been recorded living to 26 years of age. This species appears to have a long prepubertal period of three to seven years, with females averaging five years of age when they first give birth. Individual females may give birth only every other year in some cases. Although a single young is more common, twins are produced on occasion. Lactation lasts about 45 days, with the young beginning to fly and forage on their own before weaning. **Conservation Status:** China RL—LC. IUCN RL—LC.

Formosan Woolly Horseshoe Bat *Rhinolophus formosae*

台湾菊头蝠 Taiwan Jutoufu—**Distinctive Characteristics:** HB 90; T 28–39; HF 16–17; E 28–33; FA 56–61; GLS 24–28. Similar to *R. luctus*, but smaller; length of tibia 28–33 mm; fur silky and glossy; length of second phalanx of third digit less than 1.5 times that of first phalanx; third, fourth, and fifth metacarpal bones increase gradually in length; nose leaf with posterior part tapered into lancet; intermediate part with circular lateral lappets at base of sella; connecting process low; anterior part horseshoe-shaped, with deep notch in lower margin; ear, nose leaf, and wing membranes blackish. **Distribution:** Taiwan Island. Endemic. **Natural History:** Poorly known, rare form. Individuals have been found roosting in caves, buildings, tunnels, and irrigation conduits at low to middle elevations. Reported from primary forest in the central part of Taiwan. **Conservation Status:** China RL—VU B1ab(i,ii,iii) + 2ab(i,ii,iii). IUCN RL—NT.

Woolly Horseshoe Bat *Rhinolophus luctus*

大菊头蝠 Da Jutoufu—**Distinctive Characteristics:** HB 75–95; T 36–61; HF 16–18; E 28–44; FA 58–81; GLS 28–33. Size very large, largest of Chinese *Rhinolophus*; length of tibia 34–36 mm; compound (glandular) hairs slender, soft, and slightly curly; wing membrane not very elongated; length of second phalanx of third digit less than 1.5 times of that of first phalanx; third, fourth, and fifth metacarpal bones increasing in length gradually; anterior horseshoe lobe of nose leaf noticeably expanded, covering rostrum and without small adhering leaf on sides; inner and outer edges of nostrils protrude, and derive into internasal leaf; basal sellar leaf conspicuously expands into aliform toward either side, so whole sellar leaf takes on trefoil form; conjoined leaf very low and round, growing out from very underside of top of back sellar leaf; apical lobe narrow, long, and tonguelike, with round top; pelage brown or smoky gray; hair tips with light rings, hence a little gray; both ear and flying membrane heavily pigmented. **Distribution:** Widely distributed across SE China, including Hainan Island; extending to India and Nepal eastward to Vietnam and islands in the South China Sea. **Natural History:** Appears to be solitary or living in pairs and favoring tunnels and old mine shafts. Specimens have been taken in hollow trees and under thick bark in other areas. They emerge early in the evening and fly near ground level. Most have been collected in forested areas. This is a widespread species, with little ecological information available. **Conservation Status:** China RL—NT. IUCN RL—LC.

Big-Eared Horseshoe Bat *Rhinolophus macrotis*

大耳菊头蝠 Da'er Jutoufu—**Distinctive Characteristics:** HB 47–51; T 12–32; HF 9–10; E 18–27; FA 39–48; GLS 20. Size small; ears especially large; antitragus relatively small; tibia length about 18 mm; first three metacarpal bones of forelimbs short; fourth and fifth about equal in length; length of second phalanx of third digit less than 1.5 times that of first phalanx; first phalanges of fourth and fifth digits both a little shorter than their second phalanges; pelage color brown, base of hairs off-white;

ventral surface pale; horseshoe lobe of nose leaf very wide, with obvious indentation in middle and a small adhering leaf on both front sides; sellar leaf very wide, breadth about half of its length, two lateral margins parallel, basal part enlarged and forms a simple cup-shaped lobe with internasal leaf; conjoined leaf especially low and in simple arc form, growing out from underside of top of back sellar leaf; apical leaf about equal to sellar leaf in length, with slightly recessed lateral margins and blunt top; lower lip with three vertical grooves. **Distribution:** Widely distributed across SE China; extending from Pakistan through Indochina to the Philippines. **Natural History:** Known to hibernate in caves, but otherwise little is known about this species in China. It has been collected above 1,500 m in India and probably gets above that elevation in China as well. **Conservation Status:** China RL—LC. IUCN RL—LC.

Formosan Lesser Horseshoe Bat *Rhinolophus monoceros*

单角菊头蝠 Danjiao Jutoufu—**Distinctive Characteristics:** HB 40–50; T 15–27; HF 7–9; E 16–17; FA 34–40; GLS 14–16. Size relatively small; similar to *R. cornutus*, but conjoined leaf of nose leaf very sharp and slender, and projecting forward; apical lobe nearly in equilateral triangle form; basal part of sellar leaf wide. **Distribution:** Taiwan. Endemic. **Natural History:** This common form roosts in large colonies in caves and tunnels at low elevations. It is occasionally found roosting with other species but segregates from them inside the cave. **Conservation Status:** China RL—VU A1cd; B1ab(i,ii,iii). IUCN RL—LC.

Osgood's Horseshoe Bat *Rhinolophus osgoodi*

奥氏菊头蝠 Aoshi Jutoufu—**Distinctive Characteristics:** HB 52–54; T 17–21; HF 8–9; E 12–20; FA 41–46; GLS 15–16. Size medium; horseshoe lobe of nose leaf wide (6.4 mm), covering most of rostrum; sella broad, with rounded tip and parallel sides; connecting process varies from pointed to blunt triangle; lancet straight sided; metacarpals roughly equal in size; dorsal pelage pale brown with hairs gray-based; pelage paler gray below. **Distribution:** Known only from type series, from Nguluko, Yunnan. Endemic. **Natural History:** Nothing is known about this species, and apparently it has not been collected since the original type series. **Conservation Status:** China RL—EN A2cd; B1ab(i,ii,iii) + 2ab(i,ii,iii). IUCN RL—DD.

Bourret's Horseshoe Bat *Rhinolophus paradoxolophus*

高鞍菊头蝠 Gao'an Jutoufu—**Distinctive Characteristics:** HB 47; T 24; HF 10; E 26–39; FA 50–63; GLS 19–22. Similar to *R. rex*, but smaller. Ears wide, about 21 mm, and very long; antitragus large, 17 × 8 mm; nose leaf sella broad and lacking lappets; internarial cup broad, subcircular, and enclosing the base of the sella; lancet low and rounded.

Distribution: Guangxi; extending to Vietnam, Thailand, Laos. **Natural History:** A rare species, only recently reported from China. One specimen from Thailand was taken in a dry pine forest, near open plains. Other trees in the area included *Shorea*, *Pentacme*, *Xylia*, and *Ficus*. Several parasites were obtained from that animal, including trombiculid mites, nycteribiid flies, and flies in the genus *Ascodipteron*, which were embedded in the ear and wing membranes. These bats roost in caves in limestone areas of lowland rain forest. Relative to other rhinolophids, *R. paradoxolophus* uses lower-frequency echolocation sounds (22–43 kHz). **Conservation Status:** China RL—NA. IUCN RL—LC.

Pearson's Horseshoe Bat *Rhinolophus pearsonii*

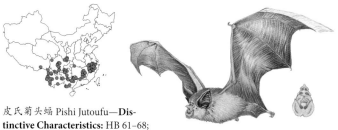

皮氏菊头蝠 Pishi Jutoufu—**Distinctive Characteristics:** HB 61–68; T 16–29; HF 12–13; E 23–29; FA 47–56; GLS 24. Similar to *R. yunanensis*, but size smaller; tail slightly shorter than tibia; third, fourth, and fifth metacarpal bones of wing membrane slightly increasing in length by turns; sellar leaf high, with blunt lateral margins; basal nose leaf not expanded into aliform; conjoined leaf low and round, extending downward from top of sellar leaf in shape of round arc, and conspicuously lower than the top level of sellar leaf; apical lobe sharp; paralabral groove (beside the lips) single; hairs long and thick, dark brown; dorsum color not distinct from ventral surface. **Distribution:** Widely distributed across SE China; extending across S Asia. **Natural History:** This species has been taken from a very broad elevational range, from 600 m to over 3,000 m. It is also known to hibernate in caves and bomb shelters, even when other species of *Rhinolophus* do not. In Thailand observed using feeding perches, from which it made short sallies, in bamboo thickets. Young have been recorded in May and June. Echolocation calls have a frequency of around 65 kHz. **Conservation Status:** China RL—LC. IUCN RL—LC.

Least Horseshoe Bat *Rhinolophus pusillus*

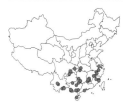

菲菊头蝠 Fei Jutoufu—**Distinctive Characteristics:** HB 38–42; T 13–26; HF 6–8; E 13–20; FA 33–40; GLS 14.8–16.8. Very similar to *R. cornutus*, but size even smaller; tibia short, length 13.5–15 mm; wing membrane not very long; length of second phalanx of third digit less than 1.5 times that of first digit; basal part of middle rictus of horseshoe lobe with two small mammillary processes; sellar leaf narrow, its basal part distinctly wider than top; connecting process triangular or hornlike; lancet hastate, varying from equilateral to elongate; hair color brown, basal portion of hair off-white. **Distribution:** Widely distributed across SE China, including Hainan Island; extending across S Asia. **Natural History:** Little known from China, but in other parts of SE Asia most specimens have come from between 1,000 and 1,500 m elevation. They are known to roost in caves in numbers up to 1,500 and in smaller colonies in houses. They have been noted foraging low over bamboo clumps in limestone areas and have also been taken in primary forest. Echolocation calls at frequencies of 90–95 kHz. **Conservation Status:** China RL—NT. IUCN RL—LC.

King Horseshoe Bat *Rhinolophus rex*

贵州菊头蝠 Guizhou Jutoufu—**Distinctive Characteristics:** HB 50; T 32–38; HF 9; E 29–35; FA 55–63; GLS 23–24. Similar to *R. paradoxolophus*, but size noticeably larger; tibia length about 21 mm; antitragus well developed; third, fourth, and fifth metacarpal bones about equal in size; length of second phalanx of third digit less than 1.5 times that of first phalanx; horseshoe lobe of nose leaf very wide, breadth 3–4 mm more than that of rostrum, with a deep indentation in middle; sides of basal part without small adhering leaf; inner edges of nostrils linked with aliform lateral leaf of basal sellar leaf to form cup-shaped lobe; sellar leaf tall, with slightly protruding lateral margins and round top; conjoined leaf undeveloped, low, and of simple arc form, growing out from very underside of top of back sellar leaf; apical lobe very short and completely covered by sellar leaf, its lateral margins slightly protruding, length about one-third that of sellar leaf; compound hairs very long, length of dorsal hairs 16 mm; dorsal pelage brown, and ventral surface light. **Distribution:** S China. Endemic. **Natural History:** Little known; one report of individuals hibernating in a cave. **Conservation Status:** China RL—EN A2cd + 3cd; B2b(i,ii,iii)c(i,ii,iii). IUCN RL—LC.

Rufous Horseshoe Bat *Rhinolophus rouxii*

鲁氏菊头蝠 Lushi Jutoufu—**Distinctive Characteristics:** HB 59; T 20–33; HF 22; E 14–22; FA 44–53; GLS 20–23. Similar to *R. sinicus*, but slightly larger; metacarpals increase slightly in size from third to fifth; horseshoe lobe of nose leaf narrow (7–9 mm), with small secondary leaflet; sella parallel-sided with round summit; connecting process rounded; lancet hastate, with narrow tip; soft, silky pelage brown to rufous dorsally and slightly paler below. **Distribution:** Known from a single record from W Yunnan; extending from Sri Lanka through India to Vietnam. **Natural History:** Nothing known of this species from China. In India, the species is restricted to forested areas with high rainfall below 1,500 m. Colonies of dozens to hundreds of individuals are known from caves, tunnels, hollow trees, wells, and temples. Females may form maternity colonies while males scatter. They have been reported to feed on grasshoppers, moths, beetles, termites, mosquitoes, and other diptera. In India, copulation occurs in December and parturition in May and June. Apparently, young are born in October in Sri Lanka. Echolocation call frequencies range from 73 to 85 kHz. **Conservation Status:** China RL—NA. IUCN RL—LC.

Shortridge's Horseshoe Bat *Rhinolophus shortridgei*

短翼菊头蝠 Duanyi Jutoufu—**Distinctive Characteristics:** HB 51–59; T 18–25; HF 9; E 16–20; FA 39–43; GLS 16.8–18.7. Size medium; tail slightly longer than tibia; wing membrane not very elongated; length of second phalanx of third digit less than two times that of first phalanx; third metacarpal bone also not elongated, its length about equal to that of fourth and fifth; nostril not completely covered by nose leaf, which possesses an indentation in the middle with a small depression on either side; basal sellar leaf wider than top, middle part slightly recessed; lower lip with three vertical grooves; hair color brown, base of hairs black-gray; ventral surface relatively pale. **Distribution:** SE China; extending to India and Myanmar. **Natural History:** Poorly known; it has been collected in seasonally dry dipterocarp forest in Myanmar. **Conservation Status:** China RL–LC. IUCN RL—LC.

Thai Horseshoe Bat *Rhinolophus siamensis*

泰国菊头蝠 Taiguo Jutoufu—**Distinctive Characteristics:** HB 38; T 14; HF 8–9; E 19–22; FA 36–41; GLS 17–18. Size small; ears large in relation to head; antitragus small; third metacarpal slightly shorter than fourth and fifth; fur short but not woolly; upperparts pale brown and venter buffy; nose leaf large and covers the upper lip; sella broad and rounded, well haired; lancet triangular; connecting process rounded on top; lower lip with three grooves. **Distribution:** Yunnan; extending to Thailand, Laos, and Vietnam. **Natural History:** Echolocation calls have been recorded at 51 kHz. **Conservation Status:** China RL—LC. IUCN RL—LC.

Chinese Rufous Horseshoe Bat *Rhinolophus sinicus*

中华菊头蝠 Zhonghua Jutoufu—**Distinctive Characteristics:** HB 43–53; T 21–30; HF 7–10; E 15–20; FA 43–56; GLS 18–23. Size medium; similar to *R. rouxii* and *R. thomasi*, but with relatively longer wings than *rouxii*; slightly larger than *R. thomasi*; second phalanx of third digit smaller than or close to 1.5 times the first phalanx in size; wing membrane attaches at heel; metacarpal bones long, the third about 33–38 mm; either side of horseshoe nose leaf has an adhering, secondary leaf; horseshoe nose leaf breadth 8–9.2 mm; lateral margins of sellar leaf nearly parallel, its top wide and round; connecting process low and round; upper part of apical lobe slender; basal two-thirds of dorsal hair brownish white, the tip reddish brown; venter brownish white. **Distribution:** C, S, and SW China; extending across the Indo-Malayan realm. **Natural History:** Reasonably common in S China and occurs as high as 2,800 m in India, where it is also known to hibernate. Colony size is variable, ranging from a few individuals to several hundred, and females form maternity colonies during the reproductive season. **Conservation Status:** China RL—LC. IUCN RL—LC.

Little Nepalese Horseshoe Bat *Rhinolophus subbadius*

浅褐菊头蝠 Qianhe Jutoufu—**Distinctive Characteristics:** HB 35–37; T 16–19; HF 7–8; E 14–18; FA 33–38; GLS 14–15. Smallest species of *Rhinolophus*; ears small to medium; sella like that of *R. pusillus*, but superior connecting process more hornlike; lancet short and broad; lower lip with three grooves; third metacarpal slightly shorter than fourth and fifth; pelage cinnamon brown dorsally, hairs with grayish bases and brownish tips; underparts slightly paler. **Distribution:** Yunnan; extending to India, Nepal, Vietnam, and Myanmar. **Natural History:** Poorly known; nothing is known of its habits in China. Extralimitally, these bats are known from lowland forests. **Conservation Status:** China RL—DD. IUCN RL—LC.

Thomas's Horseshoe Bat *Rhinolophus thomasi*

托氏菊头蝠 Tuoshi Jutoufu—**Distinctive Characteristics:** HB 48–50; T 18–28; HF 8–10; E 16–20; FA 40–48; GLS 18–20. Similar to *R. sinicus*, but size slightly smaller; metacarpal bones short, length of the third 30–34 mm; second phalanx of third digit longer than half the length of first phalanx; horseshoe lobe of nose leaf medium, breadth 7.2–8.9 mm; apical lobe short; lateral margins of sellar leaf parallel. **Distribution:** SW China; extending down the Indo-Chinese peninsula. **Natural History:** Nothing is known from China, but this species is known to roost in caves and with other species of *Rhinolophus* in other areas. **Conservation Status:** China RL—VU A1cd. IUCN RL—LC.

Trefoil Horseshoe Bat *Rhinolophus trifoliatus*

三叶菊头蝠 Sanye Jutoufu—**Distinctive Characteristics:** HB 62–65; T 30–35; HF 13; E 22–27; FA 50–54; GLS 21–25. Medium-sized and most similar to *R. luctus,* from which it differs in having a yellowish nose leaf. Base of ear also yellowish; nose leaf broad (10.5–12.4 mm); sella narrow, with basal lappets; connecting process low; lancet long and emarginated; lower lip with single groove; metacarpals increase in size from third through fifth; fur long and somewhat woolly, pale buff or brownish above, and grayish brown below. **Distribution:** Known from a single specimen from Guizhou (Jinsha); extending to NE India, Myanmar, Thailand, Malay Peninsula, Borneo, Sumatra, and outlying islands. **Natural History:** Nothing known from China, but known primarily from lowland evergreen forests in other areas. Echolocation calls were recorded at 51.2 kHz in Malaysia. **Conservation Status:** China RL—EN C2a(i,ii). IUCN RL—LC.

Dobson's Horseshoe Bat *Rhinolophus yunanensis*

云南菊头蝠 Yunnan Jutoufu—**Distinctive Characteristics:** HB 60–68; T 18–26; HF 12–14; E 23–32; FA 54–60; GLS 24–28. Size large for genus. Most similar to *R. pearsonii,* but larger. Horseshoe nose leaf broad (12.5–14 mm); sella wide at base and tapering toward tip; lancet long and triangular; lower lip with single groove; third metacarpal shortest and fifth longest; fur woolly and dense, pale brown or gray dorsally and paler ventrally. **Distribution:** Yunnan; extending to Thailand, Myanmar, and India. **Natural History:** Apparently most common at middle elevations from about 600 to 1,300 m, this species has been collected from bamboo thickets, and also from thatched roofs. **Conservation Status:** China RL—EN A2abc; B1ab(i,ii,iii) + 2ab(i,ii,iii). IUCN RL—LC.

FAMILY HIPPOSIDERIDAE—Old World Leaf-nosed Bats

蹄蝠科 Tifu Ke—蹄蝠 Tifu

Very similar to the Rhinolophidae, but nose-leaf structure different; nose leaf includes a horseshoe-shaped anterior lobe, with a few leaflets on either side of its anterior extremity; behind horseshoe lobe is a transversely protuberant middle lobe (corresponding to sellar leaf of Rhinolophidae), further behind it is a transversal apical lobe (corresponding to apical lobe of Rhinolophidae), which is sometimes separated into four sections by a longitudinal ridge; ear also without tragus. Dental formula: 1.1.1–2.3/2.1.2.3 = 28–30. Second digit of wing possesses only metacarpal bones; other digits each with two phalanges; each toe with two phalanges. Distributed in tropical and subtropical zones of the Eastern Hemisphere, east to Oceania; in China restricted to southern regions, including SW, S, and C China. Of nine genera, three are known to occur in China.

GENUS *ASELLISCUS*—Old World Leaf-nosed Bats

三叶蹄蝠属 Sanyetifu Shu—三叶蹄蝠 Sanyetifu

Size similar to that of *Hipposideros*; tail normal (not reduced); structure of nose leaf different, upper edges of apical lobe noticeably recessed, forming three linked, sharp leaflets. Of two species, only one occurs in China.

Stoliczka's Asian Trident Bat *Aselliscus stoliczkanus*

三叶蹄蝠 Sanye Tifu—**Distinctive Characteristics:** HB 40–50; T 30–40; HF 9–10; E 10–14; FA 39–44; GLS 16. Size very small; fur long; basal part of dorsal hairs nearly white, hair tips brown; ventral surface paler than dorsum; upper margin of nose leaf with three distinct points, two accessory lateral leaflets on each side of nose leaf. **Distribution:** S China; extending across SE Asia. **Natural History:** A colony in Thailand roosted in loose association in limestone caves, with individuals at least 30 cm from one another. Reproductively active females have been collected in May and June in Laos and Vietnam. **Conservation Status:** China RL—NT. IUCN RL—LC.

GENUS *COLEOPS*—Tailless Leaf-nosed Bats

无尾蹄蝠属 Wuweitifu Shu—无尾蹄蝠 Wuweitifu

Tail especially reduced; well-developed antitragus; horseshoe lobe of nose leaf very wide, separated into two broad parts by a crevice in middle, and with a long and narrow leaflet on either side of basal part. Dental formula: 1.1.2.3/2.1.2.3 = 30. Of two species, only one occurs in China.

East Asian Tailless Leaf-Nosed Bat *Coelops frithii*

无尾蹄蝠 Wuwei Tifu—

Distinctive Characteristics: HB 38–50; T 0; HF 5–9; E 11–15; FA 35–42; GLS 16. Size very small; compound (glandular) hairs slender and thick, basal part grayish black, tip brown; tips of ventral hairs slightly brownish white. **Distribution:** SE China, including Hainan Island and Taiwan; extending across Indochina. **Natural History:** In Taiwan, this species is found in man-made structures, such as old military pillboxes. May roost in caves. Basically a forest species, it has been found in small colonies in hollow trees extralimitally. Breeding females are known from January and March in Java. **Conservation Status:** China RL—VU A1cd. IUCN RL—LC.

GENUS *HIPPOSIDEROS*—Old World Leaf-nosed Bats

蹄蝠属 Tifu Shu—蹄蝠 Tifu

Form similar to that of *Rhinolophus*, but structure of nose leaf very different; each toe with only two phalanges; external ears well developed; tragus absent; anterior basal parts of ears usually with large antitragi on outer side; tail developed, longer than femur. Dental formula: 1.1.2.3/2.1.2.3 = 30. Geographical distribution matches that of *Rhinolophus*; of 67 species of *Hipposideros*, eight are known to occur in China.

Great Leaf-Nosed Bat *Hipposideros armiger*

大蹄蝠 Da Tifu—**Distinctive Characteristics:** HB 80–110; T 48–70; HF 13–17; E 26–35; FA 82–99; GLS 31–33. Size very large; third and fourth metacarpal bones about equal in length, fifth slightly shorter; calcar half as long as tibia; ears large and sharp, with recessed posterior edges; large horseshoe anterior lobe of nose leaf without indentation in middle, but with four leaflets on either side of basal part; behind it is a transverse middle lobe, which possesses a protuberant vertical ridge; behind middle lobe is apical lobe, with three vertical ridges; behind apical lobe of adult male are two thickened dermal lobes, with a frontal gland in middle; wing membrane starts at anterior extremity of tibia. **Distribution:** C and SE China (south of the Yangtze River); widely distributed in the Indo-Malayan realm. **Natural History:** A widespread, colonial species found in a variety of habitats. Inhabits caves and a variety of man-made structures. Colonies can number in the hundreds of individuals, and they co-occur with species of *Rhinolophus* and others. They forage both close to the ground and occasionally above the canopy of the forest. Breeding activity tends to be in the summer, and two young are born at a time. **Conservation Status:** China RL—LC. IUCN RL—LC.

Fulvus Leaf-Nosed Bat *Hipposideros fulvus*

大耳小蹄蝠 Da'er Xiaotifu—**Distinctive Characteristics:** HB 40–50; T 24–35; HF 6–10; E 19–26; FA 38–44; GLS 15–16; Wt 8–9 g. Size medium; ears large, with rounded tips; third metacarpal shorter than fourth; feet small; nose leaf about 5 mm wide; pelage color variable, ranging from dull yellow through pale gray to golden orange. **Distribution:** W Yunnan; extending from Afghanistan to Vietnam. **Natural History:** Nothing is known from China, but elsewhere it is common in a variety of habitats, ranging from dry plains to upland forests. It is also found in both wet and dry areas. Roosts include wells and buildings, as well as caves. Colonies may range from a few individuals to several hundred. Flight is slow and deliberate, and these bats sometimes forage close to the ground in addition to the canopy. Breeding begins in November, and parturition occurs in April and May. **Conservation Status:** China RL—NA. IUCN RL—LC.

Grand Leaf-Nosed Bat *Hipposideros grandis*

缅甸蹄蝠 Miandian Tifu—**Distinctive Characteristics:** HB 60–80; T 30–45; HF 10–15; E 20–23; FA 52–65; GLS 20–22. Size large; two color phases, dark brown and reddish brown; ventral hairs smoky gray with brownish tips; mantle pale brown; ears, nose leaf, and wings brown; glandular frontal sac on throat, most prominent in males; ears large and triangular; nose leaf with three supplementary leaflets on each side; anterior leaf simple, with medial notch. **Distribution:** Yunnan; extending to Myanmar, Thailand, and Vietnam. **Natural History:** Nothing known. **Conservation Status:** China RL—NA. IUCN RL—DD.

Intermediate Leaf-Nosed Bat *Hipposideros larvatus*

中蹄蝠 Zhong Tifu—**Distinctive Characteristics:** HB 74–78; T 37–44; HF 10–15; E 23–26; FA 56–69; GLS 23. Size medium; ears very large; horseshoe lobe of nose leaf with indentations in middle, outer sides of its basal part with three leaflets and frontal glands; wing membrane starts at the anterior one-fifth section of the tibia; pelage color nearly grayish puce; ventral surface slightly paler, hairs pale brown-gray at base. **Distribution:** S China, including Hainan Island; extending from India across Indochina. **Natural History:** Occurs from sea level up to 1,000 m. Occupies diurnal roosts in caves, mine shafts, and pagodas. Little is known of its habits in China. **Conservation Status:** China RL—VU A2abcd + 3abcd. IUCN RL—LC.

Shield-Faced Leaf-Nosed Bat *Hipposideros lylei*

鞘面蹄蝠 Qiaomian Tifu—**Distinctive Characteristics:** HB 72–95; T 48–55; HF 16–21; E 30; FA 78–84; GLS 28–29. Size large; color brownish or grayish, with buffy venter; nose leaf brownish pink; ears and wings pale brown; ears wide and triangular, without antitragus; frontal sac with winglike projections, prominent in males; lateral margins of anterior and posterior nose leaves continuous. **Distribution:** Yunnan; extending to Myanmar, Thailand, Malaysia, and Vietnam. **Natural History:** The type specimen was taken from a cave, but little else is known about this species. **Conservation Status:** China RL—NA. IUCN RL—LC.

Pomona Leaf-Nosed Bat *Hipposideros pomona*

双色蹄蝠 Shuangse—**Distinctive Characteristics:** HB 36–52; T 28–35; HF 6–9; E 18–25; FA 38–43; GLS 17–18. Size small; ears very large and blunt, with protruding anterior edges, recessed posterior edges, and a pair of small and low antitragi; nose-leaf structure simple, without leaflets on sides; horseshoe anterior lobe narrow, without indentation in middle; dorsal hair reddish brown; venter brownish white. **Distribution:** S China, including Hainan Island; extending to India, Malaysia, the Philippines, Sumatra, Java, and neighboring islands. **Natural History:** Although widespread, poorly known. **Conservation Status:** China RL—NT. IUCN RL—LC.

Pratt's Leaf-Nosed Bat *Hipposideros pratti*

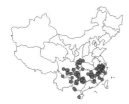

普氏蹄蝠 Pushi Tifu—**Distinctive Characteristics:** HB 91–110; T 50–62; HF 15–22; E 33–38; FA 75–90; GLS 28–35. Size similar to *H. armiger*; ears large and wide; antitragi low and small; horseshoe anterior lobe of nose leaf with only two leaflets on either side, and with concavity in middle; middle of apical lobe higher than sides; behind apical lobe are two large leaflets, with a bundle of long and straight hairs, especially developed in adult males; pelage color brown or dark smoky brown; ventral surface light. **Distribution:** C and SE China, including Hainan Island; extending to Myanmar, Thailand, Malaysia, and Vietnam. **Natural History:** A cave-roosting species; has been found roosting in the same caves as *H. armiger*. **Conservation Status:** China RL—NT. IUCN RL—LC.

Lesser Leaf-Nosed Bat *Hipposideros turpis*

丑蹄蝠 Chou Tifu—**Distinctive Characteristics:** HB 66-88; T 44-59; HF 13-18; E 26-34; FA 66-80; GLS 26-27. Size large; nose leaf simple, with four lateral leaflets; ears large, triangular, with pointed tips; wings broad, attached to ankle; color brownish; individual hairs paler basally, with darker tips. **Distribution:** S Yunnan; also known from Japan (Ryukyu Islands), Vietnam, and Thailand. **Natural History:** Has been netted in forested areas and collected from caves, but nothing is known of its life history. **Conservation Status:** China RL—VU A2abcd + 3abcd. IUCN RL—NT.

FAMILY MEGADERMATIDAE—False Vampire Bats

假吸血蝠科 Jiaxixuefu Ke—假吸血蝠 Jiaxixuefu

Ears especially large, with tragi divided; rostrum with projecting skin outgrowths, which form simple, long, narrow nose leaf; second digit with a developed phalanx; third digit with two phalanges; tail lacking. Dental formula: 0.1–1–2.3/2.1.2.3 = 26–28. Distributed in S Asia, Africa, and Australia; of three genera, only one occurs in China.

GENUS *MEGADERMA*—False Vampire Bats

假吸血蝠属 Jiaxixuefu Shu—假吸血蝠 Jiaxixuefu

Dental formula: 0.1.2.3/2.1.2.3 = 28. Distributed in S Asia, including Sumatra, Kalimantan (Indonesia), and the Philippines. Of two species, only one occurs in China.

Greater False Vampire Bat *Megaderma lyra*

印度假吸血蝠 Yindu Jiaxixuefu—**Distinctive Characteristics:** HB 70–95; T 0; HF 14–20; E 31–45; FA 56–72; GLS 30. Size medium; ears very large and ovoid; inner edges of ears join on top of forehead; nose leaf large, protuberant, and ovoid, with simple structure, length about 10 mm; tail reduced or absent; dorsum mouse brown; venter paler, with base of hairs dark gray and hair tips white; tibia longer than half of forearm length. **Distribution:** C and S China, including Hainan Island; extending from the Indian subcontinent through Indochina to China. **Natural History:** Tends to occupy more arid areas but is found in a variety of habitats. Frequently forages less than 1 m from the ground among trees and undergrowth in tropical forested habitats. Uses a variety of day roosts, including caves, pits in the ground, buildings, and hollow trees. Mating occurs from November through January, with one, or sometimes two, young born from April to June, after a gestation period of 150–160 days. Females form maternity colonies prior to parturition; otherwise both sexes occupy the same roost sites. The sex ratio is balanced at birth, and males are sexually mature by 15 months, females at 19 months. Young are nursed for two to three months, by which time they are capable of flight and foraging on their own. Females may carry the young with them during foraging until the pups are two to three weeks old, at which point they leave them behind in the day roost, or in a special night roost. Highly social animals, forming colonies of a few to dozens of animals. A seasonal colony of 1,500–2,000 was reported in India. Most individuals roost with some space between them. Mothers and offspring, however, frequently roost together more tightly. Mostly carnivorous, feeding on small vertebrates such as bats, birds, rodents, and fish, but also taking large insects and spiders. Detect prey either by passive listening for sounds made by the prey itself, or using echolocation. Usually, they take the prey from leaves or the ground and retreat to a night roost where they consume the items at their leisure. They have been known to enter houses to take lizards and insects directly from the walls. **Conservation Status:** China RL—VU A1cd. IUCN RL—LC.

FAMILY EMBALLONURIDAE—Sheath-tailed Bats

鞘尾蝠科 Qiaoweifu Ke— 鞘尾蝠 Qiaoweifu
Ears with well-developed tragus; inner edges of ears usually joined at the vertex; rostrum without skin outgrowths; tail traverses through the tail sheath of the dorsum; tail tip slightly exceeds posterior edges of sheath; second digit has metacarpal bones but lacks phalanx; third digit has two phalanges, which fold toward back of metacarpal bones at rest. Many species of Emballonuridae have glandular sacs on the anterior edges of propatagium. Dental formula: 2.1.2.3/3.1.2.3 = 30–34. Distributed in tropical zones of Eastern and Western hemispheres; but not known from Australia and New Zealand. There are two subfamilies, Emballonurinae (11 genera) and Taphozoinae (two genera), but only Taphozoinae occurs in China, where only one genus is known to occur.

GENUS *TAPHOZOUS*—Tomb Bats

墓蝠属 Mufu Shu— 墓蝠 Mufu
Size medium; ears large and straight; tragus nearly rectangular; lower lip separated by medium vertical grooves; calcaria very long; tail sheath short; tail tra-

verses dorsum of sheath ; forearm length 50–80 mm. Dental formula: 1.1.2.3/2.1.2.3 = 30. Mainly distributed in tropical zones of the Eastern Hemisphere; of 14 species, two occur in China.

Black-Bearded Tomb Bat *Taphozous melanopogon*

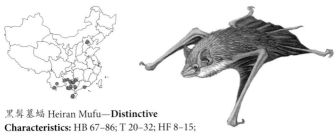

黑髯墓蝠 Heiran Mufu—**Distinctive Characteristics:** HB 67–86; T 20–32; HF 8–15; E 16–23; FA 55–68; GLS 19.4–21.9. Size small; chin with a small tuft of black beard; tail thickened toward tip and laterally compressed; wings attach to tibia, above ankle; both dorsal and ventral hairs black-brown with basal part all white. **Distribution:** S China, including Hainan Island, also Beijing; extending throughout the tropical areas of S Asia. **Natural History:** Occupies a wide variety of forested habitats in tropical regions. Forms colonies of up to 15,000 or more individuals in caves, temples, and ruins. The sexes may roost in separate colonies, or spatially separated within the same colony. The breeding season seems to be well defined, and a single young is normally born after a gestation period of 120–125 days, although twins have been recorded as well. **Conservation Status:** China RL—VU A1acd. IUCN RL—LC.

Theobald's Tomb Bat *Taphozous theobaldi*

大墓蝠 Da Mufu—**Distinctive Characteristics:** HB 88–95; T 25–35; HF 11–18; E 21–28; FA 70–76; GLS 22–24. Size large; color variable, dark brown dorsally and paler ventrally; adult males with a reddish-brown beard; uropatagium hairless; muzzle nearly naked; wings attach above the ankle; wings with well-developed wing pouch; inner edge of nostrils raised; ears large and rounded, with a small, round tragus; tail with a few long hairs at tip. **Distribution:** Yunnan; extending from C India to Vietnam. **Natural History:** A forest species, normally found roosting in caves. Colonies may number from a few hundred to several thousand individuals. Guano from this insectivorous species is mined and used as fertilizer in some areas. **Conservation Status:** China RL—NA. IUCN RL—LC.

FAMILY MOLOSSIDAE—Free-tailed Bats

犬吻蝠科 Quanwenfu Ke— 犬吻蝠 Quanwenfu

Hairs slender and soft, slightly fluffy; ears small, nearly quadrate, with thickened inner edges; ears sometimes join at front; tragi reduced, and antitragi developed;

upper lip plump and crumpled, without nose leaf; uropatagium narrow, short, and plump, second half of tail protrudes from its posterior edges; hind legs short and stout; wing membrane long and narrow; fifth digit slightly longer than metacarpal bones of third digit. Distributed in tropical and subtropical regions of the Eastern and Western hemispheres. There are two subfamilies, Molossinae (15 genera) and Tomopeatinae (one genus), but only Molossinae, represented by two genera, is known to occur in China.

GENUS *CHAEREPHON*—Lesser Free-tailed Bats

小犬吻蝠属 Xiaoquanwenfu Shu—小犬吻蝠 Xiaoquanwenfu
Size medium; tail extends beyond interfemoral membrane; tibia short; wing membranes long and narrow, but with relatively broad tips; ears joined by band over nose. Dental formula: 1.1.2.3/2.1.2.3 = 30. Distributed broadly in Africa and Eurasia, but only a single species of 18 occurs in China.

Wrinkle-Lipped Free-Tailed Bat *Chaerephon plicatus*

犬吻蝠 Quanwenfu—**Distinctive Characteristics:** HB 65–75; T 30–40; HF 9–12; E 16–21; FA 40–50; GLS 18–21. Size medium; ears join at front; upper lip with conspicuous crimps; pelage color dark brown; tips of ventral hairs slightly hoary. **Distribution:** C China, including Hainan Island; extending throughout the tropical regions of S Asia. **Natural History:** Colonies ranging from a few hundred to more than 200,000 have been reported, roosting in caves and buildings. Insectivorous, they forage high and fast, and the guano deposits under large colonies are mined and used for fertilizer in some regions. **Conservation Status:** China RL—VU A2abcd. IUCN RL—LC.

GENUS *TADARIDA*—Free-tailed bats

犬吻蝠属 Quanwenfu Shu— 犬吻蝠 Quanwenfu
Size medium or smaller; terminal half of tail protrudes from uropatagium; tibia short; wing membrane long and narrow. Dental formula: 1.1.1–2.3/1–3.1.2.3 = 26–32. Geographical distribution of this genus is widest of the Molossidae, occurring throughout the tropical and subtropical regions of both the Eastern and Western hemispheres. Of 10 species, only two are known from China.

East Asian Free-Tailed Bat *Tadarida insignis*

宽耳犬吻蝠 Kuan'er Quan-
wenfu—**Distinctive Charac-
teristics:** HB 84–94; T 48–60; HF 10–15; E 31–34; FA 57–65; GLS 22–24. Size
large; posterior margin of ear concave in center; 24–26 horny excrescences on
rhinarium; hairs bicolored, paler at base, giving frosted appearance to otherwise
uniformly pale, drab dorsum; keeled calcar; plagiopatagium attached between
one-fourth and one-third the length of tibia; tragus fringed with hair anteriorly
and dorsally. **Distribution:** SE China, including Taiwan; extending to Japan and
Korea. **Natural History:** Specimens have been taken from caves, but little else is
known about this species. **Conservation Status:** China RL—VU A2cd. IUCN
RL—DD.

La Touche's Free-Tailed Bat *Tadarida latouchei*

华北犬吻蝠 Huabei Quanwenfu—**Distinctive
Characteristics:** HB 67–72; T 41–46; HF 12–13; E
22–25; FA 53–57; GLS 20–22. Size smaller than *T.
insignis*; ears large, joined at front; upper lip with
vertical crimps; fur soft and dense; pelage color
blackish brown, basal portion of hair nearly white,
tips of ventral hairs relatively light; plagiopatagium
attached to basal third of tibia; ears thinner,
smaller, and rounder than those of *T. insignis*. **Distribution:** NE China; also
known from Thailand, Laos, and Japan. **Natural History:** Poorly known. **Conservation Status:** China RL—DD. IUCN RL—DD.

FAMILY VESPERTILIONIDAE—Vesper Bats

蝙蝠科 Bianfu Ke—蝙蝠 Bianfu
Most common, widespread, and speciose family of Chiroptera; has many widely
distributed species; development of ears normal; ears usually separated, only join
at front in a few species; tragi developed, with sharp or blunt tips; rostrum without special dermal outgrowths; second digit with normally developed metacarpal bones and a small phalanx; third digit with three phalanges, the terminal one
cartilaginous except at base; uropatagium complete, wholly encloses tail, or only
tip slightly protrudes. Dental formula: 1–2.1.1–3.3/2–3.1.2–3.3 = 28–38. Widely
distributed in Eastern and Western hemispheres and many large islands, except
polar regions; six subfamilies and 48 genera; 18 genera representing five subfamilies occur throughout China.

SUBFAMILY VESPERTILIONINAE—Vesper Bats

蝙蝠亚科 Bianfu Yake
Size medium to very small; length of ear medium, ears not funnel-shaped, lacking a keel, but with an obvious anterior basal lobe; second phalanx of third digit not elongated; nostrils not tubular. Distributed worldwide; of 38 total genera, 13 occur in China.

GENUS *ARIELULUS*—Sprites

金背伏翼属 Jinbeifuyi Shu—金背伏翼 Jinbeifuyi
Size small to medium; muzzle short, broad, and blunt; ears large, rounded, with blunt tips; ears and tragus edged with dull or yellowish white; pelage blackish brown, with individual hairs frosted with yellowish, orange, russet, copper, or brown. Dental formula: 2.1.2.2/3.1.2.3 = 34. Contains five species that are widely distributed in SE Asia, with two species known from China.

Bronze Sprite *Arielulus circumdatus*

大黑伏翼 Da Heifuyi—
Distinctive Characteristics: HB 95; T 40; HF 10; E 15; FA 41–44; GLS 15–16. Size medium; dorsal pelage black, some hairs with orange tips, giving an almost orange sheen to the head and back, hairs are soft and long; ventral surface uniform brown, paler than dorsal, hairs slightly bicolored, with the roots slightly darker than the tips; ears dark brown-black with pale anterior and posterior margins in some specimens; tragus broad, with pale margins; membranes uniform dark brown and essentially naked. **Distribution:** Yunnan; extending across SE Asia. **Natural History:** Widespread but uncommon. It has been collected from 2,000 m elevation in Nepal and appears to be a highland species, but nothing is known of its natural history. **Conservation Status:** China RL—EN A2c + 3c; C2a(i,ii). IUCN RL—LC.

Necklace Sprite *Arielulus torquatus*

黄喉黑伏翼 Huanghou Heifuyi—**Distinctive Characteristics:** FA 43–46; GLS 16–17. Size medium; dorsal pelage black tipped with bronze; ventral pelage dark tipped with silver; throat with bright ochraceous collar; ears triangular, black, without pale edging; tragus short and curved; muzzle short and broad; proximal half of uropatagium furred; plagiopatagium inserts at base of fifth toe. **Distribution:** Taiwan. Endemic. **Natural History:** The type locality is at 1,800 m elevation, and the only two other known specimens are also from the highlands. Nothing else is known of the life history. **Conservation Status:** China RL—EN C2a(i,ii); D. IUCN RL—LC.

GENUS *BARBASTELLA*—Barbastelles

宽耳蝠属 Kuan'erfu Shu—宽耳蝠 Kuan'erfu
Ears wide and short, joined at front; nostrils lie behind nasal pad, directed upward; dorsal hairs dark, with paler tips; interfemoral membrane near body sides covered with short hair. Dental formula: 2.1.2.3/3.1.2.3 = 34. Distributed across C and SE Asia, Europe, and N Africa. Of two species in the genus, one occurs in China.

Eastern Barbastelle *Barbastella leucomelas*

宽耳蝠 Kuan'erfu—**Distinctive Characteristics:** HB 47–51; T 40–47; HF 7–8; E 15–17; FA 38–45; GLS 14–16. Size small; muzzle short, flat, and broad, with glandular swellings; upper lip densely fringed with hair; ears nearly square, with no antitragal lobe; wings attach to base of outer toe; tail long. Pelage color gray, with whiter tips; compound (glandular) hairs on ventral surface near uropatagium white. **Distribution:** Across China, including Taiwan; extending widely from N Africa and the Caucasus to Japan. **Natural History:** Slow and deliberate flight; frequently seen flying low. Roosts in caves, trees, and buildings. Most colonies are relatively small and found at mid- to high elevations in oak and conifer forests. **Conservation Status:** China RL—VU A1acd. IUCN RL—LC.

GENUS *EPTESICUS*—Serotines

棕蝠属 Zongfu Shu—棕蝠 Zongfu
Form similar to *Pipistrellus*, but rostrum slightly thicker; tragus long and straight, its tip slightly acute. Dental formula: 2.1.1.3/3.1.2.3 = 32. Distributed in temperate and tropical zones of Eastern and Western hemispheres. Of 23 species, four occur in China.

Gobi Big Brown Bat *Eptesicus gobiensis*

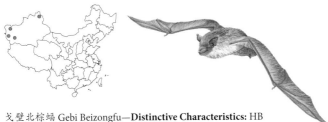

戈壁北棕蝠 Gebi Beizongfu—**Distinctive Characteristics:** HB
57–65; T 40–45; HF 9–10; E 10–15; FA 38–42; GLS 16. Size small;
dorsal pelage reddish yellow, its basal part dark brown; ventral surface brownish
white. **Distribution:** NW China; extending from Iran to Mongolia. **Natural History:** A pale desert species originally described from the Altai Mountains in the
Gobi Desert. It ranges eastward in arid mountain and desert regions as far as
Iran. Inhabits both caves and abandoned buildings. **Conservation Status:** China
RL—NA. IUCN RL—LC.

Northern Bat *Eptesicus nilssonii*

北棕蝠 Beizongfu—**Distinctive
Characteristics:** HB 54–64; T
35–50; HF 10–12; E 13–18; FA
37–44; GLS 14–16. Size small; ears
short, round, and fleshy; tragus short
and round, curving inward; fur dark brown or blackish dorsally, with some
golden-tipped hairs; venter yellowish brown; wings long and broad, with short,
rounded tips; calcar extends half the length of uropatagium; tail extends slightly
beyond uropatagium; wing membrane attaches at base of toe. **Distribution:** NE
China; extending from Europe through E Russia. **Natural History:** Frequents
boreal coniferous forests in much of its range. Diet consists mainly of diptera,
but it feeds on moths and beetles as well. Frequently roosts in buildings, including the attics of occupied houses. Gives birth in June–July. Litter size is one in
the north, but twins are more frequent in southerly regions. The young are capable of flight at two or three weeks of age. Females form maternity colonies in the
summer, and most are philopatric. Known to live for 15 years. **Conservation
Status:** China RL—LC. IUCN RL—LC.

Thick-Eared Bat *Eptesicus pachyotis*

肥耳棕蝠 Fei'er Zongfu—**Distinctive Characteristics:** HB 55–56; T 40–41; HF 8–9; E 13–14; FA 38–40; GLS 21. Size small; ears triangular, with rounded tips, and quite thick and fleshy; tragus short and round, with inward curve; head flat and muzzle short; wings attached to base of toes; color dark brown dorsally and paler ventrally. **Distribution:** C and W China; extending to Bangladesh and India. **Natural History:** Poorly known. **Conservation Status:** China RL—LC. IUCN RL—LC.

Common Serotine *Eptesicus serotinus*

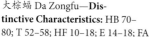

大棕蝠 Da Zongfu—**Distinctive Characteristics:** HB 70–80; T 52–58; HF 10–18; E 14–18; FA 49–57; GLS >20. Size large; dorsal pelage dark brown with gray spots; ventral surface black to brownish white. **Distribution:** Widely distributed across China; extending across N Asia and through Europe. **Natural History:** One of the largest species of *Eptesicus* and frequently is one of the first to appear in the evening, often emerging while there is still daylight. The broad wings and a leisurely, highly deliberate flight with occasional short glides or steep descents are distinctive. Flies at about treetop height (to about 10 m), often close to vegetation, and will sometimes land, wings outstretched, on the foliage to catch large insects. Feeds around street lamps and even catches prey from the ground on occasion. Breeding season is usually in September–October. In the spring, females form maternity colonies, and the young are born in June–July. The young are weaned at about six weeks of age. Colonies, frequently in buildings, are small. Individuals may live up to 19 years of age. Favored feeding areas include pasture, parkland, open woodland edge, tall hedgerows, gardens, suburban areas, and forested regions. Most foraging activity is within 2 km of the roost, although this bat may range up to 6 km. Having caught a large insect, it will fly around slowly, chewing and dropping the wings and legs. Sometimes carries prey to a feeding perch, where it hangs and eats it at its leisure. Roosts mainly in buildings, including houses and churches, but is found less frequently in modern buildings. Access to the roost is usually at or near the highest point or through the eaves. One of the most building-oriented species, hardly ever found roosting in trees. Echolocation calls range from frequencies of 15 to 65 kHz, with a peak at 25–30 kHz. **Conservation Status:** China RL—LC. IUCN RL—LC.

GENUS *FALSISTRELLUS*—False Pipistrelles

假伏翼属 Jiafuyi Shu—假伏翼 Jiafuyi

Size small to medium; similar to *Pipistrellus*, but larger. Dental formula: 2.1.2.3/3.1.2.3 = 34. *Falsistrellus* is broadly distributed in SE Asia and Australia. Of five species, two are known from China.

Chocolate Pipistrelle *Falsistrellus affinis*

茶褐伏翼 Cahe Fuyi—**Distinctive Characteristics:** HB 43–51; T 30–41; HF 7–8; E 12–15; FA 38–40; GLS 15.5. Size medium. Hair color brown, hair tips gray; ventral surface grayish white. **Distribution:** SW China; extending to NE Myanmar, Nepal, India, and Sri Lanka. **Natural History:** Roosts in trees and buildings. It frequently can be seen foraging on small flying insects around human habitations, fairly low to the ground. Occurs from sea level up to 2,000 m elevation. **Conservation Status:** China RL—NT. IUCN RL—LC.

Pungent Pipistrelle *Falsistrellus mordax*

大灰蝠翼 Dahui Fuyi—**Distinctive Characteristics:** HB 47–56; T 37–42; HF 6–9; E 14–16; FA 40–42. Size medium; dorsum rust brown with paler hair tips; venter black-brown with pale brown hair tips; anal region pale brownish yellow; tragus medium-long; wing membrane attached to base of toes; tail projects beyond uropatagium; terminal cartilage of fourth digit divided into a T. **Distribution:** Known only from Yingjiang, Yunnan; extending to Java. **Natural History:** Nothing is known. **Conservation Status:** China RL—NA. IUCN RL—DD.

GENUS *HYPSUGO*—High Pipistrelles

高级伏翼属 Gaojifuyi Shu—高级伏翼 Gaojifuyi

Size small. *Hypsugo* is found in Asia and Africa. Of 18 species, three are found in China.

Alashanian Pipistrelle *Hypsugo alaschanicus*

阿拉善伏翼 Alashan Fuyi—**Distinctive Characteristics:** HB 38; T 39–40; HF 8; E 13; FA 36–38; GLS 14. Size small; color brownish dorsally, but with hair tips paler; venter paler, but with hairs dark brown basally; outer edge of wing with distinct pale border; tragus narrow, with clearly defined basal lobe; tip of tail protrudes slightly beyond uropatagium. **Distribution:** C and N China; extending to Mongolia, Russia, and Korea. **Natural History:** Originally described from desert mountain ranges in N China, this species is now known from a variety of habitats. In spite of this, little is known of its natural history, other than that it roosts in caves. **Conservation Status:** China RL—LC. IUCN RL—LC.

Chinese Pipistrelle *Hypsugo pulveratus*

灰伏翼 Hui Fuyi—**Distinctive Characteristics:** HB 44–47; T 37–38; HF 7–8; E 12–14; FA 33–36; GLS 14–15. Size about equal to that of *Pipistrellus abramus*; ears larger; tragus short and wide; wing membrane attaches to basal part of toe; dorsal hair dark, nearly blackish brown; ventral surface relatively pale, nearly brown, hair tips a little off-white. **Distribution:** C and S China; extending to Vietnam, Laos, and Thailand. **Natural History:** Appears to inhabit forested regions but has also been found roosting in houses. Poorly known. **Conservation Status:** China RL—NT. IUCN RL—LC.

Savi's Pipistrelle *Hypsugo savii*

萨氏伏翼 Sashi Fuyi—**Distinctive Characteristics:** HB 47–60; T 30–35; HF 6–8; E 10–14; FA 32–36; GLS 13.1–14.2. Medium-sized *Hypsugo*; ear and tragus wide and short; wing membrane attaches to heel; tail extends about 5 mm from posterior margin of uropatagium; dorsal hair dark brown; ventral surface taupe. **Distribution:** Xinjiang; extending across Asia and N Europe. **Natural History:** The diet is small flying insects, which are pursued throughout the night. Occurs from sea level up to high mountain valleys across a wide range in S Europe and Asia. Roosts have been found in cracks and crevices, both natural and in buildings. May be migratory in some areas. Becomes sexually mature at about one year of age. One or two young are born in maternity roosts and are weaned at about seven to eight weeks. **Conservation Status:** China RL—LC. IUCN RL—LC.

GENUS *IA* (monotypic)

南蝠属 Nanfu Shu

Great Evening Bat *Ia io*

南蝠 Nanfu—**Distinctive Characteristics:** HB 89–104; T 61–83; HF 13–18; E 22–29; FA 71–80; GLS 27. Very similar to *Pipistrellus*, but size very large; fifth digit very short, its tip reaching only about half or two-thirds of first phalanx of

third digit. Pelage color dark, smoky brown dorsally and dark grayish brown ventrally; face hairless; ears densely haired; tip of tail extends slightly beyond uropatagium. Dental formula: 2.1.2.3/3.1.2.3 = 34. **Distribution:** S and C China; extending to Nepal, India, Thailand, Laos, and Vietnam. **Natural History:** This species is known to roost in caves and occurs at elevations to at least 1,700 m. It forages early and sometimes return to the caves early as well. It may also be migratory in some areas. It has been taken in pine forests in China. **Conservation Status:** China RL—NT. IUCN RL—LC.

GENUS *NYCTALUS*—Noctules

山蝠属 Shanfu Shu—山蝠 Shanfu
Size medium, but sturdy; ears short and wide; tragus short and curved; third digit very short, its length about equal to or a little more than length of metacarpal bone of third or fourth digit; nostrils enlarged, extending half the distance from rostrum tip to interorbital region. Dental formula: 2.1.2.3/3.1.2.3 = 34. Distributed in N Eastern Hemisphere. Of eight species known, three have been recorded from China.

Birdlike Noctule *Nyctalus aviator*

大山蝠 Dashan Fu—**Distinctive Characteristics:**
HB 80–106; T 45–62; HF 12–17; E 16–23; FA 58–64. Size large; thumb short, but with strong claw; calcar keeled; fur dense and velvety, color deep yellowish brown; muzzle broad, with gland between eye and nostril; tragus short and stubby; antitragus long and low; fifth digit shortest, third longest; wing membrane attached to ankle; tip of tail barely extends past uropatagium. **Distribution:** E China; extending to Japan, Korea, and probably Russia. **Natural History:** Inhabits mountainous areas, where it forages in deciduous forests. It leaves the roost early in the evening and forages actively for flying insects fairly high off the ground. Diurnal roosts are frequently in tree cavities. **Conservation Status:** China RL—NT. IUCN RL—NT.

Noctule *Nyctalus noctula*

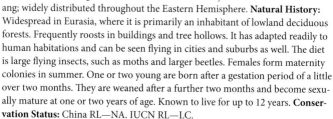

褐山蝠 Heshan Fu—**Distinctive Characteristics:** HB 60–82; T 41–61; HF 12–14; E 16–21; FA 47–60; GLS 17–19.4. Size small; pelage thick, extending onto wing membrane between basal third of fifth digit and knees. **Distribution:** Xinjiang; widely distributed throughout the Eastern Hemisphere. **Natural History:** Widespread in Eurasia, where it is primarily an inhabitant of lowland deciduous forests. Frequently roosts in buildings and tree hollows. It has adapted readily to human habitations and can be seen flying in cities and suburbs as well. The diet is large flying insects, such as moths and larger beetles. Females form maternity colonies in summer. One or two young are born after a gestation period of a little over two months. They are weaned after a further two months and become sexually mature at one or two years of age. Known to live for up to 12 years. **Conservation Status:** China RL—NA. IUCN RL—LC.

Chinese Noctule *Nyctalus plancyi*

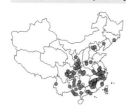

中华山蝠 Zhonghua Shanfu—**Distinctive Characteristics:** HB 65–75; T 36–52; HF 10–11; E 15–18; FA 47–50; 17–19. Size small; smaller and darker than *N. noctula*; bases of individual hairs fuscous, tips brownish, paler ventrally; fur extends onto plagiopatagium along proximal half of humerus and onto uropatagium to mid-tibia. **Distribution:** Widespread across C and E China, including Taiwan. Endemic. **Natural History:** This form enters hibernation in early to mid-November and ovulates at the end of March–early April. It exhibits delayed fertilization, and twins are normally produced in late June following a 50–60 day gestation. **Conservation Status:** China RL—LC. IUCN RL—LC.

GENUS *PIPISTRELLUS*—Pipistrelles

伏翼属 Fuyi Shu—伏翼类 Fuyilei

Form similar to that of *Myotis*, but size generally smaller; ears smallish; tragus short and blunt, unlike the narrow, long, and sharp one of *Myotis*, and with tips slightly turned forward; hind foot smallish; tail entirely enclosed in uropatagium, with only the tip slightly protruding in some species; fifth digit not contracted. Dental formula: 2.1.2.3/3.1.2.3 = 34. Widely distributed in the Eastern Hemisphere and most areas of northern Western Hemisphere; Chinese distribution also very broad. Of 31 species, eight are known from China.

Japanese Pipistrelle *Pipistrellus abramus*

东亚伏翼 Dongya Fuyi—**Distinctive Characteristics:** HB 38–60; T 29–45; HF 6–10; E 8–13; FA 31–36; GLS 12.2–13.4. Size small; dorsal hair taupe or brown. **Distribution:** Widely distributed across E China, including Hainan Island and Taiwan; extending across E Asia. **Natural History:** A common species that is frequently found in buildings and around human habitations. It regularly forms small colonies in attics or between the walls of houses and other buildings. An aerial insectivore, it can be seen feeding in open areas around lights and in disturbed habitats of various types. In spite of its being widespread and abundant, little is known of its natural history. **Conservation Status:** China RL—LC. IUCN RL—LC.

Kelaart's Pipistrelle *Pipistrellus ceylonicus*

锡兰伏翼 Xilan Fuyi—**Distinctive Characteristics:** HB 45–64; T 30–45; HF 6–11; E 9–14; FA 33–42; GLS 14.7–15.8; Wt 9–10 g. Size large; hair color dark brown or brown, hairs without gray tips. **Distribution:** S Guangxi, Hainan Island; extending across Indo-Malayan realm. **Natural History:** Although the range in China is limited, this species occupies a variety of habitats and can be locally common. It is a frequent inhabitant of populated areas, where it roosts in buildings of all types. Colonies from a few to more than a hundred individuals have been noted in caves, tree holes, wells, and similar areas. They fly early in the evening, close to the ground, and are quite deliberate. Beetles and other small insects make up the diet. Females have been shown to store sperm, thus exhibiting delayed fertilization, and the gestation period is just under two months. Twins are the rule, although singles and triplets are also known. Lactation lasts for a little over a month. **Conservation Status:** China RL—NA. IUCN RL—LC.

Indian Pipistrelle *Pipistrellus coromandra*

印度伏翼 Yindu Fuyi—
Distinctive Characteristics: HB 34–49; T 22–39; HF 3–8; E 7–14; FA 25–35; GLS 10.6–11.9. Size small; dorsal pelage uniformly mid- to dark brown, ranging from chestnut to dark clove brown; ventral surface paler, hairs with beige-brown or cinnamon-brown tips and dark roots; ears and membranes mid- to dark brown and essentially naked, with a few hairs on the uropatagium next to the body and tail, above and below. **Distribution:** Xizang; extending to Afghanistan. **Natural History:** Small colonies of a few to dozens of individuals roost in buildings and tree holes and under the bark of trees. Foraging begins at dusk, and individuals occasionally return to the diurnal roost for varying periods during the night. Flight is slow and deliberate, as the bats feed on small diptera and other insects, close to the ground. Twins are the norm, although singles are also known. May breed more than once per year, depending on the locality. **Conservation Status:** China RL—NT. IUCN RL—LC.

Javan Pipistrelle *Pipistrellus javanicus*

爪哇伏翼 Zhaowa Fuyi—
Distinctive Characteristics:
HB 40–55; T 26–40; HF 3–8; E 5–15; FA 30–36. Size medium; dorsal coloration reddish brown to darker brown, sometimes with a frosting from paler-tipped hairs; venter paler; wings and tail membranes darker brown and essentially hairless. **Distribution:** Xizang, W Yunnan; extending broadly across SE Asia and eastward to Afghanistan. **Natural History:** Uncommon resident of both forested and disturbed habitats. Roosts in buildings and other man-made structures. Occurs through a wide elevational range extralimitally, but little is known of its natural history in China. **Conservation Status:** China RL—NA. IUCN RL—LC.

Kuhl's Pipistrelle *Pipistrellus kuhlii*

古氏伏翼 Gushi Fuyi—**Distinctive Characteristics:** HB 35–49; T 30–45; HF 6–8; E 10–13; FA 31–36; GLS 13–14. Size medium; ears short and round; tragus parallel-sided; trailing edge of wing membrane frequently with whitish border;

hair color variable, but dark basally; wings narrow. **Distribution:** Known from a single record in Yunnan; extending from Kazakhstan and India eastward to C Europe. **Natural History:** Nothing is known from China, but in Europe this species is known to bear twins. Becomes sexually mature at about one year of age and lives to about eight years. Like other pipistrelles, it feeds on small flying insects. It enjoys a wide elevational range and is frequently encountered near human settlements. **Conservation Status:** China RL—DD. IUCN RL—LC.

Mount Popa Pipistrelle *Pipistrellus paterculus*

棒茎伏翼 Bangjing Fuyi—
Distinctive Characteristics: HB 42–48; T 31–38; HF 6–7; E 10–13; FA 29–34; GLS 13–14. Size small; dark brown dorsally, and bicolored ventrally, with hair tips paler; uropatagium furred for proximal one-third. **Distribution:** Yunnan; extending to India. **Natural History:** Poorly known. Occurs from sea level up to 2,400 m. Specimens have been collected from clearings in forested regions. **Conservation Status:** China RL—VU D2. IUCN RL—LC.

Common Pipistrelle *Pipistrellus pipistrellus*

伏翼 Fuyi—**Distinctive Characteristics:** HB 40–48; T 29–35; HF 6–7; E 10–12; FA 30–32; GLS 10.5; Wt 4–5 g. Size small; calcar slightly keeled; pelage color blackish gray, paler near sides of body; basal part of hair jet black. **Distribution:** Found across China, including Taiwan, and also found in Xinjiang; extending widely across both Asia and Europe. **Natural History:** These bats feed on small flying lepidoptera and diptera, which they catch by foraging in set patterns. They occupy a wide range of habitats but roost primarily in houses. One or two young are born after a gestation period of about a month and a half. The young begin to fly at about one month and are fully weaned by six to seven weeks of age. They first breed in the year following their birth, and individuals are known to live for up to 17 years. **Conservation Status:** China RL—LC. IUCN RL—LC.

Least Pipistrelle *Pipistrellus tenuis*

小伏翼 Xiao Fuyi—**Distinctive Characteristics:** HB 33–45; T 20–35; HF 3–7; E 5–11; FA 25–31; GLS 9–11; Wt 2 g. Size small; dorsal color varies from medium

to dark brown; ventral color paler, hairs with buffy tips and dark brown bases. **Distribution:** SE China, including Hainan Island; extending westward to Afghanistan. **Natural History:** A widespread species that occurs in a variety of habitats and that is also partial to towns and villages. These bats roost in attics, under roofs, in holes and crevices of walls, in tree holes, and occasionally in the foliage. Colony size is usually small, with no more than a dozen or two individuals. They fly early in the evening and feed on tiny flying insects both in forests and over clearings and fields. Pregnant females have been collected throughout the year, but in most tropical regions there are probably two peaks of activity. From one to three young are born, and weaned at 30–40 days of age. **Conservation Status:** China RL—LC. IUCN RL—LC.

GENUS *PLECOTUS*—Long-eared Bats

大耳蝠属 Da'erfu Shu—大耳蝠 Da'erfu

Size small; ear extremely large, its length much more than head length; ears joined at front; tragus relatively long; nostrils upturned; wing membrane attached to base of toes; tail length about equal to HB length; tail wholly enclosed in uropatagium. Dental formula: 2.1.2.3/3.1.3.3 = 36. Distributed in N Asia, Europe, and N Africa; in China mainly distributed in northern regions and Taiwan. Of eight species in the genus, three occur in China.

Brown Long-Eared Bat *Plecotus auritus*

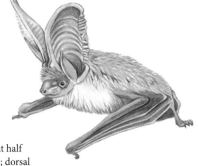

褐长耳蝠 He Chang'erfu—
Distinctive Characteristics: HB 40–45; T 48–50; HF 7–8; E 39–41; FA 36–46; GLS 16.5–18.8. Size small; length of hind foot about half of tibia length; calcar unkeeled; dorsal hair taupe; ventral surface off-white; ears very large, almost equal in surface area to the head and body; ears joined across forehead by narrow band; tail long, exceeding HB length. **Distribution:** Across N China; extending across N Asia and to W Europe. **Natural History:** This widespread species occurs in forested areas at low and moderate elevations and also frequents inhabited areas. It roosts in tree holes and a variety of buildings, as well as caves and tunnels. It has a slow,

deliberate foraging flight, feeds primarily on medium-sized moths and other insects, and occasionally gleans prey from the foliage. A single young is the norm, but occasional twins have been reported. Young are weaned at about six to seven weeks of age and become sexually mature in their second year. The maximum recorded life span is 22 years. **Conservation Status:** China RL—NT. IUCN RL—LC.

Gray Long-Eared Bat *Plecotus austriacus*

灰长耳蝠 Hui Chang'erfu—**Distinctive Characteristics:** HB 41–58; T 37–55; HF 7–10; E 37–42; FA 37–45. Size medium; ears conspicuously long; muzzle long and pointed; fur long and gray in color, with hair dark basally; tips of dorsal hairs vary from buff to brown; ventral hair tips are paler and whitish. **Distribution:** C and W China; extending eastward to Mongolia and to Europe. **Natural History:** This widespread species is frequently found around human habitations. It forages low and slowly, feeding on a variety of small lepidoptera, coleoptera, and diptera. Roosts are known from buildings as well as caves. Colonies tend to be small, and single individuals are common as well. **Conservation Status:** China RL–LC. IUCN RL—LC.

Taiwan Long-Eared Bat *Plecotus taivanus*

台湾长耳蝠 Taiwan Chang'erfu—**Distinctive Characteristics:** HB 48–50; T 47–49; HF 9–11; E 36–39; FA 37–38. Size small; fur rough and long, but with shorter hairs in mid-dorsal region; color blackish, with buffy-brown hair tips giving a golden sheen; ears about the same length as forearms; tragus long and wide, with prominent basal lobe; wings wide; calcar unkeeled; tail completely enclosed in uropatagium. **Distribution:** Taiwan. Endemic. **Natural History:** Poorly known. The holotype was collected in forest at an elevation of 2,250 m in the central mountainous region of Taiwan. **Conservation Status:** China RL–EN B2ab(i,ii,iii). IUCN RL—NT.

GENUS *SCOTOMANES* (monotypic)

斑蝠属 Banfu Shu—斑蝠 Banfu

Harlequin Bat *Scotomanes ornatus*

斑蝠 Banfu—**Distinctive Characteristics:** HB 64–85; T 52–66; HF 12–15; E 19–23; FA 50–62; GLS 20. Size large; pelage color orange-brown or nearly reddish brown; ventral surface slightly lighter; front, shoulder, and back all with white sploches or long spots; ears large; tragus broad and crescent-shaped. Form similar to that of *Scotophilus*, but its pelage is unique, orange-brown and with white spots or stripes; tragus shape similar to that of *Pipistrellus*. Dental formula same as in *Scotophilus*: 1.1.1.3/3.1.2.3 = 30. **Distribution:** C and S China, including Hainan Island; extending eastward to India. **Natural History:** The striking color pattern is likely an adaptation for roosting in the foliage, where most roosts have been found. It seems to be an inhabitant of lowland forests, but little has been recorded of its natural history. **Conservation Status:** China RL—LC. IUCN RL—LC.

GENUS *SCOTOPHILUS*—Yellow House Bats

黄蝠属 Huangfu Shu—黄蝠 Huangfu
Size quite similar to that of *Eptesicus*; form sturdy; ears short and blunt; tragus crescent-shaped; hind foot very large; calcar thick, with a narrow keel; tail tip slightly projects from posterior margins of uropatagium. Dental formula: 1.1.1.3/3.1.2.3 = 30. Distributed in S Asia and Africa; of 12 species in the genus, two are known from China.

Greater Asiatic Yellow House Bat *Scotophilus heathii*

大黄蝠 Da Huangfu—**Distinctive Characteristics:** HB 67–93; T 43–71; HF 9–15; E 13–21; FA 55–66; GLS 21–26. Size large; pelage short and fine; dorsal hair snuff colored; ventral surface light, brownish, or khaki but frequently with a distinct yellowish tint; tail tip protrudes slightly beyond uropatagium; muzzle

short and broad. **Distribution:** S China, including Hainan Island; extending through S and SE Asia. **Natural History:** A common house bat. It forages in clearings and over fields and along forest edges. It is known from sea level up to at least 1,500 m. Colony size is small, usually less than 50 individuals occupying a single roost. Males form harems of two to six females during the breeding season, but the sexes roost separately otherwise. There is evidence of sperm storage in the females. One or two young are born after a gestation period of 115 days. **Conservation Status:** China RL—LC. IUCN RL—LC.

Lesser Asiatic Yellow House Bat *Scotophilus kuhlii*

小黄蝠 Xiao Huangfu—**Distinctive Characteristics:** HB 60–78; T 40–65; HF 8–13; E 9–17; FA 44–55; GLS 16–20. Size small; dorsal hair chestnut brown; ventral surface paler, but without yellowish hue. **Distribution:** S China, including Hainan Island and Taiwan; extending from Pakistan to W Malaysia and the Philippines. **Natural History:** The similarity between *S. kuhlii* and *S. heathii* has led to confusion over their habits. They seem to be quite similar in roosting habits and foraging strategies. *S. kuhlii* colonies of up to a few hundred individuals are known from houses, other man-made structures, and hollow trees. They forage early in the evening and fly low to the ground. They can be seen foraging in inhabited areas as well as over water sources. **Conservation Status:** China RL—LC. IUCN RL—LC.

GENUS *TYLONYCTERIS*—Bamboo Bats

扁颅蝠属 Bianlufu Shu—扁颅蝠 Bianlufu
Size very small; HB length 34–46 mm; head wide and flat; ear length about equal to head length; tragus short, with blunt tip. There are round pads at base of thumbs and on soles of hind feet (fig. 8). Dental formula: 2.1.1.3/3.1.2.3 = 32. Distributed in S Asia and neighboring islands. Both species occur in China.

Figure 8. Feet of bamboo bats (*Tylonycteris*) showing the round pads at base of their thumbs and on the soles of the hind feet.

Lesser Bamboo Bat *Tylonycteris pachypus*

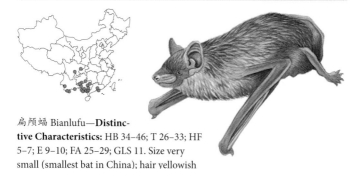

扁颅蝠 Bianlufu—**Distinctive Characteristics:** HB 34–46; T 26–33; HF 5–7; E 9–10; FA 25–29; GLS 11. Size very small (smallest bat in China); hair yellowish brown at base, tips dark brown; ventral surface brownish yellow; wing membrane attached to base of toes; ears broadly rounded; tragus short and broad. **Distribution:** S China; extending throughout the S Indo-Malayan realm. **Natural History:** These tiny bats are found roosting in the internodes of larger species of bamboo. The flattening of the skull and the pads on the feet are presumably adaptations to allow it to use this unique roosting habitat. They form colonies of up to 40 individuals and may form harems. The gestation period is about three months and usually results in twins. The young are weaned at about seven weeks of age. Bamboo bats are known to feed on swarming termites. **Conservation Status:** China RL—NT. IUCN RL—LC.

Greater Bamboo Bat *Tylonycteris robustula*

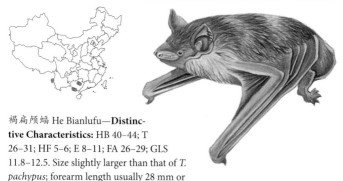

褐扁颅蝠 He Bianlufu—**Distinctive Characteristics:** HB 40–44; T 26–31; HF 5–6; E 8–11; FA 26–29; GLS 11.8–12.5. Size slightly larger than that of *T. pachypus*; forearm length usually 28 mm or more. Pelage color dark brown, darker than that of *T. pachypus*; throat and venter somewhat paler. **Distribution:** Yunnan and Guangxi; extending throughout SE Asia. **Natural History:** Habits quite similar to those of *T. pachypus*. In addition to roosting in bamboo, they are reported to use crevices in rock. Colony size is usually small; colonies consist of a single adult male and few adult females with attendant young. This species is also reported to feed on swarming termites. **Conservation Status:** China RL—VU A1acd. IUCN RL—LC.

GENUS *VESPERTILIO*—Particolored Bats

蝙蝠属 Bianfu Shu—蝙蝠 Bianfu

Size small to medium; HB length 55–80 mm; very similar to *Eptesicus*, but ears shorter and wider; pelage with bright gray spots. Dental formula: 2.1.1.3/3.1.2.3 = 32. Mainly distributed in N Europe and Asia. Both species occur in China.

Particolored Bat *Vespertilio murinus*

双色蝙蝠 Shuangse Bianfu—**Distinctive Characteristics:** HB 55–66; T 40–48; HF 8–10; E 14–16; FA 41–46; GLS 16.5. Size small; two pairs of mammae; basal part of dorsal and ventral hairs blackish brown; hair tips white; white tips of ventral hairs more distinct than those of dorsal hairs; hairs on lateral venter and throat all white. **Distribution:** N China; extending across N Asia and throughout Europe. **Natural History:** This species is widely distributed, and frequently found in and around man-made structures. Roosts are often in cracks and crevices, both natural ones in cliffs and caves and also those in attics, behind shutters, and under joists. Colonies are small, and single individuals are frequently encountered. They forage late in the evening and fly fast and high. They produce audible calls while foraging, in addition to high-frequency echolocation pulses. They feed on medium-sized beetles and moths and other insects. Two and sometimes three young are born, and lactation lasts about six or seven weeks. They breed in the year following their birth and live for up to five years. **Conservation Status:** China RL—LC. IUCN RL—LC.

Asian Particolored Bat *Vespertilio sinensis*

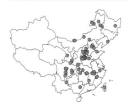

东方蝙蝠 Dongfang Bianfu—**Distinctive Characteristics:** HB 58–80; T 34–54; HF 9–16; E 14–21; FA 43–55; GLS 17.3–18. Size slightly larger than *V. murinus*; one pair of mammae; basal part of dorsal and ventral hairs all blackish brown; hair tips off-white or white; ventral surface a little paler than dorsum; hair color of lower venter wholly white. **Distribution:** Widely distributed across C and E China, including Taiwan; extending mainly across E Asia. **Natural History:** Poorly known. It has been reported roosting in foliage and is known from both mountainous and steppe regions. **Conservation Status:** China RL—LC. IUCN RL—LC.

SUBFAMILY MYOTINAE

GENUS *MYOTIS*—Little Brown Bats

鼠耳蝠亚科 Shu'erfu Yake; 鼠耳蝠属 Shu'erfu Shu—鼠耳蝠 Shu'erfu
Size medium to very small; HB length 35–97 mm; ears well developed, long, and narrow; tragus straight and slender, with sharp tip; tail length 25–60 mm, contained in uropatagium; uropatagium large, its basal part covered with hairs. Dental formula: 2.1.3.3/3.1.3.3 = 38. This subfamily and genus represent the most widely distributed of terrestrial mammals, with more than 100 species worldwide, 23 of which occur across China.

Large-Footed Myotis *Myotis adversus*

爪哇大足鼠耳蝠 Zhaowadazu Shu'erfu—**Distinctive Characteristics:** HB 51–53; T 33–48, HF 10–13; E 14–18; FA 38–45; GLS 15.5. Size very small; tibia length 18 mm, less than two times hind foot length; wing membrane stops at ankles; length of tail less than HB length; calcar long; ears short, length usually less than head length; dorsal hair reddish brown; ventral surface dark brown. **Distribution:** Taiwan; extending down Malay Peninsula to New Guinea and to Solomon Islands, Vanuatu, and eastern and northern coastal Australia. **Natural History:** In Taiwan this species occurs mainly at low to middle elevations and is known to roost in caves and tunnels. Extralimitally, it is known to feed over water, where it catches insects. The large feet and aquatic feeding habitat have led to speculation that this species might occasionally feed on fish. **Conservation Status:** China RL—NT. IUCN RL—LC.

Szechwan Myotis *Myotis altarium*

西南鼠耳蝠 Xinan Shu'erfu—**Distinctive Characteristics:** HB 55–60; T 48–50; HF 11–12; E 22–24; FA 42–46; GLS 15–16. Size medium; tail length less than HB length; hind foot large; calcar very long, length more than half of tibia length, with narrow and small keel; ears long and narrow; laid forward, ears extend beyond rostrum tip; exterior margins of uropatagium without fringe; hair color black-brown, ventral surface paler, but hairs without off-white tips. **Distribution:** S China; extending to Thailand. **Natural History:** All known specimens have been collected from caves. Other than this roosting habitat, nothing is known of the natural history of this species. **Conservation Status:** China RL—NT. IUCN RL—LC.

Hairy-Faced Myotis *Myotis annectans*

缺齿鼠耳蝠 Quechi Shu'erfu—**Distinctive Characteristics:** HB 45–55; T 39–48; HF 10; E 14–16; FA 45–48; GLS 15–17. Size medium; pelage long, dense, and soft; dorsally dark brown, and ventrally the hairs have paler tips; face covered with dark brown hair; ears small and rounded, with relatively broad tragus. **Distribution:** Yunnan (known from a single record); extending from India to Vietnam. **Natural History:** Poorly known. Most specimens have come from mid-elevations. In Vietnam, one was taken in second growth along a river valley. **Conservation Status:** China RL—NA. IUCN RL—LC.

Lesser Mouse-Eared Myotis *Myotis blythii*

狭耳鼠耳蝠 Xia'er Shu'erfu—**Distinctive Characteristics:** HB 65–89; T 53–81; HF 11–17; E 19–22; FA 53–70; GLS 21–23. Size large; dorsal hair black-brown or taupe; ventral surface brown-gray or off-white, with gray hair tips; ears long and narrow; tragus slender; wing membrane attached at ankles; calcar slender and unkeeled. **Distribution:** Scattered localities across China; extending across continental Asia and Europe. **Natural History:** Inhabit a wide variety of habitats, including disturbed areas of various types. They roost in attics of buildings and also in caves, and occasionally in tree holes as well. They may be migratory in some areas. They feed on medium to large insects, including beetles and moths. They may take occasional prey items directly from the ground. They have one or sometimes two young at a time, which are weaned at six to seven weeks of age. Maximum recorded longevity is 13 years. **Conservation Status:** China RL—VU B1ab(i,ii,iii). IUCN RL—LC.

Far Eastern Myotis *Myotis bombinus*

远东鼠耳蝠 Yuandong Shu'erfu—**Distinctive Characteristics:** HB 41–52; T 38–45; HF 8–12; E 14–19; FA 37–42; GLS 14. Size slightly small; ears long and narrow, with narrow tips; tragus narrow and markedly recurved; border of stiff bristles on free edge of uropatagium straight or very slightly curved; pelage soft, woolly, and dark, with basal part of dorsal hairs fuscous, tips paler; ventral coloration paler than that of the dorsum; wings attached to base of toes; calcar long and unkeeled. **Distribution:** NE China; extending to Japan, Korea, SE Russia. **Natural History:** Poorly known in China. Roosts in caves, in small colonies, and may be at least partially migratory. **Conservation Status:** China RL—NA. IUCN RL—NT.

Brandt's Myotis *Myotis brandtii*

埃氏鼠耳蝠 Aishi Shu'erfu—**Distinctive Characteristics:** HB 39–51; T 32–44; HF 7–9; E 12–17; FA 33–39; GLS 14. Size small; pelage long; dorsum pale brown with golden sheen; venter paler gray, sometimes with yellowish tinge; wing membrane attaches at base of outer toe; ear moderately long; tragus narrow and pointed, about half as long as ear. **Distribution:** Disjunct distribution in China (NE and SW); widely distributed in Europe and Asia. **Natural History:** Primarily a forest species; occurs along water courses. Summer maternity colonies are found in buildings, where the individuals frequently hide in cracks and behind beams. Winter roosts are known from caves, tunnels, cellars, and mine shafts. Northern populations hibernate, and some populations are partially migratory as well. They forage on small insects at low elevations and have quick, deliberate flight. One, and occasionally two, young are born in early summer, and they are able to fly at about a month of age. Maximum known longevity is nearly 20 years. **Conservation Status:** China RL—DD. IUCN RL—LC.

Large Myotis *Myotis chinensis*

中华鼠耳蝠 Zhonghua Shu'erfu—**Distinctive Characteristics:** HB 91–97; T 53–58; HF 16–18; E 20–23; FA 64–69; GLS 23. Size large; dorsal coloration dark olive brown, with lateral taupe or blackish-brown striations in transition to dark gray ventral pelage with hair tips slightly paler; calcar long and slender, unkeeled. **Distribution:** C and SE China, including Hainan Island; extending to Thailand, Myanmar, and Vietnam. **Natural History:** Occurs across a wide range of habitats from lowlands through the hill country. It is known to hibernate in caves. **Conservation Status:** China RL—VU A1abc. IUCN RL—LC.

Pond Myotis *Myotis dasycneme*

沼泽鼠耳蝠 Zhaoze Shu'erfu—**Distinctive Characteristics:** HB 57–67; T 46–51; HF 11–12; E 17–18; FA 43–49. Size medium; dorsal coloration yellowish brown; venter slaty black; tragus short, less than half length of ear; uropatagium lacking fringe. **Distribution:** Shandong; extending across Russia to W Europe. **Natural History:** Known from lowlands and foothills, this species frequents areas with abundant water. The bats are known to roost in caves and tunnels, as well as buildings and hollow trees. They may migrate between summer and winter roosts. They leave the roost to forage early and have another foraging bout just before dawn. They feed on a variety of small insects, such as craneflies, other diptera, and small lepidoptera, over the surface of the water, and may take them right off the water surface as well. One, occasionally two, young is born after a gestation period of about two months. Young are weaned after a further two months, and individuals have been known to live for almost 20 years. **Conservation Status:** China RL—DD. IUCN RL—NT.

Daubenton's Myotis *Myotis daubentonii*

水鼠耳蝠 Shui Shu'erfu— **Distinctive Characteristics:** HB 44–58; T 27–41; HF 9–12; E 11–15; FA 34–39; GLS 14. Size small; tibia length about 17 mm; length of hind foot more than half of tibia length, about 11 mm; wing membrane attached at middle part of ankle; tail short, length less than HB length; calcar slender and long, without keel; ear length medium; if turned forward, ears can exceed rostrum tip 1–2 mm; length of tragus about half of ear length; pelage short and thick; dorsal hair dark brown; ventral surface brownish gray or off-white. **Distribution:** NE China; extending across the Palaearctic realm. **Natural History:** Forages extensively over water and frequently roosts nearby. The bats are known to inhabit caves, mine tunnels, cellars, wells, and areas under rubble on the floor of caves. They hibernate in winter and migrate to summer nursery roosts in tree holes, attics, steeples, and under bridges. They fly early in the evening and fly fast and erratically. They feed on small flying insects like diptera and lepidoptera, frequently over water. One or sometimes two young are born after a 50–55 day gestation period, and they are weaned about two months later. Neonates weigh about 2.3 g. Maximum known longevity is more than 20 years. **Conservation Status:** China RL—LC. IUCN RL—LC.

David's Myotis *Myotis davidii*

须鼠耳蝠 Xushu'erfu—
Distinctive Characteristics: HB 41–44; T 30–43; HF 7–9; E 12–15; FA 31–35. Size very small; tibia length 12–13 mm; length of hind foot more than half of tibia length; tail short, barely less than HB length; wing membrane attaches to basal part of toe; calcar long, its length slightly more than half of distance to tail tip; dorsal hair dark brown, hair tips a little paler; ventral hair color same as that of dorsal hair, but tips grayish. **Distribution:** C and S China, including Hainan Island. Endemic. **Natural History:** Nothing known. **Conservation Status:** China RL—NT. IUCN RL—LC.

Fringed Long-Footed Myotis *Myotis fimbriatus*

毛腿鼠耳蝠 Maotui Shu'erfu—**Distinctive Characteristics:** HB 42–52; T 37–48; HF 8–10; E 14–16; FA 37–40; GLS 15. Size small; tibia length about 17 mm; length of hind foot more than half of tibia length; wing membrane attaches at ankles; ventral uropatagium covered with short hairs, its exterior margin also covered with comb-shaped short hairs; length of tail less than HB length; calcar unkeeled; ears about equal in length with head; pelage very short and thick; dorsal hairs black-brown and gray; ventral surface taupe, with slightly off-white hue; basal part of tail with white spots. **Distribution:** C and SE China. Endemic. **Natural History:** A colonial, cave-dwelling species; otherwise, nothing known. **Conservation Status:** China RL—VU A4cd; B1ab(i,ii,iii). IUCN RL—LC.

Hodgson's Myotis *Myotis formosus*

绯鼠耳蝠 Fei Shu'erfu—**Distinctive Characteristics:** HB 45–70; T 43–52; HF 10–12; E 16–17; FA 45–50. Size large; wing membrane attaches at basal part of toe; ears long and narrow, slightly egg-shaped; tragus sharp, long, and narrow; wing membrane along humerus and body sides covered with sparse and short hairs; hair color bright;

dorsal hair brown; ventral surface, wing membrane, and most of uropatagium bright rufous, but wing membrane between phalanges brown-black. **Distribution:** C and E China, including Taiwan; extending widely in the Indo-Malayan realm. **Natural History:** This brightly colored little bat is known to roost in foliage, which probably accounts for the striking color pattern. It has been taken from sea level up to the foothills of the Himalayas. It hibernates in caves during the winter. **Conservation Status:** China RL—VU A1acd. IUCN RL—LC.

Fraternal Myotis *Myotis frater*

长尾鼠耳蝠 Changwei Shu'erfu—**Distinctive Characteristics:** HB 43–57; T 38–47; HF 7–12; E 11–14; FA 36–42; GLS 13.5. Size slightly small; ears short, not reaching rostrum tip when laid forward; wing membrane attached at heel; length of tibia about 20 mm; hind foot length less than half of tibia length; tail length equal to or slightly less than HB length; calcar with small keel; hair dark brown. **Distribution:** C, E, and NE China; extending across E Asia. **Natural History:** Poorly known. The type series was taken from holes in bamboo stems at an elevation of 760 m. **Conservation Status:** China RL—VU A1acd. IUCN RL—DD.

Horsfield's Myotis *Myotis horsfieldii*

郝氏鼠耳蝠 Haoshi Shu'erfu—**Distinctive Characteristics:** HB 49–59; T 34–42; HF 7–11; E 13–15; FA 36–42. Size medium; dorsal coloration dark brown to black; ventral coloration deep brown with grayish tips near tail; wings attached to outer metatarsal; ears rounded and naked; tragus short and relatively broad; hind foot length more than half tibia length. **Distribution:** SE China; extending across SE Asia. **Natural History:** Frequents wooded areas and is often found near water. It roosts in abandoned tunnels, caves, buildings, and bridges, as well as occasionally in foliage. Colonies are small; groups of over 100 individuals are known but uncommon. **Conservation Status:** China RL—VU A1acd. IUCN RL—LC.

Ikonnikov's Myotis *Myotis ikonnikovi*

伊氏鼠耳蝠 Yishi Shu'erfu—
Distinctive Characteristics: HB 36–52; T 30–38; HF 7–9; E 11–13; FA 30–36; GLS 12.7. Size very small; ears short, turning forward nearly to rostrum tip and not distinctly beyond it; wing membrane attached at basal part of toe; exterior margins of uropatagium without comb-shaped fuzz; calcar keeled; dorsal hair dark brown; ventral surface brown. **Distribution:** C and NE China; extending to Russia, Mongolia, Korea, and Japan. **Natural History:** Aside from an individual found hibernating in a cave, nothing is known of the natural history of this species. **Conservation Status:** China RL—LC. IUCN RL—LC.

Chinese Water Myotis *Myotis laniger*

华南水鼠耳蝠 Hua'nanshui Shu'erfu—**Distinctive Characteristics:** HB 40–42; T 38–40; HF 8–11; E 12–16; FA 34–36. Size small; dorsal coloration dark brown; ventral hairs dark at base, with paler brown or gray tips; pelage short; face densely haired; hind foot length slightly more than half tibia length; unkeeled calcar; wing membrane attached to base of toes. **Distribution:** Widespread in C and SE China; extending to India and Vietnam. **Natural History:** Poorly known; utilizes caves. **Conservation Status:** China RL—LC. IUCN RL—LC.

Kashmir Cave Myotis *Myotis longipes*

长指鼠耳蝠 Changzhi Shu'erfu—**Distinctive Characteristics:** HB 43–46; T 37–42; HF 9–10; E 10–15; FA 36–39. Size small; pelage soft and dense; dorsally grayish brown with paler hair tips; ventrally brownish black with creamy-white hair tips; hind foot length exceeds half tibia length; ears long and narrow; tragus long and narrow, about half the ear length; third metacarpal barely exceeds fourth and fifth in length; wing attached to distal end of metatarsal. **Distribution:** Guizhou; extending to India, Nepal, and Afghanistan. **Natural History:** Large colonies in caves and underground canals have been described extralimitally. **Conservation Status:** China RL—VU D2. IUCN RL—DD.

Burmese Whiskered Myotis *Myotis montivagus*

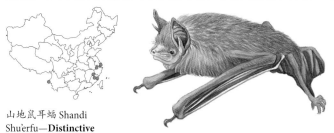

山地鼠耳蝠 Shandi Shu'erfu—**Distinctive Characteristics:** HB 56–62; T 42–48; HF 9–10; E 14–16; FA 40–49. Size medium; dorsal pelage dark brown, hairs with darker roots and paler tips; ventrally similar, with hair tips paler brown; ears short and blunt; tragus short; wings attached to base of toe; hind foot length less than half tibia length. **Distribution:** Yunnan and E China; extending to India, Myanmar, and the Malay Peninsula. **Natural History:** Poorly known; occurs primarily from low to mid-elevations. **Conservation Status:** China RL—VU A1bcd. IUCN RL—LC.

Nepalese Whiskered Myotis *Myotis muricola*

南洋鼠耳蝠 Nanyang Shu'erfu—**Distinctive Characteristics:** HB 41–47; T 25–39; HF 4–7; E 6–13; FA 31–37. Size small; pelage thick and soft; dorsal hairs black basally with paler tips; slightly paler tips ventrally; ears large and pointed; tragus narrow and half the ear length; wing attached to base of metatarsal; hind foot length less than half tibia length. **Distribution:** Across S China, Xizang to Taiwan; widely distributed in SE Asia. **Natural History:** Occupies a variety of habitats, including scrub and second growth, from sea level to moderately high elevations. Small colonies are known from caves, and it has also been recorded roosting in rolled banana leaves. Foraging begins early in the evening, and the bats fly high and fast. **Conservation Status:** China RL—NT. IUCN RL—LC.

Nepalese Myotis *Myotis nipalensis*

尼泊尔须鼠耳蝠 Niboerxu Shu'erfu—**Distinctive Characteristics:** HB 38–47; T 32–40; HF 7–8; E 12–14; FA 34–37. Size small; dorsal pelage dark basally with brown tips, or sometimes more reddish gray; ventral pelage also dark basally but with paler grayish tips; ears small; tragus long and narrow, half as long as ear; hind foot small, less than half tibia length; wing membrane attached to distal end of metatarsal. **Distribution:** C and NW China; extending from Iran to Siberia. **Natural History:** Inhabits both low- and high-elevation areas. It occurs in desert and mountainous habitats. Feeds on lepidoptera. **Conservation Status:** China RL—LC. IUCN RL—LC.

Peking Myotis *Myotis pequinius*

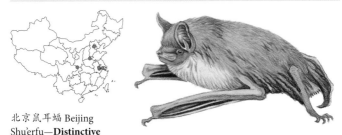

北京鼠耳蝠 Beijing Shu'erfu—**Distinctive**
Characteristics: HB 62; T 42; HF 12; E 18; FA 48–50. Size large; compound hairs long and delicate; when turned forward, ears do not go beyond rostrum tip; tragus relatively short, about half length of ears; wing membrane attached at ankle; exterior margins of uropatagium hairless or lightly fringed; tail shorter than HB length; length of hind foot more than half tibia length; fur rather short and velvety; dorsal hair gray reddish brown; ventral surface off-white. **Distribution:** C and E China. Endemic. **Natural History:** Poorly known; known to occupy caves that also contained *Miniopterus*. **Conservation Status:** China RL—NT. IUCN RL—LC.

Rickett's Big-Footed Myotis *Myotis pilosus*

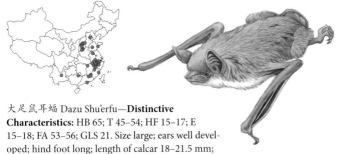

大足鼠耳蝠 Dazu Shu'erfu—**Distinctive**
Characteristics: HB 65; T 45–54; HF 15–17; E 15–18; FA 53–56; GLS 21. Size large; ears well developed; hind foot long; length of calcar 18–21.5 mm; compound hairs short and closely appressed to skin; entire hind legs and feet and basal part of tail sheath covered with short hairs; dorsal hair reddish brown; ventral surface nearly off-white, hairs with black-gray tips; hind foot length with claw equal to tibia length; wing membrane attached at mid-tibia. **Distribution:** E and S China. Endemic. **Natural History:** Feeds on fish and aquatic insects. Near Beijing a single species of fish (*Zacco platypus*) made up 60% of the diet, and beetles composed 13%. These bats have been captured foraging over water, and at cave entrances, in second-growth forest, and in limestone regions. **Conservation Status:** China RL—LC. IUCN RL—NT.

Himalayan Whiskered Myotis *Myotis siligorensis*

高颏鼠耳蝠 Gaolu Shu'erfu—**Distinctive Characteristics:** HB 40–41; T 25–38; HF 6–8; E 8–13; FA 31–36; GLS 13. Size small; tail slightly shorter than HB length; wing membrane attached at basal part of toe; length of hind foot about half of tibia length; calcar with obvious keel; dorsal hair dark smoky gray; ventral surface taupe; wing membrane black. **Distribution:** S and SE China, including Hainan Island; extending widely across the Indo-Malayan realm. **Natural History:** Collected in lowland second-growth forests over streams and at the mouths of caves. It inhabits a variety of both lowland and upland habitats. Colonies of up to 1,200 individuals have been reported from caves. The bats are reported to forage fairly high in the air but also to enter houses to feed on insects. They are active both at dusk and dawn. **Conservation Status:** China RL—NT. IUCN RL—LC.

SUBFAMILY MINIOPTERINAE

GENUS *MINIOPTERUS*—Long-fingered Bats

长翼蝠亚科 Changyifu Yake; 长翼蝠属 Changyifu Shu—长翼蝠 Changyifu
Ears short and wide; tragus slender, with tip slightly turned forward; wing membrane long and narrow; third metacarpal bone relatively short; length of second phalanx of third digit three times that of first phalanx; compound hairs short and thick. Dental formula: 2.1.2.3/3.1.3.3 = 36. Widely distributed in tropical and subtropical regions of Asia, S Europe, and N Africa. Of 19 species, three occur in China.

Western Long-Fingered Bat *Miniopterus magnater*

几内亚长翼蝠 Jineiya Changyifu—**Distinctive Characteristics:** HB 58–75; T 52–64; HF 9–13; E 11–17; FA 47–54; GLS >17. Size large; dorsal pelage long, soft, and blackish brown in color; ventral pelage dark brown, with paler hair tips. **Distribution:** S China, including Hainan Island; widely distributed in SE Asia. **Natural History:** Occupies both primary and secondary forested areas in lowlands and is common around human habitations. Roosts in caves. It forages for high-flying insects above the forest canopy and can also be seen around streetlights in settlements. **Conservation Status:** China RL—VU A2bc; B2ab(i,ii,iii). IUCN RL—LC.

Small Long-Fingered Bat *Miniopterus pusillus*

南长翼蝠 Nan Changyifu—**Distinctive Charac-teristics:** HB 45–48; T 40–48; HF 7–8; E 10–11; FA 39–42; GLS 13.5–14.5. Size small; pelage color dark brown but slightly lighter than that of *M. schreiber-sii*; fur extends slightly onto uropatagium; muzzle relatively long. **Distribution:** S China, including Hainan Island; distributed throughout the Indo-Malayan realm. **Natural History:** Nothing known. **Conservation Status:** China RL—A2bc; B2ab(i,ii,iii). IUCN RL—LC.

Schreiber's Long-Fingered Bat *Miniopterus schreibersii*

长翼蝠 Changyifu—**Distinc-tive Characteristics:** HB 67–78; T 50–62; HF 9–12; E 12–14; FA 47–50; GLS 15.7–17.2. Size large; dorsal pelage color dark brown or reddish brown; venter simi-lar, but hair tips paler; tail, uropatagium, and wings long. **Distribution:** N, SE, and S China, including Hainan Island and Taiwan; extending in a very broad distri-bution across Europe and Asia. **Natural History:** A cave-roosting species; occasionally individuals or small numbers are found in buildings or tree crev-ices. These bats begin to forage early in the evening and have a characteristic rapid, erratic flight. They catch flying beetles and other small insects, fre-quently 10 m or more off the ground. In the north they hibernate in cool caves in the winter. Some populations may also undergo seasonal migrations. They are highly gregarious, and some roosts have tens of thousands of individuals. A single young is born, and the females leave their offspring behind in com-munal nurseries when they leave to forage. **Conservation Status:** China RL—LC. IUCN RL—NT.

SUBFAMILY MURININAE—Hairy-winged Bat and Tube-nosed Bats

管鼻蝠亚科 Guanbifu Yake—管鼻蝠 Guanbifu

Nostrils elongated into tubular structures; ears more or less funnel-shaped; sec-ond phalanx of third digit not particularly elongated. Dental formula: 2.1.2.3/3.1.2.3 = 34. Occur from Pakistan and Ceylon to the Philippines, New Guinea, Australia, and northward to Siberia and Japan. Both genera of Murini-nae are found in China.

GENUS *HARPIOCEPHALUS* (monotypic)

毛翅蝠属 Maochifu Shu

Lesser Hairy-Winged Bat *Harpiocephalus harpia*

毛翼管鼻蝠 Maoyi Guan-
bifu—**Distinctive Characteristics:** HB 60–75; T 40–50; HF 11–14; E 17–18; FA 44–50; GLS 23. Size large; pelage thick and soft; dorsal hair orange-brown; ventral surface light brown; ears rounded; tragus long, with a basal notch; nostrils protuberant. Form very similar to that of *Murina*; hind legs, wing membrane, and uropatagium covered with hair in part. **Distribution:** S China, including Taiwan; extending across SE Asia. **Natural History:** Poorly known. These bats are known to feed on beetles. They have been taken at elevations from sea level up to about 1,500 m. **Conservation Status:** China RL—VU A2abcd; D2. IUCN RL—LC.

GENUS *MURINA*—Tube-nosed Bats

管鼻蝠属 Guanbifu Shu—管鼻蝠 Guanbifu
Form similar to that of *Myotis*, but nostrils prolonged into short tubes; feet small; ears wide and short; uropatagium covered with hairs. Distributed in C, E, and S Asia; of 18 species known, eight occur in China.

Little Tube-Nosed Bat *Murina aurata*

小管鼻蝠 Xiao Guanbifu—**Distinctive Characteristics:** HB 33–35; T 29–31; HF 7–8; E 10–12; FA 28–32; GLS 15.6–15.9. Size small, smallest of the *Murina*; nasal tube somewhat long, projecting forward and outward; ears short, wide, and round; wing membrane attached to base of toes; uropatagium covered with spindly hairs; base of dorsal hairs grayish black, hair tips with golden hue; base of ventral hairs also grayish black, tips off-white. **Distribution:** SW China; extending across E and S Asia. **Natural History:** This widely distributed species remains poorly known. It has been collected as high as 4,000 m. It does not seem to inhabit caves and may use foliage roosts. **Conservation Status:** China RL—VU D2. IUCN RL—LC.

Round-Eared Tube-Nosed Bat *Murina cyclotis*

圆耳管鼻蝠 Yuan'er Guan-
bifu—**Distinctive Charac-
teristics:** HB 38–50; T 32–42; HF 7–10; E 12–15; FA 30–35. Size small; nostrils tubular; ears nearly round, width close to length; tragus wiry; wing membrane attaches to base of toes along lateral margins of hind foot; tail tip dissociated; uropatagium with hairs; back of hind foot also with short hairs; base of dorsal hairs dark brown, tips smoky brown; ventral surface light brown. **Distribution:** Jiangxi and Hainan Island; extending to Zhongnan Peninsula, Philippines, and Sri Lanka. **Natural History:** Inhabits agroforestry areas at intermediate elevations. These bats roost in the foliage, where their color pattern makes them difficult to detect. They have also been taken in small caves and rock shelters. They forage near the ground and are quite deliberate in vegetated areas. **Conservation Status:** China RL—VU B2ab(i,ii,iii); D2. IUCN RL—LC.

Dusky Tube-Nosed Bat *Murina fusca*

暗色管鼻蝠 Anse Guanbifu—
Distinctive Characteristics:
HB 58; T 34; HF 8; E 18; FA
40; GLS 17. Size medium; pelage dusky brown interspersed with numerous longer whitish hairs; dorsally the effect is almost grayish; venter paler; fur extends onto uropatagium and hind feet are also quite hairy. **Distribution:** Known only from the type locality in Heilongjiang. Endemic. **Natural History:** The type specimen was collected in the house of a Russian peasant in late September, suggesting that the species might hibernate in the area. **Conservation Status:** China RL—NA. IUCN RL—DD.

Hilgendorf's Tube-Nosed Bat *Murina hilgendorfi*

东北管鼻蝠 Dongbei Guanbifu—**Distinctive Characteristics:** HB 46–70; T 32–45; HF 10–15; E 14–20; FA 40–45; GLS 16–19. Size large; fur soft, woolly, and glossy; dorsal hair four-banded: dark grayish brown basally, then paler grayish brown, then olive to orange-brown, and golden buff at tips; ventral hairs dark

brown basally, with silvery tips; dorsal surface of uropatagium, plagiopatagium, and thumb covered with hair; ear with two concavities on margin; tragus deflected outward. **Distribution:** NE China; extending to Japan, Kazakhstan, and Russia. **Natural History:** Nothing known. **Conservation Status:** China RL—NA. IUCN RL—LC.

Hutton's Tube-Nosed Bat *Murina huttoni*

中管鼻蝠 Zhong Guan-bifu—**Distinctive Characteristics:** HB 47–50; T 31–39; HF 6–10; E 16–18; FA 29–38; GLS 15–18. Size medium; pelage thick, soft, and brown; ventral surface slightly paler than dorsal hair, but not distinct from it; uropatagium and feet hairy. **Distribution:** SE China; extending from India through Indochina and SE Asia. **Natural History:** Adapted to a variety of habitats at mid-elevations. No details are available on the natural history. **Conservation Status:** China RL—VU A2bc; D2. IUCN RL—LC.

Greater Tube-Nosed Bat *Murina leucogaster*

白腹管鼻蝠 Baifu Guan-bifu—**Distinctive Characteristics:** HB 47–49; T 35–45; HF 9–10; E 14–15; FA 40–43; GLS 18–19. Size relatively large; ears relatively narrow and short; wing membrane attached to toes; fifth metacarpal bone slightly longer than fourth, so wing membrane very wide; both uropatagium and back of hind foot covered with hairs; pelage color reddish brown or brownish gray; dorsal hair mingled with off-white slender and long hairs; ventral surface white and blackish white. **Distribution:** Widely spread across E China; also extending widely across Asia. **Natural History:** Roosts in caves, trees, and houses. Forages in both forested and open areas. **Conservation Status:** China RL—LC. IUCN RL—DD.

Taiwanese Tube-Nosed Bat *Murina puta*

台湾管鼻蝠 Taiwan Guanbifu—**Distinctive Characteristics:** HB 59–61; T 32–36; HF 10–11; E 17–19; FA 34–35. Size medium; pelage long and soft; dorsal color reddish brown, hairs tricolored, with dark bases, tan intermediate zone, and reddish tips; venter paler; legs, hind feet, dorsal surface of uropatagium and tail furred. **Distribution:** Taiwan. Endemic. **Natural History:** Uncommon; apparently restricted to mountainous regions with temperate forest. **Conservation Status:** China RL—EN B2ab(i,ii,iii); D2. IUCN RL—NT.

Ussurian Tube-Nosed Bat *Murina ussuriensis*

乌苏里管鼻蝠 Wusuli Guanbifu—**Distinctive Characteristics:** HB 40; T 25; HF 10; E 13; FA 27; GLS 15. Size small; pelage short and soft; individual hairs dark basally, with pale intermediate band, and reddish-brown tips; venter paler with grayish cast; uropatagium, legs, and hind feet hairy dorsally. **Distribution:** NE China; extending to E Russia and Korea. **Natural History:** Three specimens from Korea were removed from the stomach of a snake. Nothing is known of the natural history in China. **Conservation Status:** China RL—NA. IUCN RL—LC.

SUBFAMILY KERIVOULINAE

GENUS *KERIVOULA*—Woolly Bats

彩蝠亚科 Caifu Yake; 彩蝠属 Caifu Shu—彩蝠 Caifu
Size small; length of ear medium; ears turned forward slightly exceed rostrum tip; they are not joined and are slightly funnel-shaped; tragus long and slender; nostrils normal; whole body with slender and soft hairs; wing membrane attaches to base of toe; calcar unkeeled. Dental formula: 2.1.3.3/3.1.3.3 = 38. Of 19 *Kerivoula*, two occur in China.

Hardwicke's Woolly Bat *Kerivoula hardwickii*

哈氏彩蝠 Hashi Caifu—
Distinctive Characteristics: HB 39–55; T 35–43; HF 5–10; E 11–15; FA 31–36; GLS 15. Size small; dorsal hair smoky brown; ventral surface grayish ochre, the

hairs brownish-gray at the base. **Distribution:** SE China, including Hainan Island; extending across S Asia, Indonesia, and the Philippines. **Natural History:** Widely distributed through subtropical and tropical areas. It has been collected in both forested and agricultural areas. It sometimes forages around houses and villages. It roosts in buildings and under tile roofs on occasion. **Conservation Status:** China RL—VU A2abc + 3abc. IUCN RL—LC.

Painted Woolly Bat *Kerivoula picta*

彩蝠 Caifu—**Distinctive Characteristics:** HB 40–48; T 43–48; HF 4–8; E 13–16; FA 31–38; GLS 15. Size small; compound hairs slender and soft; striking coloration unique: body hair orange; wing membrane also orange, but its interdigital membrane brownish black. **Distribution:** SE China, including Hainan Island; extending across S Asia. **Natural History:** Roosts in the foliage, frequently among dried leaves or flowers that allow it to blend in well. It apparently enters a state of torpor during the day, as it is relatively sluggish when disturbed. The fluttering, erratic flight resembles that of a large moth. **Conservation Status:** China RL—VUA2abcd. IUCN RL—LC.

ORDER PHOLIDOTA

FAMILY MANIDAE

GENUS *MANIS*—Pangolins

鳞甲目 Linjia Mu; 穿山甲科 Chuanshanjia Ke; 鲮鲤属 Lingli Shu—穿山甲 Chuanshanjia
Body covered with scales that are arranged in overlapping rows, with sparse hairs between dorsal scales (Asian forms); venter and inner sides of limbs without scales, but covered with sparse hairs; each limb with five toes; claws long, claws on middle toes of fore and hind feet especially developed; claws of forefeet turning backward; usually walk on back feet; tail long and flat. Head small, and rostrum pointed, acute, and cone-shaped; without teeth. Behavior adapted to living on ants and termites. This order contains only one family, Manidae, and one genus, *Manis*. Pangolins are distributed in S Asia and tropical and subtropical areas of Africa. There are eight species, two of which occur in China.

Indian Pangolin *Manis crassicaudata*

印度穿山甲 Yindu Chuanshanjia—**Distinctive Characteristics:** HB 450–750; T 330–460; HF to 100; GLS 101; Wt 4.7–9.5 kg. Generally similar to *M. pentadactyla* in form, but the external ear is smaller and the underside of the tail tip is

well covered with scales (fig. 9); also, the hind feet are covered with more scales. There are 11–13 rows of body scales and 14–16 scales along edge of tail. Anal glands secrete a foul-smelling yellow fluid that is apparently used as a defense mechanism. **Distribution:** W Yunnan; extending through India, Pakistan, and Sri Lanka. **Natural History:** Occupies forest and scrub habitat. Nocturnal. While terrestrial, it is also an agile climber, using its prehensile tail. The diet is almost exclusively of ants and termites, which it procures using its long, sticky tongue (which may be as long as 30 cm). The powerful forefeet assist in digging for food and in constructing burrows that may extend 1.5–6 m deep. Burrow entrances are closed when they are occupied. When alarmed, it curls up into a ball for defense. Usually a single young is produced (occasionally two); births have been reported during all seasons. Young ride on the base of the mother's tail. **Conservation Status:** China RL—NA. CITES—II. IUCN RL—NT.

Figure 9. Comparative scale patterns on the tails of Indian (*Manis crassicaudata*; a) and Chinese (*M. pentadactyla*; b) pangolins.

Chinese Pangolin *Manis pentadactyla*

穿山甲 Chuanshanjia—**Distinctive Characteristics:** HB 423–920; T 280–350; HF 65–85; E 20–26; GLS 72–94; Wt 2.4–7 kg. Dorsum, sides of limbs, and tail all covered with brown scales; only the ventral midline of the tail tip without scales (fig. 9). There are 15–18 rows of body scales and 16–19 scales along edge of tail; scales smaller than in the Indian Pangolin. Ventral surface off-white, without scales. Has a postanal depression in the skin. Head and ears small, limbs short, with long claws (claws of hind feet less than twice as long as those on forefeet); each limb with five toes. Lacks pads on the soles of its feet—a characteristic that separates it from a third species, *M. javanica*, with which it overlaps south of China. **Distribution:** Throughout SE China, including Hainan Island and Taiwan;

extending into Nepal and N Indochina. **Natural History:** Prefers environments with a thick layer of shrub and herbs growing under a tree canopy. Generally similar to the Indian Pangolin. Diet consists almost entirely of ants and termites, which are procured with a long, sticky tongue following active digging using strongly built fore-claws. Nocturnal and solitary burrowing animals, they roll into a ball for defense when threatened. Adept at climbing trees. Spend winter months in burrows as deep as 3–4 m. Reproduction occurs in late summer to early fall; generally a single young is born. **Conservation Status:** Has undergone a drastic decline and may have been extirpated in some areas due to heavy poaching for food, traditional Chinese medicine, and other products. China RL—EN A2cd + 3cd. China Key List—II. CITES—II. IUCN RL—EN A2d + 3d + 4d.

ORDER CARNIVORA—Carnivores

食肉目 Shirou Mu—食肉类 Shiroulei

Many of the animals in this order are famous for preying on other animals—but not all. Some specialize in eating fruit, insects, bamboo, or shellfish. Although body forms and sizes differ among various species, all the mammals in this order are rather robust and vigorous, with a rather high development of sense organs (hearing, sight, sense of smell). All the terrestrial species have four or five toes with sharp, curved claws on each foot, and are generally quick and agile. Some species are very well adapted to aquatic lifestyles, and the seals rarely even come to land. Many species of this order are of very high economic value. Some are important furbearers, such as sables, otters, seals, weasels, and ferret badgers. Other species such as tigers and bears have been used for traditional medicines. Recently, members of the civet and weasel families have been found to have a connection with infectious diseases acquired by humans, although the exact nature of this connection is unclear. Perhaps the most famous Chinese animal is the Giant Panda (*Ailuropoda*), an endemic rare animal of China.

Carnivores have adapted in a variety of ways for feeding on everything from large mammals to bamboo and fruit. The single most important feature, and the one that is most often cited as uniting the entire order, is a unique modification of the teeth for eating meat. Carnivores have the last premolar in the upper jaw and first molar in the lower jaw normally modified to form two vertical sharp cutting surfaces, which slide against each other in a scissor-like manner. At this location on the skull the jaws have their greatest force, making this pair of teeth—called the carnassial pair—extremely efficient as shears. However, although this is a distinguishing feature, some carnivores have further modified these teeth to best utilize different food resources. Plant-eating and fruit-eating carnivores have more horizontal crushing surfaces, and insect-eating carnivores have reduced teeth with tiny bladelike cusps that can pierce the exoskeleton of insects and get to the food inside. The incisors are relatively small, and the canines are almost always strong and sharp and adapted especially for capturing. Most terrestrial species of this order are nocturnal and solitary, although some species become more diurnal away from human disturbances. Only a few species show any social organization beyond pair bonding. Carnivores are well noted for being highly adaptable and opportunistic and can modify their behavior, home ranges, habits, and feeding to be successful in a variety of situations. For this reason, most are found in a variety of habitats. Carnivores have the most highly developed brain of any order of mammals outside of Primates. Carnivores are found on every continent except Antarctica and in nearly every type of habitat, with species found in the oceans, the Arctic, tropical rain forests, prairies, temperate forests, deserts, high mountains, and even the urban environment. They are rarely a common or abundant part of any ecosystem, usually because they are relatively large and near the top of the food chain. Carnivora is the only order of mammals that has ocean-going, terrestrial, arboreal, and semifossorial species. The order contains two suborders, both found in China. The suborder Feliformia contains the "catlike" carnivores (cats, mongooses, and civets), whereas the suborder Caniformia contains the "doglike" carnivores (dogs, foxes, bears, weasels, Red Panda, sea lions, and seals).

SUBORDER FELIFORMIA—Catlike Carnivores

猫亚目 Mao Yamu—猫 Mao
This suborder includes six families, three of which—the cats (Felidae), civets (Viverridae), and mongooses (Herpestidae)—are found in China.

FAMILY FELIDAE—Cats

猫科 Mao Ke—猫 Mao
Of all terrestrial carnivores, the felids are clearly the most carnivorous. Some species can overcome prey several times their own weight and regularly kill prey in their own weight class. Cats cannot crush food very well; their teeth consist almost entirely of sharp, scissor-like blades without flat surfaces for crushing. Two distinguishing features of felids are the horny papillae on the tongue and the presence of only one molar in each jaw. Dental formula: 3.1.2–3.1/3.1.2.1 = 28–30. They have short faces, forward-pointing eyes, and highly domed or vaulted heads. They do not show the diversity of body form prevalent in other carnivore families. The cats of China all have completely retractile claws and webbing between the toes. A black tail tip is common in most species of cats. The first toe on the forefoot is raised above the level of the others, and it is missing on the hind foot. Cats' binocular vision, unique dentition, and other modifications have been successfully adapted to a wide variety of environments, from high mountain deserts to tropical rain forests. All cats have some ability to climb trees, and all Chinese cats are stalkers or ambush killers. Most cats have good color vision and hunt principally by sight, in spite of the fact that most hunting occurs at night. Two subfamilies are recognized: the Felinae, or small purring cats, and the Pantherinae, or large roaring cats. Overall, there are 39 species of felids found worldwide, 12 of which are found in China.

SUBFAMILY FELINAE—Purring Cats

猫亚科 Mao Yake—猫 Mao
The Felinae have a completely ossified hyoid, a bone between the tongue and the larynx, which they are able to vibrate to produce a purring sound; in the Pantherinae the hyoid is not completely ossified. Feline skulls are also more rounded

than pantherine skulls and have a shorter rostrum. Of 11 genera of Felinae, five (*Catopuma*, *Felis*, *Lynx*, *Pardofelis*, and *Prionailurus*) are found in China.

GENUS *CATOPUMA*—Golden Cats

金猫属 Jinmao Shu—金猫 Jinmao

The two species of *Catopuma* are restricted to SE Asia; one of them is found in China.

Asian Golden Cat *Catopuma temminckii*

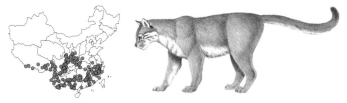

金猫 Jinmao—**Distinctive Characteristics:** HB 71–105 cm; T 400–560; HF 165–180; E 60–70; GLS 98–131; Wt 9–16 kg. Two distinctive color patterns are found. The golden pattern—from which the species derives its name—ranges from very dark brown to red, gold, or gray, with occasional melanistic (all black) individuals; normally the neck and back are a reddish or golden color, and the sides of the body are distinctly paler; in this phase the head always shows the distinctive Asian Golden Cat pattern, described below. The second pattern is the spotted pattern, resembling that found in the Leopard Cat (*Prionailurus bengalensis*). The Asian Golden Cat head coloration is distinctive: there are sharply contrasting longitudinal white interocular eye patches, and a lighter-colored stripe runs from a point medial to the interocular patches (between the eyes) to the crown; this stripe is bordered laterally with black lines. There are usually broad white cheek patches extending from just below the eyes to the cheeks, and the area below the rhinarium and the lower lips is white. The backs of the ears are dark colored (black to dark brown), with fainter coloration in the center. The tail is long (50–66% of HB length) and distinctly bicolored, dark above and whitish below, especially in the distal half of the tail. In the spotted phase, the tail may have 12–15 black bars but otherwise retains the bicolored nature of the golden phase pattern. Dental formula: 3.1.2–3.1/3.1.2.1 = 28–30. **Distribution:** Widely distributed in C, S, and SE China; extending through SE Asia, west to Nepal and south to Sumatra. **Natural History:** Occurs in dry deciduous forests, tropical rain forests, tropical savanna, shrub, and grassland as high as 3,170 m. Primary prey includes medium-sized vertebrates, including small mammals, lagomorphs, small deer, birds, and lizards. Has been known to kill some livestock, including sheep, goats, gorals, and calves of domestic water buffalo. It is a solitary nocturnal hunter and hunts mostly on the ground but is also a good climber. It breeds in tree hollows or in burrows in the ground. No specific breeding season is known. Gestation is about 85–95 days and a litter of one or two kittens is produced. Males play a role in the rearing of the young. Asian Golden Cats are sexually mature at 18–24 months. **Conservation Status:** There are an estimated

3,000–5,000 left in China. China RL—CR A3cd; C2a(i). China Key List—II. CITES—I. IUCN RL—NT.

GENUS *FELIS*—Cats

猫属 Mao Shu—猫 Mao

Of the Felidae, the genus *Felis* is perhaps most familiar to people, as it includes the domestic house cat (*Felis catus*), and indeed, all members of this genus can be mistaken for house cats. *Felis* is represented by small cats with rounded heads, short rostrums, pointed ears, and long tails. Most have spots on the back and stripes on the tail. The genus *Felis* contains six species and is widely distributed in Europe, Asia, the Americas, and Africa. There are four species in China.

Chinese Mountain Cat *Felis bieti*

漠猫 Mo Mao—**Distinctive Characteristics:** HB 600–850; T 290–350; E 58–67; GLS 94–100; Wt 5.5–9 kg. About twice the size of a domestic cat. Pelage is a uniform color but may have indistinct stripes on the legs and sides, and the basic color varies from a yellow-gray to dark brown, with the belly white to light gray. There are two indistinct brownish stripes on the cheeks, and the chin and lower lips are white. The distal portion of the relatively short tail has three or four dark rings and a black tip. The backs of the ears are close to the same color as the body, and there is a small ear tuft of dark reddish hairs. At the base of the ear is a pale reddish-brown area. Dental formula: 3.1.3.1/3.1.2.1 = 30. **Distribution:** C China. Endemic. **Natural History:** Occurs at high elevations (2,800–4,100 m) in alpine meadow, alpine bush, edges of coniferous forests, grassy meadows, and steppe. Its diet consists predominately of zokors (*Eospalax*, *Myospalax*), voles (*Microtus*), pikas (*Ochotona*), and hares (*Lepus*). It also captures birds, especially pheasants. Like most cats, it is solitary and nocturnal. Males and females live separately. They breed from January to March and have a 60-day gestation and an average litter size of two. **Conservation Status:** China RL—CR A2abc; C1 + 2a(i). China Key List—II. CITES—II. IUCN RL—VU C2a(ii) (as *F. silvestris bieti*).

Jungle Cat *Felis chaus*

丛林猫 Conglin Mao—**Distinctive Characteristics:** HB 580–760; T 218–270; HF 108–145; E 45–80; GLS 100–120; Wt 5–9 kg. Light brown, reddish, or brownish-gray cats without a distinctive pattern throughout the body except for some stripes on the legs. Melanistic individuals have been reported from several areas. There is a uniform mixture of dark-tipped hairs throughout the body

except the head, which is usually a rusty color, and there is a distinct spinal crest. The chin and upper throat, the chest between the legs, and the inguinal region are white to light gray. Ears are generally reddish, set close together, with small dark brown to black tufts beyond the ear tips. Eyes and rostrum are highlighted with white patches, and a dark rostral patch reaches to the eyes. The tail is usually around 40% of HB length and has a black tip and distinctive dark rings on the distal half. Males are significantly larger than females. Winter coat is darker than the summer coat. Dental formula: 3.1.2-3.1/3.1.2.1 = 28–30. **Distribution:** C and W China; extending from Egypt through the Middle East, Central Asia, India, and Indochina. **Natural History:** The name "Jungle Cat" is a misnomer, as these cats are found in a wide variety of habitat types, but rarely in tropical rain forests. They prefer tall grass, swamps, cattail thickets and reeds, as well as wet lowland forests around lakes, throughout most of China. Jungle Cats are also found in dry environments along riparian ecosystems and tropical deciduous forests and shrublands, and as high as 2,400 m in the Himalayas. They are very adaptable to a variety of habitat types and often found in agricultural areas. In the southern part of their range, they are often associated with sugarcane plantations. They are usually found near water and prefer dense cover, although they have been reported from desert areas with only sparse cover. The increase in the development of irrigation systems has resulted in population increases in arid regions. The cats have been reported to be associated with gardens, hedgerows, and barns, and are seen around dwellings. They feed mostly on small vertebrates, usually less than 1 kg (lagomorphs, birds, amphibians, fish, and reptiles), depending primarily on rodents. They eat birds' eggs and occasionally take the young of small ungulates such as a wild pigs, gazelles, and deer fawns. Where they live next to humans, they will take chickens, ducks, and geese. They are good swimmers and will go after fish. One study found that hares, rodents, and birds had the largest percentage of occurrence in the diet (hares 10–17%, rodents 85–92%, birds 12–44%,). They can climb and often escape humans by swimming, although they chiefly hunt on the ground. While they can be found at all times of the day or night, they are more diurnal than most cat species. They are normally solitary, and their home ranges are around 5–6 km². Breeding normally takes place from January to February, with the gestation lasting 60–70 days; however, kittens have been observed year-round. Their average litter size is two or three, and they usually have only one litter a year. Sexually mature at one to one and half years. **Conservation Status:** China RL—EN A1c; B1ab(i,iii). China Key List—II. CITES—II. IUCN—LC.

Pallas's Cat *Felis manul*

兔狲 Tusun—**Distinctive Characteristics:** HB 450–650; T 210–350; HF 120–140; E 40–50; GLS 82–92; Wt 2.3–4.5 kg. A short-legged cat about the same size as the Wildcat. However, it has very dense and thick fur, a bushy tail, and a broad forehead with the ears widely spaced apart so that they appear to sit on the sides of the head. Its coat is the longest of any species of wild cat and is a grayish color, with white tips to the hairs, which create a frosted appearance. The eyes are set forward. Forehead randomly scattered with small black spots. Six or seven narrow transverse stripes across the back extend onto the sides to varying degrees. The backs of the ears are similar to the ground color. White rings surround the eyes, and a black line outlines eye patches; there are three small black bands extending under the eyes through the cheeks, and two continue toward the neck and ears. The tail is uniformly gray above and below with a very small black tip. Dental formula: 3.1.2.1/3.1.2.1 = 28. **Distribution:** C, N, and W China; ranging to Mongolia, Russia, Central Asia, and the Middle East and as far west as Armenia. **Natural History:** These cats live on lower slopes of mountains, hilly deserts, and steppes with rock outcrops. They can be found as high as 4,000 m. They generally inhabit dry, high-mountain regions of low rainfall and shallow snow cover. They apparently cannot negotiate deep snow cover in capturing prey, as a continuous snow cover of 15–20 cm or more marks a good boundary for the range of this species. Exposed rock outcrops, talus, and south-facing slopes represent their characteristic habitat. They feed predominantly on pikas (*Ochotona*), small rodents (*Alticola, Meriones, Cricetulus*), hares (*Lepus*), marmots (*Marmota*), and sometimes partridges (*Pyrrhocorax*); they appear to be most numerous where pikas and voles are abundant and not living under deep snow cover. Nocturnal and crepuscular, solitary, and hunt by ambush. They are not fast runners and are most active at dusk and dawn. They breed in February, with a gestation of 65–70 days. The average litter size is three to six. They usually have one litter a year and are sexually mature at 12–18 months. **Conservation Status:** China RL—EN A1cd; B1ab(i,ii,iii). China Key List—II. CITES—II. IUCN RL—NT.

Wildcat *Felis silvestris*

野猫 Ye Mao—**Distinctive Characteristics:** HB 630–700; T 230–330; HF 120–160; E 60–70; GLS 80–106; Wt 3–8 kg. The domestic cat (*F. catus*) and the Wildcat are similar in behavior and appearance, and these forms are known to interbreed. The pelage color of *F. silvestris* is extremely variable, from a grayish

yellow to red, with many irregular black or red-brown spots and two small brown stripes on the cheek. The body is covered with small solid spots that are sometimes fused into stripes. The throat and ventral surfaces are usually whitish to light gray. The forehead has a pattern of four well-developed black bands that contrast against a light background color, and the eyes and rostrum are usually highlighted with white to light gray patches. There are white or light-colored fringes on the edges of the ears; and the hairs on the inner surface of the ears are yellowish white. The backs of the ears vary from being similar to the ground color to a dark brown. The tip of the tail is black, and there are some black transverse rings on the tail. The tail length is less than 50% of the HB length. Females have four pairs of mammae. In the grassland and arid regions of NW China, this is the only species in the wild that resembles the common house cat. It is easily distinguished from Pallas's Cat, which is stockier, with lower-set ears, or from the Chinese Mountain Cat, which is considerably larger, with red ear tufts. **Distribution:** NW China; ranging across Asia and Africa. **Natural History:** Lives in an extremely wide variety of habitats and prefers to live close to fresh-water sources in more arid regions. It is not found in any area with a snow cover over 20 cm. Common in plains and steppe, deserts, and semideserts and often associated with shrub desert. Often colonizes oases, gardens, and settlements, and has been found as high as 2,500 m. It feeds opportunistically on small vertebrates, preferring rodents. Activity may closely match that of the Yarkand Hare (*Lepus yarkandensis*). Known to raid agricultural areas for poultry. Small mammals compose 60–70% of diet, with ground squirrels (*Spermophilus*), gerbils (*Meriones*), and jerboas (*Allactaga*) being the most common prey items. Birds, reptiles, and insects are also common in the diet. Wildcats are mostly nocturnal but sometimes have been observed during the daytime. They are solitary and appear to be territorial. Home ranges are generally around 3–4 km². They live year-round in burrows excavated by other mammals. They can have one or two litters a year and initiate breeding in January–February, with a gestation of 56–65 days. The average litter size is three, and they become sexually mature at 18–24 months. **Conservation Status:** The Chinese population has been estimated to be more than 10,000. China RL—CR A1a. China Key List—II. CITES—II. IUCN—LC.

GENUS *LYNX*—Lynx

猞猁属 Sheli Shu—猞猁 Sheli

Lynx are easily distinguishable from other felids by their long, tufted ears and their bobbed tail. They have a ruff of long fur around the sides of their head, giving them a distinctive appearance. The four species in the genus are distributed throughout the Holarctic, with two species in North America, and two in Eurasia—one of which occurs in China. Lynx give the appearance of being rather short-bodied animals with extremely long legs (the hind limbs are longer than the forelimbs).

Lynx *Lynx lynx*

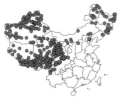

猞猁 She Li—**Distinctive Characteristics:** HB 80–130 cm; T 110–250; HF 225–250; E 80–95; GLS 145–160; Wt 18–38 kg. The largest lynx. Ground color ranges from a grizzled gray to a gray-brown. Spotting on pelage is quite variable and ranges from a few indistinct spots to large, well-defined spots. Lynx in the Himalayan region and SE China are very pale in coloration and often lack the distinct spotting seen in the more typical Lynx found across Eurasia. The throat and undersides are a white to light gray color. Lynx are noted for having the finest silky fur of any of the cat species, with a reported 9,000 hairs per cm² on their back. Lynx have distinctly long legs, with hind limbs appearing longer than forelimbs. The forefoot and hindfoot are wide, with well-developed webbing between the toes, and in winter the undersides of the feet are covered with long, dense hair. The lightness of the weight load on a track (weight/cm²) is one of the best for any species of cat and can support three times that of the domestic cat. Ears have distinctively long tufts, and the backs of the ears have a central light gray spot. There is a wide fringe of long hair from ears to throat. The inside of the ears is always covered with white hairs. The tail is very short—about equal to the hind foot length—and always has a black tip. There are three pairs of mammae. Dental formula: 3.1.2.1/3.1.2.1 = 28. **Distribution:** Widely distributed in all but SE China; extending to Europe and N Asia. **Natural History:** Principally a creature of dense, thick, boreal forests, but also occurs in deciduous forest, steppe, mountains, and alpine regions. Summer range includes steep slopes with rock outcrops and talus slopes overgrown with forests. In the Altai Mountains, Lynx are found in the taiga zone with snow cover not deeper than 40–50 cm. To a great extent, hare and small ungulate distribution determines Lynx distribution. Lynx feed predominately on hares, marmots, pikas, small ungulates, and birds. Throughout most of their range, small ungulates are the most important part of their diet. One study, when ungulates were scarce, gave occurrence in their diet of 65% hare and 21% rodents (many of which were marmots, particularly in the spring). During the winter their diet may focus more on small ungulates. They will also actively seek out and kill foxes. Solitary and nocturnal, they usually avoid water, and may travel up to about 10 km per day. They are ambush predators, and are known to migrate up and down slopes following ungulates and hares to areas of lesser snow cover. Lynx are rare where wolves are numerous. They are excellent tree climbers and use forest trails, logs, and rock out-croppings when hunting. They usually have one litter a year, with an average size of two or three. The gestation is 63–74 days. **Conservation Status:** Chinese population is estimated at around 70,000. China RL—EN A1cd. China Key List—II. CITES—II. IUCN RL—LC.

GENUS *PARDOFELIS* (monotypic)

云猫属 Yunmao Shu

Marbled Cat *Pardofelis marmorata*

云猫 Yunmao—**Distinctive**
Characteristics: HB 400–660; T 450–560; HF 115–120; E 35–40; GLS 79–91; Wt 3–5.5 kg. Shares features with the Clouded Leopard (*Neofelis*) and Snow Leopard (*Uncia*), and appears to be intermediate between the two forms. A lit-tle larger than a domestic cat; the general body shape is more elongated. The background color varies from dark gray to yellowish gray to red-brown. The legs and venter are patterned with black dots, and there are longitudinal stripes on the neck. The ground color is usually a brownish gray to reddish brown with large, irregular dark-edged blotches on the flanks and back. The feet are unusually large, resembling those of pantherines more than other felines. The ears are marked with white bars on the back. There are black stripes on the head, neck, and back, and distinctive white eye patches around the eyes. Spots are scattered on the forehead, rostrum, legs, and tail. The tail is very long and bushy, about as long as the HB. Dental formula: 3.1.3.1/3.1.2.1 = 30. **Distribu-tion:** Yunnan; extending from the southern edge of the Himalayas, throughout Indochina, the Malay Peninsula, and Indonesia (Sumatra and Borneo). **Natu-ral History:** Closely associated with lowland tropical forest, although it has been noted in recently logged forests as well. In the eastern Himalayan foot-hills it is associated with moist deciduous and semievergreen forest habitats between 1,500–3,000 m. Feeds on small vertebrates: squirrels, rats, lizards, frogs, rodents, and birds. Birds are thought to be a major part of the diet. It is nocturnal and solitary, and perhaps more arboreal than most cats. The gesta-tion is 81 days, with an average litter size between one and four young. They are sexually mature at two years. **Conservation Status:** China RL—CR A1c; B1ab(i,iii). CITES—I. IUCN RL—VU C1 + 2a(i).

GENUS *PRIONAILURUS*—Southeast Asian Spotted Cats

豹猫属 Baomao Shu—豹猫 Baomao

Prionailurus contains five species of small SE Asian cats (all about the same size as a house cat), only one of which is found in China.

Leopard Cat *Prionailurus bengalensis*

豹猫 Baomao—**Distinctive**

Characteristics: HB 360–660; T 200–370; HF 80–130; E 35–55; GLS 75–96; Wt 1.5–5 kg. Known in China as "Qian Mao," or money cat, because its spots are said to look like Chinese coins. It is the size of a small house cat but is more slender and has longer legs. Pelage has dark brown spots over a light brown or yellowish ground color in the south and a more grayish ground color in northern areas. The pattern is always distinct and usually consists of four main stripes running back from the head onto the shoulders, where they are broad and conspicuous, but down the spine they are broken up. The sides of the body are marked with spots that never fuse to form vertical stripes. Prominent white stripes run from the nose, by the medial corner of the eyes, and often up over the head. The ears are large and pointed, and the backs of the ears are black with a white spot. Two prominent dark stripes run from the inner corner of each eye to the base of the ear. There is a white streak that extends from the inner corner of each eye toward the nose, and the rostrum is white. The long tail (around 40–50% of HB length) is spotted, with some rings toward the black tip. **Distribution:** Widely distributed across China, except for the arid northern and western regions; extending from Afghanistan through the Indian subcontinent, SE Asia, Russia, and Korea. **Natural History:** These cats occur in a broad variety of habitat types from the tropical rain forests of SE Asia to the conifer forests of the Amur region. They also occur in shrub forests, but not in grasslands or steppe (except marginal areas and riparian ecosystems), and usually avoid areas of deep and continuous snow cover over 10 cm. They can be found in dense second growth, logged areas, tree plantations, and agricultural areas and can live close to rural settlements. They have been found at elevations from 1,000 to 3,000 m in the Himalayas. They feed on small vertebrates such as hares, birds, reptiles, amphibians, fish, and rodents, as well as occasional carrion. They are nocturnal and solitary and are good climbers and excellent swimmers. The average home range size for males tracked in Thailand was 3.5 km². They are often found in pairs, and the male may help in the rearing of young. They are aseasonal breeders with a gestation of 60–70 days. The average litter size is two or three, and young become sexually mature at 18–24 months. **Conservation Status:** China RL—VU A1acd. CITES—II. IUCN—LC.

SUBFAMILY PANTHERINAE—Roaring Cats

豹亚科 Bao Yake—豹 Bao

The Pantherinae subfamily of large cats is appropriately named: These are the largest members of the Felidae and contain the only carnivore known to feed on humans—the Tiger. They are all ambush predators and represent some of the most endangered carnivores in the world. Pantherines are morphologically very similar, and several authors have suggested placing all the members of this subfamily in the genus *Panthera*. Each of the three Pantherinae genera (*Neofelis*, *Panthera*, and *Uncia*) is represented in the Chinese fauna.

GENUS *NEOFELIS* (monotypic)

云豹属 Yunbao Shu

Clouded Leopard *Neofelis nebulosa*

云豹 Yun Bao—**Distinctive Characteristics:** HB 70–108 cm; T 550–910; HF 200–225; E 45–60; GLS 150–200; Wt 16–32 kg. Noted for the distinctive cloud-shaped markings on the back and sides. Its pelage has a ground color uniformly light yellowish to gray, with large, cloud-shaped dark brown spots on sides; two intermittent black stripes run down the spine to the tail base. There are six longitudinal dark brown stripes on the neck, starting behind the ears. The limbs and ventral surface are marked with large black ovals. Crown spotted; rostrum white; dark stripes from the eye and the corner of the mouth along the sides of the head. Ears are short and rounded, and the ear back is black with a light gray spot. Posteriorly, the black eye-ring continues as a black strip across the cheek. The tail is thick and plush, covered proximally with spots and becoming encircled with black rings toward the tip. Length of tail nearly equivalent to HB length. Possesses the longest canine of any felid. Dental formula: 3.1.2–3.1/3.1.2.1 = 28–30. **Distribution:** Found across S China; extending to Indochina, SE Asia, and the Indian subcontinent. **Natural History:** Closely associated with evergreen tropical rain forest, but these felids have also been found in secondary and logged forests. They have been recorded in the Himalayas up to 1,450 m and have been found in coniferous forests up to 3,000 m in Taiwan. Although less commonly, they have been found in grassland and scrub, dry tropical forests, and mangrove swamps. Reported to feed on palm civets (*Paradoxurus*), pigs, pheasants, macaques (*Macaca*), gibbons (*Hylobates*), small mammals, and birds; also known to raid chicken coops. Nocturnal and primarily solitary; most of their hunting appears to occur on the ground, although they are one of the most highly arboreal felids. They can climb down trees head first, traverse branches upside down, and hang from branches with their hind feet. They are good swimmers and may hunt in pairs. They are sexually mature at two years of age and have a gestation of 94 days. Average litter size is three. **Conservation Status:** China RL—EN A1cd; C1. China Key List—I. CITES—I. IUCN RL—VU C1 + 2a(i).

GENUS *PANTHERA*—Panthers

豹属 Bao Shu—豹 Bao
The largest catlike mammals, with the body distinctly striped or spotted in Asian species. The tail is longer than half of HB length; legs are large and muscular, especially the front legs. The rostrum is relatively long. Dental formula: 3.1.2–3.1/3.1.2.1 = 28–30. The genus *Panthera* is distributed on all the continents except Australia and Antarctica and contains four species, two of which occur widely in China.

Leopard *Panthera pardus*

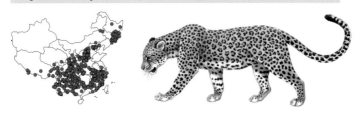

豹 Bao—**Distinctive Characteristics:** HB 100–191 cm; T 70–100 cm; HF 220–245; E 63–75; GLS 175–221; Wt 37–90 kg. The ground color is generally light brown to yellowish gray; the dorsal surface is covered with black spots that are grouped into rosettes, and single black spots occur on the head, legs, tail, and ventral surfaces. The ears appear wide set on the head, short, and rounded. Ground color of the ventral surface is white. Melanistic individuals are relatively common. Leopards have comparatively short legs, and they are the largest spotted cat in Asia. Their tail is about 60–75% of the HB length. Males are 30–50% heavier than females. Dental formula: 3.1.2–3.1/3.1.2.1 = 28–30. **Distribution:** Widely distributed in E, C, and S China; also found throughout Africa, the Middle East, Central Asia, the Indian subcontinent, Indochina, SE Asia, and Russia. **Natural History:** Very adaptable, Leopards are found in a wide variety of habitat types, from open areas with rocks and shrubs to dense tropical forests. They are absent from true deserts but are found in just about any other habitat. Most commonly associated with some type of forest cover, woodlands, scrub jungles, or rocky hills. They have been found at elevations up to 5,000 m. Leopards are predators principally of large ungulates, wild goats, Argali (*Ovis ammon*), and sheep. They are opportunistic feeders and have the amazing ability to survive even on small prey. Leopards eat a much wider range of prey than most other large cats, including rodents, rabbits, deer, antelope, pigs, foxes, monkeys, birds, partridges, and amphibians. Near humans they will eat dogs, cats, sheep, and calves. They usually focus on ungulates weighing less than 50 kg. Whatever is the most locally abundant species of ungulate prey appears to be the most important prey item in the diet. Leopards are very powerful predators and can kill prey two to three times their own weight. They will kill humans and will break into homes to eat humans. Solitary and nocturnal. They easily climb trees and swim well. They are superb climbers and can descend trees headfirst. In the tropical rain forest they will move in the daytime as well as night. Most hunt on the ground and range 3–5 km per day in areas of abundant prey and 10–20 km in areas of scarce prey. Home ranges of females have been reported to be 6–8 km² and males 17–76 km². They breed in February, and after a gestation of 90–105 days they have a litter of two or three. **Conservation Status:** Chinese populations estimated to be less than 10,000. China RL—CR A1acd; C1. China Key List—I. CITES—I. IUCN RL—NT.

Tiger *Panthera tigris*

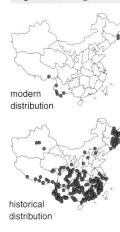

modern
distribution

historical
distribution

虎 Hu—**Distinctive Characteristics:** HB 140–280 cm; T 91–110 cm; HF 234–420; E 95–130; GLS 252–333; Wt 90–306 kg. One of the world's largest carnivores and the largest of all extant cats. It is the most easily recognizable cat, being the only striped cat, and the largest. The pelage is reddish orange to red-brown or orange-yellow with a series of narrow black transverse stripes. The stripes differ on each side of the body, and they continue onto the ventral surface. The ventral surface is white. There is a light white region above the eye. The tail usually has about 10 black rings. The hind legs are slightly longer than the front legs, and the tail is longer than half the HB and very cylindrical. Dental formula: 3.1.3.1/3.1.2.1 = 30. **Distribution:** Tigers were originally distributed widely in China, primarily in the northeastern and southeastern regions; the worldwide distribution includes the Indian subcontinent, Indochina, and Russia. **Natural History:** The Tiger is the only carnivore that regu-

South China Tiger

Amur Tiger

larly feeds on humans. Perhaps no other carnivore has played such a prominent role in the history and culture of China. Widely believed to be a symbol of power and strength, it is used not only by the Chinese culture, but by other cultures as well. According to the *I Ching*, the Tiger represents yin, or evil. Killing or capturing a Tiger is thought to bring the highest honor to the hunter. Tigers have historically been found in a wide variety of habitats from scrub forests to tropical rain forests to mangrove swamps. Found from some of the coldest areas in Siberia to the tropical rain forests of SE Asia, Tigers are clearly very adaptable to a wide variety of habitats. In China they have been found in tropical evergreen, deciduous, coniferous, scrub-oak, and birch forests, mangrove swamps, and dry thorn forests. They range as high as 3,900 m. Although opportunistic, like most carnivores, they feed mainly on large mammals, especially ungulates. They can prey on Sambar (*Rusa unicolor*) or buffalo that weigh 160–400 kg, but they usually take species that weigh between 10 and 100 kg. They are one of the few carnivores that appear to rely on prey that is many times their own size. Tigers are infamous for their strength, and there are accounts of Tigers moving large prey such as cows or horses, and one account of a Tiger moving a 770 kg Gaur (*Bos frontalis*). Wild Boar (*Sus scrofa*), roe deer (*Capreolus*), and Red Deer (*Cervus elaphus*) appear to be principal components of their diet, but they have been known to kill the Asian Black Bear (*Ursus thibetanus*) and the Brown Bear (*U. arctos*). One study in the Russian Far East showed that Wild Boar and deer constituted over 60% of their diet. They are considered ambush predators, springing onto their prey and taking them down with their muscular front limbs. Tigers kill small prey by a bite to the back of the head and neck. They kill large prey by a throat bite, causing suffocation. They may spend several days feeding on a large prey item, covering it up with leaves and grass each time they depart. Tigers forage over a large area and may range over 15–30 km in a single night of hunting. Unlike most other cats, Tigers will enter water without hesitation and are excellent swimmers. Their impact on their prey is substantial, and it is estimated that they take 10% of the available prey biomass. In undisturbed areas Tigers will hunt at any time of the day or night, but in areas disturbed by human activities they become principally nocturnal. Although Tigers are usually solitary except when in heat, mating, and rearing the young, there are reports of males associating with females and cubs. Seldom found in pairs; the usual group consists of a mother and her young. They coexist throughout most of their range with other large carnivores (Leopards and Dholes, *Cuon alpinus*), although Tigers are clearly the dominant carnivore. The average home range size varies depending on cover and prey availability but ranges from 15–51 km², with little overlap (<10%) between individuals, in tropical areas of high prey abundance to 300–1,000 km² in the Amur region (low prey abundance), where home ranges may overlap nearly completely (but not at the same time). Tigers breed in January–February and have a gestation of 90–105 days. The litter size is one to six, and two or three is more common. They are sexually mature at one to two years. **Conservation Status:** Three of the original eight subspecies of Tigers are extinct, including one in China, the far western Caspian Tiger (*P. t. virgata*) of Xinjiang. As four of the remaining five Tiger subspecies have occurred in China, conservation efforts in China are critical to the species' survival. Today, the population level for the South China Tiger (*P. t. amoyensis*) is estimated at below 30 individuals. Extensive surveys for South China Tigers over the last 10 years have failed to find direct evidence of their existence. The total population of all Chinese Tigers is estimated at less than 200. This dramatic drop in numbers is principally due to habitat destruction and hunting. Tiger bone has been an important ingredient in traditional Chinese medicine, and one Tiger on the black market can result in as much as 10 years' income for the poacher. China RL—CR D. China Key List—I. CITES—I. IUCN RL—EN A2bcd + 4bcd; C1 + 2a(i).

GENUS *UNCIA* (monotypic)

雪豹属 Xuebao Shu

Snow Leopard *Uncia uncia*

雪豹 Xue Bao—**Distinctive Characteristics:** HB 110–130 cm; T 80–100 cm; HF 265; E 61; GLS 155–173; Wt 38–75 kg. The pelage ground color is a uniformly light gray scattered with black rings or spots. Although there is variation throughout the range of the Snow Leopard, it appears to be mostly in gray, black, and white combinations. The venter is white. The spots on the head and neck are solid, whereas on the body they are broken up into irregular circles. The spots on the back coalesce to form two black lines that go from the neck to the base of the tail. The ears are short, rounded, and set on the sides of the head and wide apart. The backs of the ears are black with a pale grayish center. The eyes are distinctive among felids in that the iris is always a pale green or gray. Tail is very long and quite thick, at least 75% of the HB length, and legs seem disproportionately short. The fur is highly valued for its luxurious condition, measured at 5 cm along the back and 12 cm along the belly in winter pelage, and with a density of up to 4,000 hairs per cm^2. The front feet are larger than the hind feet. Dental formula: 3.1.3.1/3.1.3.1 = 30. **Distribution:** Western half of China; extending into Afghanistan, Bhutan, India, Kazakhstan, Kyrgyzstan, Mongolia, Nepal, Pakistan, Russia, Tajikistan, and Uzbekistan. **Natural History:** Found in high mountains, generally between 3,000 and 4,500 m and occasionally as high as 5,500 m. Prefer cliffs, rocky outcrops, and broken terrain, and terrain where the slope exceeds 40°. They will, however, use wide, flat valleys (for example, in the Kunlun Shan mountains). Normally they are found in grassland, steppe, and high-mountain arid shrubland. Snow Leopards can kill prey up to three times their own weight. Most common prey items are wild sheep, wild goats, pikas, hares, marmots, and game birds; they appear to be specialist predators on blue sheep (*Pseudois*) and ibex (*Capra*). In one study in the Taxkorgan Reserve, a spring survey yielded scats with 60% blue sheep remains and 29% marmot. Snow Leopards will kill a large prey animal every two weeks and will occasionally take livestock. There are several accounts that they appear to take advantage of snow, fog, and rain, and may hunt more intensively during those conditions. They occasionally eat vegetation, and a high incidence of tamarix has been reported in their scats. May remain in a small area for several days, then shift 1–7 km to a new part of their home range. Solitary and generally nocturnal, although they will hunt at any time of the day or night. Home ranges have been recorded from 14 to 142 km^2 in Mongolia. They can leap up to 15 m horizontally and 6 m vertically. They pair during the mating season and apparently breed during a very short interval. Birth records of over 400 captive Snow Leopards show that 89% of births occurred in April, May, and June, with 54% in May alone. Gestation lasts 90–100 days, and average litter size consists of two or three young. **Conservation Status:** Total Chinese population estimated at 2,000–2,500. China RL—CR A1cd. China Key List—I. CITES—I. IUCN RL—EN C1.

FAMILY VIVERRIDAE—Civets, Linsangs, and Binturongs

灵猫科 Lingmao Ke— 灵猫, 狸, 熊狸 Lingmao, Li, Xiongli

The general body form of viverids displays wide variation; however, almost all have extremely long cylindrical tails, which usually exceed 90% of the HB length. Chinese viverrids include the smallest (*Prionodon pardicolor*) as well as one of the largest (*Arctictis binturong*) species of the family. Viverids generally have eyes that protrude from their orbits, giving them a "bulging eye" appearance. All forms have five toes on each foot and at least some webbing between the toes. Sexual dimorphism is not pronounced within the group, males being slightly (<5%) larger, except for the some of the palm civets, in which females are larger. The feet are plantigrade or digitigrade, and the claws are semiretractile. Nearly all species have a perineal scent gland located near the genital and anal orifices. Tail rings occur in all viverrines and are reduced or absent in the other subfamilies. The paradoxurine palm civets are slightly more robust but resemble the viverrine body plan without the spots and with longer tails; the Binturong has a heavy, robust, bearlike body and a thick, prehensile, tapering tail. Dental formula: 3.1 4.2/3.1.4.2 = 40. The word "civet" comes from the Arabic word "zabat," which was used to describe the peculiar scent obtained from the glands of these animals. Viverids have been important in the perfume industry since at least the time when King Solomon imported civet oil from Africa. The "civet" secretion comes from a pouch-like perineal gland situated anterior to the anal region. The civet oil is sometimes collected by scraping around 5 g of yellowish greasy liquid from the pouch and was originally stored in antelope horns and stomachs for shipment to the perfume industry in France. Viverids do not have the capacity to squirt the secretion as do the New World skunks. The liquid, once refined, is cherished by the perfume industry because of its odor and its long-lasting properties. Civet oil is based on an alcohol compound that has been labeled "civetone" and is chemically different from the musk oil found in other carnivores. The Viverridae includes the subfamilies Viverrinae, Paradoxurinae, Hemigalinae, and Prionodontinae, with a total of 14 genera and 35 species found worldwide. There are eight genera and nine species of viverrids found in China, organized into four subfamilies, mainly occurring in provinces south of the Huang He watershed.

SUBFAMILY HEMIGALINAE—Hemigaline Civets

带狸亚科 Daili Yake—带狸 Daili
The hemigaline civets are among the rarest of all carnivores, and little is known of their natural history, ecology, or behavior. Primarily inhabiting primary-growth forests, they are more terrestrial than the paradoxurines, but not as cursorial as *Viverra*; all are semiarboreal. The civet gland is present in all species, but the group is also distinguished by the development of large anal glands. Some have speculated that the aposematic (advertising dangerous or defensive mechanisms with bright coloration or conspicuous morphological structures) coloration pattern of *Chrotogale* might indicate a noxious protective secretion of the anal glands. Of four genera in the Hemigalinae, only one is known definitively from China.

GENUS *CHROTOGALE* (monotypic)

带狸属 Daili Shu

Owston's Palm Civet *Chrotogale owstoni*

长颌带狸 Changhe Daili—**Distinctive Characteristics:** HB 400–660; T 350–490; HF 70–90; GLS 102–113; Wt 2.4–3.4 kg. Pelage uniformly yellowish brown, with five blackish-brown wide and transverse stripes on back. The venter and limbs have blackish-brown spots, and the nape has two dark black longitudinal bands. The distal half of the tail is black, and its base has two white rings. There are rows of small black spots on the neck, sides, and limbs. **Distribution:** Guangxi, Yunnan; extending into Laos and Vietnam. **Natural History:** Prefer densely vegetated habitats near water sources in both primary and secondary forests below 500 m. They feed principally on the ground but will climb trees in search of food. They are nocturnal and solitary and nest in large trees or dense brush. Although very little is known of their diet, anecdotal information indicates that it principally consists of earthworms. However, they may also eat small vertebrates (squirrels), invertebrates, and some fruit. Dens are constructed under large tree trunks and in dense brush or may be located in natural holes in trees, rocks, or the soil. Their scent secretion may also be used in predator defense. They breed between January and March, and after a gestation of 60 days have an average litter of three. Breeding may occur twice a year. **Conservation Status:** Occurs in several protected areas in China (the Dawei Mountain National Reserve, Jinping Divide National Reserve, and Huanlian Mountain National Reserve). Chinese population estimated at 300. China RL—EN B1ab(v); D. IUCN RL—VU A1cd.

SUBFAMILY PARADOXURINAE—Palm Civets

长尾狸亚科 Changweili Yake—长尾狸 Changweili
The paradoxurines are medium to large civets with an elongated body, short legs, and an extremely long tail. The tail is equal to or longer than the HB and is cylindrical except in the Binturong (*Arctictis*), which has a tapering, muscular tail. This subfamily contains one of the largest civets (Binturong) and one of the most widely distributed (Common Palm Civet, *Paradoxurus hermaphroditus*). The head has a long rostrum and pointed, catlike ears. The rhinarium is large and connected to the lip by a medial groove. The vibrissae are prominent and can be either white or black or a combination of both. The young have pale or white eyespots located above and/or below the orbits. The eyespots disappear in some species with age. The development of the scent gland (a saclike depression surrounded by two labia) varies slightly from species to species. The feet in the paradoxurines have extensive hairless interdigital webbing and are subplantigrade. The paradoxurines occur throughout the Indo-Malayan realm, primarily in tropical forests. The Paradoxurinae comprises five genera, four of which occur in China; of these, three are monotypic (*Arctictis, Arctogalidia, Paguma*).

GENUS *ARCTICTIS* (monotypic)

熊狸属 Xiongli Shu

Binturong *Arctictis binturong*

熊狸 Xiong Li—**Distinctive Characteristics:** HB 522–900; T 520–890; HF 100–135; E 45–65; GLS 113–155; Wt 9–14 kg. The largest viverrid in Asia. A stout, bearlike animal with long, shaggy hair, usually black. The ears are tipped with long, tufted hairs that extend beyond the ears. The Binturong is the only placental mammal in the Old World with a true prehensile tail, although other palm civets use their tail as an accessory limb. Its form is stout and strong, with a body color of black mixed with light brown hairs. Females are normally 20% heavier and larger than the males. Anterior margin of the ear is often white. Their eyes are usually a reddish brown. **Distribution:** Yunnan and Guangxi; ranging throughout SE Asia. **Natural History:** Arboreal animals that live in dense tropical and monsoon rain forests below 800 m. They subsist primarily on fruit, especially figs. They also eat eggs, young shoots, and leaves, and hunt birds, rodents, and other small animals. Will dive into water to pursue fish. They are critical seed dispersers in SE Asia. They are slow-moving nocturnal, arboreal animals that live alone or in small groups of adults with immature offspring. Almost always, the female is dominant. Males sometimes stay with the females after mating, even after they have given birth. Young can suspend themselves by their tail. Awkward on the ground, they spend most of their time in trees. They are aseasonal breeders, usually with one litter a year of two or three. Their gestation is 90–92 days, and they are sexually mature at two to two and a half years. **Conservation Status:** Population in China estimated at 200 in S and SW Yunnan. China RL—CR A1cd; B1ab(i,ii,iii); C1. China Key List—I. IUCN RL—VU A2cd.

GENUS *ARCTOGALIDIA* (monotypic)

小齿狸属 Xiaochili Shu

Small-Toothed Palm Civet *Arctogalidia trivirgata*

小齿狸 Xiao Chi Li—**Distinctive Characteristics:** HB 440–600; T 510–690; HF 74–80; E 38–42; GLS 100–118; Wt 2–2.5 kg. Head and back are brownish gray; the venter is a light brown. There is a white stripe running from the nose tip to the forehead. The back has three distinct black or dark brown stripes running along the length of the body (the species is sometimes called by the name Three-striped Palm Civet). The median stripe is complete, but the lateral stripes are discontinued, alternating with broken spots or absent. Feet and tail tip blackish brown. Only the females have the perineal scent gland, located near the vulva. The tail is longer than the HB. **Distribution:** S Yunnan; extending to India, Myanmar, Bangladesh, Thailand, Laos, Vietnam, Indonesia, and Malaysia. **Natural History:** Inhabit tropical rain forests at elevations below 1,200 m. They are nocturnal, solitary, and arboreal, and found in primary- and secondary-growth forests, even in areas where there is considerable logging. They generally stay away from human habitation, although they have been reported in coconut plantations. Lack of records may be the result of their confinement to the top layers of the evergreen forest canopy. Little is known about their food habits; based on their highly modified dentition, fruit must be the most important item. They will also eat insects, small mammals, birds, frogs, and lizards. They are aseasonal breeders, with some having two litters a year of two to three young. The gestation has been reported to be 45 days. **Conservation Status:** Probably extinct in China. China RL—NA. IUCN RL—LC.

GENUS *PAGUMA* (monotypic)

花面狸属 Huamianli Shu

Masked Palm Civet *Paguma larvata*

花面狸 Hua Mian Li—**Distinctive Characteristics:** HB 400–690; T 350–600; HF 65–120; E 40–60; GLS 100–130; Wt 3–7 kg. Possesses a distinctive facial pattern that varies geographically but usually consists of a medial longitudinal stripe from the forehead to the rhinarium, a small white or pale eyespot below the eye, and a larger, more distinctive white patch above the eye that may extend to the base of the ear. The rostrum is black. There are no traces of spots on the body, and the guard hairs are rusty brown to dark brown, with the underwool generally light brown to gray. In some young juveniles, a faint spotting pattern can be detected. The tail is the same color as the body, with the distal-most portion often dark. Females, which have two pairs of mammae, are slightly larger than males. **Distribution:** Widespread across C and SE China, including Hainan Island and Taiwan; extending to Bangladesh, Myanmar, Cambodia, India (and S Andaman Islands), Indonesia (Kalimantan, Sumatra), Japan (introduced), Laos, Malaysia (Sabah, Sarawak, West), Nepal, Pakistan, Singapore, Thailand, Vietnam. **Natural History:** Found in a variety of forest habitats, from primary-growth evergreen to second-growth deciduous forest, and they frequent agricultural areas. They eat mostly fruits but will also eat birds, rodents, insects, and roots. They will attack chickens and waterfowl in farmland. They are arboreal, solitary, and nocturnal and spend the daytime sleeping in a den in a tree. They dwell in burrows and live in small family groups of 2–10. Home range is around 3.7 km². The litter size varies from one to five, with a gestation of 70–90 days. They are sexually mature at one year. **Conservation Status:** China RL—NT. IUCN RL—LC.

GENUS *PARADOXURUS*—Palm Civets

椰子狸属 Yezili Shu—椰子狸 Yezili
Paradoxurus contains three species, of which only one occurs in China.

Common Palm Civet *Paradoxurus hermaphroditus*

椰子狸 Ye Zi Li—**Distinctive Characteristics:** HB 470–570; T 470–560; HF 67–85; E 42–58; GLS 90–118; Wt 2.4–4 kg. Similar in size to the domestic cat, with the tail about equal to the HB length. The pelage contains at least five rows of spots; however, the spots are indistinct and usually lost in adults and in some geographical subspecies. The color is mostly light brown, with several dark brown long stripes on back; spots on sides; white spots on face; most of the tail is black (although there may be faint traces of tail rings). The feet are also black. There are three pairs of mammae. **Distribution:** S China, including Hainan Island; extending to Bhutan, Myanmar, Cambodia, India, Indonesia, Laos, Malaysia, Nepal, New Guinea, Philippines, Singapore, Sri Lanka, Thailand, Vietnam; scattered records in Sulawesi, Moluccas, and Aru Islands, probably resulting from introductions. **Natural History:** Occur in montane, tropical, and subtropical forests. They are also abundant in second growth and on plantations (coconut, coffee, mango, pineapple, banana). One study reported a home range of 17 km^2 and a daily movement of 1 km; there is considerable overlap of home ranges among individuals. They are nocturnal and solitary and seek out the largest trees in an area to nest. They may use the same nesting trees or holes for several days in a row. Their affinity for the fleshy hull of coffee beans and palm sap is well known. Palm sap is sometimes made into a drink called "toddy," and sometimes they are referred to as the "Toddy Cat" because of their affinity for palm sap. An expensive coffee is sometimes marketed from the beans collected from their scats. It is believed that they select the best and ripest beans to eat; this coffee can sell for more than $100 per pound. They are opportunistic omnivores but depend heavily on nuts, berries, and fruits. They are considered pests on fruit and coffee plantations. Local hunters often set snares for *Paradoxurus* and *Paguma* by placing them at the bases of *Ficus* or palm trees with freshly ripe fruit. They also feed on small vertebrates, eggs, and insects. In Thailand they are known as rat-catchers around plantations. They are sexually mature at one year and breed year-round. Average litter size is three, born after a 60-day gestation. **Conservation Status:** China RL—VU A2cd + 3cd. IUCN RL—LC.

SUBFAMILY PRIONODONTINAE

灵狸亚科 Lingli Yake
The Prionodontinae contains a single genus, which is represented in China.

GENUS *PRIONODON*—Linsangs

灵狸属 Lingli Shu—灵狸 Lingli
Of the two species within this genus, one is represented in China.

Spotted Linsang *Prionodon pardicolor*

斑灵猫 Ban Lingmao—**Distinctive Characteristics:** HB 350–400; T 300–375; HF 60–68; E 30–35; GLS 65–75; Wt 4.1–8 kg. Distinguished from all other Viverridae by the absence of the scent glands in both sexes; the smallest viverrid in China. The general body form is distinctly slender, with short limbs; thin

short, and dense fur; and a very long neck. The color pattern on the sides consists of large spots and two black longitudinal stripes running down from forehead to shoulder. The ground color tends to be light, and the spots do not form transverse bands. There are two rows of spots adjacent to the middle of the back, which sometimes fuse into a mid-dorsal line near the tail. Each side of the body has three to four rows of spots. The tail is long (nearly as long as the HB), with 8–10 tail rings and a white tip. Has completely retractile claws and hairy claw sheaths. Dental formula: 3.1.4.1/3.1.4.2 = 38. **Distribution:** S China; extending to Bhutan, Myanmar, India, Laos, Nepal, Thailand, Vietnam. **Natural History:** Prefer evergreen broadleaf rain forests, subtropical evergreen forests, and monsoon forests below 2,700 m. They have also been reported hunting in disturbed forests and forest-edge habitats. They feed mainly on small vertebrates (frogs, rodents, lizards), birds' eggs, insects, and berries. They are arboreal, solitary, and nocturnal and appear to be rare throughout their range. They spend a large part of their time in the hollows of trees and will come to the ground in search of food.

They breed from February to August and have an average litter size of two to four young. **Conservation Status:** China RL—VU A2cd. China Key List—II. CITES—I. IUCN RL—LC.

SUBFAMILY VIVERRINAE—Civet Cats

灵猫亚科 Lingmao Yake—灵猫 Lingmao

This subfamily has the widest distribution among the Viverridae, being found throughout all of Africa (excluding the Saharan region), in S Europe (southwest of the Rhine River), from the western edge of the Indian subcontinent eastward throughout most of SE Asia, and north into C China (including Taiwan). Of the five genera, two occur in China. These civets are terrestrial and are all nocturnal solitary foragers inhabiting dense vegetation or open woodland. They are ambush killers and occupy an ecological niche similar in certain aspects of food habits and behavior to that of some of the smaller canids. All foraging is done on the ground, although most will climb trees when threatened. They do not form established nesting sites but live in burrows, rock crevices, or thick vegetation during the day. They are all general omnivores and eat small mammals, birds, eggs, frogs, toads, lizards, carrion, fruit, insects, and snails. Because of their opportunistic foraging, they may chance upon temporary abundant food sources such as termite mounds, carrion, or ripening fruit, upon which they will concentrate for limited periods of time.

GENUS *VIVERRA*—Civet Cats

大灵猫属 Dalingmao Shu— 大灵猫 Dalingmao

Viverra species are about the size of mid-size domestic dogs. Their general color is gray, and they have a black spinal stripe running from behind the shoulders to the root of the tail. The front of the rostrum on each side has a whitish patch. The rostrum, chin, and throat are blackish. The sides and lower surface of the neck are conspicuously banded with black stripes set off by white interspaces. The tail has a variable number of complete black-and-white rings, with the black much broader than the white. The genus *Viverra* is distributed in S Asia and contains four species, two of which occur in China.

Large-Spotted Civet *Viverra megaspila*

大斑灵猫 Daban Lingmao—**Distinctive Characteristics:** HB 770–900; T 320–400; HF 70–80; E 40–50; GLS 130–135. Form and size similar to those of *V. zibetha*, but with two black transverse stripes under the neck; the back gray-brown, with a black stripe running down from shoulder to rump; large, dark brown spots on the sides; and complete absence of the skin lobes on the third and fourth digits on the forefoot. The posterior portion of the body has well-defined round to quadrangular spots, which are arranged in rows and appear pale in the center of the spot. The mid-dorsal stripe is black and distinctly separate from the spots. The tail has four black rings, and the distal section of the tail is black. **Distribution:** S China; extending to Myanmar, Cambodia, Laos, W Malaysia, Thailand, Vietnam. **Natural History:** Poorly known. It is believed that its natural history and diet closely resemble those of the Large Indian Civet (*V. zibetha*). It seems to prefer subtropical and monsoon forests with thick vegetation and riparian ecosystems. It is nocturnal and solitary and has not been observed in trees. **Conservation Status:** Only eight furs have been obtained in China since the 1970s. China RL—NA. IUCN RL—VU A2cd + 3cd.

Large Indian Civet *Viverra zibetha*

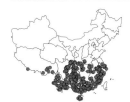

大灵猫 Da Lingmao—**Distinctive Characteristics:** HB 500–950; T 380–590; HF 90–145; E 35–65; GLS 135–150; Wt 3.4–9.2 kg. The largest terrestrial civet in Asia. The ground color is gray to gray-brown, with numerous black spots on the body and legs. The facial region is unmarked except for a small dorsal eyespot and a large white rhinarial patch. The neck stripes on this civet have the most contrast of any civet: the two broad, pure white bands reach from ear to ear around the throat, and these are surrounded by broad black bands. There is a black mid-dorsal stripe that runs from the back of the external pinnae to the base of the tail. The four to seven black tail rings are separated by smaller, complete white rings. The third and fourth digits of the forefoot have protecting claw sheaths (absent from the hind foot). **Distribution:** Widespread throughout C and SE China, including Hainan Island; extending to Myanmar, Cambodia, India, Indonesia, Laos, W Malaysia, Nepal, Thailand, and Vietnam. **Natural History:** Found in forests, scrub, and agricultural lands. They are mostly carnivorous and will eat birds, frogs, snakes, small mammals, eggs, crabs, fish, fruit, and roots. Solitary and nocturnal. Although they spend most of their time on the ground, they can climb in search of food. They spend much of their time during the day sleeping in burrows that have been dug by other animals and abandoned. They are territorial and mark their territories with excretions from their anal glands. One Thai study reported a home range of 12 km^2 and a daily movement of 1.7 km. They are often found adjacent to villages and agricultural areas. Like *Viverricula*, this civet has been used as a source of civetone, an oil-like substance secreted by the perineal gland. Civetone has been used in the production of perfume for centuries. They are more active during the day than most civets. Large Indian Civets are aseasonal breeders and can have two litters a year of one to five young. **Conservation Status:** Formerly abundant in China, but since the 1950s the population has declined in most areas by 94–99%. Based on the rate of decline, the total population is probably around 3,000. China RL—EN A2acd. China Key List—II. IUCN RL—NT.

GENUS *VIVERRICULA* (monotypic)

小灵猫属 Xiaolingmao Shu

Small Indian Civet *Viverricula indica*

小灵猫 Xiao Lingmao—**Distinctive Characteristics:** HB 500–610; T 280–390; HF 65–120; E 25–43; GLS 90–105; Wt 1.6–4 kg. The body hair is short, coarse, and dense. The head is small, with a short, acutely pointed muzzle and large, rounded external pinnae. Because of the narrow skull, the external pinnae are close set on top of the head. The ground color is gray to brown, the feet dark brown or black. The lateral neck stripes are not as pronounced as in *Viverra*. The two black stripes are very narrow and not always clearly separated from the body spotting pattern. The mid-dorsal line is black, and there are four to five rows of small spots on each side. The spots run together toward the midline and are more distinct ventrally. The tail has six to nine complete black tail rings, and the tip is usually white. There are no skin lobes over the semiretractile claws. The interdigital webbing is extensive and sparsely covered with hair. There are three pairs of mammae. **Distribution:** Widespread throughout C and SE China, including Hainan Island and Taiwan; extending from Yemen and Afghanistan to the Malay Peninsula and Indonesia; also found on many islands in SE Asia (many of these populations have been introduced). **Natural History:** Occur in grassland and scrub, but also often in agricultural areas and near villages. Feed on rats, squirrels, small birds, lizards, insects, grubs, and fruit. If given the opportunity they will eat domestic poultry. Solitary and nocturnal, although they will occasionally hunt by day. They prefer to seek food on the ground, though they can climb trees with agility. They dig readily and prefer to sleep in burrows. They are aseasonal breeders, with an average litter size of two to five. The home range is 3.1 km². Often kept in captivity for the purpose of harvesting the secretion of the perineal gland. This yellowish fluid can be collected by scooping out the gland. The secretion has been used as the basis of perfume for centuries. **Conservation Status:** China RL—VU A2cd. China Key List—II. IUCN RL—LC.

FAMILY HERPESTIDAE—Mongooses

獴亚科 Meng Yake—獴类 Menglei

Once considered a subfamily of the Viverridae, the mongooses are now generally separated into their own family. They are small carnivores with grizzled fur and a long, tapering tail. They are terrestrial in nature and have nonretractile claws. They are distributed throughout Asia and Africa. Some species are famous for their rat-catching abilities. This is a large family represented by 14 genera; of these only one genus and two species are found in China.

GENUS *HERPESTES*—Mongooses

獴属 Meng Shu—獴类 Menglei

Mongooses are small, weasel-like animals with grizzled fur, conical heads, and short ears. The rounded ears do not protrude above the head profile. They have a well-developed anal sac around the anus, and some species can squirt its secretion in defense. Mongooses have the general form of a slender animal with a pointed head, short rounded ears, short legs, and a long, tapering tail. Except for distinguishing features around the throat, they are generally of one color. Mongooses, at quick glance, have a general appearance similar to some weasels of the family Mustelidae. They can be distinguished from typical viverrids by the lack of spots or stripes or facial masks on the pelage and the lack of protruding ears. Terrestrial in nature, all are very poor tree climbers, and all can swim well when forced to do so. The Crab-eating Mongoose spends more time in the water than most and can be considered semiaquatic. The genus *Herpestes* is widely distributed in tropical and subtropical areas of Asia and contains 10 species, two of which occur in China.

Small Indian Mongoose *Herpestes javanicus*

红颊獴 Hongjia Meng—**Distinctive Characteristics:** HB 250–370; T 240–270; HF 50–65; E 12–27; GLS 66–77; Wt 0.6–1.2 kg. Smallest mongoose in Asia; it can be distinguished from *H. urva* by its size. Form small and slender; back, limbs, and tail all brownish gray; ventral surface chestnut. Tail length about equal to HB length; no distinctive tail tip. **Distribution:** S China, including Hainan Island; extending to Afghanistan, Bangladesh, Bhutan, Myanmar, Cambodia, India, Indonesia, Malaysia, Nepal, Pakistan, Thailand, and Vietnam, and widely introduced worldwide. **Natural History:** Often found in dry forests, grasslands, and secondary scrub forests; also around human habitation and agricultural areas. It is a cautious diurnal creature that generally remains around cover. It digs and lives in burrows, hedgerows, thickets, groves of trees, and cultivated fields. Primarily an insectivore, though it also feeds opportunistically on small vertebrates. Contrary to popular belief, mongooses are not immune to snake venom; instead, they rely on their skill, agility, and thick fur to avoid being bitten. However, the Small Indian Mongoose appears to be highly resistant to cobra venom. Easily tamed and often kept as a pet and a destroyer of household vermin. Aseasonal breeders, they have a gestation of 50 days, with litter size averaging between two and six. They usually have one litter a year and are sexually mature at 6–12 months. **Conservation Status:** China RL—VU A1cd. IUCN RL—LC.

Crab-Eating Mongoose *Herpestes urva*

食蟹獴 Shixie Meng—**Distinctive Characteristics:** HB 360–520; T 240–336; HF 80–102; E 20–30; GLS 88–100; Wt 1–2.3 kg. Size larger than *H. javanicus*. Fur is long, coarse, and somewhat ragged; wool underfur dark brown at the base and pale brownish yellow at the tips. Back is gray, mixed with yellowy-white color; two white longitudinal striations on the region from cheek to shoulder; all four legs dark brown. Tail tip pale; tail short, length up to two-thirds HB length. **Distribution:** Widely distributed in SE China, including Hainan Island and Taiwan; extending to Myanmar, India, Laos, Malaysia, Nepal, Thailand, Vietnam. **Natural**

History: Poorly known. Found in evergreen forests near streams and terraced rice fields at low elevations. In Laos there are reports from more mountainous areas. More aquatic than most species, it is an expert swimmer and diver. It feeds mainly on frogs, fish, and crabs and hunts along the banks of streams. Despite its name, its food habits have never been extensively studied, and it is unknown how important crabs are to its diet. Recent records indicate that it is crepuscular and diurnal. Normally solitary, it can squirt out a fetid fluid from its anal gland as a means of defense. **Conservation Status:** China RL—NT. IUCN RL—LC.

SUBORDER CANIFORMIA—Doglike Carnivores

犬亚目 Quan Yamu—犬 Quan
This suborder includes nine families, six of which—the canids (Canidae), bears (Ursidae), eared seals (Otariidae), earless seals (Phocidae), Red Panda (Ailuridae), and weasels (Mustelidae)—are found in China.

FAMILY CANIDAE—Canids

犬科 Quan Ke—犬 Quan
Medium-sized carnivores with a long rostrum; limbs are slender and adapted for fast running; digitigrade stance, with nonretractile claws. The forefoot has five digits, but the first digit is small and set high above the rest; four digits on hind foot. Dental formula: usually 3.1.4.2/3.1.4.3 = 42. Olfaction and auditory senses well developed; lives on animal foods but also usually eats plants. This order contains 13 genera, of which four occur in China.

GENUS *CANIS*—Dogs and Wolves

犬属 Quan Shu—犬, 狼 Quan, Lang
The genus *Canis* includes animals that are strong and vigorous and similar in appearance to the domestic dog (included in this genus). Their front shoulder and head are held relatively high; ears are upstanding, and tail extents to about 66% the HB length. These are the largest representatives of the Canidae. Dental formula: 3.1.4.2/3.1.4.3 = 42. The distribution of this genus extends nearly all over the world and contains six species. Only one wild species occurs in China.

Wolf *Canis lupus*

狼 Lang—**Distinctive Characteristics:** HB 100–160 cm; T 330–550; HF 200–250; E 90–120; GLS 214–250; Wt 28–40 kg. The wolf is the largest species of the Canidae. The common dog was domesticated from this form and is considered the same species. Color generally grayish yellow, brownish gray, or grizzled gray, but varies widely. The winter coat can conserve body heat so well that wolves can function at temperatures below –40°C. Characterized by relatively thin bodies on long legs, and a long rostrum and forward-pointing ears and eyes.

Dental formula: 3.1.4.2/3.1.4.3 = 42. **Distribution:** Wolves have been recorded across China, and the largest populations are in NE China. It is still widely distributed in China except for Taiwan, Hainan, and Shandong; extending across Asia, Europe, and North America. **Natural History:** Occupies a wide range of habitats, including mountainous regions, tundra, forests, plains, deserts, alpine zone, and agricultural areas. It is abundant on the Tibetan Plateau and found at very high elevations. However, it is not found in rain forests. One of the few carnivores in China that feeds mainly on large mammals—Red Deer (*Cervus elaphus*), roe deer (*Capreolus*), sheep (*Ovis*). Wolves are highly adaptable and will feed on small animals such as lagomorphs, marmots (*Marmota*), and game birds, and also on fruit. Most food habit studies have shown that wolves consume mostly the young, the old, and other susceptible members of the prey. Wolves are social animals and usually run in family groups called "packs" of five to eight or larger. They mark their territory by scent marking, scratching, and howling. The order within the pack is maintained by a dominance hierarchy centered around the alpha male and alpha female. Wolves are good swimmers and do not hesitate to swim. They travel extensively, mostly at night, within their home range, which can vary from 130 to 13,000 km^2. They are monogamous, and both parents help raise the young. The gestation period is 60–63 days, and the young are born in late spring. The normal litter size is six. Sexual maturity is reached at two years of age. **Conservation Status:** Now mainly restricted to NE China, Nei Mongol, and the Tibetan Plateau, with a population estimated at 6,000. China RL—VU A2abc. CITES—II. IUCN RL—LC.

GENUS *CUON* (monotypic)

豺属 Chai Shu

Dhole *Cuon alpinus*

豺 Chai—**Distinctive Characteristics:** HB 88–113 cm; T 400–500; HF 70–90; E 95–105; GLS 150–170; Wt 10–20 kg. Similar to *Canis*, but with shorter rostrum and shorter tail. Color can range from a deep red to a grayish brown or yellowish red, with white on the throat, legs, and face. Ears are large, rounded, and filled with white hair. The tail tip is almost always black, and the tail is <50%

HB length. Males and females are approximately the same size. Six or seven pairs of mammae. Dental formula: 3.1.4.2 /3.1.4.2 = 40. **Distribution:** Occurs across China; extending to Indonesia (Java, Sumatra), Malaysia, India, Pakistan, Indochina, Korea, Mongolia, and Russia. **Natural History:** Found in nearly every habitat (except desert), from open country in Xizang to dense forests and thick scrub jungles as high as 2,100 m. They hunt in packs and can kill animals up to 10 times their own size. Packs focus on large prey and will eat Wild Boar (*Sus scrofa*), muntjacs (*Muntiacus*), Sambar (*Rusa unicolor*), wild sheep (*Ovis*), wild goat (*Capra*), small deer, rodents, and lagomorphs. Packs consist of 5–12 individuals, but groups of 40 have been reported. Home range can be from 40 to 84 km², the size of which is determined by the availability of food and water. Primarily diurnal and crepuscular, but occasionally active at night. In many packs that have been studied, there were twice as many males as females. The dens are usually ones that were occupied by other animals. All members of the pack care for the cubs and carry food back for them from a hunt. The gestation period is 60–62 days; births occur in spring, with four to six cubs in a litter. They become sexually mature in one year. **Conservation Status:** China RL— EN A2abcde. China Key List—II. CITES—II. IUCN RL—EN C2a(i).

GENUS *NYCTEREUTES* (monotypic)

貉属 He Shu

Raccoon Dog *Nyctereutes procyonoides*

貉 He—**Distinctive Characteristics:** HB 450–660; T 160–220; HF 75–120; E 35–60; GLS 100–130; Wt 3–6 kg. A small canid with disproportionately short legs, fox-like in appearance, and with a distinctive face mask. The forehead and muzzle are white, while the eyes are surrounded by a black ocular region. The cheeks are covered with shaggy, long hairs, forming a ruff; there is a cross-shaped pattern on the anterior part of the back; chest, legs, and feet are dark brown. Their general form is relatively stout, with the tail <33% of HB and covered with shaggy hairs. Dorsal and distal hairs of tail tipped in black; dorsal hair brownish gray, mingled with hairs with black tips. Dental formula: 3.1.4.2/3.1.4.3 = 42. **Distribution:** C, S, and E China; extending to Japan, Mongolia, North and South Korea, Russia; introduced into Europe. **Natural History:** Inhabit open broadleaf forests near water or open meadows, thick bushy areas, and reeds. They are seldom found in dense forests of high mountains and are usually associated with water. Prefer to forage in woodlands with an abundant understory—especially ferns. Their diet consists of amphibians, mollusks, insects, fish, small mammals, birds and their eggs, fruit, and grains. Rodents form the bulk of their diet, although they rely more heavily on plants than most canids and eat roots, stems, leaves, bulbs, berries, seeds, and nuts. They are nocturnal and solitary, but sometimes live in family groups and will often forage in pairs. Home ranges vary from 5 to 10 km². They use at least 10 different latrine sites. This is the only canid that hibernates in the northern parts of its range. Monogamous; establishes a permanent pair bond when mating begins in February–March. The gestation period is 59–64 days. There are 5–8 young per litter, but sometimes as many as 12. **Conservation Status:** China RL— VU A2abcd. IUCN RL—LC.

GENUS *VULPES*—Foxes

狐属 Hu Shu—狐狸 Huli
These are long, slender, doglike canids with a thick tail that is >50% of HB length. The hairs on the tail are dense and shaggy. Limbs are relatively short and usually darker than the body color. The rostrum is noticeably slender. Dental formula: 3.1.4.2 / 3.1.4.3 = 42. Widely distributed in Asia, Africa, Europe, and North America. This genus contains 12 species, three of which occur in China.

Corsac Fox *Vulpes corsac*

沙狐 Sha Hu—**Distinctive Characteristics:** HB 450– 600; T 240–350; HF 90–120; E 50–70; GLS 95–118; Wt 1.8–2.8 kg. Smaller than *V. vulpes* but with longer legs; chest and groin white; dorsal hair brownish gray; ears short; color of the back of the ears and tail base the same as that of the back. The tail tip is black, which can be used to distinguish it from *V. ferrilata*, which has a white tail tip. Tail approximately 50% of HB length. **Distribution:** Found across N China; extending to N

Afghanistan, Kazakhstan, Kyrgyzstan, Mongolia, Russia. **Natural History:** Inhabits open steppes and semideserts and does not live in forests, areas of dense brush, or cultivated lands. It is not found in mountainous regions or in areas where snow depth exceeds 15 cm. Feeds chiefly on pikas (*Ochotona*), rodents, birds, insects, and lizards. One study reported the percentages of occurrence in scats of pika (55%), vole (22%), hamster (16.5%), marmot (44%), other rodents (85%), carnivores (5.5%), other mammals (16.5%), birds (5.5%), and insects (22%). Apparently well adapted to deserts, these foxes can go without water for extensive periods of time. They live in burrows, and several individuals may share dens. May form small packs in winter and inhabit burrows abandoned by marmots. Home ranges have been reported from 1 to 3.7 km². They are nocturnal in habit, and mating occurs from January to March. Gestation lasts 50–60 days, and the young are born in late spring–early summer. Females produce one litter of three to six pups per year; sexual maturity is attained at the age of two. **Conservation Status:** China RL—VU A2cd. IUCN RL—LC.

Tibetan Fox *Vulpes ferrilata*

藏狐 Zang Hu—**Distinctive Characteristics:** HB 490–650; T 250–300; HF 110–140; E 52–63; GLS 138–150; Wt 3.8–4.6 kg. Size similar to *V. vulpes*, but has brownish-red back and white venter; body sides have grayish broad bands, distinct from back and venter. Has a conspicuously narrow reddish muzzle and reddish color on crown, neck, back, and lower legs. The backs of the small ears are tan, and the insides white; undersides are whitish to light gray. The tail is bushy and gray, except for a white tip. Tail <50% of HB length. **Distribution:** Tibetan Plateau; extending to Nepal. **Natural History:** Found in semiarid to arid areas of alpine meadow, alpine steppe, and desert steppe and hills from about 2,000 to 5,200 m. The principal diet consists of pikas and rodents. One scat study showed the occurrence of 95% pika (*Ochotona curzoniae*) and small rodents and the remainder insects, feathers, and berries. Other studies have noted lizard species (*Phrynocephalus*), hares (*Lepus oiostolus*), marmots (*Marmota himalayana*), musk deer (*Moschus*), Blue Sheep (*Pseudois nayaur*), and livestock as prey items. Diurnal and solitary, although they can be seen together in family groups of a mated pair with young. Most active in the morning and evening but can be seen out during the day. Burrows are found at the base of boulders, along old beach lines, low on slopes, and at other such sites. There may be one to four entrances to a den, the entrance about 25–35 cm in diameter. Mating occurs in late February, and litters of two to five young appear in Apri–May. **Conservation Status:** China RL—EN A4d. IUCN RL—LC.

Red Fox *Vulpes vulpes*

赤狐 Chi Hu—**Distinctive Characteristics:** HB 500–800; T 350–450; HF 115–155; E 74–102; GLS 130–150; Wt 3.6–7 kg. The largest fox in the genus. Usually reddish brown, with long, slender black legs. The dorsal hair is normally reddish brown, with shoulders and body sides more yellowish; backs of ears are black or brown; venter is white. The color variance is very large, ranging from yellow to brown to crimson, etc. The bushy tail is 60–70% of HB length and the same color as the body, with a white tip. A 20-mm-long subcaudal gland on the upper portion of the tail gives off a "foxy" odor. **Distribution:** Across China; distribution extends widely across Asia and Europe. **Natural History:** Live in all kinds of habitats, from deserts and forests to major metropolitan areas. They prefer brushy habitats with a mix of open areas and cover. They are found in semideserts, high mountain tundra, forests, and farmland. Their diet consists principally of small ground-dwelling mammals, including lagomorphs and sciurids. Other items taken are galliformes, frogs, snakes, insects, berries, and vegetables. Carrion may be seasonally important to some populations. The Red Fox is nocturnal and will cache surplus food. Very mobile, often covering 10 km per day, with non-overlapping territories. Territories are larger in winter than in summer. Dispersal occurs in the fall, with the males generally dispersing farther than females. Monogamous; males help with parental care. Mating occurs from late December to late March. The young are born from March to May. Litter size 1–10, occasionally up to 13. **Conservation Status:** China RL—NT. IUCN RL—LC.

FAMILY URSIDAE—Bears

熊科 Xiong Ke—熊 Xiong
Representatives of the bear family exceed in size all other species of the Carnivora, and they have among the largest distributions for any species. Bears are strong, possess a very short tail, have large heads with a projecting rostrum, and display relatively small eyes. They are plantigrade, with five digits on each foot. The front feet have long and inflexible claws. Dental formula: 3.1.3–4.2/3.1.3–4.3 = 38–42. Bears are terrestrial and can climb trees and swim. They are generally herbivorous by nature but are also opportunists and will take advantage of nearly any source of food: carrion, small mammals, large herbivores, and fish. They are solitary and nocturnal. There are five genera and eight species of bears worldwide, three genera and four species of which occur in China.

GENUS *AILUROPODA* (monotypic)

大熊猫属 Daxiongmao Shu

Giant Panda *Ailuropoda melanoleuca*

大熊猫 Da Xiong Mao—
Distinctive Characteristics:
HB 150–180 cm; T 120–150; HF 140–200; E 70–110; GLS 280–300; Wt 85–125
kg. Perhaps there is no other mammal that is so identified with China as the
Giant Panda. It is a bear with a wide and massive head with a short rostrum.
The body is uniformly white; the limbs and shoulders are black; the head bears
a pair of upstanding round black ears, large black eyes and ocular patches, and
a sharply contrasting black nose. Males are larger than females. The forefoot
and hind foot have five digits, and they are semiplantigrade. A notable feature
on these animals is an extra, opposable sesamoid structure (called the panda's
thumb) in the hand (this structure is also enlarged in the foot). Dental formula: 3.1.4.2/3.1.4.3 = 42. **Distribution:** C China. Endemic. The Giant Panda's
former range covered almost all of the southern half of China and some of
Myanmar, but its numbers have been reduced significantly to six distinct populations. **Natural History:** Inhabit montane forests (generally mixed coniferous and broadleaf forests) at elevations of 1,200–3,900 m where bamboo stands
are present. They sometimes descend to lower elevations during the winter.
They feed on gentle slopes with a high forest canopy. Feed almost entirely on
the leaves of 30 or more species of bamboo, and bamboo can account for up to
99% of their diet. It is believed that the panda's thumb (the operative sixth digit
in the hand) evolved to facilitate their feeding on bamboo. The digestive tract
is extremely muscular and covered with a thick layer of mucus to help digest
the woody diet and protect against splinters. Other foods eaten include fruits,
fir bark, vines, small mammals such as bamboo rats (*Rhizomys*), fish, insects,
and leaves. Adults consume 12–15 kg of food per day. They shelter in trees and
caves. They are primarily terrestrial, although also good climbers and capable
of swimming. They are solitary, nocturnal, and crepuscular. Home ranges of
females do not overlap, while male home ranges may overlap with those of several females. Home range size is 4–8.5 km^2 and is largely dependent on the
quantity and quality of bamboo resources. Sexual maturity occurs at four and a
half to six years, and the breeding season extends from March to May. There is
a delayed implantation of 45–120 days, followed by a gestation of 112–163
days. Although up to three cubs may be born in a litter, normally only one cub

survives to adulthood. **Conservation Status:** Total population estimated at <1,600. China RL—EN A2c + 3c; E. China Key List—I. CITES—I. IUCN RL—EN C2a(i).

GENUS *HELARCTOS* (monotypic)

马来熊属 Malaixiong Shu

Sun Bear *Helarctos malayanus*

马来熊 Malaixiong—**Distinctive Characteristics:**
HB 100–140 cm; T 30–70;
HF 180–210; E 40–60; GLS 230–290; Wt 25–65 kg. The smallest living bear species in the world, and the only bear characteristic of the tropical forests of SE Asia. Its name comes from the tan crescent-shaped mark (shape is variable) on its chest. This sharply contrasting crescent is white, tan, or orange and stands out against the almost pure black background. The Sun Bear has a very short, dense coat that is jet black with light markings on the face. It has very small, rounded ears set low on the heads. The muzzle is short and lighter in color than body color; muzzle color varies from orangish tan to gray or a silver color. The rhinarium continues downward and unites with the lips. Forelimbs are distinctively bowed, and the forefoot is turned inward. Males are generally 20% larger than the females. **Distribution:** May be extinct in China. Historic distribution in SW China; extending to Indochina, Sumatra, and Borneo. **Natural History:** The most arboreal bear; they live predominantly in lowland tropical dipterocarp rain forests but have also been reported in coconut plantations and low montane and swamp forests up to 2,400 m. They have been reported to eat termites, fruits, insects, bees, earthworms, small mammals, birds, coconuts, and the hearts and growing tips of coconut palms. They will sometimes cause damage to coconut plantations. They are known in some areas as the "honey bear" for their attraction to bee nests. Normally solitary. They are usually nocturnal in disturbed areas and largely diurnal in undisturbed areas. They are aseasonal breeders, with a gestation of 95–96 days. Litters are of one or two cubs. **Conservation Status:** The Sun Bear's existence in China today is doubtful. No Chinese bears have been reported from the wild or kept in captivity since the 1970s, although the species has been reported in Laos directly across the border. China RL—EN D. China Key List—I. CITES—I. IUCN RL—VU A2cd + 3cd + 4cd.

GENUS *URSUS*—Bears

棕熊属 Zongxiong Shu—熊 Zongxiong

The genus *Ursus* contains the world's largest terrestrial carnivores. Chinese *Ursus* are massive and are usually brown, dark brown, or black. The heads are robust, and the rostrum is very long. Ears are disproportionately small. Cubs have a V-shaped light stripe on breast, which usually disappears in adults. Of the four *Ursus* species, two occur in China.

Brown Bear *Ursus arctos*

棕熊 Zongxiong—**Distinctive Characteristics:** HB 115–119 cm; T 80–130; HF 190–280; E 100–170; GLS 250–380; Wt 125–225 kg. The world's largest terrestrial carnivore, with massive head and shoulders and a dish-shaped face with a long rostrum. There is considerable variability in the size of Brown Bears from different populations, depending on the food available and the habitat. They show the greatest variation in color and size of any ursid—from shades of blond to black to red. The ears are small and project laterally; males are larger than females. The front foot pad is about half the size of that of the Asian Black Bear (fig. 10). **Distribution:** At one time the Brown Bear was one of the most widely distributed land mammals on Earth. Today its populations are greatly reduced and fragmented. They were widespread across C, W, and NE China; extending across most of the Holarctic. **Natural History:** Occupy a wide range of habitats including dense forests, subalpine mountain areas, and tundra. Mainly eat vegetation—such as grasses, sedges, bulbs, roots, tubers, herbaceous

Figure 10. Comparative front paws of Asian Black (a) and Brown (b) bears.

a   b

312 — **URSIDAE**

plants, corn, berries, fruits, and nuts—which composes 60–90% of their diet. Common animal matter consumed includes insects, rodents, hoofed mammals, fish, and carrion. In some areas they have become significant predators of large hoofed mammals such as moose (*Alces*), reindeer (*Rangifer*), and Red Deer (*Cervus elaphus*). In spite of their large size, they can sprint at almost 50 km/h. They are nocturnal and crepuscular. Under most circumstances, they are solitary, except for females accompanied by their cubs and during the breeding season. Occupy overlapping home ranges; male home ranges are larger than those of females. There is no territorial defense. In the northern parts of their range they will hibernate for six or seven months. They have been known to cache food. Sexual maturity occurs at four and a half to seven years of age. Mating occurs from early May to July, but implantation does not occur until about October or November. The young are born from about January to March. The litter size averages two. Female bears are induced ovulators. A male bear may father more than one litter of cubs a year. **Conservation Status:** Total Chinese population estimated at 7,000–8,000, mostly found in scattered isolated populations. China RL—VU C1. China Key List—II. CITES—I. IUCN RL—LC.

Asian Black Bear *Ursus thibetanus*

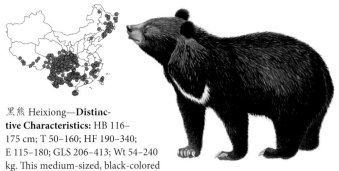

黑熊 Heixiong—**Distinctive Characteristics:** HB 116–175 cm; T 50–160; HF 190–340; E 115–180; GLS 206–413; Wt 54–240 kg. This medium-sized, black-colored bear has a lightish muzzle and ears, which appear large in proportion to the rest of its head, especially when compared with other species of bears. There is a distinct white patch on the chest, which is sometimes in the shape of a V, and white on the chin. Although the chest crescent patch can occur in Brown Bears (especially in the young), it is never as distinctive in the adult as in the Asian Black Bear and is usually absent in adult Brown Bears. A brown color phase also occurs. Hairs on sides of neck rather are long and form a distinctive crest of hairs down each side of the neck. The front foot pad is large compared with that of the Brown Bear (fig. 10). Dental formula: 3.1.4.2/3.1.4.3 = 42. **Distribution:** Widespread in C, S, and NE China, including Hainan Island and Taiwan; extending to Afghanistan, India, Indochina, Japan, Korea, Laos, Nepal, Pakistan, Thailand, Russia, Vietnam. **Natural History:** Occupy oak, broadleaf, and mixed forests and prefer forested hills and mountains. They are well adapted to tropical rain forests and oak forests. In summer, they have been reported at elevations over 3,000 m, descending to lower elevations during winter. They are principally herbivorous, with one study showing that 89% of food consists of plant matter.

In the spring, there was a greater reliance on bark, lichen and moss, and acorns and other nuts (21%). During the summer a diet shift occurs toward berries, buds, invertebrates, and small vertebrates, and at this time they enlarge their home ranges, moving to ripe patches of berries. They are also known to eat carrion. They have been reported to feed on early spring bamboo shoots. They occasionally kill domestic livestock, but the amount to which they prey on wild hoofed mammals is unknown. In fall they frequently climb nut-bearing trees and pull down branches to feed on the acorns and nuts, then deposit the branches in the tree to serve as a crude platform for further feeding. Solitary and nocturnal, although they are often seen in the daytime when fruits are ripening. Apparently, they den for winter sleep in the northern parts of their range. It has been suggested that in the southern limits of their range, where it is quite hot, they do not undergo winter sleep, but this has not been confirmed. In Russia the home range is reported to be 10–20 km²; an adult male in Tangjiahe, China, had a home range of 37 km². Gestation lasts seven or eight months; on average they give birth to two cubs. Sexual maturity of females is thought to occur at three to four years of age. In Russia, mating is reported to occur in June–July, with births occurring between December and March. **Conservation Status:** Total population in China estimated at 12,000–18,000. This species is commonly kept in bear farms throughout China to provide bile for use in traditional Chinese medicine. China RL—VU C1. China Key List—II. CITES—I. IUCN RL—VU A2cd + 3d + 4d.

FAMILY OTARIIDAE—Eared Seals

海狮科 Haishi Ke—狮 Haishi
This is the family of aquatic carnivores normally referred to as sea lions and fur seals. Otariids can be distinguished from seals in the family Phocidae based on a variety of external morphological features. Also known as the eared seals, otariids retain a small external pinna. As a group, they are more likely to haul out on the shore than phocids, have the ability to support the front half of their body on their pectoral girdle, and can turn their hind feet forward. They use their front limbs as the principal means of locomotion in the water. Of seven genera within the Otariidae, two are present in China.

GENUS *CALLORHINUS* (monotypic)

海狗属 Haigou Shu

Northern Fur Seal *Callorhinus ursinus*

海狗 Hai Gou—**Distinctive Characteristics:** HB 140–250 cm; Wt 175–275 kg (males), 30–50 kg (females). Adult males are a rich dark brown to gray; females are more grayish dorsally and a lighter gray ventrally. There is a light-colored patch on the chest; the ears are almost hidden beneath the fur; the flippers have sparse hair, and their inner sides are naked. Newborn pups are entirely black. Dental formula: 3.1.3.2/2.1.3.2 = 34. **Distribution:** Vagrant populations reported off the eastern coast of China, including Taiwan; extending broadly across N Pacific coastal regions from the United States and Canada to Japan. The primary breeding grounds are on the Pribilof Islands (United States). **Natural History:** Have been used extensively for fur coats. They spend most of the year at sea and rarely come ashore during the nonbreeding period. They migrate south during the winter. During migration they do not travel in large herds, but in small groups of 1–10 animals. Feed at sea during the evening, night, and early morning and sleep during the day. Deepwater "seal fish" (*Bathylagus callorhinus*) have been found in stomach contents. The most common food items are squid, herring, pollack, lantern fish, and mollusks. Predators include sharks, Killer Whale (*Orcinus orca*), and Steller's Sea Lion (*Eumetopias jubatus*). Breeding rookeries are generally near the continental slope and are rocky. Males arrive first in May and establish territories eventually occupied by 10–50 cows. The females arrive in mid-June and give birth within two days of arrival. Nearly all seals are infected with nematodes, and the hookworm (*Uncinaria lucasi*) is one of the chief causes of pup death. Mating occurs within one week of giving birth, followed by a delayed implantation of three to four months, yielding a total gestation period of one year. Females become sexually mature at age three; males at five to six. They breed at about eight years of age but do not establish harems until around 12. Adult females normally migrate south in late October–November. **Conservation Status:** Over 3,000 fur seals are caught and drowned annually in Japanese gill nets, and the Japanese fishing industry uses some 7,000 animals for food. China RL—VU A2cd + 3cd. IUCN RL—VU A2b.

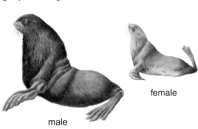

female

male

GENUS *EUMETOPIAS* (monotypic)

北海狮属 Beihaishi Shu—北海狮 Beihaishi

Steller's Sea Lion *Eumetopias jubatus*

北海狮 Bei Haishi—**Distinctive Characteristics:** HB 230–330 cm; GLS 325–400; maximum Wt 350 kg (females), 1,120 kg (males). The largest otariid; displays marked sexual dimorphism. Yellowish brown to reddish brown and slightly darker on the chest and abdomen; pups are dark brown to black; adult males have long, coarse hair on the chest, shoulders, and back of the neck; neck is narrow and slim in females. Dental formula: 3.1.3.2/2.1.3.2 = 34. **Distribution:** Vagrant populations found off the northeastern coast of China. An abundant, widely distributed sea lion of the cooler regions of the N Pacific, the worldwide distribution includes the N Pacific coastal regions of Canada, Japan, Russia, and the United

States. The center of abundance is probably the Aleutian Islands. **Natural History:** Opportunistic feeders, foraging mostly near the shore and over the continental shelf for fish and cephalopods. They are very gregarious and will form rafts of several hundred individuals while floating on the water. Their diet consists of squid, herring, halibut, flounder, rockfish, cod, and lamprey. Food is normally swallowed whole. Cephalopods are a major portion of the diet, but they will occasionally take Northern Fur Seal pups. Most usual cause of death of young pups is drowning, however, nematodes are a serious problem. Pups are born between May and July and stay close to mothers for about a week, then gather in groups and play and sleep together. Pups will not voluntarily go into the open ocean. Bulls arrive at the rookery first and become sexually mature at three to eight years (females between two and eight). Mating occurs in late May and early July. During the breeding season, females remain on land during the day and feed principally at night. They are gregarious and polygynous and use traditional rookeries and haul-out sites, usually on remote islands. **Conservation Status:** China RL—EN A1b + 2cd + 3cd. IUCN RL—EN A2a.

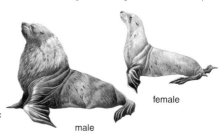

female

male

FAMILY PHOCIDAE—True Seals

海豹科 Haibao Ke—海豹 Haibao

The the true seals, or earless seals, are the most highly aquatic carnivores, with little ability to walk on land. Their hind limbs are modified into flippers and extend backward and cannot be bent forward. On land they move with a wriggling motion by forelimbs and body. They propel themselves through the water principally with their hind limbs. They are all carnivorous and distributed in sea areas of the Northern Hemisphere. Three of the 13 genera of Phocidae are found in Chinese waters.

GENUS *ERIGNATHUS* (monotypic)

髯海豹属 Ranhaibao Shu

Bearded Seal *Erignathus barbatus*

髯海豹 Ran Haibao—**Distinctive Characteristics:** HB 210–230 cm; Wt 200–250 kg. The largest phocid in Chinese waters. No sexual dimorphism in color. Gray, slightly darker down the midline, brownish on the proportionally small head; lighter ventrally; great profusion of long, very sensitive, glistening-white vibrissae; two pairs of mammae; fore flippers square-shaped, the third digit is slightly longer than the others. **Distribution:** Vagrant populations have been reported from Zhejiang. Worldwide, Bearded Seals are circumpolar in their distribution and are found in all circumpolar Arctic seas and coastal regions, with vagrant populations wandering as far south as Japan, Spain, and the United States. **Natural History:** Prefer shallow waters near coasts that are free of fast ice in winter. Mostly found in seasonally ice-covered waters less than 200 m deep. Inhabit areas of broken pack ice and drifting ice floes but are quite versatile and also occur in areas of shore-fast ice and thick ice, where they are able to maintain breathing holes. Many of the seals move long distances to follow the receding ice in the summer. Feed on decapod crustaceans (such as shrimps and crabs), holothurians (sea cucumbers), mollusks (such as clams and whelks), octopus, and bottom fish. Prefer to feed at the bottom in areas with water depths of less than 130 m. They are solitary and are not found in very large numbers in any one locality. They do not concentrate during breeding; pups are born in the open on ice floes. Delayed implantation of two months; gestation about 11 months. Most pups are born from mid-March to early May, later in the north than in the south. **Conservation Status:** China RL—NA. IUCN RL—LC.

GENUS *PHOCA*—Common Seals

海豹属 Haibao Shu—*海豹* Haibao
There are only two species in *Phoca*, one of which occurs off the Chinese coast.

Spotted Seal *Phoca largha*

斑海豹 Ban Haibao—**Distinctive Characteristics:** HB 140–170 cm; GLS 218; Wt 85–150 kg. Tail is short; pelage is grayish yellow or dark gray with numerous spots; pelage has a pale silver background with a darker gray area along the dorsal surface; superimposed on the pale and dark areas is a scattering of brown-black oval spots. Round head and large eyes; digits of the fore flipper decrease very slightly in length from first to fifth. Dental formula: 3.1.4.1/2.1.4.1 = 34. **Distribution:** Coastal China; worldwide associated with pack ice in coastal N Pacific off Canada, Japan, Russia, United States (Alaska). **Natural History:** The only phocid that breeds in China (Bohai Sea), where some give birth on land; this is the most southerly latitude of its breeding areas. There is an annual migration in the fall and winter to the edge of the pack ice, where the seals haul out on floes. They may ascend rivers, possibly including the Yangtze. Usually breed in association with pack ice. The diet includes crustaceans, cephalopods, and fish such as herring, capelin, pollack, eelpout, sand lance, and cod. Known predators are sharks, Killer Whale (*Orcinus orca*), Walrus (*Odobenus rosmarus*), Steller's Sea Lion (*Eumetopias jubatus*), Brown Bear (*Ursus arctos*), Wolf (*Canis lupus*), foxes, and some large birds. Mating occurs in March. In the beginning of November the seals enter Liaodong Bay in pairs. A single pup is born from January to February after a gestation of 11–12 months (two to three months delayed implantation). Females sexually mature at two years, males at four to five years. **Conservation Status:** China RL—EN C2a(i,ii); E. IUCN RL—DD.

GENUS *PUSA*—Ringed Seals

环斑海豹属 Huanbanhaibao Shu—环斑海豹 Huanbanhaibao
This genus includes three allopatric species: the Ringed Seal, the Caspian Seal, and the Baikal Seal, of which only one is represented in China.

Ringed Seal *Pusa hispida*

环斑海豹 Huanban Haibao—**Distinctive Characteristics:** HB 140–150 cm; Wt 45–90 kg. Light gray background spotted with black; many of the spots are surrounded by ring-shaped lighter marks. Appropriately named because of these ring-shaped marks on its coat. **Distribution:** Vagrant populations appear along northeastern coast of China; generally found only in waters north of 35°N latitude. **Natural History:** Animals of inshore waters, they are rarely encountered in the open sea or on floating pack ice. They may remain in contact with drifting pack ice or shore-fast ice for much of the year. During winter they may dig caves into snow that has gathered above breathing holes. They are opportunistic feeders, feeding on fish (cod, smelt, herring), pelagic crustaceans and invertebrates, and squid. It is believed that they can go as deep as 91 m when feeding. Normally fairly solitary, but one of the most common seals of the Arctic. Killer Whales (*Orcinus orca*), Polar Bears (*Ursus maritimus*), Arctic Foxes (*Vulpes lagopus*), and sometimes Walruses (*Odobenus rosmarus*) eat pups. Pups are born in March–April after a delayed implantation of two to three months (total gestation about 11 months). Males are mature at five years; females at four to seven. They are born with a pure white coat, which they shed within four to six weeks. Mating takes place about a month after parturition. **Conservation Status:** China RL—EN C2a(i,ii); E. IUCN RL—LC.

FAMILY MUSTELIDAE—Weasels, Badgers, Martens, and Otters

鼬科 You Ke—鼬类, 獾类, 貂类, 水獭 Youlei, Huanlei, Diaolei, Shuita
Mustelids are small to medium-sized carnivores and make up the largest family of the carnivore order. Their form is either slender and short-legged (otters, weasels) or robust and stout (badgers, Wolverine). All have five toes on each foot. They all have well-developed anal glands that give them a powerful and distinctive odor called musk. The usual condition is to have two glands that empty into a sac that can be discharged through the anus. Some mustelids can discharge the fluid as a reflex reaction as a secondary defense function. Most of the Mustelidae are highly carnivorous, but some specialize in eating insects and fruit. In most species, the sexes live separately throughout the year, and sexual dimorphism is the rule rather than the exception. Copulation is vigorous and usually associated with induced ovulation. Many mustelids have delayed implantation of the developing embryo. Mustelids are found on all continents except Australia and Antarctica; both subfamilies—Lutrinae and Mustelinae—occur in China.

SUBFAMILY LUTRINAE—Otters

水獭亚科 Shuita Yake—水獭 Shuita
Otters are the only truly aquatic members of the Mustelidae. Of the seven genera, three occur in China. They have long, cylindrical bodies and a thick muscular tail used in swimming that is fully haired. The foot is wider than the hand, and both have well-developed webbing. The fur is thick, smooth, and waterproof; facial vibrissae are noticeably long and stiff; the muzzle is short and blunt; nostrils and ears are valvular and can be closed underwater.

GENUS AONYX—Small-clawed Otters

非洲小爪水獭属 Feizhouxiaozhuashuita Shu—小爪水獭 Xiaozhuashuita
Aonyx is distributed in S Asia and Africa. It contains two species, one of which occurs in China.

Asian Small-Clawed Otter *Aonyx cinerea*

小爪水獭 Xiaozhua Shuita—**Distinctive Characteristics:** HB 400–610; T 290–350; HF 75–95; E20–25; GLS 84–94; Wt 2–4 kg. The smallest species of otter; however, it is relatively stouter than other otter species. Its color is uniformly brown except the light throat and venter; vibrissae are long and dense; small, rounded ears are on sides of head (which is more rounded than in other otters); eyes are proportionately large (when compared to head size in other otters); in profile, rhinarium has two concavities on the upper border; hand is partially webbed and has vestigal claws; base of tail is thick but tapers quickly to a narrow tip and is flattened dorsoventrally; female has two pairs of mammae. Dental formula: 3.1.3.1/3.1.3.2 = 34. **Distribution:** S China, including Hainan Island and Taiwan; extending to Bangladesh, Myanmar, India, Indonesia, Laos, Malaysia, Philippines (Palawan Island), Thailand, Vietnam. **Natural History:** Found in small streams, ponds, rice paddies, marshes, swamps, mangroves, and freshwater wetlands up to 2,000 m. They can coexist with the Eurasian Otter (*Lutra lutra*) and the Smooth-coated Otter (*Lutrogale perspicillata*), but they are more frequent in smaller bodies of water than the other species. They regularly scent mark distinct territories and are principally diurnal and crepuscular. They feed on aquatic animals such as crabs, snails, shellfish, crayfish, insects, and frogs and are mainly known as crab eaters. They leave shellfish in the sun to bake and will eat it after the shells have opened. They forage in groups of up to 12–15, although 4–12 appears to be normal. They are monogamous and mate for life, and both parents help to raise their offspring. Young may stay with the family unit for more than one year, and unrelated individuals may join the group. Gestation is 60 days, and they may have two litters a year. Average litter size is four. Age at sexual maturity is two and a half years. **Conservation Status:** China RL—EN A2cd. China Key List—II. CITES—II. IUCN RL—VU A2acd.

GENUS *LUTRA*—Otters

水獺属 Shuita Shui—水獺 Shuita
Of the three species of *Lutra*, only one is present in China. The genus is widely distributed in Asia, Europe, and Africa.

Eurasian Otter *Lutra lutra*

水獺 Shui Ta—**Distinctive Characteristics:** HB 490–840; T 243–440; HF 88–125; E 15–30; GLS 90–120; Wt 2.5–9 kg. Body elongate; dense, thick, brownish fur; legs short. Pelage color is lighter on the neck and venter. Conical, thick, muscular tail; feet are webbed and have well-developed claws; large nasal pad, when facing forward and upward in dorsal profile shows noticeable concavities; anal glands are present. Dental formula: 3.1.4.1/3.1.3.2 = 36. **Distribution:** Distributed across China, including Hainan Island and Taiwan; extending throughout Eurasia. **Natural History:** Live in freshwater areas such as rivers, lakes, ponds, streams, marshes, swamps, and rice fields, from sea level up to 4,120 m. They avoid areas of deep water. Eat two or three times a day, sometimes consuming up to 25% of their own body weight. They feed principally on fish, which sometimes makes up more than 80% of their diet. Other occasional food items include frogs, birds, crustaceans, crabs, waterfowl, lagomorphs, and rodents. Solitary, nocturnal and crepuscular; males and females come together only to mate. They are territorial, marking the boundaries of their home ranges with their anal glands. Males have larger home ranges than females. The population density is around one otter per 1–5 km of river. These aseasonal breeders, with delayed implantation; they reach sexual maturity at two to three years. Gestation lasts 63 days, and litter sizes range from two to three. Sometimes used to herd fish into nets. **Conservation Status:** China RL—EN A2cd. China Key List—II. CITES—I. IUCN RL—NT.

GENUS *LUTROGALE* (monotypic)

印度水獭属 Yindushuita Shu

Smooth-Coated Otter *Lutrogale perspicillata*

江獭 Jiang Ta—**Distinctive Characteristics:** HB 650–750; T 400–450; HF 100–140; E 20–30; GLS 122–128; Wt 5–12 kg. The largest species of otter in Asia. It has smooth and sleek pelage of a deep blackish-brown color; a pale neck and venter; small, rounded ears that are set low on the head; white lips; flat upper margin of nasal pad (in *Lutra* there are noticeable concavities); higher domed head than *Lutra*. Feet are large, with webbing that extends to the second joint of each digit. Tail >50% of HB length and flattened toward the tip. Males are significantly larger than the females; females have two pairs of mammae. Dental formula: 3.1.4.1/3.1.3.2 = 36. **Distribution:** S China; extending throughout S and SE Asia, India, and Indonesia. **Natural History:** Found in many different kinds of lowland habitats: mangroves, wetlands, rivers, swamps, and rice fields (they prefer rice fields). They usually require forest cover adjacent to the water and are excellent swimmers; they are able to swim underwater for long distances. They do not hesitate to travel long distances over land. Feed predominantly on fish and use their large vibrissae to help find prey; in some populations fish make up 90% or more of their diet. Diet may include small mammals, crustaceans, frogs, turtles, and birds. They hunt in wetlands, streams, rivers, and open ocean. Depending on the habitat, may hunt by day or by night. Cooperative hunting techniques have been observed; a typical group consists of a dominate male and female and three to five young. They are monogamous and aseasonal breeders. Males and females jointly raise the altricial young. **Conservation Status:** There are no recent records from China. China RL—EN A2cd + 3cd. CITES—II. IUCN RL—VU A2acd.

SUBFAMILY MUSTELINAE—Weasels, Wolverine, Martens, and Badgers

鼬亚科 You Yake—鼬类, 獾类, 貂类 Youlei, Huanlei, Diaolei

Mustelinae are generally long-bodied and short-limbed carnivores with dense fur. They have five well-developed digits and claws on all feet. The Chinese forms fall naturally into two groups: (1) the weasels, Wolverine, and martens; and (2) the badger-like mustelids. The weasels represent some of the smallest carnivores—all weighing less than 2 kg—and the Least Weasel (*Mustela nivalis*) is the smallest species of carnivore. They are principally terrestrial hunters and are purely carnivorous. They feed on small vertebrates, birds' eggs, and insects. Males are considerably larger than females. The martens are an arboreal counterpart to the weasels. They are medium-sized carnivores and spend a great deal of time hunting in the trees. They are solitary predators and are opportunistic hunters that focus on small vertebrates, carrion, and sometimes fruits and nuts. The Wolverine is the largest mustelid and will eat large prey—even caribou and deer. They are adept scavengers and sometimes rely on carrion. They are generally restricted to more northern latitudes, and they use the high snow levels to their advantage in capturing prey. The badger-like mustelids are well represented in China with three genera. They are more omnivorous than the other mustelines and correspondingly have more crushing dentition. They are powerfully built and have a long snout and short tail. They eat a variety of foods and have well-developed musk glands. Badgers rely more on roots, fruit, invertebrates, and nuts than do other mustelines. Of 15 genera of Mulstelinae, seven occur in China.

GENUS *ARCTONYX* (monotypic)

猪獾属 Zhuhuan Shu

Hog Badger *Arctonyx collaris*

猪獾 Zhu Huan—**Distinctive Characteristics:** HB 317–740; T 90–220; HF 55–135; E 21–45; GLS 80–140; Wt 9.7–12.5 kg. Named for its piglike snout; otherwise, it is similar to the Asian Badger (*Meles leucurus*), although usually larger (the largest badger in China). The head is elongate and conical in shape and the face is mostly white, with two black stripes extending from the nose, over the eyes, and over the whitish ears to the neck. Feet, legs, and venter dark brown to black; throat white (in *Meles* it is black); claws on front feet are white (in *Meles* these are also black); the tail is whitish in color. Dental formula: 3.1.4.1/3.1.3.2 = 36. **Distribution:** Widespread in C and E China; ranges from Assam (India) and Myanmar to Indochina, Thailand, Sumatra, and probably Perak in Malaysia. **Natural History:** Reported principally from forested areas within its range, from lowland jungles to wooded highlands 3,500 m in elevation. In India it has been reported as common in grasslands. It is solitary, crepuscular, and terrestrial. It is omnivorous, with a diet that consists principally of tubers, roots, earthworms, snails, and insects; occasionally will feed on small mammals. Earthworms appear to be the principal item in its diet. It uses its long, hoglike nose to root through the forest floor. Little is known of its behavior or ecology. Adult females have been observed foraging with offspring. Preyed upon by Tiger and Leopard. Hog Badgers will dig their own burrows. Females will have their young in a burrow and produce one litter per year in February or March of two to four young. **Conservation Status:** China RL—VU A2c; C1. IUCN RL—NT.

GENUS *GULO* (monotypic)

狼獾属 Langhuan Shu

Wolverine *Gulo gulo*

貂熊 Diao Xiong—**Distinctive Characteristics:** HB 675–780; T 180–195; HF 180–195; E 45–55; GLS 140–165; Wt 6.5–14 kg. The largest and most powerfully built mustelid (females are 10–12% smaller than males). It has proportionately short limbs and tail, and hairs on body sides are conspicuously longer than dorsal hairs. The body is uniformly dark brown; limbs and venter blackish brown; and there is a broad, light-colored stripe from neck to base of tail on sides of body. Variable white patches on the chest are common. There are four pairs of mammae; and anal, abdominal, and plantar scent glands. Wolverines have short, round ears. The plantigrade feet are large, with powerful, bearlike semiretractile claws. Dental formula: 3.1.4.1/3.1.4.2 = 38. **Distribution:** NE and NW China; distribution Holarctic. **Natural History:** Major predators in mixed conifer, larch, and taiga forests. They are opportunistic feeders that focus on carrion, large ungulates (*Rangifer*, *Capreolus*, *Cervus*), rodents (*Marmota*, *Myodes*), lagomorphs, and forest game birds. They will eat small quantities of berries, nuts, and fungus. Carrion is an important part of their diet, and their massive teeth are adapted for crushing bones and obtaining bone marrow. For a stocky animal, they are very swift when attacking prey and can reach speeds of

45 km/h. They are mostly nocturnal (although in some areas will be active at any time) and solitary, and they can climb and swim readily. They do not appear to be hindered by deep snow and are active year-round. Their fur is especially valued because of its frost-resisting properties and is often used to line parkas. They have a very light loading factor on snow, with a weight load of 27–35g/cm², which gives them an advantage in attacking ungulates in deep snow cover. They are highly territorial and practice food caching. Sexually mature at two and a half years, they normally breed in May–August and average one litter every two years of two to four altricial young between January and April. Wolverines have delayed implantation. **Conservation Status:** Total population in China estimated to be less than 400. China RL—EN A1acd; D. China Key List—I. IUCN RL—LC.

GENUS *MARTES*—Martens

貂属 Diao Shu—貂 Diao
The eight species of marten have a principally Holarctic distribution; three species occur in China. Their tail is bushy and its length is usually >50% of HB length. Their limbs are short and the feet are semi-digitigrade. Dental formula: 3.1.4.1/3.1.4.2 = 38.

Yellow-Throated Marten *Martes flavigula*

青鼬 Qing You—**Distinctive Characteristics:** HB 325–630; T 250–480; HF 70–130; E 24–53; GLS 90–103; Wt 0.8–2.8 kg. Distinctly different from other martens in body proportions, with the appearance of a remarkably elongated body with a long neck and a long, slim tail. Anterior half of body is light brown to yellowish brown; posterior half blackish brown; throat distinctively bright yellow; limbs and tail black; darker hair on head and back side; venter is light yellow. The long tail is all black, not bushy, and 60–75% of the HB length (fig. 11). There is hair between the rhinarium and upper lip (medial rhiniarial groove is lacking); a dark stripe runs along the side of the neck. Females have two pairs of mammae. **Distribution:** Widely distributed in China (except the northwestern region), including Hainan Island and Taiwan; extending across to India, Indonesia (Sumatra, Java, and Borneo), North and South Korea, Pakistan, E Russia, Vietnam. **Natural History:** Found in tropical pine, other coniferous, and moist deciduous forests at elevations of 200–3,000 m. Diet consists of rodents, pikas, game birds, snakes, lizards, insects, eggs, frogs, fruit, nectar, and berries. In some places it has been reported that they prey on musk deer (*Moschus*), and the young of wild boar, deer, and gorals. May hunt in pairs or small family groups. Mostly crepuscular and diurnal, but become nocturnal near human habitations. A mean annual range size of

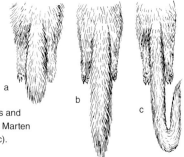

Figure 11. Comparative tail lengths and bushiness of the Sable (a), Beech Marten (b), and Yellow-Throated Marten (c).

7.2 km² was reported in one study. Average number of young per litter is two or three. They have a gestation of 220–290 days. **Conservation Status:** China RL—NT. China Key List—II. IUCN RL—LC.

Beech Marten *Martes foina*

石貂 Shi Diao—**Distinctive**
Characteristics: HB 340–480; T 220–330; HF 45–100; E 18–25; GLS 75–90; Wt 0.8–1.6 kg. General coloration a solid pale grayish brown to dark brown with a bushy tail about half of HB length (fig. 11), and most specimens have a prominent white or pale neck patch. The upper lip has medial rhinarial groove. Tail and limbs are darker than the back. Sexual dimorphism is not noticeable. **Distribution:** From C through NW China; extending from Europe and some islands of the Mediterranean eastward to the Middle East, Kazakhstan, Mongolia, and Russia. **Natural History:** Prefer rocky and open areas in the mountains up to 4,000 m, and they are generally found in more open environments than other martens. In more lowland areas, they prefer highly fragmented forests, hedgerows, and cultivated areas and are often found around human habitations. They appear to avoid conifer forests. They will use rocky crevices, stone heaps, abandoned burrows of other animals, and hollow trees for resting. This marten's opportunistic diet consists of rodents, birds, eggs, and berries. Vegetable matter forms a major part of the late summer and early fall food in some areas. A good climber but rarely goes high in trees. It is active at all times away from human habitations but primarily nocturnal and crepuscular. Male territories overlap those of females. They breed once a year in midsummer, yielding litters usually containing three or four, but as many as eight, altricial young that are cared for by the female.

They have delayed implantation. **Conservation Status:** China RL—EN A2cd + 3cd. China Key List—II. IUCN RL—LC.

Sable *Martes zibellina*

紫貂 Zi Diao—**Distinctive Characteristics:** HB 340–460; T 110–180; HF 60–90; E 32–50; GLS 68–85; Wt 0.4–1.1 kg. The winter pelage is long, silky, and luxurious, making it one of the most highly prized furs in the fur industry. Its color varies, but is generally yellowish brown to dark black-brown. Legs and tail color similar to back, but usually darker. Sometimes there is an ill-defined light patch on chest. Top of head usually lighter than back. The summer pelage is shorter, coarser, duller, and darker than the winter coat. The tail is bushy and short (length about one-third HB; fig. 11). **Distribution:** NW and NE China; extending across N Asia. **Natural History:** Occupies both coniferous and deciduous forests, sometimes high in the mountains, and preferably near streams. It prefers dense tree canopy of mixed species but with a high density of larch. The diet consists mostly of rodents (one study reported 72% occurrence in diet in summer), but also includes pikas, birds, fish, insects, honey, nuts, vegetation, and berries. Nuts and berries become more important in its diet during the winter. It is mainly terrestrial but can also climb. An individual may have several permanent and temporary dens, located in holes among or under rocks, logs, or roots. A burrow several meters long may lead to the enlarged nest chamber, which is lined with dry vegetation and fur. Hunts either by day or by night. It tends to remain in one part of its home range for several days and then move on. There may be migrations to higher country in summer and also large-scale movements associated with food shortage. Reported population densities vary from one Sable per 1.5 km^2 in some pine forests to one per 25 km^2 in larch forests. Individual home range is usually several hundred ha but may be as great as 3,000 ha. Mating occurs from June to August, and young are usually born in April or May; because of delayed implantation, the total period of pregnancy is 250–300 days. The number of young per litter ranges from one to five; sexual maturity occurs at 15–16 months. **Conservation Status:** Estimated population in China of 6,000. China RL—EN A2acd. China Key List—I. IUCN RL—LC.

GENUS *MELES*—Badgers

獾属 Huan Shu—獾类 Huanlei
Meles and *Arctonyx* have a superficial resemblance to each other, with their long, narrow heads and extended rhinarium. *Meles* is widely distributed in the Palaearctic realm except N Africa; of three species, one occurs in China.

Asian Badger *Meles leucurus*

狗獾 Gouhuan—**Distinctive Characteristics:** HB 495–700; T 130–205; HF 85–110; E 35–50; GLS 110–128; Wt 3.5–9 kg. A large mustelid with a pronounced long nose ending in a large external nose pad. The stout body is set on short, thick legs, with a short and thick tail. The face is elongated and cone-shaped; small, round, white-tipped ears are set low to the sides of the head. The fur is coarse, dense, and of medium length. It is grizzled gray on the body, a darker gray to almost black on the legs. The head has distinct markings: the majority of their face is white, and two black stripes, one on each side of the head, run longitudinally across the face, from the nose, over the eyes, to the base of the ears. The white facial markings contrast with the all-black throat and venter. The rostrum is long and has a cartilaginous nasal pad, and the region between nasal pad and upper lip is covered with hairs. Musk glands are present just outside the anal opening underneath the tail, which are used for scent marking. The feet are digitigrade, with five toes on each foot, and the soles of the feet are devoid of hair. Long, black, curved claws are present on all digits, and are longer on the forefoot. Three pairs of mammae are present. Dental formula: 3.1.3.1/3.1.3.2 = 34. **Distribution:** Distributed across China; extending to Kazakhstan, North and South Korea, and Russia (from the Volga River through Siberia). **Natural History:** Most available information comes from studies of the Eurasian Badger (*Meles meles*). It is presumed that there are few differences in basic natural history between these species. They occupy a large range of habitats throughout their range and prefer densely forested areas adjacent to areas of wide, open fields at elevations up to 1,600–1,700 m. They are found in deciduous, mixed, and coniferous woodland, hedges, scrub, riverine habitat, agricultural land, grassland, steppes, and semideserts. They are also occasionally found in suburban areas. They live in social groups of 2–23 animals, with an average of six. In warmer climates, they tend to be solitary or live in pairs. In colder climates, the clans are larger and more closely knit. The group is lead by a dominant pair, a male and a female. They live in large underground catacombs called "setts," which are interlocking tunnels that contain the nesting chambers and that often have around 20 entrances and exits to the ground above. They are very territorial and will defend their home range from other badgers. Distribution of setts varies depending on soil and landscape. Deciduous and mixed woodlands are preferred for digging setts, followed by hedgerow-scrub and coniferous woodland; they sometimes dig setts under buildings. They prefer to live in areas with well-drained soil that is easy to dig, has minimal disturbance by humans and their animals, and a good food supply. Badgers are opportunistic feeders and will feed on invertebrates (earthworms, insects, mollusks, beetles, and wasp larvae), small mammals (mice, rabbits, rats, voles, shrews, moles, hedgehogs), ground-nesting birds, small reptiles, frogs, carrion, plant matter (acorns, nuts, berries, fruits, seeds, cereal grains, tubers, roots, bulbs), and mushrooms. In many areas of their range, earthworms are a staple in their diet. Nocturnal or crepuscular. They only have one litter per year, and females take sole responsibility for the care of the young. They are induced ovulators and experience delayed implantation, which usually occurs in December or early January. Gestation lasts for seven weeks after the delayed implantation. **Conservation Status:** China RL—CR A2cd. IUCN RL—LC.

GENUS *MELOGALE*—Ferret Badgers

鼬獾属 Youhuan Shu—鼬獾 Youhuan
More robust than *Mustela*. Face with white stripes, a cartilaginous, long nose, and a snout that projects considerably beyond the lower jaw; their rostrum is terminated by a large, subcircular rhinarium that has no philtrum; claws relatively well developed; tail about 50% of HB length. Dental formula: 3.1.4.1/3.1.4.2 = 38. The subtropical genus *Melogale* is distributed throughout S Asia. It contains four species, two of which occur in China.

Chinese Ferret Badger *Melogale moschata*

鼬獾 You Huan—**Distinctive Characteristics:** HB 305–430; T 115–215; HF 45–65; E 20–40; GLS 70–84; Wt 0.5–1.6 kg. Smaller and more slender than true badgers, but more heavily built than weasels. The limbs are short, and the snout is long and cartilaginous and projects well beyond the lower jaw. There is no philtrum dividing the upper lip. The fore and hind foot have five digits and long, nonretractile claws, and the soles are naked to the heel. The face is basically dark in color (grayish or brownish), but with large, whitish patches on the cheeks and a white band between the eyes; there is considerable variation in the white facial coloration. A small black spot is present on each cheek; a pale stripe runs from the top of the head between the ears to the shoulders and then gets thinner and fades out toward the middle of the back; there is a black band across the rostrum and another across the forehead. The body color is dark gray or brown; venter yellow. The tail is short (≤50% HB length), bushy, and brown with a white tip. There are two anal glands and two pairs of inguinal mammae. **Distribution:** C and SE China, including Hainan Island and Taiwan; extending to India, N Laos, N Vietnam. **Natural History:** Live in subtropical forest, grasslands, and agricultural areas. They are omnivorous, and their diet includes small mammals, birds, bird eggs, frogs, insects, snails, earthworms, fruit, and carrion. They use their probing snouts to dig for roots and earthworms. They are nocturnal, solitary, and have a home range of 4–9 ha. They usually live in preexisting burrows and are terrestrial, although they will occasionally forage in trees. Mating occurs from May to October; gestation from 60 to 80 days; average litter size of two; no delayed implantation. Fur is used for collars and jackets. **Conservation Status:** China RL—NT. IUCN RL—LC.

Burmese Ferret Badger *Melogale personata*

缅甸鼬獾 Miandian Youhuan—**Distinctive Characteristics:** HB 390–410; T 175–180; HF 60–70; E 30–35; GLS 80–85; Wt 0.9–1.6 kg. In general appearance, *M. personata* is very similar to *M. moschata*. Head color is also similar, except the forehead black band is thinner. The back is grayish brown to blackish. A white dorsal stripe runs down the back, frequently all the way to the base of the tail. The tail is dark, bushy, and with a white tip, however, it is considerably longer (>50% HB) than in *M. moschata*. **Distribution:** S China; extending to Myanmar, Nepal, India (Assam), W Malaysia, Thailand, Vietnam. **Natural History:** Occupies forests, grasslands, and agricultural areas throughout its range. It forages principally on the ground, and males are believed to have home ranges that enclose several female home ranges. It is principally insectivorous and eats cockroaches, grasshoppers, earthworms, and snails. It also preys upon small vertebrates (lizards, frogs, rodents, small birds) and consumes fruits and nuts. It is nocturnal, crepuscular, and believed to be solitary. During daylight hours it stays in preexisting burrows or natural shelters, which it may then enlarge. It can climb trees readily, assisted by the rough ridges on the soles of its feet. **Conservation Status:** China RL—NA. IUCN RL—DD.

GENUS *MUSTELA*—Weasels and Ferrets

鼬属 You Shu—鼬类 Youlei
Weasels are characterized by a very long, slender body with exceptionally short limbs and ears that do not protrude above the head profile. They are all terrestrial and highly carnivorous. Dental formula: 3.1.3.1/3.1.3–4.2 = 34–36. Seventeen species occur worldwide on all continents except Australia, seven of which occur in China.

Mountain Weasel *Mustela altaica*

香鼬 Xiang You—**Distinctive Characteristics:** HB 105–270; T 66–162; HF 22–47; E 11–28 GLS 36–50; Wt 80–280 g. Similar to *M. sibirica* in general color but smaller; back and tail a pale brownish yellow or reddish brown; venter yellow to yellow-white, sharply contrasting with the back. Head grayish brown, with lips and chin white. Have a spring and autumn molt, with the summer coat being darker brown than the pale or straw-colored winter coat. Tail >40% of HB length and not bushy or tipped with black; limbs like the back, but the feet white, contrasting with the back and legs. The two smallest weasels in China are *M. nivalis* and *M. altaica*. They can be externally distinguished from each other based on the length of the tail (*M. nivalis* tail <33% of HB). **Distribution:** Throughout China except southeastern region; extending across Asia. **Natural History:** Prefer alpine meadow, live among the rocky slopes, and have been found from 1,500 to 4,000 m. They may live near human habitation and occasionally attack domestic fowl. They feed mainly on pikas (*Ochotona*), hamsters (*Cricetulus*), and voles (*Alticola*), and their numbers are positively correlated with the density of pikas. They also eat a variety of small vertebrates, including rodents, rabbits, birds, lizards, frogs, fish, and insects. They occasionally eat berries. They may undergo extreme fluctuations in populations from year to year, perhaps related to variability in food supply. They are principally nocturnal; however, they may hunt during the day as well. They can climb and swim well. It is believed that they are polygynous breeders. Gestation of 35–50 days. There is no direct evidence of delayed implantation. Altricial young appear in early July, and only the female cares for the young. **Conservation Status:** China RL—NT. IUCN RL—NT.

Ermine *Mustela erminea*

白鼬 Bai You—**Distinctive Characteristics:** HB 190–220; T 42–80; HF 30–40; E 12–20; GLS 38–45; Wt 60–110 g. Widely valued for the characteristics of its fur, the color of which changes along with seasons. The summer coat is reddish brown or yellowish brown, but the feet are whitish and contrasted, and there is a sharp demarcation between venter and dorsal surface. The foot pad is totally covered with fur. The winter coat is all white in northern areas—in more southern areas it may stay a yellowish brown with white venter. Size sexual dimorphism large, with males weighing up to 150% of female weight. Tail >33% of HB length, and terminal third is black; four or five pairs of mammae. **Distribution:** NW and NE China; extending widely across Europe, Asia, and North America. **Natural History:** Occupies a wide habitat range from tundra, alpine meadow, woodland (coniferous, mixed), marsh, mountains, and riverbanks, to farmland and hedgerows. Key components for habitat appear to be prey abundance and ground cover. Found at elevations of up to 2,000–3,000 m year-round. These weasels have voracious appetites and will eat up to 40% of their own weight in a single day. Their diet consists of lagomorphs, microtine rodents, squirrels, rats, birds, eggs, lizards, frogs, snakes, insects, earthworms, and fruit. Mostly nocturnal and solitary; may be more diurnal in winter; climb and swim well; male territory may include several female territories. During winter they may hunt under the snow. May exhibit considerable fluctuations in population number from year to year. Males and females have separate territories that they defend against members of the same sex. They will use hollow logs, rocks, and rodent burrows for dens and will cache surplus prey. A delayed implantation of 9–10 months is followed by a four-week gestation. Ermines mate once a year, producing litters of four to nine altricial young. Average natural life span of one and a half years. Ermines are preyed upon by raptors and other carnivores. **Conservation Status:** China RL—EN A2cd + 3cd. IUCN RL—LC.

Steppe Polecat *Mustela eversmanii*

艾鼬 Ai You—**Distinctive Characteristics:** HB 315–460; T 90–200; HF 45–68; E 15–35; GLS 62–73; Wt 460–1,198 g. Largest species of *Mustela* in China and the only member of the genus in which the feet, tail, and venter are black. The body has long black guard hairs against a yellowish-brown underfur. There is a dark brown mask on the light-colored muzzle. Tail tip dark brown to black (may cover half of tail); tail about 33% of HB. **Distribution:** C, NW, and NE China; extending widely across Asia and through E Europe. **Natural History:** Occupies open steppe environments through most of its range and avoids forests. It is primarily nocturnal but can also be seen active during the day in areas away from humans. Solitary; occupy burrows made by other animals. It may use a single burrow year-round and enlarge it and refurnish it daily. Feeds on small vertebrates (murine rodents, ground squirrels, voles, birds, reptiles), as well as birds' eggs and insects, consuming 100–150 g of meat daily. On the Tibetan Plateau it is a dietary specialist on Plateau Pikas (*Ochotona curzoniae*). Year-to-year population fluctuations can be considerable. Mating occurs early, such that young are born in early spring (April–May). Gestation is around 36–40 days. Litter size ranges from 4 to 10 young. **Conservation Status:** China RL—NT. IUCN RL—LC.

Yellow-Bellied Weasel *Mustela kathiah*

黄腹鼬 Huangfu You—**Distinctive Characteristics:** HB 205–334; T 165–182; HF 22–46; E 12–21; GLS 43–54; Wt 168–250 g. Back and tail dark brown, venter and mandible yellow-white, forming a distinct division from head to rump on sides of body. Edge of upper lip, the chin, and a little of the throat whitish, but the rest of the underside a deep yellow; tail about 66% of HB length. The foot pads are well developed and exposed. **Distribution:** C and SE China, including Hainan Island; extending to S Asia. **Natural History:** Poorly known. They eat rodents, birds, birds' eggs, lizards, frogs, fruit, and insects. They are nocturnal, solitary, and territorial. Mating occurs in late spring or early summer. Births occur in April–May, with litter sizes ranging from 3 to 18. Adults are sexually mature in one year. **Conservation Status:** China RL—NT. IUCN RL—LC.

Least Weasel *Mustela nivalis*

伶鼬 Ling You—**Distinctive Characteristics:** HB 130–190; T 20–53; HF 16–25; E 9–13; GLS 27–37; Wt 28–70 g.
The smallest carnivore. Males are about twice the size of females. Hair color changes seasonally; summer coat is brownish red with sharply offset white or pale venter; winter pelage is uniformly white in northern parts of the range, paler than summer coat in southern parts. Tail tip same as body color (in some specimens, the very tip of the tail is black); tail <35% of HB length; females have three or four pairs of mammae. **Distribution:** NW, C, and NE China; extending widely across Asia, Europe, and North America. **Natural History:** Found in a wide range of habitats: forests, steppe, meadows, mountains (up to 4,000 m), villages, gardens, and farmlands. However, generally avoid any habitat that lacks good cover. May spend the whole winter under snow. Prey abundance and dense cover determines distribution. Feeds principally on microtine rodents but also rats, hares, birds, and birds' eggs. They must eat frequently, about a third of their body weight per day. They store food for winter. Do not make their own burrows. Solitary and primarily nocturnal, although they can be active during the day. Separate territories for males and females. *M. nivalis* and *M. erminea* display character displacement and geographically overlap. When prey numbers are high, both species can coexist. Home range of males varies from 0.5 to 25 ha, and the population may fluctuate seasonally in response to microtine rodent abundance. Climb trees and swim well. Mate from February to August and may have two litters of four to six annually. No delayed implantation; gestation of 34–37 days. **Conservation Status:** China RL—VU A2cd + 3cd. IUCN RL—LC.

Siberian Weasel *Mustela sibirica*

黄鼬 Huang You—**Distinctive Characteristics:** HB 220–420; T 120–250; HF 45–65; E 15–25; GLS 50–72; Wt 500–1,200 g. Body color reddish brown to dark

brown, gradually changing to a yellowish-brown venter; face and front dark brown; upper lip white; an indistinct dark mask, tail about 50% of HB length, may have darker tip; sexual size dimorphism. Dental formula: 3.1.3.1/3.1.3.2 = 34. **Distribution:** Widespread in NW, C, and E China, including Taiwan; extending across Asia. **Natural History:** Found in dense primary and secondary forests, forest steppe, and mountains. Often found in river valleys, near swamps and areas with dense ground vegetation. May occur in villages and in cultivated areas. Feed principally on small mammals, especially murine rodents. Also reported to eat domestic fowl, amphibians, birds, fish, berries, nuts, and invertebrates. May store prey for later consumption. Nocturnal and crepuscular, but may be active during the day in thick vegetation. They are solitary and maintain territories. They have been observed moving up to 8 km in a single night and swim well. They will often swim in pursuit of water voles.

Mating occurs in March–April. Gestation period is 33–37 days. Young are born in late May; usually five or six individuals per litter. **Conservation Status:** China RL—NT. IUCN RL—LC.

Back-Striped Weasel *Mustela strigidorsa*

纹鼬 Wen You—**Distinctive Characteristics:** HB 275–340; T 145–205; HF 47–54; E 20–23; GLS 57–65; Wt 443–1,200 g. Basic body color is brown with a thin, whitish to silvery median dorsal stripe that goes from head to base of tail; bushy tail <50% of HB length; lip, cheeks, chin, and throat pale yellowish. There are two pairs of mammae. Dental formula: 3.1.3.1/3.1.4.2 = 36. **Distribution:** S China; extending throughout SE Asia. **Natural History:** Poorly known. It has been reported to live in river valleys at elevations between 1,200 and 2,200 m. It has also been found in evergreen forests, farmland, and around villages. **Conservation Status:** Total Chinese population estimated at 10,000. China RL—EN A2cd + 3cd. IUCN RL—LC.

GENUS *VORMELA* (monotypic)

虎鼬属 Huyou Shu

Marbled Polecat *Vormela peregusna*

虎鼬 Hu You—**Distinctive Characteristics:** HB 300–400; T 150–210; HF 24–88; E 15–30; GLS 52–65; Wt 370–700 g. Back a yellowy-white color mixed with a mosaic of brown and white stripes and spots. The face, limbs, and venter all blackish brown; tail all white with blackish-brown tip; tail long, its length up to half of HB length. Noticeably large ears. The underparts are dark brown, and the facial mask is dark brown. Females have five pairs of mammae. **Distribution:** NW and NC China; extending widely across Asia and Europe. **Natural History:** Most commonly found in steppe and dry, open hill and valley habitats. Has been found as high as 2,100 m. Like most mustelids, *Vormela* possesses anal scent glands, from which a noxious substance is emitted. When threatened, it throws its head back, erects its body hairs, curls its tail over its back, and emits musk from the anal glands. It excavates deep, roomy burrows and is nocturnal and crepuscular. It has been reported to be a good climber, although it is the most fossorial of weasels. It preys on rodents and focuses on *Meriones* colonies. It will also eat birds (including poultry), reptiles, and lagomorphs. Solitary except during the breeding season. Births occur from February to March after a gestation period of about nine weeks. **Conservation Status:** China RL—VU A2cd + 3cd. IUCN RL—VU A2c.

FAMILY AILURIDAE

GENUS *AILURUS* (monotypic)

小熊猫科 Xiaoxiongmao Ke; 小熊猫属 Xiaoxiongmao Shu
The Red Panda has been placed in the Ursidae, the Procyonidae, a family by itself, and in a family with the Giant Panda. Recent evidence suggests that *Ailurus* is most closely related to a group that contains the mephitids (skunks) and procyonids (raccoon-like mammals) of the New World; resemblances to the Giant Panda could be due to convergence in their dietary habits.

Red Panda *Ailurus fulgens*

小熊猫 Xiaoxiongmao—**Distinctive Characteristics:** HB 510–730; T 370–480; HF 95–115; E 50–80; GLS 100–120; Wt 2.5–5 kg. Form as stout as that of a domestic cat; pelage uniformly reddish brown; rostrum white; cheek, brow, and ear margin all covered with white hairs; ears are large, erect, and pointed; tail long, thick, and shaggy, with 12 alternating red and dark rings; tail tip dark brown. Head round; rostrum shortened; four pairs of mammae; plantigrade; fore and hind foot each contain five digits; no sexual dimorphism. Dental formula: 3.1.3.2/3.1.4.2 = 38. **Distribution:** C and SW China; extending to N Myanmar, Nepal, India (Sikkim). **Natural History:** Found in the temperate forest zone of the Himalayan ecosystem at heights of 1,500–4,000 m in mixed forest habitat with a dense understory of bamboo. It lives in evergreen broadleaf, evergreen mixed, and coniferous forests, but mainly in bamboo scrub near valleys and ranges with temperatures lower than 20°C in summer and 0°C in winter. Copes with low-temperature environments by lowering its metabolic rate; it has one of the lowest metabolic rates of any carnivore. Prefers south- and west-facing steep slopes in conifer forests with a high amount of logs and stumps. Red Pandas focus on places where the basal diameter of bamboo is small and the humidity is high. The bulk of the diet consists of bamboo (*Chimonobambusa, Giongzhuea, Phyllostachys, Sinarundinaria,* and *Thamnocalamus*), and they focus on the tender and young shoots and leaves. They may also eat small vertebrates, eggs, blossoms, berries, and seeds (*Acer, Fagus, Morus*). Solitary and nocturnal. Sometimes form small groups of two to five individuals. They can rapidly climb high trees and move through trees when a threat appears; foraging, however, often occurs on the ground. Adults rarely interact with one another outside of the mating season, and latrines are used to mark territories. Breeding is seasonal (February–March), and gestation is 120–150 days. One litter averaging one to four is produced annually. **Conservation Status:** The Chinese population has been estimated to be between 3,500 and 7,000. China RL—VU A2acd. China Key List—II. CITES—I. IUCN RL—VU C1.

ORDER PERISSODACTYLA

FAMILY EQUIDAE

GENUS *EQUUS*—Horses, Zebras, and Asses

奇蹄目 Qiti Mu; 马科 Ma Ke; 马属 Ma Shu—马, 斑马, 驴 Ma, Banma, Lü
Perissodactyls are large animals possessing an odd number of toes, with hooves on the tip—essentially these animals support their body weight on the median

third toe of their feet, and their locomotion is unguligrade. The skulls tend to be elongated. Unlike the artiodactyls (even-toed ungulates), they possess a third trochanter on their femur. All forms are herbivorous and have a simple stomach and large caecum. Once a flourishing order, the Perissodactyla are now represented by only three families, six genera, and 17 species. Only one family, the Equidae, occurs in China, although two species of rhinoceros (family Rhinocerotidae) come close to the southern border. The Equidae, all genus *Equus*, includes eight species distributed across Asia and Africa, although domesticated forms have been introduced worldwide; three species occur in China. Equids are the most cursorial of the perissodactyls. The neck is long and laterally compressed, and there are long forelocks on the forehead and manes on the neck in some species; ears are sharp and upstanding; tail long, with tail hairs hanging down as far as the middle part of the hind leg. Dental formula: 3.0–1.3–4.3/3.0–1.3.3 = 36–42.

Horse (Przewalski's Horse) *Equus caballus*

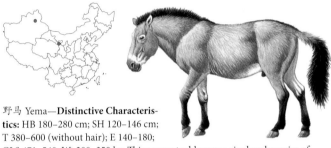

野马 Yema—**Distinctive Characteristics:** HB 180–280 cm; SH 120–146 cm; T 380–600 (without hair); E 140–180; GLS 471–540; Wt 200–350 kg. This account addresses a single subspecies of horse, the wild horse or Przewalski's Horse, *E. c. przewalskii*. Compared with domestic horses, the head is large, the legs thicker; pelage uniformly light brown in summer and lighter in winter; ventral surface yellowish; long hair on forehead absent; mane brown, short, and upstanding; rostrum milk white; a blackish-brown stripe runs down spine from middle of back to base of tail; several inconspicuous transverse striations are visible on limbs in summer. **Distribution:** Formerly NW China; extending into Mongolia and Central Asia. **Natural History:** Przewalski's Horse apparently survived in the wild longer than any other of the lineages of horse, largely because it inhabited remote areas in Central Asia. The morphology of Przewalski's Horse indicates that it evolved adaptations for cold climate in tundra and steppe environments—thus that its last known habitat in the semidesert steppes of Central Asia represents an environment to which it was not well adapted. It frequently had to survive drought conditions, digging holes with its hooves to access water or migrating to areas with potential water sources. The social order of wild horses probably matches that of feral domestic horses: there is a dominant male who remains close to five or six females in a harem-like association and separate groups of bachelor males. Mating occurs in August–September, and parturition in May–July. Only one foal is normally produced. **Conservation Status:** The general history of this species has been one of the spread of domesticated forms and the gradual elimination by interbreeding or persecution of wild forms. The last subspecies to hold out was *przewalskii*, due to its remote locale. It was rare at the time the first specimens were made available to science, and it is now felt that the subspecies is extinct in the wild. The last confirmed sighting, in Mongolia just north of the Chinese border, occurred in 1969. Between these events 12 founders were successfully brought into captivity and bred. The breeding program was rife with problems, from inbreeding, undesirable artificial selection, and introgression with nonpure lineages. Conservation geneticists have been cleaning up this captive population, and the form is now being reintroduced to parts of its former range in the Dzungarian Basin and near Dunhuang in the Gansu corridor. The Dzungarian population is being managed in the Kalamaili Reserve, where 27 horses were released in 2001 and an additional 10 in 2004. China RL—EW. China Key List—I. CITES—I (as *E. przewalskii*). IUCN RL—EN D (as *E. ferus przewalskii*).

Kulan *Equus hemionus*

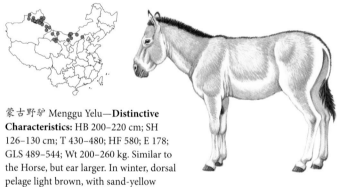

蒙古野驴 Menggu Yelu—**Distinctive Characteristics:** HB 200–220 cm; SH 126–130 cm; T 430–480; HF 580; E 178; GLS 489–544; Wt 200–260 kg. Similar to the Horse, but ear larger. In winter, dorsal pelage light brown, with sand-yellow color; short, erect mane; ventral surface yellowish white; inner sides of all four legs milk white; rostrum white; a brown median dorsal stripe runs down from shoulder to base of tail; shoulder blade with brown transverse pectoral stripe. Summer fur dark brown. **Distribution:** NW China; extending into Mongolia and formerly Kazakhstan and S Russia, to Syria, N Iraq, Iran, Afghanistan, Pakistan, and NW India; now survives in isolated populations in India, Turkmenistan, and C Iran. **Natural History:** Occupy xeric steppes and mountainous areas. Diurnally active. Primarily grazers when grass is abundant but may also feed on a variety of desert shrubs; they apparently can go for long periods without water. Normally a single male controls access to a small harem; occasionally found in large groups. The birthing season begins in May, and mating extends to the end of September; in any one population births normally extend over a two- or three-month period. Gestation lasts 11 months and may result in twins. **Conservation Status:** Severely depleted throughout its range; the most extensive population resides in S Mongolia and extends into N China. Here it is perceived that they cause rangeland damage. They are also heavily poached for meat and hides. China RL—EN A1acd. China Key List—I. CITES—I. IUCN RL—EN A2abc + 3bd.

Kiang *Equus kiang*

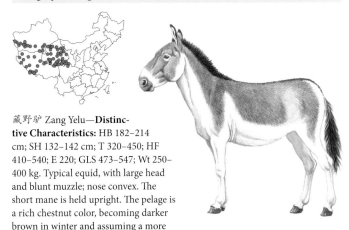

藏野驴 Zang Yelu—**Distinctive Characteristics:** HB 182–214 cm; SH 132–142 cm; T 320–450; HF 410–540; E 220; GLS 473–547; Wt 250–400 kg. Typical equid, with large head and blunt muzzle; nose convex. The short mane is held upright. The pelage is a rich chestnut color, becoming darker brown in winter and assuming a more reddish hue in late summer. Legs and undersides are white. There is a dark dorsal stripe that extends from the mane to the terminus of the tail. Ear tips are black, as is a narrow band along the margin of the hooves. **Distribution:** Tibetan Plateau; extending into Ladakh and Sikkim (India), and Nepal. **Natural History:** Inhabit open country and may range as high as 5,300 m, but are also found in adjoining desert steppe as low as 2,700 m. Their diet consists almost entirely of grasses and sedges, primarily *Stipa*; forbs are rarely eaten. Their social dynamics are variable; many solitary, but they may also be seen in small groups or in extremely large assemblages of hundreds of animals. The mating season usually commences in late July and may extend to September; young are born from mid-July to August following a 355-day gestation. **Conservation Status:** Populations are becoming increasingly fragmented and negatively impacted by current development priorities, primarily fencing, on the plateau. China RL—EN A1acd. China Key List—I. CITES—II. IUCN RL—LC.

ORDER ARTIODACTYLA—Even-toed Ungulates

偶蹄目 Outi Mu—偶蹄类 Outilei

Artiodactyls comprise medium to large hoofed animals. All four legs possess an even number of toes, nearly equal in size, that are arranged around the axis formed by the highly developed third and fourth toes; the limb axis supports the body on these two toes. Toes two and five, or rudiments thereof, are smaller and face backward. Most species are strictly herbivorous (except the omnivorous pigs), fast running, and social living. Some species have horns or antlers growing from the frontal bone. Canines are reduced in most species that have horns or antlers and highly developed in those that do not. Stomachs complex, with two to four chambers; several families possess a ruminant three- or four-chambered stomach. Face or other external secreting glands are a common characteristic. The Artiodactyla represents a diverse lineage composed of 10 families (six of which occur in China), 87 genera, and over 220 species. They are distributed throughout the world, naturally or through introduction.

FAMILY SUIDAE—Pigs

猪科 Zhu Ke—猪 Zhu

The Suidae represents an Old World family of nonruminant ungulates comprising pigs and the babirusa (*Babyrousa*) of Indonesia. Pigs are medium-sized with thickset bodies and sparse, bristly hair. The rostrum is long, and its anterior extremity forms a bare nasal disk or snout. The lower canine is large and tusk-like, being constantly sharpened by wear against the upper canine. Stomach is simple and two-chambered; females bear three to six pairs of mammae. Young are striped, and pigs live in small social herds. There are five genera, of which only one, *Sus*, occurs in China.

GENUS *SUS*—Pigs

猪属 Zhu Shu—猪 Zhu

Among the eight species of *Sus* is the ubiquitous Wild Boar, *S. scrofa*, the form that ranges across most of China. All pigs live in herds that roam forests and wild lands as well as raiding farmland in search of worms, fruits, and other foods. They have a unique snout designed to root about under the surface of the ground, both sniffing out and digging up their favored foods.

Wild Boar *Sus scrofa*

野猪 Ye Zhu—**Distinctive Characteristics:** HB 90–180 cm; SH 59–109 cm; T 200–300; HF 250–350; E 114; GLS 295–350; Wt 50–200 kg. Distinctive brown or blackish heavyset pig with coarse hair. Male has ridge of hair from crown down back of neck. Northern races are long-haired, those in tropics rather sparsely haired. Their hind toes generally leave prints, unlike deer, on most substrates. Toes sometimes rather blunt compared to those of deer, and associated rooting signs and sloppy black dung are diagnostic signs. Dental formula: 3.1.4.3/3.1.4.3 = 44; males have prominent tusks. **Distribution:** Occurs across China except the driest deserts and high plateau areas; extending to Europe, N Africa, through Asia to the Malay Peninsula, Sumatra, and Java. **Natural History:** Found in all wild habitats from forest to scrub, grasslands, and swamps, raiding cultivation areas and ranging far into mountains. Mainly crepuscular and nocturnal. Omnivorous, feeding on plant material, mushrooms, seeds, and fruit, especially acorns, but also worms, snails, insects, small vertebrates, and carrion. When feeding, they rummage through the topsoil with their flat sensitive snout, sniffing out delicacies. Can become predatory, sometimes attacking snakes upon encounter. Male canine teeth rub together to give very sharp tusks used in defense and aggressive status fighting. Travel in small herds, although some males are solitary. Good swimmers. Make piles of broken-off saplings as a nursery nest. One litter of four to eight young is born in spring following a four-month gestation. **Conservation Status:** Much reduced in numbers due to hunting but still widespread, sometimes common, and even becomes an agricultural pest in some areas. In Taiwan hunting of Wild Boars to prevent crop damage has severely reduced their population. China RL—LC. IUCN RL—LC.

FAMILY CAMELIDAE—Camels

骆驼科 Luotuo Ke—骆驼 Luotuo
The Camelidae is a small South American, African, and Asian family comprising the camels, vicuñas, guanacos, alpacas, and llamas. These are large ungulates with no horns and a long neck. Their muzzle is split to form a harelip. Toes two and five are absent, and the end of toes three and four is expanded into a broad pad (they do not possess hoofs) to allow effective movement in sand and on rocks; the foot posture is digitigrade. The stomach has three chambers. Several species have been domesticated. Of three genera, only *Camelus* occurs in the Old World and in China.

GENUS *CAMELUS*—Old World Camels

骆驼属 Luotuo Shu—骆驼 Luotuo
Large camelid with one or two large dorsal humps. Dental formula: 1.1.3.3/3.1.2.3 = 34. Two species occur, of which only one occurs in China.

Bactrian Camel *Camelus bactrianus*

双峰驼 Shuangfeng Tuo—**Distinctive Characteristics:** HB 320–350 cm; SH 160–180 cm; Wt 450–680 kg. Very large ungulate with two prominent humps on back. Head small, neck long and curved upward. Color golden to bark brown, darkest on thighs. In winter has long, shaggy hair on neck and humps. Has double row of long eyelashes and hair in ears to protect it from sandstorms. Its slit-like nostrils can close during dust storms. The wild Bactrian Camel is relatively small and lithe when compared to the domesticated form; its humps appear significantly smaller and are more conical in shape. Its fur coat is not as thick. **Distribution:** NW China; extending into Mongolia and Central Asia. **Natural History:** Occupies steppe grassland, montane desert, semidesert, and arid scrub. Can occur at up to 4,000 m elevation. Domesticated for over 4,000 years, and more domesticated animals now remain than wild. Eats a wide variety of desert plants and leaves of thorn trees and bushes. Can eat salty, halophytic plants. In times of food scarcity will eat bones, meat, shoes, canvas, etc. The humps store fat and enable the camel to live for many days without food. Water-filled chambers surround the stomach and enable the camel to live for several weeks without water. The camel can drink slightly saline water and can urinate concentrated salt. It can hold over 100 liters of water. The camel can vary its body temperature facultatively, so it does not need to sweat or expend energy to thermoregulate. The overall suite of adaptations allows it to withstand winter temperatures many degrees below zero and extremely hot summer temperatures. Lives in small herds of 6–20 animals; seasonal migrants. During the mating season, males fight, bite, spit, snort, and try to push each other to the ground. Gestation is about 400 days, and one or two young are born per litter. Young stay with the mother for three to five years. Adults live up to 30 years. **Conservation Status:** Only about 500–1,500 wild Bactrian Camels remain globally, about half in China. These herds are threatened by habitat alteration, illegal hunting, and hybridization with domestic camels. China RL—EN A1acd. China Key List—I. IUCN RL—CR A3de + 4ade.

FAMILY TRAGULIDAE—Chevrotains and Mouse-deer

鼷鹿科 Xilu Ke—鼷鹿 Xilu
The Tragulidae are the world's smallest deer. They show several primitive features, such as a lack of antlers or horns, the presence of large canines (in males the canine is a well-developed long, curving, narrow sharp tusk; in females the upper canine is very small), and the retention of slender but well-formed second and fifth digits. They are mostly nocturnal and frugivorous, feeding on fallen fruits in forest. They possess a three-part stomach. Dental formula: 0.1.3.3/3.1.3.3 = 34. Of three genera, only *Tragulus* reaches SE Asia and China.

GENUS *TRAGULUS*—Mouse-deer

鼷鹿属 Xilu Shu—鼷鹿 Xilu
The mouse-deer have short forelegs and long hind legs, and usually sport light spots on their throat and breast. *Tragulus* is a SE Asian genus composed of two to six species ranging from Indochina to Borneo; only one species has been recorded in China.

Java Mouse-Deer *Tragulus javanicus*

 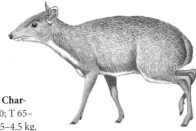

小鼷鹿 Xiao Xilu—**Distinctive Characteristics:** HB 430–500; SH 350; T 65–80; E 35–50; GLS 92–103; Wt 2.5–4.5 kg. Tiny deer lacking antlers and having long, curved canines in both sexes—reflecting the general trend in deer for males to possess either antlers or large canines. General pelage reddish brown with characteristic three white bars under the throat joined under the chin in a neat T shape. Underparts yellowish white. Footprints and dung are tiny compared to those of other Chinese ungulates. **Distribution:** Found only in Xishuangbanna prefecture of S Yunnan; ranging to the Greater Sunda Islands and Indochina. **Natural History:** Inhabits tropical evergreen lowland forests, using crown-gap areas with dense undergrowth as foraging sites and ridge areas as resting sites. Feeds largely on fallen fruits, especially figs, but also eats young shoots. Once thought to be nocturnal; recent studies have shown it to be diurnally active and to rest at night. Solitary. Eyes very reflective at night. Runs to water when chased by dogs. Hunters can attract mouse-deer by patting the ground in imitation of the female's thumping behavior. Makes shrill, squeaky whistle on contact. Runs with jerky, stiff-legged gait and sits hunched on haunches. Gestation is five or six months, and new pregnancy may almost immediately follow birth of the single (sometimes two) young, so that the reproductive rate is high. **Conservation Status:** Rare and restricted in China. China RL—CR A1cd; B1ab(i,ii,iii). D. China Key List—I. IUCN RL—DD.

FAMILY MOSCHIDAE

GENUS *MOSCHUS*—Musk Deer

麝科 She Ke; 麝属 She Shu—麝 She
These are small deer without antlers; instead, both genders sport prominent canines. Dental formula: 0.1.3.3/3.1.3.3 = 34. Their hair is very stiff and bristly. Most forms live in mountains. Musk deer are very agile and can jump into trees where they balance on small branches. Toes long and sharp. While they lack infraorbital glands, male musk deer have a musk scent gland on their underbelly that is extremely valued both in the perfume industry and for traditional Chinese medicine. This has led to severe persecution and snaring of all species, driving them close to extinction. However, musk deer can be farmed with moderate success, although captive animals remain very wild and nervous. Of seven *Moschus* species, six are recognized in China.

Anhui Musk Deer *Moschus anhuiensis*

安徽麝 Anhui She—**Distinctive Characteristics:** HB 696–765; SH <500; T 18–32; HF 192–195; GLS 141–151; Wt 7.1–9.7 kg. Body gray-brown; lower hind legs nearly black. The ear is fringed with white and blackish on the back; the black coloration extends to the cheeks and forehead. The chin and throat are white, and a white stripe extends up to the cheek, while two white stripes run backward along the underside of the neck, forming a ring on the upper breast. Young (one to two years old) possess 13 orange stripes crossing the body between the shoulder and the hip, although these gradually disappear, becoming many spots that form three lines on sides of the back in adults. The rump is dusky brown, and the rump patch insignificant. **Distribution:** Found only in Mt. Dabie area of W Anhui. Endemic. **Natural History:** Poorly known, but its natural history is likely similar to that of *M. berezovskii* and *M. moschiferus*. It is more likely to produce twins than single births. Females mature rapidly and are capable of breeding in their first year of life. **Conservation Status:** Threatened in China due to restricted distribution. China RL—EN B1ab(i,ii,iii) + 2ab(i,ii,iii). China Key List—II. CITES—II. IUCN RL—EN A2cd.

Forest Musk Deer *Moschus berezovskii*

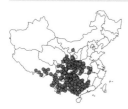

林麝 Lin She—**Distinctive Characteristics:** HB 630–800; SH <500; T 40; GSL 102–146; Wt 6–9 kg. Pelage dark olive brown, without spotting on back of adult; nearly black on the rump; legs and venter yellow to orange-brown. Inside of ears and eyebrows whitish; ears black at tip and orange-brown at their base. Lower jaw with cream stripe; cream patches on side of throat join to two broad cream stripes running down the front sides of neck to breast; contrasting band up median of neck dark brown. Juveniles spotted. Forms from Sichuan, Qinghai, and Xizang are larger and darker brown with orange-yellow underparts and brownish-yellow neck stripes; those from S Yunnan, Guangxi, and Guangdong are the smallest and palest form and have more fulvous pelage; forms from the Yunnan-Guizhou highland, Hunan, and Jiangxi are intermediate in color and also small; and those from NW Yunnan are large in size, paler brown on the back and with grayish-white neck stripe and spot. **Distribution:** Widely distributed in C and S China; extending to the E Himalayas and into NE Vietnam. **Natural History:** Inhabits coniferous or broadleaf forests, or mixed forests at high elevations (1,000–3,800 m). Most active between dusk and dawn, alternately resting and feeding. Animals share communal latrines, leaving large piles of tiny pellets. These animals are shy, sedentary, and remain within a defined home range throughout the year. Males utilize their large musk gland to defend their territory and attract mates. When alarmed they make great leaps with wild changes of direction. Diet consists of leaves, grasses, moss, lichens, shoots, twigs. They can adroitly jump into trees to forage. Their main predators include Leopard, marten, fox, Wolf, Lynx, and especially humans. Gestation lasts six and a half months, after which one or two young are born. During the first two months, the young deer lie hidden in secluded areas, independent of their mother except at feeding times. They are weaned within three to four months and reach sexual maturity by 24 months. Animals may live up to 20 years. **Conservation Status:** China RL—EN A1cd. China Key List—II. CITES—II. IUCN RL—EN A2cd.

Alpine Musk Deer *Moschus chrysogaster*

马麝 Ma She—**Distinctive Characteristics:** HB 800–900; SH 500–600; T 40–70; HF 270; GSL 140–170; Wt 9.6–13 kg. A large musk deer. Pelage light brown with sandy yellow hue, and hair on back of neck distinctively whorled, giving a banded appearance. Juvenile has white spots on back, but these are rarely visible in adults. Throat with noticeable white stripes or single broad creamy band; throat pelage often a red-gold color. Inside ears lined with long sandy hairs; distinctive orange eye-ring. **Distribution:** Highlands of C China and south to the Himalayas; extending to Nepal, India (Sikkim), and Bhutan. **Natural History:** An animal of barren plateaus at high elevations, where it occupies meadows, fellfields, shrublands, or fir forests. In W Sichuan, where it overlaps the distribution of *M. berezovskii*, the *M. chrysogaster* inhabits the higher elevations (above 3,000 m), compared with the 1,000–2,500 m altitudinal range of *M. berezovskii*. Feeds mainly on grasses and shrubs. Solitary and crepuscularly active. Densities may be as low as two to three animals per km². One to two young (normally one) born in June following a six-month gestation. **Conservation Status:** This species has been heavily poached for its musk. China RL—EN A1d + 2cd + 3cd. China Key List—II. CITES—II. IUCN RL—EN A2cd.

Black Musk Deer *Moschus fuscus*

黑麝 Hei She—**Distinctive Characteristics:** SH <500; GLS <150; Wt 8 kg. Small, dark musk deer; smaller and darker than the similar *M. berezovskii*. Unspotted, with no white markings on face or neck. Sometimes lighter brown patch on shoulders. Throat dark, frequently with two incomplete yellow collars. Limbs black, and hind limbs longer than forelimbs. **Distribution:** E Himalayas; extending to Bhutan. **Natural History:** Occurs in coniferous forests, forest edges, and rocky ridges at high elevations (2,600–4,200 m). Poorly known form; all life-history attributes are likely similar to those of *M. chrysogaster*. **Conservation Status:** China RL—EN A2cd + 3cd. China Key List—II. CITES—II. IUCN RL—EN A2cd.

Himalayan Musk Deer *Moschus leucogaster*

喜马拉雅麝 Ximalaya She—**Distinctive Characteristics:** HB 86–100 cm; SH 51–53 cm; T 40–60; GLS 150–180; Wt 11–16 kg. Similar to *M. chrysogaster*; hair on back of neck distinctively whorled. Dorsal pelage a grizzled dark brown, rump paler, with only an indistinct yellowish stripe up front of neck and onto lower jaw; throat dark. Ears are long and rounded, lined white inside and with yellowish tips and edges at rear; eye-ring poorly expressed. **Distribution:** SW Xizang; extending in the W Himalayas to west of Chumbi divide on south side of Himalayas. **Natural History:** Inhabits high, alpine environments; while poorly known, its natural history is likely to be similar to that of *M. chrysogaster*. **Conservation Status:** Rare in China. China RL—NE. China Key List—II. CITES—I. IUCN RL—EN A2d.

Siberian Musk Deer *Moschus moschiferus*

原麝 Yuan She—**Distinctive Characteristics:** HB 650–900; SH 560–610; T 40–60; GLS 130–160; Wt 8–12 kg. Soft pelage is dark brown with a rufous tinge; many distinctive pale yellow spots on back. The lower jaw is white, and there are two white stripes running down from neck to shoulder. **Distribution:** NE and NW China; extending to Siberia, Korea, Mongolia. **Natural History:** Occupies broadleaf and coniferous forests, or mixed forests, where it is solitary and primarily active at dusk and dawn. Diet consists of leaves, herbs, and lichens. One to three, generally two, young are born in May–June following a six-month gestation. **Conservation Status:** The form *M. moschiferus* disappeared from Xinjiang by the end of the 19th century, and the species has generally retracted throughout its range in China. China RL—EN A1cd. China Key List— II. CITES—II. IUCN RL—VU A2d + 3d + 4d.

FAMILY CERVIDAE—Deer

鹿科 Lu Ke—鹿 Lu

The Cervidae is a large family in which males typically have branched, bony antlers with no horny sheath that are shed periodically. Females of some species have smaller antlers, but usually these are absent. Males of small species or species without antlers have long, tusklike upper canines. Otherwise, the upper canine is reduced or absent. Many species have external secretion glands—infraorbital, digital, and/or inguinal. There are three subfamilies worldwide, all of which are represented in China.

SUBFAMILY CAPREOLINAE—Deer, Moose, and Reindeer

狍亚科 Pao Yake—鹿, 驼鹿, 驯鹿 Lu, Tuolu, Xun Lu

The Capreolinae is comprised of nine genera found throughout the Holarctic and Neotropical realms. In China it is comprised of three genera of northern cervids, all characterized by at least partly hairy noses and irregular antler form.

GENUS *ALCES*—Moose

驼鹿属 Tuolu Shu—驼鹿 Tuolu

Moose are the largest members of the deer family. Adult males have wide, sweeping, upturned palmate antlers with many tines. Their nose is large and camel-like. A moose's life span can exceed 20 years. Predators include humans, tigers, wolves, and bears. A home range varies in size from 20–40 km² to a maximum of 300 km². In winter, when much of the diet consists of branches and other dry, woody materials, the scat is in pellet form. Both moose species can be found in China. Dental formula: 0.0.3.3/3.1.3.3 = 32.

Eurasian Elk *Alces alces*

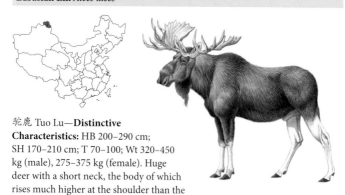

驼鹿 Tuo Lu—**Distinctive Characteristics:** HB 200–290 cm; SH 170–210 cm; T 70–100; Wt 320–450 kg (male), 275–375 kg (female). Huge deer with a short neck, the body of which rises much higher at the shoulder than the rump. The lip is inflated, and the nose is large and camel-like. The face is long and narrow. Bulls carry antlers that become palmated (flat and extended) after the third year; a front tine branches from the trunk, which is then flattened to form a wide palm with many upward-pointing small tines. Antlers can spread up to 2 m wide. These are shed in January–February. Bulls have a small, beard-like tassel on the throat. Pelage is rich reddish brown above, grayer on flanks and underside; browner in summer; grayer and woollier in winter. **Distribution:** Xinjiang (Altai); extending to W Siberia and to Scandinavia. **Natural History:** In the spring and summer they eat branches, shoots, and leaves from various broadleaf trees—birch, ash, mountain ash, and willow, as well as clover, rape, grain, different herbs, and water-lily roots. During the autumn and winter the diet changes to blueberry bushes and heather, and later to mostly pine branches, as well as juniper, the bark and branches from broadleaf trees (ash, willow, mountain ash), and occasionally the bark from spruce trees. Their long legs and spreading hooves help them in marshes and deep snow. They have poor eyesight, but great senses of smell and hearing. They are also excellent swimmers and have been known to cross lakes more than 1 km wide. During winter they form small family groups of four to eight individuals. The cow is in heat from the end of September to the middle of October, and gestation lasts eight months. Cows usually give birth to one or two calves weighing 8–15 kg at birth. Calves start to browse at three weeks and are fully weaned at five months, staying with their mother until they are a year old. They become sexually mature after two years, and the life span is 20–25 years. **Conservation Status:** Very rare, with a limited distribution in China, though widespread and common across boreal Eurasia. China RL—EN A2acde. China Key List—II. IUCN RL—LC.

Moose *Alces americanus*

美洲驼鹿 Meizhou Tuolu—**Distinctive Characteristics:** HB 240–310 cm; SH 170–220 cm; T 80–120; Wt 360–600 kg (male); 270–400 kg (female). Similar to *A. alces*, but slightly larger, redder, and with a more prominent neck tassel (dewlap). **Distribution:** NE China (Greater and Lesser Xing'an mountains); extending to E Siberia, Canada, United States. **Natural History:** An animal of the

boreal evergreen and mixed hardwood forests. Eats a massive amount of twigs and other browse. Most aspects of its natural history are similar to those of *A. alces*. **Conservation Status:** Extremely rare and of limited distribution in China. Common in Siberia and North America. China RL—EN A2acde. IUCN RL—LC.

GENUS *CAPREOLUS*—Roe Deer

狍属 Pao Shu—狍类 Paolei

Capreolus represents an ancient northern genus of only two species, one of which occurs in China. Roe deer are small. The antler is unusual, lacking a brow tine, but having a forward tine on the upper half of the main trunk of the antler. The main trunk has a further simple fork giving a maximum of three tines. The entire antler is covered in many small protuberances. The nose has a black moustache stripe that contrasts with two white nose spots. The tail is short and concealed by hair. The upper canine is absent. Roe deer are unique among ungulates in employing delayed implantation to ensure birthing at the optimal time of year. Fertilized embryos remain unattached in uterus for up to five months.

Siberian Roe *Capreolus pygargus*

西伯利亚狍 Xiboliya Pao—**Distinctive Characteristics:** HB 95–140 cm; SH 65–95 cm; T 20–40; E 128–140; GLS 210–250; Wt 20–40 kg. Small, stocky deer. Back horizontal, neck vertical. Male antlers are compact and vertical, with three tines. The form from Xinjiang is larger than animals from C and NE China. Pelage in winter is gray-brown, becoming more yellow-brown to red in summer; underparts yellowish. White on chin contrasts with their black muzzle. Rump and undertail white, and tail is raised when alarmed. **Distribution:** Widespread

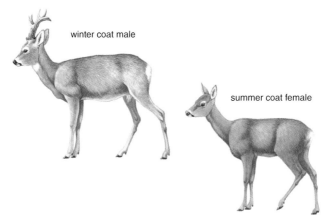

winter coat male

summer coat female

throughout C, NW, and NE China; extending to the Ural Mountains, eastward across Siberia, Mongolia, and to Korea, and south into NE Myanmar. **Natural History:** A deer of dark woodlands that feeds on open meadows and farmland at night. Diet includes grass, browse, and tree bark. Normally solitary, or found in small feeding parties. A shy, retiring, mostly crepuscular and nocturnal species. Mating takes place in August–September. Gestation is 294 days, including the period of delayed implantation of four to five months. Calves (normally twins) are dropped in June. Maturity is reached by 13 months, and adults live 10–12 years. **Conservation Status:** China RL—VU A2bcd. IUCN RL—LC.

GENUS *RANGIFER* (monotypic)

驯鹿属 Xunlu Shu

Reindeer *Rangifer tarandus*

驯鹿 Xun Lu—**Distinctive Characteristics:** HB 120–220 cm; SH 94–127 cm; T 70–210; Wt 91–272 kg. *Rangifer* is an old northern genus of deer (also called Caribou in North America) adapted to life in tundra conditions. These are compact, medium-sized deer with antlers in both sexes. Antlers variable, sometimes complex, rarely symmetrical. Front tines long and horizontal, often palmate. Pelage gray and woolly, browner and finer in summer; underparts whiter. Has long, beard-like hair below throat. **Distribution:** Nei Mongol (extreme north of Greater Xing'an Mountains); extending to Alaska, Canada, Greenland, and across the N Palearctic from E Siberia to Europe. **Natural History:** Occupies taiga forest and tundra where it eats mostly browse, bark, mosses, lichens, grasses, herbs, and ferns. A social deer; forms large herds. Able to make long migrations between summer and winter feeding areas. Rutting takes place about

summer coat male

winter coat female

October. Young are born in May–June after a gestation of about 228 days. One or two young born; reach maturity at two and a half to three and a half years. Thick fur and short tail are adaptations to extreme cold winters. Ability to smell and find lichens and other food under snow is a special adaptation. **Conservation Status:** Rare; only a few hundred animals remain in China. Most of its habitat was burned in great fires in 1986. A few semidomestic herds still range free. China RL—NA. IUCN RL—LC.

SUBFAMILY CERVINAE—Deer and Muntjacs

鹿亚科 Lu Yake—鹿, 麂 Lu, Ji
The Cervinae represents a group of small to large deer ranging in size from small muntjacs to the huge Red Deer. All males bear antlers, and many boast a fine spread. Eld's Deer and Père David's Deer are extinct in the wild, but releases of the latter may be now creating new wild breeding populations. Most species are now rare and threatened due to hunting pressure. Of nine genera in the Cervinae, eight are found in China.

GENUS *AXIS*—Axis Deer

豚鹿属 Tunlu Shu—豚鹿 Tunlu
A genus of smallish deer with trifurcate antlers with an obtusely angled front tine. Very similar to *Cervus*, with which they are sometimes combined (the primary difference being lack of an upper canine in *Axis*). Of three species, only one occurs marginally in China.

Hog Deer *Axis porcinus*

豚鹿 Tun Lu—**Distinctive Characteristics:** HB 105–115 cm; SH 60–72 cm; T 200; Wt 36–50 kg. Smallish, short-legged, dark brown deer, becoming grayer in winter. Underparts are paler; throat and long hairs inside ears are white. Antlers three-tined as in the Sambar, but smaller and more gracile, and the brow tine meets the beam at a more acute angle. Male lacks mane of Sambar, and young are always spotted. Lateral rows of small white spots may persist in some adults. Male has dark band across lower forehead and on hocks. Lacks upper canines. **Distribution:** S Yunnan; extending to Assam (India), Myanmar, and N Indochina; introduced to Sri Lanka. **Natural History:** Prefers low-lying rather open, grassy habitat, especially along riverbanks, on floodplains, and in swamps. Much more a grazer and less a browser than the Sambar. Originally diurnal and herd forming, now these deer have become usually nocturnal and solitary as a response to hunting pressure. They run like pigs through brush with their head held low, rather than leaping as other deer do; hence their common name. They rut between September and February in China, and one to two fawns are born between April and October. **Conservation Status:** Now certainly extinct in the wild in China; however, they may occur as a trade item from neighboring Myanmar and Laos. China RL—CR D. China Key List—I. CITES—I (as *A. p. annamiticus*). IUCN RL—EN A2bcd.

GENUS *CERVUS*—Red Deer and Elk

鹿属 Lu Shu—鹿 Lu

Cervus are typically medium- to large-sized deer with many-tined antlers. Antler length more than twice the length of skull. Possess an infraorbital gland, but not a digital gland. They tend to live in large herds with serious fighting of stags during a rut period over access to harems of females. Both *Cervus* species occur in China.

Red Deer *Cervus elaphus*

马鹿 Ma Lu—**Distinctive Characteristics:** HB 165–265 cm; SH 100–150 cm; T 100–220; GLS 400–450; Wt 75–240 kg. Large, stately deer with wide antlers sporting many (up to six per antler) tines. Antlers with the second tine originating close above the brow tine. Pelage varies with season, being reddish brown in summer and darker brown and thicker furred in winter. Rump patch large, conspicuous, and light reddish yellow, its upper margin dark brown. **Distribution:** Widespread in temperate mountain ranges of NE, NW, and C China; extending through most of the N Holarctic (across Siberia and Europe to Canada and W United States), and NW Africa. **Natural History:** A deer of temperate

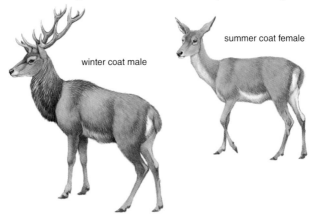

winter coat male

summer coat female

woodlands, moorlands, and grassy meadows. Mostly found in mountain ranges up to 5,000 m with combination of conifer forests and open alpine meadows. Animals come lower into valleys in winter. Eat grass, herbs, lichens, mosses, and bark of trees. Live in small herds of females and young, gathering into larger herds in winter. Stags live singly or form all-male herds in summer but gather harems in rut season in late summer, without obvious territories. Antlers are shed in spring. New antlers form during summer in time for the next rutting season. Males rub trees to strip off velvet. Natural life span is about 15 years, but a captive animal lived to almost 27 years. Stags give deep roars and fight with clashing antlers, sometimes blinding or otherwise injuring one other in dominance disputes over females. A single calf is born in late spring following an eight-month gestation. Young mature at one and a half to two and a half years. **Conservation Status:** Very rare and restricted in China. China RL—VU A2cd + 3cd. China Key List—II. IUCN RL—LC.

Sika Deer *Cervus nippon*

梅花鹿 Meihua Lu—**Distinctive Characteristics:** HB 105–170 cm; SH 64–110 cm; T 80–180; GLS 260–290; Wt 40–150 kg. Smallish, elegant deer with rich, reddish pelage and many irregular rows of white spots along dorsum and on sides. The lower jaw is white, and the undertail and sides of tail are white. There is a dark brown line down the back broadening into a dark patch above tail. Center of tail is reddish brown. In winter the coat is thicker and more chestnut and the white spots are less conspicuous. Male antlers generally sport only three to four tines. Regional variation includes a form that is tall and dark, with black-edged white patch on outer side of hind feet in Shanxi; a taller form with no white spots on neck and spots on body more conspicuous in winter in NE China; a form in SE China with inconspicuous dark dorsal line and spots on neck inconspicuous; a dark brown form with white spots on neck and a dark dorsal stripe in Hebei and Beijing; and one that is shorter, with reddish hue on neck and inconspicuous spots in winter in Taiwan. **Distribution:** Widespread across C and E China, including Taiwan; extending to SE Siberia, Korea, Ryukyu Islands (Japan), and formerly N Vietnam; introduced to Europe, United States, and New Zealand.

summer coat female

winter coat male

Natural History: Prefers woods and forest with dense understory but forages in open grassy areas. Eats grass, some browse, and even fruit. Crepuscular, but sometimes active by day and night. Forages singly or in small herds. Adults can live up to 25 years. Herds move down to lower valleys in winter. Large males are territorial and mark territory with urine and ground thrashing. Lesser males are driven out during the rut by fights involving both antlers and hooves. Dominant males round up females into a harem. Mating occurs in autumn, and gestation is about 210–223 days, with young being born in April–May. Stags shed their antlers around April–May. **Conservation Status:** Heavily depleted in the wild. The form in Taiwan was extirpated in 1969 but reintroduced in 1988 from captivity to Kenting National Park. Large herds exist in captivity to meet the demand for velvet antlers used in traditional Chinese medicine. China RL—EN A2cd + 3cd. China Key List—I. IUCN RL—LC.

GENUS *ELAPHODUS* (monotypic)

毛冠鹿属 Maoguanlu Shu

Tufted Deer *Elaphodus cephalophus*

毛冠鹿 Maoguan Lu—**Distinctive Characteristics:** HB 85–170 cm; SH 49–72 cm; T 70–130; HF 440; E 80; GLS 166–190; Wt 15–28 kg. These small deer possess long canines in males, prominent suborbital glands, and a bushy, dark tuft of hair on the forehead that hides the short, thin pedicels and tiny antlers of the male. The fur is very coarse, almost spinelike, giving a shaggy appearance. Undertail is white, and there are white hairs on ear tips, base of ears, and sides of muzzle. The form found in Qinghai, W Sichuan, Guizhou, and Yunnan is large, with uniform dark chocolate-brown pelage, darkest in winter and somewhat reddish in summer; the form in Shanxi, E Sichuan, and Hubei is smaller but also dark brown; and the form in SE China is smaller but grayish black. Young show a line of faint white spots along the median dorsum. **Distribution:** Widespread in C and SE China; extending to N Myanmar. **Natural History:** Lives in high, damp forests up to the tree line and close to water. Lives between 300 and 800 m in SE China, between 1,500 and 2,600 m in the middle of its range, and to as high as 4,750 m in W Sichuan. Diet is grass, some browse, and fruits. Secretive and crepuscular; usually solitary or found in pairs. Feeds on grassy meadows above tree line in early morning. Lives within a well-defined home territory, where it travels along well-established paths, rendering it vulnerable to snares. Barks like a muntjac when alarmed and in the mating season. Rut occurs between September and December. Single or twin fawns are born in April to July after about a six-month gestation. **Conservation Status:** China RL—VU A2bcd + 3bcd. IUCN RL—NT.

GENUS *ELAPHURUS* (monotypic)

麋鹿属 Milu Shu

Père David's Deer *Elaphurus davidianus*

麋鹿 Mi Lu—**Distinctive Characteristics:** HB 150–200 cm; SH 114 cm; T 500; GLS 400–420; Wt 150–200 kg. A large, elegant, rufous-brown deer with long, wavy guard hairs and unique antler formation. The antler lacks a brow tine but has a long rear branch almost parallel to the back. All tines of both branches are swept backward. Antlers are sometimes dropped more than once per year. The summer antlers are the larger set and are dropped in November, after the June–August rut. The second set, if they appear, are fully grown by January and are dropped a few weeks later. Summer coat ochre to reddish tan throughout the year. Winter coat is woollier, duller gray, with the undersides a bright cream. There is a darker stripe along the shoulders and down the spine. Head is long and slender, with large eyes and small, pointed ears. Males have a throat mane. The long tail ends in a black tuft, with long hairs drooping over the back of the hind legs. **Distribution:** Originally, marshy habitats of NE China. Endemic. **Natural History:** Formerly lived in low-lying grasslands and reed beds, often in seasonally flooded areas such as the lower Yangtze River valley and coastal marshes. Eats grass, reeds, and leaves of bushes. Generally lives in single-sex or maternal herds, although dominant and sometimes other adult males may be found with females and calves in both breeding and nonbreeding seasons. Fond of water and can swim well and spend long periods in water. Rather tame. During the breeding season, stags fast as they spar for the right to mate. When fighting, males not only use their antlers and teeth but also rear up on their hind legs and "box." Animals reach maturity during second year. Gestation is 270–300 days. One, rarely two, young born. Young are weaned in 10–11 months. Adults live up to 18 years. Long legs and hooves adapted to walking on wet, marshy land. **Conservation Status:** Père David's Deer became extinct in the wild in China about 1900, and today it remains entirely conservation dependent. The first captive herd was maintained by the Chinese emperor at Nanhaizi Park. French missionary Père Armand David saw this herd and obtained specimens for description of the species. The Chinese herd was destroyed by a combination of flood and insurgents associated with the Boxer Rebellion, but by that time several animals had been sent to Europe. A captive herd was assembled at Woburn Abbey, U.K. The Duke of Bedford donated this founder stock back to the Chinese government in two groups between 1985 and 1987, primarily to the Beijing Milu Park (38 animals). In 1986, 39 deer were sent from European and American zoos (mostly from the London Zoo) to the Dafeng Nature Reserve. Both captive herds are thriving, and a few accidental and deliberate releases to the wild have taken place. China RL—EW. China Key List—I. IUCN RL—EW.

GENUS *MUNTIACUS*—Muntjacs

鹿属 Ji Shu—鹿类 Jilei

Muntjacs are small deer. Males have small, simple antlers that emerge from long pedicels. Females have small bony pedicels only, covered with tufts of hair. Both sexes have long canine teeth in their upper jaw that protrude when the mouth is closed. Dental formula: 0.1.3.3/3.1.3.3 = 34. In males the upper canine is tusk-shaped, but not as slender as the tusks of *Moschus* or *Hydropotes* species. Muntjacs forage just before sunrise and in the late evening. They are browsers, feeding on twigs, grasses, leaves of trees, herbs, and fallen fruit. They regularly visit salt licks in search of minerals. Muntjacs travel alone, in pairs, or occasionally in groups of up to four animals. They are territorial and use secretions from a gland located in front of their eyes to scent mark territorial boundaries. They can live to be more than 10 years old. Muntjacs are constantly on the lookout for predators. When alarmed, they give a series of deep, barking sounds; hence the name "barking deer." The female makes high-pitched mewing sounds, and the male barks during the mating season. Hunters imitate these calls to lure males within gunshot range. Of 11 species of *Muntiacus*, four occur in China.

Black Muntjac *Muntiacus crinifrons*

黑麂 Hei Ji—**Distinctive Characteristics:** HB 98–132 cm; SH 62–78 cm; T 165–240; HF 280; E 105; GLS 200–235; Wt 21–28.5 kg. A large, dark muntjac. Body color dark blackish brown with yellowish orange on sides of nose, top of head, ears, crown tuft, and long-haired pedicels. Insides of ears are white. Sometimes yellowish hairs appear on shoulders. Tail is long and black and contrasts sharply with white undertail. Both antlers and pedicels are of medium length. Antlers single or two-tined. **Distribution:** Confined to a small area of S Anhui and W Zhejiang and adjacent SE Jiangxi and Mt. Wuyi in N Fujian. Endemic. **Natural History:** Occupies rolling hills in mountainous areas at about 1,000 m in a variety of forest formations. Eats twigs, leaves of trees, herbs, and grasses; also some fruit, but less fruit than *M. reevesi*. Single fawns are born following a six- or seven-month gestation. The reproductive cycle is aseasonal, and some females conceive new litters while still lactating. **Conservation Status:** Rare and persecuted, with a limited distribution. China RL—EN A2bcd. China Key List—I. CITES—I. IUCN RL—VU A2cd.

Gongshan Muntjac *Muntiacus gongshanensis*

贡山鹿 Gongshan Ji—**Distinctive Characteristics:** HB 95–105 cm; SH 55–57 cm; T 90–160; GLS 190–205; Wt 16–24 kg. A medium-sized, dark muntjac. Coloration is similar to *M. crinifrons*, being dark brown with pale orange on head, but this animal differs in various ways: It is smaller, less black, has longer hooves, has a shorter tail, has a short, thick pedicel, lacks a crown tuft, and has white "sock" rings. **Distribution:** Gong Shan region of extreme NW Yunnan; extending into N Myanmar. **Natural History:** Believed to be similar to that of *M. crinifrons*. **Conservation Status:** China RL—EN A2cd + 3cd; B1ab(i,ii,iii). IUCN RL—DD.

Red Muntjac *Muntiacus muntjak*

赤鹿 Chi Ji—**Distinctive Characteristics:** HB 98–120 cm; SH 50–72 cm; T 170–200; GLS 176–220; Wt 17–40 kg. Medium-sized reddish-colored muntjac with long, narrow pedicel. Has very large preorbital gland. Different races vary as to size and extent of black marking on outer foreleg, but all have black on forehead and front side of pedicels. Undertail is white, and top side of tail is the same reddish as the body. Usually has white socklets. There is no dark dorsal stripe down neck. **Distribution:** S China, including Hainan Island; extending into India, Pakistan, Indochina, Greater Sunda Islands. **Natural History:** Occupies mountain forests, where it lives singly or sometimes in small groups of two to four individuals. The diet consists of flowers, buds, and leaves of woody plants. As with other muntjacs, reproduction is aseasonal, and females mate shortly after giving birth to a single young. **Conservation Status:** China RL—VU A2bcd + 3bcd. IUCN RL—LC.

Reeves' Muntjac *Muntiacus reevesi*

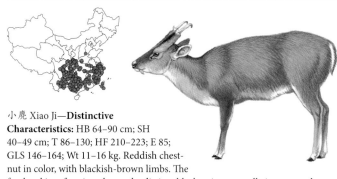

小麂 Xiao Ji—**Distinctive Characteristics:** HB 64–90 cm; SH 40–49 cm; T 86–130; HF 210–223; E 85; GLS 146–164; Wt 11–16 kg. Reddish chestnut in color, with blackish-brown limbs. The forehead is rufous in color, and a distinct black stripe generally is present along the nape of the neck onto back. The throat and chin are white. The tail is short and reddish; undertail white. Pedicel is short and antler medium length. The form in Taiwan is darker and richer in color than the mainland China forms. **Distribution:** C, S, and SE China, including Taiwan. Endemic. **Natural History:** Similar to that of other muntjacs. They occupy brush-clad rocky places and open woodlands of pine and oak. Seek cover in steep ravines and usually have well-defined areas to which they retreat. Head and neck are carried low when running. They are basically solitary, although sometimes found in pairs or small family groups. Home ranges average about 100 ha, overlap considerably, and do not vary in size by gender. Female core areas also overlap, indicating they are not territorial, whereas male core areas overlap minimally, suggesting territoriality. Females mature within first year. In the wild, mating takes place throughout the year. The gestation period lasts 209–220 days. Fawns remain hidden in dense vegetation until they can move around with their mother. They have spots to aid in their camouflage, which slowly disappear as they reach adult size. **Conservation Status:** China RL—VU A2bcd. IUCN RL—LC.

GENUS *PRZEWALSKIUM* (monotypic)

白唇鹿属 Baichunlu Shu

White-Lipped Deer *Przewalskium albirostris*

白唇鹿 Baichun Lu—**Distinctive Characteristics:** HB 155–210 cm; SH 120–140 cm (male), 115 cm (female); T 100–130; HF 330–520; E 210–280; GLS 340–404; Wt 180–230 kg (male), <180 kg (female). A large, robust deer, very similar to *Cervus*. Pelage is grayish brown with a dark ridge from the crown and down the back; underparts creamier. Tail is short; fringe of ears, nose, lips (giving rise to the common name), chin, and rump patch are white. Fur becomes dense, woolly, and paler in winter. The large antlers are strongly flattened toward the top; large stags have a brow tine branching from close to the base, and normally three branches originating from farther up the beam; these in turn may also fork. Stout hooves and limbs are adaptations for high elevations. **Distribution:** Confined to eastern half of the Tibetan Plateau. Endemic. **Natural History:** Inhabits conifer forest, rhododendron and willow scrub, and alpine grasslands from 3,500 to 5,100 m; somewhat lower in winter. Compared with other cervids on the plateau, most likely to be found in open habitats. Feeds on grass, herbs, lichens, and leaves and bark of trees and bushes. Typical of large social cervids, it lives in small groups, but seasonally it can be found in herds of 200–300 animals. Males and females live separately except during the breeding season. The single young are born between late May and late June following a seven- to eight-month gestation; animals mature at an age of three years. **Conservation Status:** Lost from much of its former range, it has been heavily depleted due to hunting for young antlers. Extensively farmed in China (and in other countries, such as New Zealand). China RL—EN A2cd + 3cd. China Key List—I. IUCN RL—VU A2c.

GENUS *RUCERVUS*—Deer

坡鹿属 Polu Shu—坡鹿 Polu

Small Asian genus containing three species of large cervids with complex antlers spreading from a very short beam. Includes the extinct Schomburgk's Deer (*R. schomburgki*; original range primarily in Thailand, although one specimen has been recorded from Yunnan, and it may still occur in Laos), and the Indian Barasingha (*R. duvaucelii*). *Rucervus* is closely related to *Cervus*. A single species occurs in China.

Eld's Deer *Rucervus eldii*

坡鹿 Po Lu **Distinctive Characteristics:** HB 150–170 cm; SH 120–130 cm; T 220–250; E 136–170; HF 350–400; GLS 290; Wt 64–100 kg. Large, reddish-brown, elegant, long-headed deer with light spots along median dorsum and characteristic male antlers in which the front brow tine joins the main beam at an obtuse angle to form a sweeping continuous curve; no anal spot. **Distribution:** Formerly distributed in tropical zone of SW Yunnan and S China (but now extinct there), survives in China only in captive herds at western end of Hainan Island; extending to Myanmar, Cambodia, N India, Laos, Thailand, and Vietnam. **Natural His-**

tory: Formerly lived in rather open, seasonal forests at low elevation. The Chinese form occupies seasonally dry grasslands, although some other forms may be secondarily specialized to life in swampy terrain. Feeds on grass and some browse; also fallen fruits and flowers. Will raid rice fields. Lives in small to large herds. Outside of the breeding season male groups form. In the breeding season males fight for dominance and collect harems of females. Males give barking grunt or roar during this period, and many suffer eye injuries during fighting. Although they can live without water for several days, males are fond of wallowing in mud. Regularly visit salt licks. Rutting is in the spring (unlike other large Chinese deer that rut in autumn), and a single young is born about eight months later. Unusually broad antlers are effective for fighting but appear to be a liability in forested terrain (thus its preference for open country). **Conservation Status:** Extinct in the wild in China. Several hundred exist in captive herds in Datian and Bangxi nature reserves in large fenced compounds. There is little suitable habitat remaining and no protection from hunting, so wild releases are not currently planned. China RL—CR A3e; B1ab(i,ii,iii). China Key List—I. CITES—I. IUCN RL—EN A2cd + 3cd + 4cd.

GENUS *RUSA*—Deer

水鹿属 Shuilu Shu—水鹿 Shuilu
A small genus of four large Indo-Malayan deer centered mostly on Malaysia and the Philippines. Very closely related to *Cervus* and sometimes included in that genus. A single species is found in China.

Sambar *Rusa unicolor*

水鹿 Shui Lu—**Distinctive Characteristics:** HB 180–200 cm; SH 140–160 cm; T 250–280; E 180–220; GLS 370–390; Wt 185–260 kg. Large, brown deer with sparse, coarse hair and usually three tines on male antlers. Adult males develop longish hair as mane on neck and forequarters. Ears large and broad; and tail densely covered with black, shaggy long hair, making it look thick. Undertail is white and flashed in alarm. Bare glandular patch on throat. Fawns generally not spotted. Females lack antlers, and young males may have a single-tined, almost straight antler. Antlers are stouter than in most cervids. They are cast annually, breaking from a short pedicel that grows into a broad, roseate base. **Distribution:** Through tropical and subtropical zones of SE China, including Hainan Island and Taiwan; extending to E India and Sri Lanka along S Himalayas, through Indochina to Borneo and Sumatra, and north into the Philippines. **Natural History:** Lives in tropical forests, scrub, hills, and secondary-growth marshes up to 3,700 m, also venturing into agricultural fields. Eats grass, browse, ferns, leaves of small trees, and some fruits; more of a browser than grazer. Crepuscular and nocturnal, it occupies a wide range of wooded habitats, hiding in dense vegetation by day and feeding in more open areas at night. Generally solitary, or mother with young in small parties. Uses salt licks, especially when growing new antlers. Males roar and rut in winter months; a single fawn is born after about eight months. In Hainan, the reproductive cycle may be aseasonal. **Conservation Status:** Widely hunted but still widespread. China RL—VU A2cd + 3cd. China Key List—II. IUCN RL—VU A2cd + 3cd +4cd.

SUBFAMILY HYDROPOTINAE

GENUS *HYDROPOTES* (monotypic)

獐亚科 Zhang Yake; 獐属 Zhang Shu

Chinese Water Deer *Hydropotes inermis*

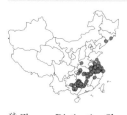

獐 Zhang—**Distinctive Characteristics:** HB 89–103 cm; SH 45–57 cm; T 60–70; GLS 150–170; Wt 14–17 kg. A small cervid with no antlers in either sex. The male upper canines are long and laterally compressed; fur is dense and thick; the tail is very short. Pelage is rich reddish brown. Young with two rows of small white spots on sides. **Distribution:** E China; extending to Korea. **Natural History:** Lives in low-lying grasslands and reed beds, often in seasonally flooded areas such as the lower Yangtze River valley and coastal marshes. Feeds on grass, reeds, and leaves of bushes. Can swim well. Rather tame. Occurs at low densities (0.5–3.2/km²) and may be either solitary or found in small groups. Mates in winter to give birth to two to five young (usually two to three) in May–June. **Conservation Status:** Known population approximates 10,000 individuals and is increasingly fragmented, mostly distributed along the lower reaches of the Yangtze River and its associated lake system. China RL—VU A2bcd. China Key List—II. IUCN RL—VU A2cd.

FAMILY BOVIDAE—Antelope, Cattle, Bison, Buffalo, Goats, and Sheep

牛科 Niu Ke—羚羊, 牛, 野牛, 水牛, 山羊, 绵羊 Lingyang, Niu, Yeniu, Shuiniu, Shanyang, Mianyang

The bovids represent a large family of herbivorous ungulates ranging from small to large and from stocky to gracefully elongate. Rostrum tip hairy except for *Bos*; lateral toes (the second and fifth) reduced or replaced by hooflets. Both sexes have horns, but horns absent among some females; horns grow from frontal bone, are never branched or shed, and are covered in a keratin (proteinaceous) sheath surrounding a core of living bone. Surface of horn may be smooth or annulated (ringed), and may be curved or twisted but never forked. Dental formula: 0.0.3.3/3.1.3.3 = 32. Ruminant stomach with four chambers; possess one to two pairs of mammae. Widely distributed in North America and the Old World; of eight subfamilies worldwide, only three are found in China.

SUBFAMILY ANTILOPINAE—Gazelles and Saiga

羚羊亚科 Lingyang Yake—羚羊 Lingyang

A diverse subfamily of smaller antelopes and gazelles. Antilopinae tend to be slender and agile animals. They are mostly social grazers. The horns are placed near the back of the skull and are heavily annulated. Of 15 genera in the Antilopinae, three occur in China.

GENUS *GAZELLA*—Gazelles

羚羊属 Lingyang Shu—羚羊 Lingyang

Medium-sized antelopes; both sexes have horns, except horns absent in females of *G. subgutturosa*. Tail short but not <12 cm. Have stripes on face. Social, herd-living grazers of open grassland and deserts of Africa, E Europe, and Asia. Of 10 species of *Gazella*, only one occurs in China.

Goitered Gazelle *Gazella subgutturosa*

鹅喉羚 E'houling—**Distinctive Characteristics:** HB 88–109 cm; SH 60–70 cm; T 120–175; GLS 170–215; Wt 29–42 kg. Elegant gazelle with pale head, underparts, and inner legs. Dorsal pelage light sandy brown; the brownish-black tail contrasts with the white rump patch. Some races have prominent dark facial stripes. The strongly annulated horns divide and sweep backward before curv-

ing slightly forward at tips (fig. 12). Lump at front of neck gives the species its English name. Tarim Basin form large, with bold facial stripes and a brown rostrum; Dzungarian Basin form also large but with shorter horns (ca. 27 cm); Nie Mongol, Gansu, and N Shaanxi forms smaller, with brown facial stripes below eyes and a white rostrum; and Qaidam Basin form larger, with horns ca. 30 cm long and pelage a sandier color. **Distribution:** Confined to lower-elevation deserts of N and NW China; extending to Mongolia, Pakistan, and Arabia. **Natural History:** Inhabits steppes, alpine grasslands, and semidesert vegetation at low to moderate elevations. Feeds on many herbs and grasses, including halophytic (salt-adapted) vegetation. Lives in small herds of 1–12 animals wandering over large areas seasonally.

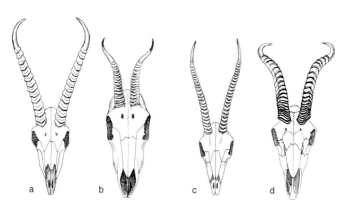

Larger herds of up to 30 may form in winter. Mates in winter, and single or twin calves are dropped in May or June after a gestation of five to six months. **Conservation Status:** Once considered an important game species; its range and numbers have declined as a result of uncontrolled hunting and habitat degradation. Extirpated from parts of former range such as Ordos Plateau. China RL—EN A1d + 2cd + 3cd. China Key List—II. IUCN RL—VU A2cd.

Figure 12. Skull and horn profiles of Goitered (a), Mongolian (b), Tibetan (c), and Przewalski's (d) gazelles.

GENUS *PROCAPRA*—Central Asian Gazelles

原羚属 Yuanling Shu—原羚 Yuanling
Medium-sized antelopes with short tails and slender legs; only males have horns, and these are long and slender. These are herd-living grazers of open grasslands and deserts. All three *Procapra* species are found in China.

Mongolian Gazelle *Procapra gutturosa*

黄羊 Huang Yang—**Distinctive Characteristics:** HB 108–160 cm; SH 54–84 cm; T 50–120; E 97; GLS 220–270; Wt 25–45 kg. Medium-sized, elegant gazelle with male horns short (20 cm) and reclined, bending backward then turned upward and inward at the tip (fig. 12). Pelage is orange-buff in summer with cinnamon sides; much richer in color than the sandy brown of *Gazella subgutturosa*. White underparts and a white rump patch. Dark tail contrasts conspicuously when wagged from side to side. Pelage is paler in winter. **Distribution:** Dry steppes and semidesert of central N China; extending into Mongolia and adjacent parts of Siberia. **Natural History:** Inhabits dry, grassy steppe, semidesert, and formerly moister northeastern grasslands. Feeds on mostly grasses with some browse. Lives in large herds. Has been observed to gather in even larger herds (6,000–8,000) for the spring northern migration. Males separate from herds on summer pastures. Mates in late autumn and winter. Males develop a swollen throat at this time. Single or twinned young are dropped in June after a gestation of 186 days. Young reach maturity at two years, and captive animals live up to seven years. **Conservation Status:** Persecuted by hunters and limited by fencing and farming of grasslands. The herds of C and W Mongolia have largely vanished. Endangered in Russia and rare in China. The range of Mongolian Gazelles in China is about 25% of what it was in the 1950s–1970s (they are now found only in E Nei Mongol), and the population has decreased dramatically during that interval from approximately 2,000,000 to 250,000 (only about 85,000 of which reside permanently in China and do not migrate into Mongolia). China RL—VU A2cd + 3cd. China Key List—II. IUCN RL—LC.

Tibetan Gazelle *Procapra picticaudata*

藏原羚 Zang Yuanling—**Distinctive Characteristics:** HB 91–105 cm; SH 54–65 cm; T 80–100; GLS 170–190; Wt 13–16 kg. Smallish, stocky gazelle. Pelage gray-brown, with thick, saddle-like hair on the back. Underparts and rump patch are

white. Lacks conspicuous facial markings. Small tail is fluffy and black; it is raised when alarmed. Male horns grow upward then sweep backward before rising again toward the tip (fig. 12). The heavily annulated horns are almost parallel to each other, not splayed as in other gazelles. **Distribution:** Tibetan Plateau. Endemic. **Natural History:** Inhabits cold northern deserts, semideserts, grasslands, and mountain shrublands at high elevations (up to 5,750 m). Occupies more mountainous habitat than Przewalski's Gazelle in their area of range overlap. Feeds mostly at dusk and dawn on grasses, forbs, and lichens. Generally found in small herds of 3–20 animals, gathering in larger herds during migrations to higher summer pastures. A wary and speedy animal. Scrapes out a depression for shelter in bad weather. Mating takes place in winter, and single (or occasionally twin) young are dropped in June. **Conservation Status:** Formerly very common, and huge herds used to migrate with the seasons across the Tibetan Plateau. Today the Tibetan Gazelle is much reduced in numbers due to uncontrolled hunting and deterioration of habitat caused by domestic herds. They remain mostly where humans and livestock are scarce. China RL—VU A2cd + 3cd. China Key List—II. IUCN RL—NT.

Przewalski's Gazelle *Procapra przewalskii*

普氏原羚 Pushi Yuanling—**Distinctive Characteristics:** HB 109–160 cm; SH 50–70 cm; T 70–120; GLS 185–220; Wt 17–32 kg. Medium-sized, rather stocky gazelle with sandy-brown pelage, white underparts, and white rump patch divided into two spots by dark median line. Male horns relatively stubby, bowed backward and splayed apart before growing upward and toward each other near tips (fig. 12). **Distribution:** Central N China; now largely confined to the area near Qinghai Lake. Formerly was more widespread in N Qinghai, Gansu (Loess Plateau), and Nei Mongol (W Ordos Plateau). Endemic. **Natural History:** Inhabits high-elevation steppe plateau, including open valleys, undulating terrain, dunes, and some wetland grasslands. Eats mostly grass and reed tips, and a few other herbs such as the legume *Astragulus*, which is poisonous to most domestic animals. Behavior similar to that of other steppe gazelles. Lives in small herds; exhibits a polygynous mating system typical of most ungulates. Age at first reproduction is two years. The single young (sometimes twins) are born in May–June. **Conservation Status:** Critically endangered as a result of hunting and heavy domestic grazing and disturbance on its habitat. Only 114 animals estimated in 1997, compared with 200 in 1994 and 350 in 1984; currently confined to four subpopulations near Qinghai Lake. Additionally, grassland fencing beginning in 1999 has led to further dramatic declines in the population and the calving rate. China RL—CR A2bce + 3bce; C1; D. China Key List—I. IUCN RL—EN C2a(i).

GENUS *SAIGA* (monotypic)

高鼻羚羊属 Gaobilingyang Shu

Steppe Saiga *Saiga tatarica*

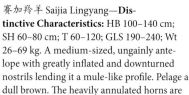

赛加羚羊 Saijia Lingyang—**Distinctive Characteristics:** HB 100–140 cm; SH 60–80 cm; T 60–120; GLS 190–240; Wt 26–69 kg. A medium-sized, ungainly antelope with greatly inflated and downturned nostrils lending it a mule-like profile. Pelage a dull brown. The heavily annulated horns are quite short, nearly straight, and have forward-bending tips; they are amber or whitish, in contrast to the black horns of other antelopes. **Distribution:** NW Xinjiang (Dzungarian Basin); current distribution now restricted to S Ukraine, E Kazakhstan, and SW Mongolia. Formerly widespread from grasslands of Europe and Central Asia to Mongolia and Siberia (in the Pleistocene to Alaska). **Natural History:** Inhabits temperate grassy plains, often in arid areas. Eats mostly grass as well as mosses, lichens, some browse, and tree bark. Active throughout the day; never observed far from water. Runs at high speed. Some populations undertake large seasonal migrations. Summer herds may consist of 30–40 animals, but migration herds formerly numbered hundreds of thousands. In mating season in early winter males become territorial and fight to gather a harem. Many males die in fights or of exhaustion by end of winter. Single or twin young are dropped in April–May after gestation of 139–152 days. Young mature after their first year; captive animals can live up to 12 years. The strange nose with downward-pointing nostrils and extensive internal convolutions and membranes seems to serve a temperature-regulation function, as well as giving the animal exceptional olfactory ability. **Conservation Status:** The horns are believed to have strong medicinal properties, and trade of these items has caused the species to become endangered. The Steppe Saiga is now considered extinct in the wild in China, although some animals may cross the border from Kazakhstan. Neighboring populations in Kazakhstan and Mongolia are extremely rare and declining. Additionally, the sex ratio is highly skewed, and most herds remaining in Central Asia are nearly all female, due to heavy harvesting of males for their horns; correspondingly, breeding has been sharply curtailed. Reintroduction efforts are being made. China RL—EW. China Key List—I. CITES—II. IUCN RL—CR A2acd.

SUBFAMILY BOVINAE—Wild Cattle and Spiral-horned Antelopes

牛亚科 Niu Yake—牛 Niu
Generally large animals with massive or spiral horns, including cows, buffalo, spiral-horned African antelopes, Indian Nilgai (*Boselaphus tragocamelus*), and the aberrant Indochinese Saola (*Pseudoryx nghetinhensis*). Horns are not annulated; muzzle broad; nostrils lateral; without facial glands. Of nine genera, only one occurs in China. Wild Buffalo (*Bubalus arnee*) may formerly have roamed into S Yunnan and SE Xizang.

GENUS *BOS*—Cattle and Yak

野牛属 Yeniu Shu—野牛 Yeniu
Large size and stubby legs; long tail, with tip covered with long hairs; both sexes have smooth-surfaced, outward- then upward-sweeping horns. Of six species of *Bos*, two occur in the wild in China. Both have been domesticated and crossbred with domestic cattle.

Gaur *Bos frontalis*

野牛 Ye Niu—**Distinctive Characteristics:** HB 250–330 cm; SH 165–220 cm; T 70–105 cm; E 300–350; GLS 500; Wt 650–1,500 kg. Large, dark, wild cattle with grayish or yellow-white "socks" on lower legs; no whitish rump patch. Both sexes are mostly blackish brown; calf is brown. Insides of ears are white. Male has heavy horns that sweep outward then curve upward, growing from massive, pale-colored crown hump. Male has a dewlap. Female has more delicate horns. A stouter version of Gaur with massive outspreading horns is sometimes traded from Myanmar across the W Yunnan border. This is the Mythan or Gayal, a domesticated animal sometimes also crossed with domestic cattle. **Distribution:** Central S China; extending to the Indian subcontinent through Myanmar and Indochina to the Malay Peninsula. **Natural History:** Inhabits dense to open tropical forests at low to moderate elevations. Lives in denser forest than other Asian cattle. Feeds on grass and browse, favors bamboo shoots and the leaves of the dwarf bamboo *Arundinella*. Diurnal and nocturnal but rests in shady places during the heat of the day. Can sleep standing but usually lies down like a domestic cow. Lives in small herds and regularly visits salt licks. Emits an oily sweat, which it rubs on trees in a form of scent marking. In breeding season males fight like bulls for dominance, with much roaring and snorting. Gestation is almost 10 months. A single young is born to each female in the herd; females come back into heat a few weeks later. **Conservation Status:** In China rare, restricted in range, and endangered by hunting and habitat loss. China RL— EN A1bc; B1ab(i,ii,iii); D. China Key List—I. CITES—I (as *B. gaurus*). IUCN RL—VU A2cd + 3cd + 4cd.

Yak *Bos grunniens*

野牦牛 Ye Maoniu—**Distinctive Characteristics:** HB 305–380 cm; SH 170– 200 cm (male), 137–156 cm (female); T 100 cm; GLS 500; Wt 535–821 kg (male), 306–338 kg (female). Large, black cattle with long, shaggy hair that almost reaches the ground; long wisp of hair on tail (over 100 cm long). Long, sharp horns, colored gray to black, spread laterally then twist upward and backward at tips. Horns of males longer, wider, and more massive than those of females. **Distribution:** Tibetan Plateau; extending to N India (Ladakh), Nepal; apparently in Kazakhstan, Mongolia, and S Russia until the 13th–18th centuries. **Natural History:** Inhabits high-elevation grasslands and cold desert from 4,000–6,100 m. Descends into lower valleys in winter. Feeds mostly on grass as well as some herbs and mineral-rich soil. Lives in small groups of two to six animals, but sometimes forms large herds. Most Yaks on the plateau today are domesticated, and some are crossed with cattle; wild Yaks are much larger. Run with a jerky, bouncing gait. Single young are dropped in May–June after 258 days of gestation. Females give birth at only two-year intervals but can live for 25 years. The stout, compact body, thick woolly coat, and richness of the milk are all adaptations to the harsh conditions in which this species lives. The bushy tail is an adaptation to flick away summer flies. Domestic yaks provide meat, milk, cheese, leather, bones for carvings, and jewelry to Tibetan pastoralists. The sheared hair is woven into coarse cloth and rope and used to make tents. The dung is used for fuel. **Conservation Status:** Rare and much restricted from its former range into W Sichuan. China RL—EN A1c; B1ab(i,ii,iii); C2a(ii). China Key List—I. CITES—I (as *B. mutus*). IUCN RL—VU A2ac + 3c + 4c.

SUBFAMILY CAPRINAE—Goats and Sheep

羊亚科 Yang Yake—山羊, 绵羊 Shanyang, Mianyang
Caprinae is a diverse subfamily of goat-antelopes, musk ox, goats, and sheep. Horns usually carried by both sexes, but those of females are small. Muzzle narrow and hairy. Members of the group vary considerably in length, from just over 100 cm for a goral to almost 250 cm for a Musk Ox (*Ovibos moschatus*). Their social dynamics vary, and species range from solitary territorial types with daggerlike horns that use scent marking for territorial defense of small home ranges to social grazers that live in large herds, have butting horns, establish dominance hierarchies, and wander over large tracts of open land. Of 13 genera of Caprinae, eight are recognized in China.

GENUS *BUDORCAS* (monotypic)

羚牛属 Lingniu Shu

Takin *Budorcas taxicolor*

羚牛 Ling Niu—**Distinctive Characteristics:** HB 170–220 cm; SH 107–140 cm; T 100–216; HF 267–444; E 101–149; GLS 350–460; Wt 250–600 kg. A large, sturdy goat-antelope that appears rather like a Musk Ox (*Ovibos moschatus*), with stocky legs, broad hoofs, and strong dewclaws. The coat is dense and shaggy, with a stripe along the back. Coat color varies with race, age, and sex, ranging from whitish yellow to reddish gray, gold, or darker brown. The tail is short and bushy. A bull's face is often dark, while only the nose is dark on females and calves. All have arched noses and hairy snouts. Males are much larger than females. Profile of face convex. Both sexes have horns that arise from the midsection of their massive head, quickly curve outward, and then sweep backward and upward to a point. Horns may reach up to 64 cm in length. Horn bases may show transverse ridges. **Distribution:** Central S China; extending to the E Himalayas (Bhutan, Sikkim) and through N Myanmar. **Natural History:** In summer, feed in alpine meadows up to 4,000 m. In winter they descend into the valleys and forests to as low as 1,000 m. They feed on a variety of grasses, bamboo shoots, forbs, and leaves of shrubs and trees. Forage in early morning and late afternoon and regularly visit salt licks, which renders them very vulnerable to poachers who lay in ambush. Although mostly slow moving, they can move

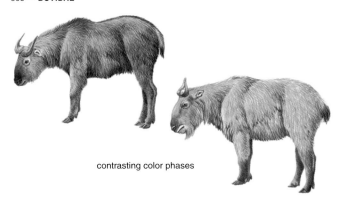

contrasting color phases

quickly over short distances when required. They can leap from rock to rock on steep slopes as a means of escape. If cornered they can fiercely attack their pursuers with their dangerous horns. Surprised at close range, they can charge humans, and some hunters have been killed by Takin. They may nibble the walls of deserted buildings for minerals and have been known to enter and climb to the second floor of buildings. They emit a loud warning cough in alarm. Rutting males give a low bellow. Migrate seasonally to preferred habitats. During spring and early summer months, they begin to gather in large herds of up to 100 animals at the uppermost limits of tree line. During cooler autumn months, when food is less plentiful at higher elevations, herds disband into smaller groups of up to 20 individuals and move to forested valleys at lower elevations. Groups mainly comprise females, subadults, young, and some adult males. Older males usually remain solitary throughout most of the year but gather with females during the rutting season. Sexually mature at about three and a half years of age. Rutting occurs in late summer, followed by a gestation of 200 to 220 days. Single young are born in March or April. Longevity is about 16–18 years. Although without skin glands, their entire body secretes an oily, strong-smelling substance that serves as a moisture barrier on the animal's coat, protecting it from fog and rain. **Conservation Status:** Increasingly rare as a result of hunting, forest loss, bamboo die-off after flowering, road construction, and disturbance from tourism. China RL—EN A1c; B1ab(i,ii,iii)cd); C2a(ii); China Key List—I. CITES—II. IUCN RL—VU A2cd.

GENUS *CAPRA*—Goats

羊属 Yang Shu—羊 Yang
The true goats, *Capra* are of medium size and both sexes have horns, although the male's are much longer, some reaching over 100 cm. Horn surface has broad transverse ridges in males but is smooth in females. Infraorbital gland absent; only forefoot has digital gland. There are eight species of *Capra* found in arid and mountainous regions of N Africa, Europe, Central Asia, the Indian subcontinent, China, and Siberia. Only one species occurs in China.

Siberian Ibex *Capra sibirica*

北山羊 Bei Shanyang—**Distinctive Characteristics:** HB 115–170 cm; SH 65–105 cm; T 100–200; GLS 230–306; Wt 80–100 kg (male), 30–50 kg (female). Large goat with spectacular, large, back-curved horns. Male horns up to 100 cm long. Pelage is light brown with pale underparts; a black longitudinal stripe runs along midline of dorsum. Fronts of legs have dark brown stripes. Males have long beard; females short. In winter, color becomes yellowish white or pure white, and the venter gray-brown. **Distribution:** NW China; extending to Central Asia, N India, N Pakistan, S and W Mongolia, Russia. **Natural History:** Occupies mountainous regions from 3,000 to 6,000 m in bare, rocky terrain and open meadows. Its diet consists of alpine grasses and herbs, and it feeds in early morning and evenings. Lives in small parties of 4–10 but sometimes forms large herds. Uniquely massive, recurved horns used in territorial fights between males. Mates in winter months, with a gestation of 147–180 days. Usually one, sometimes two, kids are born in spring. Mature at two to three years. **Conservation Status:** Highly threatened by poaching, habitat degradation, and competition from domestic stock. Extirpated from E Kunlun, Qiling (Qinghai), and W Gansu; vulnerable elsewhere. China RL—EN A2cd + 3cd. China Key List—I. IUCN RL—LC.

GENUS *CAPRICORNIS*—Serows

鬣羚属 Lieling Shu—Lieling
Serows are tall, dark-colored goats with a short body and tall legs; hind legs longer than front legs; coat coarse, with little underwool; some species have a long mane of hair on the neck. The horns are recurved and narrowly annulated basally. Of six species of *Capricornis*, three exist in China.

Chinese Serow *Capricornis milneedwardsii*

甘南鬣羚 Gannan Lieling—**Distinctive Characteristics:** HB 140–170 cm; SH 90–100 cm; T 115–160; E 175–205; GLS 280–320; Wt 85–140 kg. A tall, long-legged, dark goat-antelope with short, recurved horns and a long, shaggy mane down back of neck and extending as ridge of coarse hair down back. Ears are large, and there are prominent glands in front of eyes. Tail is short and bushy. Pelage is blackish with grayish or reddish grizzling, especially on the long mane and legs. The hair is coarse and rather thin. The horns are longer, stouter, and more heavily annulated than those of any goral (*Naemorhedus*). Much larger than a goral and much smaller than a Takin (*Budorcas taxicolor*). Forms found through the Himalayas and eastern parts of Tibetan Plateau and through Sichuan, Yunnan, S Gansu, S Shaanxi to Hubei have a black mane, while forms in SE China south of the Yangtze River have a grayish-white mane. **Distribution:** Widespread across C and SE China; extending through the Himalayas to Indochina. **Natural History:** Inhabits rugged steep hills and rocky places, especially limestone regions at elevations up to 4,500 m. They normally winter in the forest belt and move to higher-elevation cliffs during summer. Feeds on a wide range of leaves and shoots; visits salt licks. Mostly nocturnal and solitary. Has regular sleeping scrapes and sometimes rests on promontories with a good view. **Conservation Status:** China RL—VU A2cd + 3cd. IUCN RL—NT.

Taiwan Serow *Capricornis swinhoei*

台湾鬣羚 Taiwan Lieling—**Distinctive Characteristics:** HB 80–114 cm; SH 50–60 cm; T 70–120; Wt 17–25 kg. Smaller and more goral-like than mainland serows, and has brown fur. Has shorter mane than mainland serows, but this is more erectile. Has pale creamy patch extending from chin to throat. Horns smaller and more gracile than those of mainland serows. **Distribution:** Taiwan. Endemic. **Natural History:** Inhabits rugged forest and rocky slopes along the main mountain chain on Taiwan between 1,000 and 3,000 m. Feeds on grass and browse, young twigs, and some fruits. Generally solitary. Uses rock shelters. Crepuscular. Single young born after seven months of gestation. Mating takes place in October–November. **Conservation Status:** China RL—EN A2cd. China Key List—I. IUCN RL—LC.

Himalayan Serow *Capricornis thar*

尼泊尔鬣羚 Nibo'er Lieling—**Distinctive Characteristics:** Similar to *C. milneedwardsii*, but some specimens reddish. **Distribution:** Xizang; extending into the Himalayas, Bhutan, Bangladesh, and parts of Assam and Sikkim (India). **Natural History:** Similar to that of *C. milneedwardsii*, although it is normally found at lower elevations (2,000–3,000 m) in the forested belt of high mountains. **Conservation Status:** China RL—NE. China Key List—II. CITES I. IUCN RL–NT.

GENUS *HEMITRAGUS*—Tahrs

塔尔羊属 Tǎ'ěryáng Shǔ—塔尔羊 Tǎ'ěryáng

The tahrs are a small genus of three goatlike species, living in barren rocky or mountainous areas of Arabia, Nilgiri Hills of India, and the Himalayas. Legs are relatively short; head small; ears small and pointed; eyes large; horns found in both sexes and are triangular in cross section. Only one species occurs marginally in China.

Himalayan Tahr *Hemitragus jemlahicus*

喜马拉雅塔尔羊 Xǐmǎlāyǎ Tǎ'ěryáng—**Distinctive Characteristics:** HB 130–170 cm; SH 62–106 cm; T 90–120; Wt 50–108 kg. Medium-sized goatlike animal with reddish to dark brown hair; males have a shaggy mane around the neck extending to the knees, especially long in winter. Males lack a beard, have a bare muzzle, and possess digital glands. Small horns in both sexes sweep upward and backward then inward; laterally flattened to give triangular cross section; not twisted and not ringed. Horn length up to 45 cm. **Distribution:** S Xizang border; extending south into the Himalayas and can be expected in extreme W Xizang adjacent to known populations in India. Introduced into New Zealand. **Natural History:** Inhabits steep, rocky mountainsides between 3,000 and 4,000 m with woods and rhododendron scrub. Eats grass, other herbs, and some fruits. Lives in small parties of 2–20 animals. Mating occurs from October to January. Males lock horns in dominance fights. One or occasionally two kids born in June–July after a gestation of 180–242 days, depending on duration of delayed implantation. Animals become mature after one and a half years. A captive animal lived up to 22 years. Show extreme agility in jumping among steep rocks. **Conservation Status:** Endangered within China; threatened by small range, heavy hunting pressure, and competition and disturbance from domestic grazers. China RL—EN D. China Key List—I. IUCN RL—NT.

GENUS *NAEMORHEDUS*—Gorals

斑羚属 Banling Shu—斑羚 Banling

Naemorhedus includes several small goat-antelope species, the gorals. These have coarse, shaggy hair with a woolly undercoat. They are stockier than serows, with smaller horns; front legs and back legs of similar length; infraorbital glands small. The genus is found through the Himalayas and from Siberia to N India and Indochina. All four species occur in China and live in rugged mountainous terrain.

Red Goral *Naemorhedus baileyi*

红斑羚 Hong Banling—**Distinctive Characteristics:** HB 93–107 cm; SH 57–61 cm; T 80–100; E 95–106; HF 200–250; GLS 168–199; Wt 20–30 kg. Small goral with small, slender recurved horns. Distinguished from other species by foxy-red pelage with no black ticking. Narrow, dark brown stripe runs down back to the short, blackish, tufted tail. Sometimes pale on forehead. Lacks pale throat patch. Ears shorter than in other gorals. **Distribution:** SE Xizang and extreme NW Yunnan; extending into NE Assam (India) and N Myanmar. **Natural History:** Inhabits forest, ragged crags, scrub, and meadows from 2,000 m up to 4,500 m in summer. Most aspects of its natural history are similar to those of other gorals, although it is supposedly rather tame. Mates in December, and young are born in June after a six-month pregnancy. **Conservation Status:** Uncommon within narrow distribution and much threatened by hunting and forestry operations. China RL—EN A1cd. China Key List—I. CITES—I. IUCN RL—VU C2a(i).

Long-Tailed Goral *Naemorhedus caudatus*

中华鬣羚 Zhonghua Lieling—**Distinctive Characteristics:** HB 106–120 cm; SH 69–75 cm; T 130–160; E 130–170; HF 270–320; Wt 32–42 kg. Gray, goatlike antelope with a pale throat patch. Pelage mostly gray-brown with no black overlay. Much smaller and paler than serows and lacking a long mane, although it does have an inconspicuous dark dorsal stripe. Legs paler than body, but with less sharp transition than in *N. griseus*. Distinguished from *N. goral* by its bushier tail and black stripes of foreleg passing to outer leg below "knee" rather than down median. Recurved black horns are basally annulated but more gracile than in serows; horn length short (127–178 mm typical, but as long as 235 mm). Has inconspicuous glands in front of eyes. Undercoat more woolly than in serow. The throat is particularly broadly white, this color extending to the chin; tail is long and appears longer, as it is bushy throughout. **Distribution:** NE China; extending to E Russia and Korea. **Natural History:** Inhabits steep and rocky terrain in evergreen and deciduous forests, especially with exposed grassy ridges from about 500 to 2,000 m elevation. Eats a wide range of plant material: grass, herbs and shoots, leaves of small trees, and even some fruit. Lives singly or in small groups. Diurnal and crepuscular. Keeps to steeper slopes, where it is very agile over rocky crags and cliffs. Has resting scrapes in sheltered places under rock sides; also rests on rock ledges. Visits salt licks. Gives hissing sneeze call when alarmed. Mates in early winter; one or two kids born about six months later. Small, rather vertical toes allow for great agility and good grip on steep, rocky slopes. **Conservation Status:** Much reduced by hunting, snares, habitat degradation, and grazing competition. China RL—VU A2cd + 3cd. China Key List—II. CITES—I. IUCN RL—VU A2cd.

Himalayan Goral *Naemorhedus goral*

斑羚 Banling—**Distinctive Characteristics:** HB 100–120 cm; SH 59 cm; T 80–150; HF 240–275; GLS 196–214; Wt 35–42 kg. Large, grizzled-gray to brownish-gray goral with thick woolly undercoat, covered by longer, coarser black guard hairs, and a short, semierect mane on male. Coat becomes shaggy in winter. Legs light brown or tan; even white on forelegs; dark dorsal stripe weak or absent; throat generally variably white; underparts grayish white. Distal half of tail is black and not bushy. Horns 12–18 cm in length. **Distribution:** Only marginally present in China along the northern flanks of the Himalayas; extending from Kashmir to the Changbi Valley between Sikkim and Bhutan. **Natural History:** Feeds on grassy ridges and steep, rocky slopes but hides in forest or rock crevices; shelters under rock overhangs. Eats grasses, herbs, and twigs with some fruits. Males usually single; otherwise found in pairs or small parties. Active in early morning and at dusk; resting through midday, but more active in cloudy weather. Usually finds drinking water in small streams. Gives a hissing sneeze in alarm. One or two young are born after a gestation of six to eight months. Young are weaned by eight months of age, and mature by three years. May live up to 15 years. **Conservation Status:** China RL—EN A2cd + 3cd. China Key List—II. CITES—I. IUCN RL—NT.

Chinese Goral *Naemorhedus griseus*

川西斑羚 Chuanxi Banling—**Distinctive Characteristics:** HB 88–118 cm; SH 61–68 cm; T 115–200; E 117–150; HF 235–285; GLS 184–225; Wt 22–32 kg. Tallish, dark brown, fawn, or grayish goral with some black overlay. Has short, dark crest and clear, thick, dark dorsal stripe. Legs are sharply paler than body. Forelegs sometimes reddish with black stripe; pale patch on throat is edged orange; chin is dark. Underparts light gray. Tail not long but bushy. Animals in C China are a dark brown and their throat patch is buff-edged reddish yellow; form from Yunnan is darker, with a reddish-brown edge to whitish throat patch and a brown tail base. **Distribution:** C and S China; extending to NE India, W Myanmar, NE Thailand, E Bangladesh. **Natural History:** Similar to other gorals. **Conservation Status:** China RL—EN A2cd + 3cd. China Key List—II. CITES—I. IUCN RL—VU A2d.

GENUS *OVIS*—Sheep

盘羊属 Panyang Shu—盘羊 Panyang

Ovis includes domestic sheep and their wild allies. These are stocky caprines with shortish legs. Both sexes have horns; those of males much larger and usually spiraling, roughly circular in cross section, and ribbed with many rings. They have infraorbital, digital, and inguinal glands. Five species are distributed in the Palaearctic and Nearctic regions; only one species occurs in China.

Argali *Ovis ammon*

盘羊 Panyang—**Distinctive Characteristics:** Male: HB 180–200 cm; SH 110–125 cm; T 100–180; HF 430–500; E 100–150; GLS 290–360; Wt 95–140 kg, rarely up to 180 kg. Females much smaller; weight about one-third that of males (68 kg). Very large sheep with small ears and tail and long, silky fur. Pelage grayish brown with yellowish breast and white underparts, lower legs, and rump patch. Males carry massive horns up 100–170 cm long, with heavy annulations and broad base, that increase in length and mass with age. The horns curve down and forward more than 360 degrees. Female horns are much smaller and only slightly curved. **Distribution:** Widespread in mountains of W China; extending to Pakistan, N India, Nepal, Central Asia, Mongolia, and S Siberia. **Natural History:** Lives on alpine grasslands between 3,000 and 5,000 m, descending lower in winter. Prefers to occupy open areas with a gentle slope; females occupy steeper (cliff) terrain following lambing. Feeds on grasses and some herbs and lichens, and regularly drinks from open springs and rivers. Where sympatric with Blue Sheep (*Pseudois nayaur*) they are more likely to occur in forb-dominated communities, compared to the grass-dominated communities occupied by Blue Sheep. Populations are reported to be small and sporadically distributed across their range. They are gregarious and live in groups of 2–150 individuals. One, rarely two, lambs are born in May–June after a 150–160-day gestation. Massive horns are used for head-butting fights during the rut and for protection. The thick, woolly coat provides protection during cold winters. **Conservation Status:** Endangered in China; most populations are small and severely fragmented. China RL—EN A2cd + 3cd. China Key List—II. CITES—I (*O. a. hodgsoni*); II (other subspecies). IUCN RL—NT.

GENUS *PANTHOLOPS* (monotypic)

藏羚属 Zangling Shu

Tibetan Antelope *Pantholops hodgsonii*

藏羚 Zang Ling—**Distinctive Characteristics:** HB 100–140 cm; SH 79–94 cm; T 130–140; E 120–150; GLS 216–278; Wt 24–42 kg. The single representative of a rather aberrant caprine genus (*Pantholops*). This is a largish antelope with sandy-brown to reddish-fawn pelage and white underparts. The coat is dense and woolly. Males have black markings on the front of their face, with a contrasting white patch on the upper lip. A black patch is found on the front of their neck. In winter the pelage lightens, such that at a distance males may appear white.

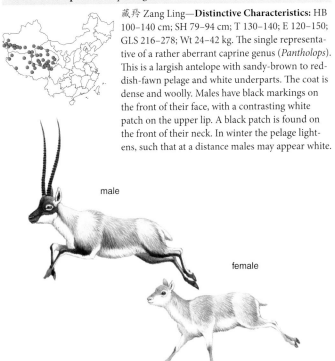

male

female

Males have diagnostic very tall horns (50–71 cm) held almost vertically, but curving slightly forward at tips. Unlike other caprines, females are hornless. Both males and females possess large inguinal glands in the groin, with an opening 5 cm long and a pouch 6 cm deep; this pouch contains a smelly, peanut-butter-like, waxy yellow substance. **Distribution:** Tibetan Plateau; extending to Ladakh and Kashmir. **Natural History:** Inhabits cold deserts and alpine grasslands of the Tibetan Plateau, including the lower-elevation Qaidam Basin. Feeds on grass, herbs, and lichens. Lives in large herds. Males and females almost completely segregate during their seasonal migration; females move long distances to a few traditional birthing grounds, whereas males may travel only a short distance from their wintering areas. Single calves are born in June after a gestation of six to seven months. It is believed that females first reproduce at one and a half to two and a half years of age. The fleecy undercoat so prized for making shatoosh wool is an adaptation for extremely cold winters. **Conservation Status:** Seriously endangered by poaching for its valuable, soft shatoosh wool; also vulnerable to the railroad and highway corridors that disrupt its migration path. Population size has undergone a drastic decline in recent decades. China RL—EN A2cd + 3cd. China Key List—I. CITES—I. IUCN RL—EN A2d.

GENUS *PSEUDOIS*—Blue Sheep

岩羊属 Yanyang Shu—岩羊 Yanyang

A small genus of medium-sized sheep found in China and the Himalayas; both species occur in China. Similar to *Ovis*, but differ in horn structure and some morphological characteristics. Their horn does not spiral, but rather twists outward from the head, is roughly triangular in cross section, and has a ridge on the inner margin. Inguinal and digital glands are poorly developed, and the infraorbital gland is absent.

Blue Sheep *Pseudois nayaur*

岩羊 Yanyang—**Distinctive Characteristics:** Male: HB 120–165 cm; SH 69–91 cm; T 130–200; E 90–130; HF 70–100; GLS 198–258; Wt 50–70 kg. Females are smaller (Wt 35–45 kg). Winter pelage is thick and woolly; shorter and finer in summer. Upper parts brownish gray with slaty-blue tinge; whitish underparts and inner legs. Outer legs marked with black. Has a broad, flat tail with a bare central surface, large dewclaws, no inguinal glands, no preorbital glands, and usually no digital glands. The rounded, smooth horns curve backward over the neck, then flare outward with a twist. Both sexes have horns, but those of males are much larger, reaching up to 82 cm. **Distribution:** W China; extending south into Bhutan and N Myanmar and across the Himalayas into Nepal, N India, Pakistan, and Tajikistan. **Natural History:** Inhabit open, grassy slopes in high mountains from 2,500 to 5,500 m. They feed on grass, alpine herbs, and lichens and live in small to rather large herds, alternately resting and feeding on steep, grassy slopes of alpine meadows. Males sometimes form all-male herds and sometimes mix with family herds. Sentinels watch out for Snow Leopards (*Uncia uncia*), their primary predator. Mates during winter, followed by a 160-day gestation. Single lamb (rarely twins) is born in early summer; weaning occurs in six months, and young reach maturity at one and a half years. **Conservation Status:** China RL—VU A2cd + 3cd. China Key List—II. IUCN RL—LC.

Sichuan Blue Sheep *Pseudois schaeferi*

矮岩羊 Ai Yanyang—**Distinctive Characteristics:** HB 109–160 cm; SH 50–80 cm; T 70–120; GLS 208–247; Wt 28–65 kg (male), 17–40 kg (female). Similar to but generally smaller than *P. nayaur*, and has a drabber coloration with a silvery sheen. Horn thinner and with less of a curl. **Distribution:** Confined to a narrow area along the Sichuan-Xizang border. Endemic. **Natural History:** Live among very steep rocky slopes at elevations between 2,700 and 3,200 m; occasionally range into conifer forest and forest clearings. *P. nayaur* may live in same region at higher elevations. Diet consists of grasses, low shrubs, club mosses, and lichens. Feed and rest alternately throughout the day on the grassy slopes of mountains. Groups formerly of 10–36 animals, but now usually less than 15 as a result of overhunting. Males sometimes form all-male groups or sometimes mix with females and young. Usually single young (rarely twins) is born in May–June after a gestation of 160 days. Young are weaned within six months and reach maturity at one and a half years. Males may take seven years to reach full size. **Conservation Status:** Population has drastically declined as a result of hunting, with group size dropping from a former range of 10–36 to only 3–8 by 1990. Protected on religious grounds by Baiyu minority in Sichuan. China RL—CR B1ab(i,ii,iii,v). China Key List—II. IUCN RL—EN A2cd.

ORDER CETACEA—Whales, Porpoises, and Dolphins

鲸目 Jing Mu—鲸, 海豚 Jing, Haitun
The Cetacea are completely aquatic mammals. Both form and structure are highly adapted for aquatic life; body pisciform; neck inconspicuous; body surface with no hair or scales; forelimb (flipper) finlike; hind limbs absent; most have dorsal fins; tail very long, ending in two flat fins (flukes); both dorsal fin and fluke composed of connective tissue, without bone or fin ray; tail is the main locomotor organ; head without external ear; auditory sensation very developed; both smell and vision reduced; nostrils elevated, with valves that can open and close; eyes very small.

All members of this group live in seas except a few freshwater species; usually gregarious; food habits carnivorous, living on invertebrates, fish, and plankton; classified into two suborders: Odontoceti, with teeth in mouth; and Mysticeti, with no teeth but with long strips of baleen (keratinized plates used for straining marine organisms from water) on the upper jaw. Mysticeti includes about 13 species; size generally large or very large; HB length more than 10 m; the largest, the Blue Whale (*Balaenoptera musculus*), is about 30 m long and weighs more than 180,000 kg; with hundreds of inserted corneous baleen strips in upper jaw, which filter plankton in the water; nostril with two openings; forelimb with four digits. Odontoceti includes about 72 species; tooth number usually very large (about 100, with 260 the most numerous), the smallest with only a pair of homodont teeth; HB length generally only several meters; nostril with one opening; skull asymmetrical; forelimb with five fingers. Cetaceans are distributed over all seas and many rivers. Of about 11 families, 40 genera, and 85 species, approximately eight families, 24 genera, and 32 species may occur in coastal waters of China (see also Appendix I). As most of these species have wide distributions and are commonly treated, here we present only those three species, belonging to separate odontocete families, that occur commonly in China's inland waters.

FAMILY DELPHINIDAE—Dolphins

海豚科 Haitun Ke—*海豚* Haitun
The Delphinidae is the most diverse family of whales, with 35 species in 17 genera. Dolphins are small to medium-sized cetaceans that are gregarious and form large social groups. Most species have a dorsal fin and a distinctive beak (a snout that is sharply differentiated from the forehead) or a long snout. Up to 15 species of dolphin are known from the coastal waters of China.

GENUS *SOUSA*—Humpback Dolphins

白海豚属 Zhonghuabai Shu
Sousa are characterized by a sloping "forehead" and a double-step dorsal fin marked by a smaller fin that sits on an elongated hump on the dolphin's back. The beak is long and slender and is usually exposed when surfacing. Of two species of *Sousa*, one occurs in China; the other occurs in the Atlantic Ocean.

Indo-Pacific Humpback Dolphin *Sousa chinensis*

中华白海豚 Zhonghuabai Haitun—**Distinctive Characteristics:** HB 250 cm; GLS 575; Wt 250 kg. The robust body is uniformly white or off-white, sometimes almost reddish in hue; may have some black spots on body, particularly males. Young are a deep gray and conspicuously darker than adults. The sexual dimorphism (males larger) found throughout much of the species range is not evident in Chinese populations. The species is characterized by a distinctive hump at the base of the small dorsal fin, although this is not as pronounced or may be lacking in Chinese forms. They have a relatively long, slender beak, clearly set off from the melon. Possesses many homodont teeth (tooth counts = 30–36 upper jaws; 24–37 lower jaws). **Distribution:** Found along coastline of SE China, in major river mouths from the Yangtze River south and in Taiwan; extending to coastlines along N and W Australia to India, and all the way to the tip of South Africa. **Natural History:** Generally occur in shallow, nearshore waters less than 20 m in depth. They swim up into fresh water in Chinese rivers and as far out as 50 km into the ocean where depths remain shallow. Normally swim in pods of fewer than 10 individuals; the maximum group size appears to be 20–30. Strong social bonds among pod members are uncommon. Diet consists primarily of fish and cephalopods. While the single calves may be born year-round, calving is most common in the spring to summer months following a gestation of 10–12 months. **Conservation Status:** Population numbers are very small in China and appear to be negatively affected by marine pollution, major development projects, and fishing activity.

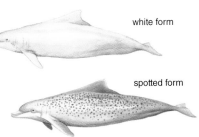

white form

spotted form

In 1996, 60 individuals were spotted in the Xiamen area, but these have been decreasing with subsequent comprehensive surveys. Only 1,000 are known to live in the Pearl River estuary region. China RL—EN A1ac. China Key List—I. CITES—I. IUCN RL—NT.

FAMILY PHOCOENIDAE—Porpoises

鼠海豚科 Shuhaitun Ke—海豚 Haitun
Porpoises are small cetaceans that largely occupy Northern Hemisphere seas and coastlines. The teeth are laterally compressed and spade-like; the head has short jaws and no beak. The dorsal fin is not prominent, being short or absent. There are six species represented in three genera, only one of which is found in Chinese waters.

GENUS *NEOPHOCAENA* (monotypic)

江豚属 Jiangtun Shu

Finless Porpoise *Neophocaena phocaenoides*

江豚 Jiang Tun—**Distinctive Characteristics:** HB 100–230 cm; Wt 25–50 kg. Anterior body thicker than posterior; head rounded; protruding forward; no fin on back; flipper sickle-like; whole body pale gray with a bluish tinge on the back and sides; 15–21 shovel-shaped teeth on each side of the jaw. **Distribution:** In China found along coastal waters and in bays from the Korean Peninsula to Vietnam, including Taiwan; extending throughout Indo-Pacific shorelines from the Persian Gulf to Japan. **Natural History:** Occupies warm seas and coastal inland waters; a freshwater population inhabits the middle-lower reaches of the Yangtze River and its adjacent lake systems. Prefers sandy areas with reedy swamps for feeding. Diet of fish and squid. Swims alone or in pairs, although groups of 12–15 individuals have been observed. Can swim upstream for a very long distance. Produces a characteristic vocalization with a narrow sonar band that can be used to accurately census populations with detection devices rather than direct observation. In the Yangtze River population, mating occurs from May through June, and normally a single calf is born during late April of the following year. **Conservation Status:** Thought to be seriously depleted due to heavy fisheries bycatch; the decline of the ocean-dwelling subspecies may be as great as 95% in some areas. The total Yangtze River population has been estimated at 2,000–3,000, and there is every indication that it is declining precipitously. China RL—EN A1acd. CITES—I. IUCN RL—VU A2cde.

FAMILY INIIDAE—River Dolphins

河豚科 Hetunke—河豚 Hetun

Possess a long rostrum and many repetitive teeth, reduced eyes, and ability to locate food by echolocation. Of the three genera in *Iniidae*, only one occurs in China.

GENUS *LIPOTES* (monotypic)

白暨豚属 Baijitun Shu

Yangtze River Dolphin *Lipotes vexillifer*

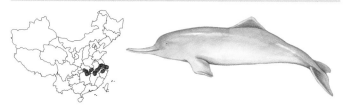

白暨豚 Baiji Tun—**Distinctive Characteristics:** HB to 220 cm (male), to 250 cm (female); Wt 135–160 kg (male), 240 kg (female). Rostrum narrow and long, its tip slightly upturned; dentition of uniform cone-shaped teeth ranges from 32 to 34 above and 31 to 34 below; roots laterally compressed; eyes small; flipper relatively wide, with blunt tip; dorsal fin low and triangular; blowhole longitudinal and somewhat rectangular; back light blue or off-white; ventral surface white. **Distribution:** Recently found only in the middle and lower reaches of the Yangtze River between two large tributary lakes, Dongting and Poyang. In the past it occupied these lakes and extended as far as 1,900 km up the Yangtze River, and occurred in the separate drainages of the Qiantang and Fuchun rivers. Endemic. **Natural History:** Inhabits fresh water, including major rivers and tributaries; prefers sandy substrates to estuarine habitats. Historically, swam in small groups of two to six individuals, with a maximum pod size of 15. Now that it is becoming increasingly difficult to find, most sightings are of solitary individuals, and maximum group size approaches four individuals. Commonly swims with fin exposed above water surface; breathes at intervals of 10–30 seconds. Swims at a speed of 7.5–9.7 km/h, and has been known to travel up to 200 km. Diet of fish. Vocalizations consist of whistles as well as broadband sonar signals. Reproductive season February–April; interbirth interval two years; gestation 10–11 months; a single young is born. **Conservation Status:** Likely the most endangered of all cetaceans, if not extinct. China RL—CR A1acd; C2b; D. China Key List—I. CITES—I. IUCN RL—CR C2a(ii); D.

APPENDIX I

Cetaceans Found off the Coast of China

Not covered in text

ORDER CETACEA
  SUBORDER MYSTICETI
    FAMILY BALAENIDAE
      North Pacific Right Whale *Eubalaena japonica*
    FAMILY BALAENOPTERIDAE
      Common Minke Whale *Balaenoptera acutorostrata*
      Sei Whale *Balaenoptera borealis*
      Bryde's Whale *Balaenoptera edeni*
      Blue Whale *Balaenoptera musculus*
      Fin Whale *Balaenoptera physalus*
      Humpback Whale *Megaptera novaeangliae*
    FAMILY ESCHRICHTIIDAE
      Gray Whale *Eschrichtius robustus*
  SUBORDER ODONTOCETI
    FAMILY DELPHINIDAE
      Short-Beaked Common Dolphin *Delphinus delphis*
      Pygmy Killer Whale *Feresa attenuata*
      Short-Finned Pilot Whale *Globicephala macrorhynchus*
      Risso's Dolphin *Grampus griseus*
      Fraser's Dolphin *Lagenodelphis hosei*
      Pacific White-Sided Dolphin *Lagenorhynchus obliquidens*
      Killer Whale *Orcinus orca*
      Melon-Headed Whale *Peponocephala electra*
      False Killer Whale *Pseudorca crassidens*
      Pantropical Spotted Dolphin *Stenella attenuata*
      Striped Dolphin *Stenella coeruleoalba*

        Spinner Dolphin *Stenella longirostris*
        Rough-Toothed Dolphin *Steno bredanensis*
        Bottlenose Dolphin *Tursiops truncatus*
    FAMILY PHYSETERIDAE
        Pygmy Sperm Whale *Koiga breviceps*
        Dwarf Sperm Whale *Koiga sima*
        Sperm Whale *Physeter catodon*
    FAMILY ZIPHIIDAE
        Baird's Beaked Whale *Berardius bairdii*
        Blainville's Beaked Whale *Mesoplodon densirostris*
        Ginkgo-Toothed Beaked Whale *Mesoplodon ginkgodens*
        Cuvier's Beaked Whale *Ziphus cavirostris*

APPENDIX II

Hypothetical Mammals

Those found close to China but without known representation in the Chinese mammal fauna

ORDER PRIMATES
    FAMILY CERCOPITHECIDAE
        Gee's Golden Langur *Trachypithecus geei*
        Capped Langur *Trachypithecus pileatus*

ORDER RODENTIA
    FAMILY SCIURIDAE
        Bhutan Giant Flying Squirrel *Petaurista nobilis*
        Yellow Ground Squirrel *Spermophilus fulvus*
    FAMILY DIPODIDAE
        Lesser Fat-Tailed Jerboa *Pygeretmus platyurus*
        Thomas's Pygmy Jerboa *Salpingotus thomasi*
        Mongolian Three-Toed Jerboa *Stylodipus sungorus*
    FAMILY SPALACIDAE
        Altai Zokor *Myospalax myospalax*
    FAMILY CRICETIDAE
        Gobi Altai Mountain Vole *Alticola barakshin*
        Korean Red-Backed Vole *Myodes regulus*
    FAMILY MURIDAE
        Kashmir Field Mouse *Apodemus rusiges*
        Greater Marmoset Rat *Hapalomys longicaudatus*

ORDER SORICOMORPHA
    FAMILY SORICIDAE
        Hill's Shrew *Crocidura hilliana*

Pale Gray Shrew *Crocidura pergrisea*
Van Sung's Shrew *Chodsigoa caovansunga*
Anderson's Shrew *Suncus stoliczkanus*

ORDER CHIROPTERA
FAMILY VESPERTILIONIDAE
Tickell's Bat *Hesperoptenus tickelli*
Intermediate Long-Fingered Bat *Miniopterus medius*
Scully's Tube-Nosed Bat *Murina tubinaris*

ORDER CARNIVORA
FAMILY FELIDAE
Fishing Cat *Prionailurus viverrinus*
FAMILY VIVERRIDAE
Otter Civet *Cynogale bennettii*
FAMILY CANIDAE
Golden Jackal *Canis aureus*

ORDER PERISSODACTYLA
FAMILY RHINOCEROTIDAE
Sumatran Rhinoceros *Dicerorhinus sumatrensis*
Javan Rhinoceros *Rhinoceros sondaicus*
Indian Rhinoceros *Rhinoceros unicornis*

ORDER ARTIODACTYLA
FAMILY SUIDAE
Pygmy Hog *Sus salvanius*
FAMILY TRAGULIDAE
Greater Mouse-Deer *Tragulus napu*
FAMILY CERVIDAE
Schomburgk's Deer *Rucervus schomburgki*
FAMILY BOVIDAE
Banteng *Bos javanicus*

APPENDIX III

Introduced Alien, Feral, or Free-ranging Domestic Mammals

ORDER RODENTIA
FAMILY CRICETIDAE
Common Muskrat *Ondatra zibethicus*
FAMILY MURIDAE
House Mouse *Mus musculus*
Brown Rat *Rattus rattus*
FAMILY MYOCASTORIDAE
Coypu *Myocastor coypus*

ORDER CARNIVORA
  FAMILY FELIDAE
    Domestic Cat *Felis catus*
  FAMILY CANIDAE
    Domestic Dog *Canis lupus familiaris*
  FAMILY MUSTELIDAE
    American Mink *Neovison vison*

ORDER PERISSODACTYLA
  FAMILY EQUIDAE
    Ass *Equus asinus*
    Horse (domesticated) *Equus caballas*

ORDER ARTIODACTYLA
  FAMILY SUIDAE
    Wild Boar (domesticated) *Sus scrofa vittatus*
  FAMILY CAMELIDAE
    Bactrian Camel (domesticated) *Camelus bactrianus*
  FAMILY BOVIDAE
    Yak (domesticated) *Bos grunniens*
    Aurochs (domesticated cattle) *Bos taurus*
    Water Buffalo *Bubalus bubalis*
    Goat (domesticated) *Capra hircus*
    Red Sheep (domesticated sheep) *Ovis aries*

GLOSSARY

aliform. Shaped like a wing.

allogrooming. Grooming directed at another individual.

allopatric. Geographical separation of populations; occurring in different places.

altricial. Born relatively helpless and in need of extensive parental care.

annulation. A ringlike structure.

anthropogenic. Relating to human impact on the environment.

antitragus. Small lobe at the base of the ear, opposite to the tragus (plural *antitragi*).

apical. At the tip, or apex (as in apical lobe of a nose leaf on some bats).

axillary. Pertaining to the armpit, the cavity beneath the junction of the arm and the body.

brachiation. Arboreal locomotion involving swinging from one handhold to another, usually through trees.

brow tine. The first tine above the base of an antler.

calcar. A bony or cartilaginous medial projection from the ankle of microchiropteran bats, used to support the uropatagium (plural *calcaria*).

callosities. Thick, hardened areas of the skin.

canine. Cuspid, or eyetooth, situated between incisors and premolars.

cannon bone. A bone formed of fused metacarpals or metatarsals.

carpal. Any one of the group of bones forming the wrist joint in the skeleton of the forelimb.

coprophagy. Feeding upon feces.

crepuscular. Active primarily at dawn and dusk.

cuneal. Wedge-shaped.

cursorial. Adapted for running.

dewclaw. A vestigial digit of the foot.

digit. Finger or toe.

digitigrade. Walking on the digits, with the wrist or heel held off the ground.

distal. Situated away from the point of attachment.

diurnal. Active during the day.

dorsum. Back or upper surface.

endemic. Found in a given geographic region and not found elsewhere.

estivation. Process of going into torpor in summer, mainly due to lack of water.

estrus. The period during which a female is receptive to copulation (adj., *estrous*).

foliverous. Feeding on leaves.

fossorial. Adapted to digging and burrowing; a fossorial animal conducts most of its activity underground.

frugivorous. Feeding on fruit.

guard hairs. Outer layer of coarse, protective hairs.

halophytic. Adapted to living in a saline environment

hastate. Like a spear point, with flaring, pointed lobes at the base.

heterodont. Having teeth that vary in structure in different parts of the jaw; in mammals represented by the different morphologies of the canines, incisors, premolars, and molars.

hibernation. Seasonal torpor in response to winter cold temperatures.

Holarctic realm. Northern distribution; a combination of the Nearctic and Palaearctic realms.

homodont. Having teeth that are repetitive in morphology.

humerus. Upper arm bone connecting the forearm to the shoulder.

incisor. Tooth adapted for cutting or gnawing, located at the front of the mouth along the apex of the dental arch.

Indo-Malayan realm. Biogeographic region encompassing India, S China, the Malay Peninsula, the Philippine islands, and the islands of Indonesia to Wallace's line (also *Oriental realm*).

inguinal. Pertaining to the region of the groin.

insectivorous. Feeding on insects.

interfemoral membrane. Membrane stretching between the thighs in bats (also *uropatagium*).

internarial. Between the nostrils.

ischial swelling. A patch of thickened, hairless, and often brightly colored skin on the buttocks of many apes (also *ischial callosity*).

labial. Pertaining to the lips; on the side proximal to the lips.

lancet. On *Rhinolophus* bats, tip of nose leaf projecting upward between the eyes.

lappet. Small flap of skin.

lingual. Pertaining to the tongue; on the side proximal to the tongue.

mammae. Milk-producing glands.

mammillary. Breastlike or breast-shaped.

metacarpal. Any bone in the hand between the carpals and phalanges; only one metacarpal per digit.

metatarsal. Any bone in the foot between the tarsals and phalanges; only one metatarsal per digit.

molars. Teeth with broad crowns used to grind food, located behind the premolars.

monestrous. Having a single estrous cycle per year.

nose leaf. Accessory flap attached to top of nostrils.

Palaearctic realm. Biogeographic region encompassing N Africa, Europe, the Middle East, and N Asia.

parapatric. Pertaining to geographic ranges of species that are contiguous but not overlapping.

paraphyletic. A taxonomic group that includes some but not all of the descendants of a common ancestor.

parturition. The process of giving birth.

patagium. A thin membrane of skin between the limbs that provides a gliding surface; the wing membrane of a bat.

pedicel. A bony supporting structure for an antler.

pelage. Collectively, all the hairs on a mammal.

perineum. Portion of the body between the genitals and the anus (adj., *perineal*).

phalanx. Any one of the distal two or three bones in each finger or toe (plural *phalanges*).

philopatric. Remaining close to one's birthplace.

philtrum. The area from below the nose to the upper lip.

pinna. External part of the ear (plural *pinnae*).

pisciform. Fish-shaped.

piscivorous. Feeding on fish.

plagiopatagium. The membrane of a bat wing that extends between the body and hind limbs to the arm and fifth digit.

plantar pad. The soft portion on the sole of the foot.

plantigrade. A form of locomotion in which the entire foot touches the ground.

polyestrous. Having several estrous cycles during a single breeding season.

polygynous. One male mating controlling access to and mating with multiple females.

postpartum. After birth; postpartum estrus is a cycle beginning shortly after a female gives birth.

precocial. Describes young that at birth are relatively independent of parental care.

premolars. Bicuspids, or the teeth between canine and molars.

proboscis. Long, tubular snout.

propatagium. The small portion of a bat's wing membrane that extends from the shoulder to the wrist.

radius. One of the two bones of the forearm.

rhinarium. The area of hairless skin surrounding the nostrils.

rostrum. Beaklike projection of the anterior part of the head or skull.

sagittal crest. Ridge running lengthwise along the top of the braincase.

saltatorial. Adapted to leaping locomotion.

sella. The characteristic posterior nose leaf of bats of the genus *Rhinolophus* (also *sellar leaf*).

sellate. Saddle-shaped.

sympatric. Occurring in the same place; describes an area of overlap in the distribution of two species.

synanthropic. Ecologically associated with humans.

synonym. Each of two or more names applied to the same taxon.

tapetum lucidum. A reflective layer in the eyes of nocturnal mammals aiding in night vision; yields "eyeshine."

tarsal. Toe bone.

tibia. The shin bone; the inner and usually larger of the two bones between the knee and the ankle.

torpor. A generalized state during which heart rate, body temperature, and respiration are reduced.

tragus. The cartilaginous projection anterior to the external opening of the ear in microchiropteran bats (plural *tragi*).

ulna. One of the two bones of the forearm.

ultrasonic. Wavelengths above the frequencies of audible sound, normally any wavelengths over 20,000 Hz.

unguligrade. A type of locomotion in which only the hoofs touch the ground.

uropatagium. The flap of skin found between the hind legs and the tail of most bats.

venter. The belly surface.

vestigial. Reduced; atrophied; remnant.

vibrissae. Long, stiff hairs found on the snout of most mammals that serve as tactile receptors; whiskers.

viviparous. Giving birth to live young.

FURTHER READING

Allen, G. M. 1938–40. *The Mammals of China and Mongolia (Natural History of Central Asia)*. W. Granger, editor. Central Asiatic Expeditions of the American Museum of Natural History, New York, 11:part 1:1–620[1938]; part 2:621–1350[1940].

Corbet, G. B., and J. E. Hill. 1992. *Mammals of the Indomalayan Region: A Systematic Review*. Oxford University Press: Oxford.

Francis, C. M. 2008. *A Guide to the Mammals of Southeast Asia*. Princeton University Press: Princeton.

MacKinnon, J., and N. Hicks. 1996. *Wild China*. The MIT Press: Cambridge, Massachusetts.

Pan, Q., Y. Wang, and K. Yan. 2007. *A Field Guide to the Mammals of China*. China Forestry Publishing House: Beijing. [In Chinese.]

Schaller, G. B. 1998. *Wildlife of the Tibetan Steppe*. University of Chicago Press: Chicago.

Sheng, H. L., O. Noriyuki, and H. J. Lu. 1999. *The Mammalian of China*. China Forestry Publishing House: Beijing.

Smith, A. T., and Y. Xie (editors). 2008. *A Guide to the Mammals of China.* Princeton University Press: Princeton.

Wang, S., and Y. Xie (editors). 2009. *China Species Red List Volume 2: Reptiles, Birds and Mammals.* High Education Press, Beijing. [In Chinese and English.]

Wilson, D. E., and D. M. Reeder (editors). 2005. *Mammal Species of the World: A Taxonomic and Geographic Reference.* Third edition. Johns Hopkins University Press: Baltimore.

Xie, Y., S. Zhang, and W. Wang (editors). 2009. *Biodiversity Atlas of China.* Hunan Education Press: Changsha, Hunan. [In Chinese.]

INDEX TO SCIENTIFIC NAMES

INDEX TO COMMON NAMES